"An outstanding rebuttal of the myth that leaders somehow have different DNA than ordinary people. Koehn's profiles of legendary figures reveal that, in fact, *none* of these people were leadership naturals—rather, their abilities were forged by the challenges they confronted. During trying times, they kept an unwavering resolve and put others' needs before their own. Their example ought to inspire every aspiring leader to rise to the occasion."

> —William P. Lauder, executive chairman, the Estée Lauder
> Companies

"A powerful and timely treatise on leadership, *Forged in Crisis* presents five compelling portraits of individuals who made a lasting impact on the world in times of extraordinary challenge. Nancy Koehn is a seriously talented historian who has a gift for mining the past to elucidate the present. She writes with verve and vivid detail."

> —Graham Allison, former assistant secretary of state
> and author of *Essence of Decision* and *Destined for War*

"Koehn's well-written and incisive study helps to show us the way to a better nation. Wisely, she chooses to portray people from different races, genders, and eras, [carving] out a new and clearer definition of leadership in the world. In many ways, the book is like John F. Kennedy's *Profiles in Courage*. This is a very perceptive look at leadership in the modern era that taps leadership qualities from the past."

> —Bruce Chadwick, author of *Law and Disorder, James and
> Dolley Madison*, and *The General and Mrs. Washington*

"Vividly re-creates the anguish and urgency felt by five trailblazing leaders in times of great adversity. With spirited prose that highlights crucial moments of testing and triumph, Nancy Koehn breathes life into the past as she shows what it takes to lead. In challenging times, this book is an essential read."

> —Zoë Baird, CEO and president, the Markle Foundation

FORGED IN CRISIS

THE POWER OF
COURAGEOUS LEADERSHIP
IN TURBULENT TIMES

Nancy Koehn

SCRIBNER
New York   London   Toronto   Sydney   New Delhi

Scribner
An Imprint of Simon & Schuster, Inc.
1230 Avenue of the Americas
New York, NY 10020

First Scribner hardcover edition October 2017

SCRIBNER and design are registered trademarks of
The Gale Group, Inc., used under license by Simon & Schuster, Inc.,
the publisher of this work.

For information about special discounts for bulk purchases,
please contact Simon & Schuster Special Sales at 1-866-506-1949
or business@simonandschuster.com.

The Simon & Schuster Speakers Bureau can bring authors to
your live event. For more information or to book an event, contact the
Simon & Schuster Speakers Bureau at 1-866-248-3049 or visit
our website at www.simonspeakers.com.

Interior design by Kyle Kabel

Manufactured in the United States of America

1   3   5   7   9   10   8   6   4   2

ISBN 978-1-5011-7444-5
ISBN 978-1-5011-7446-9 (ebook)

CHAPTER-OPENING PHOTOGRAPHS—SOURCE CREDITS
The photograph on page 11 appears courtesy of the Royal Geographical Society.
The photograph on page 77 appears courtesy of the Library of Congress. The
photograph on page 201 appears courtesy of the National Portrait Gallery,
Smithsonian Institution. The photograph on page 279 appears courtesy of
bpk-Bildagentur/Art Resource, New York. The photograph on page 369 appears
courtesy of the NCTC Archives Museum.

To Kelly Close,
who has always understood that the impossible
is made possible by resilience, courageous leadership,
and an abiding faith that right makes might

Contents

The Call of History

Picture in your mind three snapshots from the past. The first is from late 1915. Ernest Shackleton, an explorer from Great Britain, and his twenty-seven men are trapped on an iceberg off the coast of Antarctica. Their ship, the *Endurance*, has gone down through the ice, and he and his crew are marooned a thousand miles from civilization with three lifeboats, canned food, and no means of communicating with the outside world. Shackleton's mission is somehow—against all odds—to bring his entire team home safely. But he doesn't know how he will do this. At night, when he can't sleep, he slips outside his tent and paces the ice as he considers his next move. Sometimes, he doubts his ability to do what he knows he must.

The second snapshot is from the summer of 1862. Abraham Lincoln, the president of the United States, is also uncertain about how he will accomplish his purpose: to save the Union in the midst of a civil war. He, too, has trouble sleeping and often spends the hours after midnight walking up and down the second-floor hall of the White House. The conflict is going badly for government armies and is proving much bloodier than anyone could have imagined. The commander in chief knows that slavery is at the heart of the contest. But he's unsure exactly what to do about the almost 4 million black Americans held in bondage. He's also living with intense personal grief following the death of his son Willie four months earlier. In certain moments, Lincoln staggers under the weight he carries.

The third image is from the winter of 1961. It's late at night, and Rachel Carson, a scientist and bestselling author, is alone in her study, trying to finish a manuscript titled "Silent Spring," about the dangers of widespread pesticide use. Her subject is controversial, and she knows that large chemical companies, the US Department of Agriculture, and other powerful institutions are poised to make war on her and the book as soon as it's published. Despite the threats, Carson believes deeply in the work's integrity and larger message: that humankind has an obligation to protect the earth and that this obligation involves a sweeping call to citizen awareness and action. She writes as carefully as she can, her work given urgency not only by the importance of her subject, but also by her medical situation. For more than a year, she has been battling aggressive, metastasizing cancer. Carson realizes she may not have much time left, and in certain moments, she doubts she can actually complete her book and say what must be said. When her anxiety rises, the author walks around the room, staring out into the darkness.

Each of these three snapshots shows us a leader poised to take a critical step forward. Shackleton, Lincoln, and Carson found themselves in a position to make an enormous difference, and each rose to the challenge. Their stories, like those of the two other leaders here, Frederick Douglass and Dietrich Bonhoeffer, are as astounding as any from the great myths, adventure novels, and films that we remember and return to again and again. The difference is that these five stories are real; *they actually happened*. They're part of our past, and while each of these stories mattered a great deal in their respective eras, they also have much to offer our generation and those that come after.

The five leaders in this book are important to us today because we live in a moment when our collective faith in national figures—be they from government, business, or religion—is waning. When we think about the latest election or most recent financial scandal and take stock of the people we call leaders, we grow concerned that the men and women capable of tackling the problems and delivering on the promise of this age aren't among their ranks.

History helps us here. It gives us perspective on how other people, in other times, dealt with huge challenges and large opportunities.

It provides a sharp lens through which to view ordinary people doing extraordinary things. It also exposes the fallacies in some of our current assumptions about leadership. For example, these five stories make it clear that leaders can emerge from many different backgrounds, genders, races, and personality types. A shy, reserved person such as Rachel Carson turns out to be as authoritative as the president of the United States. Charisma and aggressiveness, two attributes we often associate with important leaders, aren't essential to making a big, worthy impact. Nor is real leadership primarily a result of specific endowments with which a few special people are born. The truth, it turns out, is quite different.

As the examples from the past here demonstrate, courageous leadership is actually a result of individual people committing to work from their stronger selves, discovering a mighty purpose, and motivating others to join their cause. In the process, each of the leaders and the people they inspire are made more resilient, a bit bolder, and, in some instances, even more luminous. When this happens, impact expands, and the possibility grows for moving goodness forward in the world.

This book is about the making of five unforgettable leaders who lived, worked, struggled, and triumphed in different circumstances toward different ends. With one exception, their paths did not cross. Four of the five knew during their lifetimes that they'd accomplished their respective missions. But none knew the full power of their influence—influence that continues to reverberate.

What each person *could* see was that he or she was in the midst of a profound personal crisis. It was not of his or her making. And none of the five had seen such turbulence coming. But once they were in the middle of calamity, they recognized that they couldn't falter and then fail to recover; they couldn't give up. Rather, each resolutely navigated through the storm and was transformed.

Each of these leaders—Ernest Shackleton, Abraham Lincoln, Frederick Douglass, Dietrich Bonhoeffer, and Rachel Carson—was thus forged in crisis. Intentionally, sometimes bravely, and with the messy humanity that defines all of us when we're at our most vulnerable, these people made themselves into effective agents of worthy change.

They worked from the inside out—*from within themselves*—making a commitment to a bigger purpose, summoning the courage to adhere to this purpose in the face of huge setbacks, and harnessing the emotional awareness to navigate the turbulence around them. They then used the internal assets and insights they gleaned about their own leadership to try to change the world in important, positive ways.

The book is laid out story by story. It opens with explorer Ernest Shackleton's expedition to the South Pole in 1914 and reconstructs the slow-motion disaster that unfolded when his ship became trapped in pack ice and then sank, leaving the leader to try to get his twenty-seven men safely back home to Britain. He could rely on few physical assets other than three lifeboats and some canned goods. His most important resources turned out to be his own resilience and a commitment to survive that he inspired in his men.

The second story begins with Abraham Lincoln's experience as president during 1862, the second year of the Civil War. This was an extraordinarily difficult period for the Union, the federal forces fighting to preserve the United States as one nation, and the thoughtful, calculating, and worry-laden man who was commander in chief. Union generals wouldn't aggressively attack Confederate forces. The government was running out of men, money, and political capital to prosecute the war. Lincoln had few cards left to play.

The third leader whom we meet, the escaped slave and abolitionist Frederick Douglass, lived and worked during the same time as Lincoln (indeed, the two met several times and grew to respect each other). Douglass's story opens in 1847, when he returned to the United States from Great Britain, where he had sought safety from death threats and potential recapture. Once back in America, he staked out a bold, self-determined path as a speaker, writer, and political agitator for the cause of black freedom. His ability to walk this path owed a great deal to what he'd learned as a slave in Maryland—one who'd escaped from bondage in 1838—and as an orator for the growing abolition movement.

The fourth section takes up Dietrich Bonhoeffer, who was a young German minister in Berlin in 1933 when the National Socialists came to power. Almost immediately, he recognized the grave threat that

Hitler and his regime posed to Jews, civil and ecclesiastical liberties, and world peace. Long before his fellow countrymen understood the extent of Nazi ambitions, Bonhoeffer was determined to resist the Third Reich. The story here charts the development of that commitment and the man who sustained it—over and over again—as the noose of Nazi evil tightened. Bonhoeffer started his leadership journey as a church spokesperson working for pacifism and nonviolent resistance to Hitler. By 1943, when the Gestapo arrested and imprisoned him, he'd become involved in a network of government officials trying to assassinate the Führer and overthrow the Third Reich.

The final leader in the book is Rachel Carson, who came of age in the 1930s and '40s. At a time when few women made their living in the sciences, she was an experienced marine biologist. By the mid-1950s, she was also a bestselling author. In 1962, this quiet, reserved woman set the world on fire by publishing *Silent Spring*, a book that forced government, business, and American citizens to confront the dangers of synthetic pesticides such as DDT and the larger issue of man's long-term relationship with the earth. The story here concentrates on Carson's race against the clock as she struggled to finish her book while fighting cancer.

At the broadest—and perhaps most obvious—level, these stories are connected by the strength, pluck, and deep sense of obligation to do right that the protagonists found within themselves. The stories are also knit together by the specific lessons that these people learned as they tried to advance their cause in the face of enormous obstacles. The insights that the five individuals stumbled upon, cultivated, and honed were not radically new or unusually bold; they wouldn't easily slot into a modern executive's dashboard to be used in autopilot fashion. They made no pretense of forming some kind of winning playbook for leaders.

No, the insights that these four men and one woman absorbed were often subtle. Early in his presidency, for example, Lincoln discovered the power of mastering his emotions in a specific situation carefully enough to take no immediate action or, in some instances, to do nothing at all. In our own white-hot moment, when so much of our time and attention is focused on instantaneous reaction, it seems almost inconceivable that *nothing* might be the best something we can offer. But Lincoln came to understand this well, and he and the country benefited from his understanding.

Equally subtle, in 1937, when Carson assumed an editorial position for the agency that became the Fish and Wildlife Service, she quickly realized that her bureaucratic commitments at work and her caretaking responsibilities at home would prevent her from doing nearly as much freelance writing as she hoped. In the wake of this disappointment, she came to see the importance of her work in the "gathering years," in preparing herself for what she was meant to do in the future, when the larger opportunity arrived. The concept that, at times, the most powerful thing one can do is to invest in oneself, without signs of great outward progress, is another that is difficult for us to grasp today. We're so keen to arrive right *now*, to check this or that objective off our lists and move on, that we have trouble realizing that periods of gathering—our strength, tools, and experiences—are as significant as the big, external leaps forward along our paths. Indeed, as the stories in this book demonstrate, the latter rarely happen without the former.

One of the most important threads connecting these stories is that all of these leaders were *made*. They were not *born*. Nothing was genetically or divinely ordained about what they accomplished, or how they motivated other people to meet serious challenges. The four men and one woman here became effective leaders by dint of working on themselves: intentionally choosing to make something better of who they were, even in the midst of crisis, and never losing sight of the larger, dynamic stage on which they found themselves. Relatively early in their lives, each came to see his or her setbacks as classrooms in which they could sharpen their skills, improve their emotional strengths, and minimize specific weaknesses. With experience, they learned to detach themselves enough from the immediacy of their circumstances to observe the bigger landscape and their place in it, and to take action—within themselves and in relation to external goals—from this perspective.

The work they did on themselves wasn't some kind of formal bildungsroman brought to life. No, the self-development work that these protagonists did was generally unnamed and unforeseen. It was often accomplished ad hoc, in response to an obstacle in their way or a new realization. But once learned, the particular skill, aspect of emotional mastery, or powerful insight became a part of the individual leader's tool belt—to be used and strengthened going forward. And as all five individuals came to realize, the harder they worked on themselves, the more effective they became as leaders.

In my experience as a scholar and executive coach, the concept of leaders being made rather than born is often difficult to appreciate. We live in an age that assumes that individuals of great vision and impact are the result of rare, valuable endowments: all nature, little nurture. Whether these gifts are magnetism, strategic planning, public-speaking abilities, or something else, we tend to assume they're divinely ordained. (Perhaps this assumption explains some of the very destructive run-up in executive compensation during the last thirty years.) So we search ardently—if vainly—for these haloed men and women, only to find ourselves angry and disappointed when so many leaders from different walks of life turn out to be incompetent, greedy, or worse.

This book eschews such a view. In its place, it features five selected stories of the self-conscious making of effective leaders. *Effective leadership* is a term much bandied about today. But it's often used in frustratingly vague, and, at times, self-serving, ways. The best definition I've encountered is from the American writer David Foster Wallace. Wallace became famous for his novels, including *Infinite Jest*, but he also wrote thoughtful essays. In 2000, he published an article in *Rolling Stone* about the first John McCain presidential campaign. In the piece, Wallace riffed on the broader subject of real leadership, including how the word *leader* has become a cliché that is so boring our eyes glaze over when we see it. This is weird, he continued, because "when you come across somebody who actually *is* a real leader, that person isn't boring at all; in fact he is the opposite of boring."

Wallace then went on to define "real"—what I call courageous or effective—leaders as individuals "who can help us overcome the limitations of our own individual laziness and selfishness and weakness and fear and get us to do better, harder things than we can get ourselves to do on our own." This definition captures a whole lot about courageous leaders—men and women from whom we can learn and draw credible inspiration—including their ability to see the intersection of human agency and larger historical forces and then, from this perspective, to incite others to right action. Consider, for example, Lincoln's Second Inaugural Address, which is an extraordinary distillation of the meaning of the Civil War. Here, in 701 words, the sixteenth president connected the history and violence of slavery with the bloodshed of the war, linking both with the transformation the country had undergone as a result of the conflict. He closed the speech by calling his fellow citizens to forgiveness and a new relationship with one another.

Wallace's conception of effective leaders also explains why they command influence and exercise impact—one-on-one, as well as in groups and institutions:

> A leader's true authority is a power you voluntarily give him, and you grant him this authority not in a resigned or resentful way but happily; it feels right. Deep down, you almost always like how a real leader makes you feel, how you find yourself working harder and pushing yourself and thinking in ways you wouldn't be able to if there weren't this person you respected and believed in and wanted to please.

Each of the five people in this book became a courageous leader of the kind that Wallace has described. The authority of these individuals stemmed partly from that granted them by others who recognized their leadership, partly from the experience each accumulated along his or her respective journey, and partly from the commitment and emotional intelligence they each brought to their mission—a mission deemed critical amid the larger moment. All five raised the bar for their followers, moving these people to do better, harder things than they could have accomplished on their own. Two of the individuals in this book, Frederick Douglass and Dietrich Bonhoeffer, found their purpose early in their lives and pursued it with focus and determination for many years. The other three, Shackleton, Lincoln, and Carson, stumbled into their life's work after following other leads and learning from both success and failure. Once these two men and one woman saw what they had to do, they brought all their strength and self-knowledge to bear on the work at hand.

Many years ago, I made a short film for the Harvard Business School about the lessons that Abraham Lincoln's life offered for modern leaders. I interviewed a range of CEOs, asking them what they'd learned from the sixteenth president. Their responses were wide-ranging and profound; many continue to influence my work on effective leadership. I was particularly struck by what A. G. Lafley, CEO of Procter & Gamble at the time, said about how leaders are made. He pointed to three main ingredients. The first is an individual's strengths and weaknesses and the cumulative experience a person acquires walking his or her path. The second is that an individual recognizes a moment has arrived that *demands* his or her leadership. The third is that the individual has to consciously decide "to embrace the cause and get in the game."

As we shall see, making oneself into a courageous leader, in the way Lafley describes, is perilous, compelling, and exhausting work that is also some of the most satisfying one can do. Like the months that Shackleton and his crew spent stranded on the ice, the four years of terrible, turbulent civil war that Lincoln found himself at the center of, or the decades of large-scale, untested chemical use that Carson took up in *Silent Spring*, our own time—the early twenty-first century—cries out for effective, decent leaders. People of purpose and commitment who want to make a positive difference and who choose to rise: first within themselves, by claiming their better selves, and then on the larger stage, by staking out the higher ground.

Are you ready to hear the call to action contained in each of these stories? Ernest Shackleton, Abraham Lincoln, Frederick Douglass, Dietrich Bonhoeffer, and Rachel Carson have something important to offer each of us right now, as we try to craft lives of purpose, dignity, and impact. Read these stories and get to work. The world has never needed you and other real leaders more than it does now.

PART ONE

Bring the Team Home Alive

ERNEST SHACKLETON'S CHALLENGE

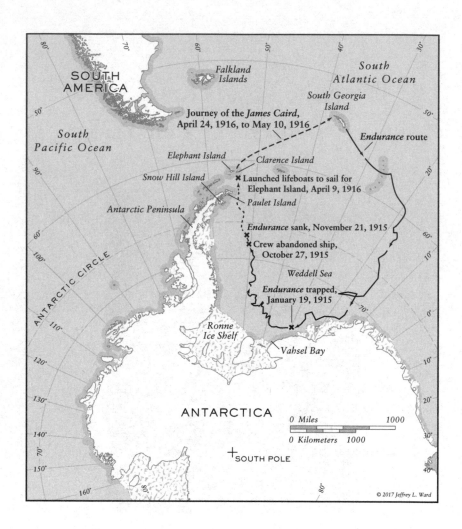

SOUTH AMERICA

South Pacific Ocean

Falkland Islands

South Atlantic Ocean

Journey of the *James Caird*, April 24, 1916, to May 10, 1916

South Georgia Island

Endurance route

Elephant Island

Clarence Island

Snow Hill Island

✗ Launched lifeboats to sail for Elephant Island, April 9, 1916

Antarctic Peninsula

Paulet Island

Endurance sank, November 21, 1915

✗ Crew abandoned ship, October 27, 1915

ANTARCTIC CIRCLE

Weddell Sea

Endurance trapped, January 19, 1915

✗

Ronne Ice Shelf

Vahsel Bay

ANTARCTICA

0 Miles 1000

0 Kilometers 1000

✛ SOUTH POLE

© 2017 Jeffrey L. Ward

CHAPTER ONE

No Hope of Rescue

In late October 1915, Ernest Shackleton, leader of the celebrated British expedition to Antarctica, surveyed the crisis unfolding around him. Shackleton had originally planned to sail his ship, the *Endurance*, through the Weddell Sea to the South American side of the continent, land on the coast, and then march a team of five men, supported by dogs and sledges, to the South Pole and then onto the Ross Sea on the side closest to Australia. Completing this mission would make the explorer the first to cross the entire continent. In the context of other Antarctic expeditions, this achievement held out the promise of enduring fame for Shackleton and glory for Great Britain.

But in late January 1915, pack ice had locked the *Endurance* about eighty miles from land, holding the ship and her crew hostage to the drifting floes; by October, the currents had carried the boat almost seven hundred miles north and west. The floes—large masses of floating ice, some weighing several tons—alternately broke apart and came back together in the ocean's mighty swells. Caught in this shifting mosaic, the wooden ship creaked and groaned under the immense pressure. It seemed only a matter of time before the *Endurance* would succumb and sink.

Toward the end of October, the ice suddenly rose and fell, driving the vessel starboard (rightward) to a thirty-degree tilt. The ship righted itself when the ice loosened some. But in the ensuing days, the floes continued to press on the hull, opening planks on the ship's sides.

Crew members manned the pumps round the clock as they tried to stanch the inflowing water. The captain, Frank Worsley, still hoped the *Endurance* might break free of the moving pack and sail into open water. But Shackleton was less optimistic and made plans to move the men and supplies onto the ice. "A strange occurrence was the appearance of eight Emperor [penguins]," Worsley noted in his diary on October 26. After issuing a few ordinary cries, he wrote, the birds "proceeded to sing what sounded like a dirge for the ship."

The next day, the ice intensified its assault on the *Endurance*, squeezing her like a vise. The vessel was "in her death agony," wrote the expedition's surgeon, Alexander Macklin, in his diary. "It was a pitiful sight. To all of us she seemed like a living thing—we had sworn at her and cursed her antics in a seaway, but we had learned to love her as we now realised, and it was awful to witness her torture." Late that afternoon, Shackleton ordered his men to abandon ship and take refuge in tents on the shifting ice floe. That night, the temperature fell to -15° Fahrenheit (-26° Celsius).

While the men tried to sleep amid the vessel's cracking timbers, Shackleton paced the ice. He thought about the dying ship. He took stock of his men and options for getting them all home alive. Like other leaders in a crisis, Shackleton understood that achieving his mission depended critically on how he managed himself—mentally, emotionally, and physically. He realized that the path ahead was likely to be long and arduous, and as he later remembered, "an ordered mind and a clear programme were essential if we were to come through without loss of life."

Early the next morning, Shackleton, his second-in-command, Frank Wild, and expedition photographer Frank Hurley prepared hot powdered milk for breakfast. As the men emerged from their tents, Shackleton gathered them round and announced a new goal: "ship and stores have gone—so now we'll go home." He did so "without emotion, melodrama or excitement," Macklin remembered, even though "it must have been a moment of bitter disappointment" for the leader. He'd "lost his ship, and with her any chance of crossing the Antarctic Continent." As always with him, Macklin added, "what had happened had happened: it was in the past and he looked to the future." A day later, in the privacy of his own diary, Shackleton was more candid about the challenge ahead. He knew that circumstances had altered his mission from one of exploration to one of survival. "A man must shape himself to a new mark directly the old one goes to ground," he wrote. "I pray God, I can manage to get the whole party to civilization."

From his Antarctic experience, Shackleton knew that one of the most important tools he had in accomplishing his mission was his presence. How he showed up each day in front of his men—what kind of energy he gave off, how determined he looked, even how he carried his body—had a huge impact on the team. He used what we would today call his emotional intelligence to maintain his determination and bravery; when these flagged, he never let his men know.

This is an important lesson for our time. Leaders often forget that all eyes are on them—as they give a speech, sit in a meeting, walk down a hallway, or glance furtively at their smartphone during dinner. This is especially true when the volatility of a situation increases. In these moments, people instinctively look to leaders, searching their words, actions, and body language for guidance. This means that individuals in positions of authority must learn to embody their mission not only in what they say and do, but also in how they show up. When a leader appears assured and levelheaded, others are more likely to respond to the call.

As the forty-one-year-old commander worked to exude confidence, he kept his men's focus trained on the task ahead. It was no use considering what had been lost or what might have been; the new goal was to get everyone home safely. The morning after abandoning ship, Shackleton announced the team would march across the pack ice toward a former explorer's base on Snow Hill Island, some three hundred miles northwest. He estimated the men could walk five to seven miles a day. He was sure that when they arrived there, they would find emergency stores cached by past expeditions. From Snow Hill Island, the commander and a smaller party would travel an additional 130 miles west to Deception Island, where whaling ships were known to dock.

The trek across the broken ice would be difficult for a group hauling two of the ship's three lifeboats, food supplies, and other stores. But Shackleton was in a hurry to get his team moving, partly to improve the men's morale. "It will be much better for the men in general to feel that even though progress was slow," he noted privately, "they are on their way to land, than it will be simply to sit down and wait for the tardy north-westerly drift to take us out of this cruel waste of ice." A second reason of Shackleton's for taking action now was to avoid damage to the lifeboats; this might occur if the men waited for open water and ended up sailing in choppy seas amid shifting icebergs.

On October 30, 1915, three days after evacuating the *Endurance*, the men set out for Snow Hill Island. Some hauled the lifeboats, others drove dog teams pulling supplies. The long, plodding caravan headed away from the ship and the site the men called Dump Camp. The team moved at a crawl, owing to their heavy loads and the difficulty of moving across uneven ice—a landscape defined by jagged ridges and huge blocks as far as the eye could see. After two tedious hours, the men had traveled only a mile. They were exhausted. The next two days were worse, and on the third day, November 1, Shackleton called off the march.

The twenty-eight men had traveled less than four miles toward their destination. The commander knew that at the current pace, their supplies would give out long before they reached Snow Hill Island. He ordered the men to move their gear to a solid ice floe not far from the battered ship. Shackleton planned to have the men camp there while he considered his next move.

On November 21, 1915, the commander saw what remained of the *Endurance* sinking through the ice. "She's going, boys!" he shouted, and the men quickly clambered out of their tents to watch. "There was our poor ship a mile and a half away struggling in her death-agony," a crew member recorded in his diary. "She went down bows first, her stern raised in the air. She then gave one quick dive and the ice closed over her forever." A strange silence fell over the camp. With the ship gone, the men could see nothing but ice, extending endlessly in all directions. There was no line on the horizon, no sign whatsoever of the outside world. Without the *Endurance*, one man wrote, "our destitution seems more emphasized, our desolation more complete." Shackleton himself was stunned by the ship's sinking. He recorded the event only briefly in his diary, adding, "I cannot write about it."

The leader knew there was no hope of rescue. Not only were the men seven hundred miles northwest of where he'd originally planned to build base camp, but he'd also told family and colleagues not to expect any communication from him before early 1916. The leader understood that he'd have to get the crew to safety on his own, and he knew how difficult this would be.

Shackleton had been to Antarctica twice before. The first time, as a member of the British National Antarctic Expedition (1901–4), he'd come close to death—a result he attributed as much to the team's weak commander as to the continent's harsh conditions. The second time, he'd led his own expedition (1907–9). His crew hadn't achieved its objective of discovering the South Pole, but he'd learned a great deal about himself and his authority. He knew that cohesion, including the men's faith in themselves and their leader, was as important to survival as adequate nutrition. Shackleton also understood that as the head of the expedition, *he* was responsible for these elements. Now, in 1915, against extraordinary odds, he had to advance his mission and keep his men believing they could achieve it with him.

How exactly was the explorer going to accomplish his goal? How was he to keep his own courage and confidence levels high to feed those of his men? In November 1915, as the *Endurance* sank and the ice closed over her, the answers to these questions were anything but clear. What Shackleton *did* know was that he was committed to bringing all his men home alive, and he was willing to do whatever it took to accomplish this. In the midst of disaster, he'd made a conscious choice to lead. He was all-in, and his story offers up key leadership lessons for moments when disaster strikes.

CHAPTER TWO

Shackleton's Early Life

S hackleton was born on February 15, 1874, in County Kildare, Ireland, the second child and first son of Henry and Henrietta Letitia Sophia Gavan Shackleton. Ernest grew up in a solidly middle-class family. As a boy, he devoured adventure magazines, enthralled by the idea of man mastering nature. He also loved poetry, especially the heroic strains of Robert Browning. (When he was a sailor, Shackleton would wile away the hours off duty reading poetry in his cabin. "Old Shack's busy with his books," shipmates commented.)

At sixteen, Ernest convinced his parents to allow him to go to sea, and the elder Shackleton found his son a position as a ship's boy on a merchant vessel. The lowest-ranking member of the crew, the teenager spent his time scrubbing decks and polishing brass railings. After this voyage, the ship's captain wrote that the young sailor was "the most pig-headed, obstinate boy I have ever come across." But Shackleton was also attentive and observant and soon had a rising career in the merchant marine. By age twenty-four, he'd attained the rank of full master, which qualified him to command a commercial vessel. Unlike in school, where his performance had been consistently below average, at sea, supervisors praised his intelligence and skills, noting "his brother officers considered him to be a very good fellow."

Among other seamen, Shackleton developed a reputation for not flaunting his rank. He was a "departure from our usual type of young officer," a colleague observed. "He was contented with his own company—at the same time he never stood aloof in any way, but was eager to talk—to argue as sailors do." Shackleton usually spoke in a quiet drawl, intimate in voice and manner. But with subjects that engaged him, the same colleague remembered, "his features worked, his eyes shone, and his whole body seemed to have received an increase of vitality." Regardless of his energy level, the seaman concluded, Shackleton was "very human, very sensitive."

As he scaled the maritime ladder, the young man grew restless. He complained that he needed an "opportunity of breaking away from the monotony of method and routine—from an existence which might eventually strangle his individuality." In March 1900, at age twenty-six, he saw such an opening when he learned about a proposed expedition to Antarctica. Shackleton knew the son of the principal benefactor of the enterprise and, through this connection and subsequent interviews, won an appointment as a member of the National Antarctic Expedition (NAE), which set sail aboard the ship *Discovery* in 1901.

The ambitious mariner had another reason for wanting to join the voyage. In 1897, he had met Emily Dorman, the daughter of a prosperous London solicitor. He was immediately smitten with the tall, attractive, soft-mannered woman. Determined to win her hand, he sought a pathway to fame, fortune, and social status; the NAE appeared to be such an opportunity, and he grabbed for it with both hands.

At the turn of the century, Britain was one of many countries engaged in a fierce competition to discover the South Pole. In 1895, after the Sixth International Geographical Congress had declared that developing a better understanding of Antarctica was the most urgent scientific issue of the era, many nations launched expeditions to the southernmost continent. In 1899, for example, Norwegian explorer Carsten Borchgrevink became the first man to winter in Antarctica. He returned to Europe in 1900, suggesting that the region might be an economic prize, complete with enormous fishing stocks and mineral stores. Other explorers quickly followed in the name of science, commerce, and nationalism. For these men, the combination of international rivalry, scientific discovery, patriotism, and high-risk adventure was a seductive elixir that held out the possibility of glory and national honor.

But as this global competition intensified, Britain suffered from several disadvantages. None of the members of the NAE, including its commander, Major Robert Falcon Scott of the Royal Navy, had any previous polar experience. As important, previous Norwegian expeditions had used dog teams and skis to move efficiently over ice, yet few British explorers were practiced at either form of transport. As a result, many of the country's expeditions to the South Pole ultimately relied on man-hauling, in which crew members tramped across the ice pulling supply-laden sledges. Proper nutrition had also proven to be a serious problem; on past expeditions, British leaders frequently rationed food inadequately and relied primarily on a diet of canned foods. Without fresh meat or produce, many explorers suffered from scurvy, a condition that resulted in bleeding gums, swollen joints, and skin damage, and which, we know today, was caused by vitamin C deficiency.

Despite the challenges, the NAE arrived on the Antarctic coast in early 1902. Even at its most temperate, Antarctica was (and is) a forbidding place. Temperatures at the South Pole average about 20° Fahrenheit (-28.8° Celsius) in the summer and about -76° Fahrenheit (-60° Celsius) in the winter. The lowest recorded temperature on earth, -128.6° Fahrenheit, which is -89.2° Celsius, belongs to Antarctica. Strong, cold winds and constantly changing conditions added to the dangers, creating an environment in which there was literally no margin for error. Scott and his men knew this before they left Britain; they understood it even more clearly once they had spent a winter at base camp.

On November 2, some six weeks into spring in the southern hemisphere, Scott, Shackleton, and colleague Edward Wilson set off from base camp for the South Pole. From the beginning, their journey was marred by logistical and other difficulties. Man-hauling sledges weighing up to five hundred pounds across uneven terrain in subzero temperatures—for as many as ten hours each day—sapped the men's strength and confidence. Inadequate clothing, gear, and food stocks also greatly hindered progress. Further exacerbating the explorers' troubles were frequent clashes between Scott and Shackleton over routes, supplies, and traveling speeds. By late December, the three men were undernourished and dispirited.

On December 30, when the team reached 82°17'S, about five hundred miles north of the South Pole, Scott gave the order to turn back. Hungry, physically debilitated, and strained by interpersonal tensions, the three men almost died on the return trek. Shackleton suffered from breathlessness, a wracking cough, and chest pains; on a few occasions, he could not walk and had to be pulled on one of the sledges. Sheer willpower pushed him on. On February 3, 1903, the polar party made it back to base camp. They had gone a much shorter distance than they had hoped and failed to claim the Pole, but they had traveled farther south than any previous expedition.

In 1905, Scott published an account of the trip, titled *The Voyage of the Discovery*. The book portrayed Shackleton as an invalid who was all but responsible for the expedition's failure to reach the Pole. Shackleton was furious at what he regarded as Scott's fraudulent account. Determined to prove the naval commander wrong and rehabilitate his reputation, Shackleton began planning his own Antarctic voyage.

To do this, he needed both scientific support and aristocratic patronage. The expedition would cost at least £30,000 (almost $4 million today), but could easily run much higher. To win approval from the experts, Shackleton reached out to the Royal Geographical Society (RGS), an organization founded in 1830 to advance geographical science. To solicit financing from London elites, he used family connections, writing letters and paying personal calls. By 1907, he'd raised the necessary money, secured a vessel, the *Nimrod*, and selected his crew. The expedition set sail from Britain that summer.

The voyage took two years, and it made Shackleton a national hero. Although the explorer and his three companions—Frank Wild, Jameson Adams, and Eric Marshall—did not reach the South Pole, the foursome succeeded in trudging to within one hundred miles of it, reaching 88°23'S in early January 1909. This was the farthest south any man had ever been.

By that time, however, the men were plagued by hunger, frostbite, and what may have been scurvy. Shackleton realized that if they pushed on to the Pole, they would indeed discover it, but would probably not survive the return trip. He knew another explorer was likely to reach the Pole and claim the prize before he could return to Antarctica, but nonetheless, Shackleton made the wrenching choice to turn back. "Better a live donkey than a dead lion," he later wrote his wife.

Still, he was terribly disappointed. As the leader and his exhausted companions tramped northward, Shackleton tried to console himself. "Whatever [our] regrets may be we have done our best," he wrote in his diary. "Beaten the Southern Record [set by Scott in 1902] by 366 miles, the North by 77 miles [set by Robert Peary trying to reach the North Pole in 1906]. Amen."

As the four men dragged themselves 650 miles north to base camp, they knew they were marching for their lives. Shackleton was often short of breath, dizzy, and, at times, nearly unable to keep going. But he remained focused on the group's survival, turning vigilant attention to each of his companions' well-being. Several weeks into their return trek, he noticed Frank Wild was especially weak with hunger. The commander, Wild recorded in his diary,

> privately forced upon me his one breakfast biscuit and would have given me another tonight had I allowed him. I do not suppose that anyone else in the world can thoroughly realise how much generosity and sympathy was shown by this; I DO by GOD I shall never forget it. Thousands of pounds would not have bought that one biscuit.

By February 27, 1909, the party had trudged to within thirty-three miles of their destination. But Adams and Marshall were too weak to go any farther; Shackleton and Wild set out for help. The two walked for thirty-six hours, and on March 1, they were reunited with members of the larger expedition, many of whom had given up the polar party for dead. Shackleton, who had hardly slept in fifty hours, quickly organized and then led a group to rescue Adams and Marshall out on the ice. Within two days, all of the men were safely back in base camp, and on March 4, 1909, the commander and his crew set sail for home.

The historical record is silent on how Shackleton grappled with his failure to achieve a burning ambition. What *is* clear in hindsight is that, in the life-threatening conditions of the Antarctic, the explorer had relied not only on courage and a steely will, but on the consistent responsibility he felt for his men's survival. Shackleton understood that in moments of great turbulence when the stakes are high, the fate of a particular enterprise comes down—briefly and critically—to the energy and actions of the individual leader.

This is a key lesson for leaders today, who have to own the power of their agency in the midst of volatility and then act from this place. We all have witnessed examples of such leadership in emergency situations: firefighters rushing into a burning building to rescue people trapped inside; an amateur sailor caught in an unexpected storm; or a parent whose child is taken violently ill. The individuals in each of these situations know they must act decisively because a great deal hangs in the balance. In these moments, they have no hesitation, no thought of turning back. They realize they must move forward—into the turbulence. And as they do, they often work from previously unknown reserves of fortitude and resilience.

In 1909, Shackleton returned to Britain, where he was knighted, enjoying widespread fame as the man who had come closest to the Pole. Inspired by this feat, Norwegian explorer Roald Amundsen resolved to lead his own expedition to discover the South Pole. And two years later, on December 14, 1911, he and four companions did just that. Amundsen's meticulously planned journey, which relied on well-trained sled dogs and expert skiers, went so well that he and his team arrived back at base camp ahead of schedule and without anyone's suffering significant injury or illness. When Shackleton learned of the Pole's discovery, he was impressed. For his part, Amundsen credited the leader of the *Nimrod* expedition with showing him "what one man's will and energy can accomplish."

In 1911–12, Amundsen was not the only explorer trying to discover the South Pole. A British expedition, led by Shackleton's nemesis, Robert Falcon Scott, was also trying to be the first to reach it. Scott and his polar party took a different route south to the Pole than Amundsen and, once again, relied on man-hauling. In January 1912, when Scott and his four companions reached the South Pole and saw the Norwegian flag planted there, they realized they had been beaten. Bitterly disappointed, the British polar party turned north for the long march back to base camp. By now, they were malnourished and weak; bad weather also slowed their progress. By mid-March, two of the five men had perished. Debilitated and hungry, Scott and his two remaining companions marched on; by March 20, they were just eleven miles south of a food depot when a severe blizzard trapped them in their tent. The three men died there. Their bodies were discovered eight months later.

In early 1913, news reached Britain that Scott and his teammates had died on the return journey from the Pole. In one year, the explorer had lost as many men as all the expeditions to Antarctica in the previous fifteen years combined. Nonetheless, the British press and public made him a martyr; virtually overnight, the dead captain became a national hero. For Shackleton, who had experienced firsthand what he saw as Scott's vacillating and often irresponsible leadership, and who himself had not lost a man in Antarctica, the lionization of his former rival was a difficult pill to swallow. He understood all too well that Amundsen's discovery of the Pole and the heroism accorded Scott by the public had eclipsed Shackleton's own achievement and, with it, his dreams of enduring fame.

Perhaps this injury rekindled Shackleton's interest in heading south again. Perhaps it was his desire to make a bold, patriotic gesture. Then again, it may have been the innate restlessness that the explorer always experienced when he was not on the ice. Whatever the impetus, Shackleton began contemplating another journey—this time *across* the southernmost continent. "The discovery of the South Pole will not be the end of Antarctic exploration," he had written in the London newspaper the *Daily Mail*. "The next work [is] a transcontinental journey from sea to sea." Now, in late 1913, Shackleton nursed his wounded pride and made plans to lead a new expedition.

It was a daring proposition. As Shackleton explained to the Royal Geographical Society in early 1914, "there is not one person in this room tonight, and there is not one individual who is under the Union Jack in any part of the Empire, who does not wish the British Flag to be the first national flag ever carried across the frozen waste." The explorer also had personal reasons for going south again. "I feel much older and a bit weary," the thirty-nine-year-old explained to Elspeth Beardmore, wife of a former patron, "but perhaps the Antarctic will make me young again."

CHAPTER THREE

Preparing to Cross Antarctica

As 1914 opened, Shackleton pushed ahead with preparations for the expedition. His plan called for two ships. One would sail into the Weddell Sea and deposit a shore party, which would establish base camp and prepare for the upcoming journey. From this point, a smaller group, consisting of Shackleton and five men, would travel south to the Pole; they would then descend the Beardmore Glacier and head north to McMurdo Sound on the Ross Sea.

A second ship would sail directly to the Ross Sea, establish its own base camp, and dispatch a team to lay depots of food and other supplies that would sustain the overland party during the second half of their journey. The second vessel would then await the transcontinental team's arrival on the Ross Sea coast.

In all respects, Shackleton's expedition was a formidable undertaking. For one thing, there were the logistical challenges of organizing two crews and equipping two polar vessels. For another, there was the Weddell Sea itself, which was infamous for its large, unpredictable ice floes and swirling currents. It was hardly surprising that most expeditions to Antarctica had traveled south to the other (Australian) side of the continent. As for the overland journey—about eighteen hundred miles—many considered it impossible. Shackleton calculated that he and his five companions could travel about fifteen miles a day—only one mile a day slower than the impressive pace set by Amundsen, the fastest polar explorer of the time. But the Norwegian had relied primarily on skis and dog sleds, and the British explorer had little experience with either. As he planned his enterprise, he arranged to carry dogs and dog sleds to Antarctica. But he showed little passion in learning how to use these resources and then perfect such use.

In retrospect, the scant attention Shackleton paid to travel by skis or dogsleds was a mistake. If he and his men had been proficient in either of these methods, they might have mitigated the crisis in which they found themselves by late 1915. And it seems likely that as disaster unfolded, the explorer recognized that he'd committed a serious oversight. The point here is that even great leaders don't get it right all the time. Truly courageous leadership, as we shall see, announces itself in the way a given individual accepts responsibility for his or her errors and then recovers from them, learning all the while.

In 1913, raising money for polar exploration proved tough going. Given the complexities of the two-ship plan, Shackleton estimated he would need at least £50,000 ($6.6 million today), and possibly as much as £80,000 ($10.6 million). As Britain and other European nations prepared for war, investors were wary of all kinds of ventures, even those they had once financed. The Royal Geographical Society was still interested in polar exploration, but officials were critical of Shackleton's plans, granting him a symbolic donation of only £1,000 (about $132,000 today). Many other potential backers considered his proposal too dangerous, declining to lend money or public endorsement.

Shackleton approached fund-raising with the verve and creativity of a determined entrepreneur. He hired a photographer with an eye to selling images and film footage taken on the expedition. In the months leading up to the expedition's launch, he also formed a syndicate to monetize the moving-picture rights and sold an official account of the expedition to the London-based *Daily Chronicle*. Shackleton also cultivated friendships with newspaper reporters who promoted him and his voyage. With persistence, money came in, much of it from wealthy supporters. For example, Dame Janet Stancomb Wills, heiress to a tobacco fortune, made a generous donation and became a lifelong friend. Birmingham industrialist Dudley Docker gave £10,000 for one of the two ships. Another important gift came from Sir James Key Caird, a Scottish magnate who was struck by Shackleton's determination and confidence. Caird promised £24,000 (about $3.2 million today), the single largest donation the explorer received. (As a sign of gratitude, Shackleton named the three lifeboats aboard the main ship after the three benefactors.) By the summer of 1914, the explorer had raised or borrowed most of the money he needed.

At the same time, Shackleton turned his attention to the equipment and supplies the voyage would demand. Polar ships required special construction. In an era when most vessels were made of steel and iron, ships going to Antarctica needed the strength and pliability of reinforced wood hulls to resist the relentless pressure of ice floes without cracking or splitting. And Shackleton demanded even more customization. He needed a darkroom for a photographer and berths on deck for sled dogs.

In a Norwegian shipyard, he found a wooden craft of three hundred tons equipped with extra cabin space and a darkroom. Priced at £11,600, she was a bargain, and Shackleton bought her on credit, renaming the ship *Endurance* after his family motto, By Endurance We Conquer. He intended this vessel to travel through the Weddell Sea, carrying the transcontinental party and other crew members to the coast of Antarctica, where they would set up base camp. For the Ross Sea side of the expedition, Shackleton bought the *Aurora*, a tried-and-tested polar ship.

Shackleton also organized supplies, including clothing and camping gear. He bought the latest technology in polar wear: windproof Burberry coats, Jaeger woolen long underwear, mufflers, balaclavas, and reindeer-fur-lined finnesko boots. He purchased the best available tents and sleeping bags.

Then there was the matter of feeding his men. In the late-nineteenth and early-twentieth centuries, proper nourishment presented serious challenges to Antarctic polar expeditions. If the men did not eat enough, they would die; if they did not eat the right combinations of food, they would grow seriously ill. But what amounts and which varieties of food provided the best fuel? With the science of nutrition still in its infancy, opinion varied widely.

Many polar expeditions, including Robert Falcon Scott's final venture in 1911–12, probably saw severe cases of scurvy. Since his first trip south, Shackleton had believed that fresh meat was a preventive to the disease; this time, he intended to feed expedition members with large amounts of freshly killed seal and penguin. He also commissioned capsules of lime juice. (Later scientific research would corroborate Shackleton's faith in both fresh meat and lime juice; the vitamin C in each has been found to help ward off scurvy.) The explorer also consulted with a chemist, and together, the two men devised the "composition cake." Something akin to today's energy bars, the composition cakes were made from oatmeal, sugar, beef powder, oleo, and casein (milk protein). Each cake supplied nearly three thousand calories, or about three-quarters of the caloric total that Shackleton calculated each man would need per day. He planned to supplement daily rations with sugar, powdered milk, nut food, tea, salt, and Marmite (a brown paste made from yeast extract). Like other effective leaders, Shackleton was comfortable moving between the big actions demanded by his mission and the small details essential to achieving it.

Legend has it that to attract potential crew members, Shackleton placed the following newspaper advertisement: "Men wanted for Hazardous Journey. Small wages, bitter cold, long months of complete darkness, constant danger, safe return doubtful. Honour and recognition in case of success." This certainly makes for compelling reading in our time, and it is conceivable that Shackleton placed the notice. He was searching for men with a specific outlook and orientation, and this ad would have appealed to such individuals. But no record of it has survived, and as polar historian Roland Huntford has pointed out, the explorer did not need to spend his money on advertising. The press had made much of his latest enterprise, and once Shackleton had publicly announced his expedition in late 1913, applicants showed up in droves at his London office. According to his friend Hugh Robert Mill, hundreds of men applied to join the venture; another source put the number of candidates at five thousand.

Bridges Adams, an acquaintance who directed an acting company, remembered a conversation in which Shackleton explained his views on hiring. The leader, Adams recalled, "was fascinated when I described the formation of a repertory company, and how character and temperament mattered quite as much as acting ability; just *his* problem, he said—*he* had to balance his types too, and their science or seamanship weighed little against the kind of chaps they were." As he read the candidates' letters, Shackleton divided them into three categories: "Mad," "Hopeless," and "Possible." He met face-to-face with those in the Possible category, searching for cheerfulness, a sense of humor, and other qualities he associated with optimism, a personal trait he deemed essential for men on a daring, dangerous mission. One applicant recalled that his interview with Shackleton was less than ten minutes long. During this time, the commander

> asked me if my teeth were good, if I suffered from varicose veins, if I had a good temper, and if I could sing. At this question I probably looked a bit taken aback, for I remember he said, "O, I don't mean any [opera singer Enrico] Caruso stuff; but I suppose you can shout a bit with the boys?" He then asked me if my circulation was good. I said it was except for one finger, which frequently went dead in cold weather. He asked me if I would seriously mind losing it. I said I would risk that. . . . After this he put out his hand and said "Very well, I'll take you."

When Shackleton reviewed the qualifications of applicants who had previously been to the Antarctic, he looked for perseverance and stamina. For example, he hired Tom Crean, a sinewy Irishman who had saved the lives of two men on a past polar expedition by traveling thirty miles without stopping to eat or sleep. When it came to hiring crew hands, Shackleton wanted men who had worked on fishing trawlers in the North Sea. He knew these sailors were accustomed to spending long hours on frozen, windswept decks and believed they would be able to tolerate the harsh conditions off the Antarctic coast.

The leader's most important hire, however, did not interview for the job at all. Frank Wild, one of Shackleton's colleagues on the *Nimrod* voyage, volunteered as soon as he learned of the transcontinental journey. Having trekked to within one hundred miles of the South Pole together in 1908, both men had unshakable confidence in each other. The explorer appointed Wild his second-in-command.

Here is another key insight for modern leaders: hire for attitude, train for skill. Shackleton understood that the more volatile and uncertain the environment, the more important it is to have individuals who can and *want* to embrace the disruption, who understand how to thrive in ambiguity and respond quickly to its unforeseen challenges. These aspects, the leader realized, depend more heavily on an individual's temperament and outlook than they do on professional rank, technical expertise, or specific job history. Like Shackleton, today's leaders need team members and other stakeholders who can acknowledge turbulence, embrace its opportunities, and meet its challenges with confidence and effect.

In July 1914, the *Endurance* was docked in London, loading supplies and sixty-nine sled dogs while the crew readied the vessel for the journey south. As preparations advanced, the rumblings of war grew louder. On July 28, Austria-Hungary declared war on Serbia, following the assassination of Archduke Franz Ferdinand, heir to the throne, by a Yugoslav nationalist. Britain vowed to join the conflict against Austria-Hungary and its ally Germany, and World War I began.

Almost immediately, Shackleton sent a telegram offering to turn his entire expedition over to the British military effort, but the government declined. First Lord of the Admiralty Winston Churchill wrote back, explaining that the expedition had been organized with the support of authorities, and thus the government did not want to interfere. On August 4, 1914, the day Britain declared war on Germany, Shackleton received royal approval from King George V, and *Endurance* set sail. By midmonth, it was heading to Buenos Aires, where it would take on additional crew and provisions before heading south.

Sailing separately for South America—some six weeks after the *Endurance* had departed—Shackleton arrived in Buenos Aires to discover his expedition was not ready to depart. For one thing, Frank Worsley, captain of the *Endurance*, had proved largely incapable of keeping discipline during the journey to South America. Observing this, Shackleton restructured the expedition's command to reduce the captain's discretionary authority. For another, the dog trainer scheduled to join the venture dropped out at the last minute because of a contract dispute. Left with few alternatives, the commander elected to head for Antarctica without a trainer, even though he and his men had little experience driving dog teams.

From Argentina, the ship sailed for South Georgia Island, a British territory roughly two thousand miles southeast and home to a Norwegian whaling station. There, Shackleton planned to post letters and obtain his last supplies. In November, when the ship arrived at the island, the commander confronted new, unexpected obstacles. Whalers reported that ice floes in the Weddell Sea were the farthest north they could remember, advising Shackleton to remain in South Georgia until the southern summer set in. Initially, Shackleton agreed and waited for the pack ice to recede. But a month later, with conditions unchanged, he decided to set sail for the bottom of the world. It was December 5, 1914.

Within days, the *Endurance* met the dreaded pack ice. The number and density of the floes surprised the leader and his crew. The ice and the conditions created by it were constantly shifting. Sometimes, as Roland Huntford has written, the pack seemed "frankly malevolent, it was closed and impenetrable." At other moments, it would slacken, apparently "cunning and deceptively friendly." From the bridge, Shackleton kept watch on the ocean's changing surface.

As the ship navigated through the jigsaw puzzle of ice, the commander and his crew took their measure of each other. "Shackleton afloat" was "a more likeable character than Shackleton ashore," the expedition's physicist, Reginald James, later remembered. Most of the men knew the famous explorer only from their short interviews and did not realize until they were well under way just how tightly he ran his ship. He expected good work, efficiently done. He demanded unquestioning loyalty and responsiveness to his orders. The men on board felt his careful eye upon them, whether they were on duty or off.

But Shackleton didn't lead solely by dint of his authority. He believed he had to earn his men's trust and loyalty, and he did this by connecting personally with each expedition member. "When [Shackleton] came across you by yourself," Dr. Macklin recalled,

he would get into conversation and talk to you in an intimate sort of way, asking you little things about yourself—how you were getting on, how you liked it, what particular side of the work you were enjoying most. . . . Sometimes when you felt he'd been perhaps a bit ruthless, pushing you round a bit hard, he seemed to have the knack of undoing any bad effect he'd had with these little intimate talks; he immediately put you back on a feeling of rightness with him.

Shackleton worked to find common ground, often discussing history, sports, and other subjects. To crew members, moments alone with their leader seemed extemporaneous, unique, and often validating. "One found it rather flattering at the time, to have him discussing Thackeray, for instance, or asking you if you'd ever read Browning," Macklin observed. As a shrewd student of human psychology, Shackleton knew he needed to build strong relations with all his team, regardless of rank and grade. On earlier expeditions to Antarctica, he had seen the dangerous consequences of discord. Now, on the *Endurance*, he endeavored to gain his team members' confidence and respect, fostering cohesion among them as he did. The crew responded positively; the men soon gave him the good-natured nickname of Boss.

For all his bonhomie, however, the leader brooked no arguments or negotiations. Instead, Wild, his second-in-command, became, as Macklin put it, a "sort of foreman." "When we wanted things," the ship's surgeon recalled, "instead of going to Shackleton we went to Wild." The commander's right-hand man always listened carefully to the men, fielding their questions and complaints, and noticing that the opportunity to vent frustration frequently sufficed to ease whatever tensions had arisen. Wild's role as a sounding board and sometime mediator enabled Shackleton to create distance between himself and the crew, and this, in turn, helped preserve his authority.

As the *Endurance* made its way south, the ice thickened, and the pace slowed. By Christmas Eve 1914, floes closed in around the ship, immobilizing it. There was little to do but wait for the ice to loosen. Wanting to maintain positive energy among his team, the Boss ordered a holiday celebration. The men decorated the mess room, feasting on soup, mince pies, plum pudding, and canned goods such as herring and rabbit. After a time, the pack ice broke, and the ship sailed on. But on New Year's Eve, two floes jammed the *Endurance*, upending the ship six degrees and threatening to sink her. The crew hauled her out of the pressure zone using an ice anchor and chain, and the journey south continued. The expedition was now more than half-way to Shackleton's intended destination along the Antarctic coast.

After weeks of skirting, ramming, and circumnavigating ice floes, in early January 1915 the expedition approached the coast of the continent. During the next five days, the *Endurance* sailed south-west, along the continent's edge, coming within sight of an inlet that might have served as a landing place. But the commander did not want to stop there. He hoped to reach Vahsel Bay, where the crew would set up base camp. From this point, the overland party would have an efficient route to the Pole, and then across the remainder of Antarctica. By January 15, Shackleton was sure he had a clear run to his destination.

But it was not to be. Three days later, moving ice locked the vessel in its grip. To conserve coal, Captain Frank Worsley decided to stop trying to ram through the pack ice and instead wait for open water. The next day, the floes closed around the ship, and the *Endurance* was trapped. It was January 19, 1915.

CHAPTER FOUR

A New Mission

Shackleton and his crew watched for signs of an opening in the ice, but none appeared. He directed the men to keep the boilers going, so the *Endurance* could move quickly if the pack loosened. But on January 27, after eight days of the ship's being locked in the floe, the commander ordered the engine fires put out. Now the ship was captive in the ice, moving with the currents. The team prepared to spend the summer aboard the ship, waiting for the pack to thaw and release the vessel into open water.

Circumstances shifted dramatically for the crew. Routines changed; there was simply less to do aboard the trapped, drifting ship, and this discomfited the team. As crew members tried to come to grips with their new situation, tensions occasionally flared. Small stuff that would not have mattered under ordinary conditions became a source of irritability and potential antagonism. The ship's storekeeper, Thomas Orde-Lees, for example, began criticizing the table manners of carpenter Henry "Chippy" McNish. "At scooping up peas with his knife," Orde-Lees recorded in his diary, "he is a perfect juggler." McNish himself disapproved of the coarse language favored by certain members of the overland party. Even the ship's fare came under attack. Serving fresh seal meat was "a . . . cheap way of running the expedition," griped seaman Walter How.

The twenty-seven men under Shackleton's leadership had different jobs: officers who directed the expedition, scientists who conducted experiments, and sailors who kept the vessel running. They also came from various social and economic backgrounds. In the face of these distinctions, Shackleton worked to minimize differences among the men. He knew from his own experience in Antarctica that friction and mistrust could kill the enterprise. What the group needed most in the crisis they now confronted was unity and faith in their collective ability to navigate through it.

To promote such solidarity and confidence, the leader used several tactics. For example, in a deviation from maritime norms, he divided the daily manual tasks equally among officers, scientists, and sailors. Orde-Lees, who had held a major's commission in the British army, worked "to put aside pride of caste," asserting that "scrubbing floors is not fair work for people who have been brought up in refinement." Despite his grumbling, he admitted that sharing labor worked well to minimize jealousies among the crew. "As a disciplinary measure," he wrote in his diary, "it humbles one & knocks out of one any last remnants of false pride."

To foster camaraderie, Shackleton insisted that everyone gather each evening after dinner in the ship's wardroom. Sometimes the men looked at lantern slides (progenitors of 35 mm slides and today's digital photographs) that the ship's photographer Frank Hurley had collected. They played parlor games and talked politics and books. Shackleton was always there, taking charge of sing-alongs, interjecting jokes, or demonstrating his mastery at Animal, Vegetable, Mineral. The leader's involvement was not a function of inherent bossiness or a need for control. Rather, his purpose was to keep the men engaged in ongoing interaction. He regarded socialization as a vital safeguard against doubt, despair, and moral collapse.

The leader soon discovered that he had other psychological issues to contend with; idleness, boredom, and ennui were almost as dangerous among men whose planned work had largely disappeared. Shackleton battled these threats to collective morale by insisting that, as far as possible, every man maintain his ordinary duties. These included swabbing the decks, organizing supplies, taking care of the sled dogs, and watching for navigable breaks in the ice. He asked the scientists to collect specimens from the ice and make meteorological observations. Whenever stocks of fresh meat ran low, the commander appointed teams to hunt for seal and penguin, insisting that meals and entertainment continue on a strict schedule.

Still, the men had time on their hands. To help fill the days and keep his crew and dogs fit, Shackleton set up a dog-training schedule. He divided the animals into six teams, assigning one crew member as the driver of each. The men and dogs often conducted their training runs out on the ice as the sun was setting, returning to the ship by moonlight. Shackleton even approved racing among the teams. In June, for example, the crew held the "Antarctic Derby." The men wagered cigarettes, chocolates, and money; the Boss laid down five pounds on Frank Wild's team and was thrilled when his bet paid off. The men loved working with the dogs. And as Huntford has pointed out, all this labor held out the possibility that the overland crossing was still ahead.

Shackleton wanted to keep his men as optimistic as possible. He recognized that how he showed up before them had a great effect on their outlook. So he was always prepared to locate himself at the center of spontaneous entertainment. One day, for example, he surprised his men by waltzing across the pack ice with Worsley. Such a display, Orde-Lees noted, was typical:

> That is Sir Ernest all over. . . . He is always able to keep his troubles under and show a bold front. His unfailing cheeriness means a lot to a band of disappointed explorers like ourselves. In spite of his own great disappointment and we all know that is disasterous [sic] enough, he never appears to be anything but the acme of good humour and hopefulness. He is one of the greatest optimists living.

We know from Shackleton's diary, and from later accounts by Wild and Worsley, that such optimism was by no means the entire story. Like many leaders in great turbulence, the commander was anxious about larger conditions. Almost as soon as the *Endurance* was caught in pack ice, for example, he worried that the Weddell Sea's unpredictable currents would carry the ship to a place that would make the transcontinental trek all but impossible.

But Shackleton never let his men see this concern—or his bigger fears. He understood very well the effect his demeanor would have on his men. If he appeared hesitant or fearful, this would diminish the team's confidence in him and in their ability to stay alive on the icebound ship. Whether he was on the bridge scanning the horizon, giving orders, or talking with an individual crew member, the commander appeared engaged and confident. Over and over, he used his presence and energy to convey resolve and assurance.

In mid-February 1915, a crack appeared in the ice ahead, creating a two-hundred-yard vein of water in which the ship might sail. The men jumped from the deck with picks and shovels in hopes of extending the opening. But after a full day of hard labor, they had made almost no progress, and Shackleton gave the order to stop. Careful to minimize the apparent setback, the Boss presented the overall situation as one of delay rather than disaster. He explained to the men that the ship might remain stuck in the ice through the approaching winter, and that now he would plan for a landing the following summer.

The days became weeks, and the weeks became months, and still the ice held the ship. As April passed, daylight hours waned; in early May, the men found themselves in the complete darkness of the Antarctic winter. Before the light faded completely, the crew had hunted aggressively for seals, stockpiling five thousand pounds of meat and blubber. Now, with daylight gone, outside temperatures plummeted to an average of -17° Fahrenheit (-27° Celsius). The men converted the ship's main hold into communal living quarters kept comfortable by the heat of a coal stove and the light of a paraffin lamp that hung from the ceiling.

In the darkness, there was little outside work to be done, so the men passed their spare time by writing in diaries, reading, listening to music from a hand-crank phonograph, and playing cards and chess. They continued to congregate after dinner for conversation and the occasional amateur vaudeville. Still, Shackleton worried constantly about collective morale and, in late May, ordered everyone to cut one another's hair. In the ceremonial shearing, Shackleton himself was the first to go under the scissors. Worsley described the scene:

The amateur barber seizes his victim with the air of a man about to do a mighty deed. He brandishes the clippers aloft, they descend & a yell of protest rises from the unfortunate object of his attentions. . . . Each as he looks across at his neighbour goes off into fits of laughter. All now look so irresistibly quaint, comical or criminal, that the camera is called in to perpetuate this evening & to cure us, where necessary, of conceit of our personal appearance.

Beginning in June, the ocean currents grew more turbulent. While the skies above appeared relatively calm, huge ice flocs banged and pressed against the ship. By July, Shackleton and his men could feel the vessel quivering between the plates; her timbers groaned, her hull shifted. The commander doubted the *Endurance* could withstand the force much longer. In mid-July, he took Wild and Frank Worsley, the expedition captain, into his confidence, telling them, as the latter remembered, that the ship was near her end. "You had better make up your mind that it is only a matter of time," he said. "It may be a few months, and it may only be a question of weeks, or even days. . . . What the ice gets . . . the ice keeps."

For the next four months, the *Endurance* continued to drift. She had now traveled almost seven hundred miles west and then north from Shackleton's intended landing point in Vahsel Bay. The ship was heading into softer, but also potentially more dangerous, ice—floes that were as likely to break her into pieces as they were to split apart and release the vessel into open water.

On October 23, the ice began its final attack on the ship. The pressure intensified, and her iron plates buckled. Beams bulged, and the vessel began to leak. Gallons of water poured in. The steam pumps could not keep pace. While the ship's carpenter, "Chippy" McNish, worked furiously belowdecks to build a dam, Shackleton ordered his men to the hand pumps. "Every spell on [the pumps] was an agony," Macklin remembered. The men's efforts held the boat intact for four days.

But on October 27, 1915, the "stout little ship," that "bride of the sea," as the men had dubbed her, finally gave in. The decks warped and splintered; the sternpost broke. And the keel, a key component of the ship's structural frame, tore off. More water rushed in. Standing on the quivering deck, Shackleton looked down through a skylight. "[I] saw the engines dropping sideways as the stays and bed-plates gave way," he remembered. "I cannot describe the impression of relentless destruction that was forced upon me as I looked down and around. The floes, with the force of millions of tons of moving ice behind them, were simply annihilating the ship."

The Boss ordered his men to abandon the *Endurance*. In plans laid down weeks before, crew members moved the dogs, the three lifeboats, stores, and essential gear onto the floe. Shackleton insisted on taking meteorologist Leonard Hussey's banjo, calling it "vital mental medicine." The men and dogs spent the night on thick ice nearby; but no one slept much. On the deck of the *Endurance*, a light went on and off intermittently. "You could hear the ship being crushed up," Chief Officer Lionel Greenstreet recalled, "the ice being ground into her, and you almost felt your own ribs were being crushed, and suddenly a light [on the ship's deck] went on for a moment and then went out. It seemed the end of everything."

While his men tried to sleep, Shackleton spent the night prowling the ice. Hurley observed the leader:

Sir Ernest was ever on the watch and, as I took refuge in one of the tents from the stabbing wind, the last sight I had that night was of a sombre figure pacing slowly up and down in the dark. I could not fail to admire the calm poise that disguised his anxiety, as he pondered on the next move. What was the best thing to do? How should he shape his tactics in the next round of the fight with death, with the lives of twenty-eight men at stake? I realised [then] the loneliness and penalty of leadership.

Early the next morning, Shackleton called his crew together, quietly explaining that he would get them home. "His first thought," Greenstreet observed, "was for the men under him. He didn't care if he went without a shirt on his back so long as the men he was leading had sufficient clothing. He was a wonderful man that way; you felt that the party mattered more than anything else."

To keep his team active and spirits high, the Boss ordered them to march three hundred miles northwest across the ice to Snow Hill Island, where he believed they would find emergency stores. The team set out as planned, but made such slow progress that Shackleton called off the march after only two days.

CHAPTER FIVE

Life on the Ice

As soon as Shackleton ordered the march to stop, the team began preparing to spend the southern summer on the ice, naming their new home Ocean Camp. The commander divided the men into five tents and, with an eye to keeping morale high and discipline intact, chose a strong, optimistic leader for each. He assigned three of the more difficult expedition members to his own tent: the physicist Reginald James, whose clumsiness and academic demeanor had made him the focus of much teasing; Second Officer Hubert Hudson, who was prickly and argumentative; and the photographer Hurley, whose energy and ingenuity could sometimes slide into arrogance. Shackleton had long understood the saying "keep your friends close and your enemies closer." Now, to neutralize disagreement and sustain group morale, he put this understanding to good use.

As always, the leader was intent on keeping the crew busy. Days began with an early breakfast of seal steak, porridge, or canned provisions, after which each man set about his assigned chores. While the cook, Charles Green, prepared the next meal, others melted ice into drinking water, repaired equipment, or tended the dogs. Most of the men spent long hours hunting seals, whose meat was the mainstay of the team's diet, and whose blubber fueled the specially constructed stove that Hurley had rigged up.

Lunch consisted of bannocks, which were fried lumps of flour flavored with lentils and whatever else Green could find, as well as tea and jam. At 5:30 p.m., the men ate dinner, which usually consisted of more bannocks, hoosh—a stew made from a mix of dried meat, fat, and cereal to which fresh seal or penguin had been added—and watery hot cocoa. In the evenings, the men played cards, read, or talked until lights-out at 8:30 p.m. (November above the antarctic circle meant nearly sixteen hours of sunlight each day, so the crew often crawled into their sleeping bags before dark.) Topics of conversation included the weather, the movement of the ice, and when they were likely to set sail in the lifeboats. By 10:00 p.m., the camp was still and quiet; the only sounds and movements were those of the designated night watchman as he made his rounds.

During the weeks after establishing Ocean Camp, the men and their dog teams traveled back and forth between the wreck of the *Endurance* and their new home, salvaging supplies. In total, the crew recovered more than three tons of stores, including flour, sugar, rice, walnuts, barley, lentils, canned vegetables, and jam. They also pried boards and nails from the vessel, turning these over to the carpenter, who used them to reinforce the lifeboats.

After most of the foodstuffs had been brought to Ocean Camp, Hurley tried to rescue his negatives and moving-picture film from the wrecked ship. Without Shackleton's knowledge, Hurley and one of the sailors hacked their way through the broken timbers. "I made up my mind," the photographer remembered, "to dive in after them. It was mighty cold work groping about in the mushy ice in the semi-darkness of the ship's bowels, but I was rewarded in the end and passed out three previous tins [that held the images]. While Seaman [Walter] How was massaging me vigorously to restore my circulation, the vessel began to shake and groan ominously. We sprang for our lives and leaped onto the ice." The commander agreed to let Hurley keep some of the moving film and negatives. The photographer chose 120 images from a total of 400, smashing the remaining ones on the ice to remove any possibility of changing his mind.

Nearly four weeks after the men had abandoned the *Endurance*, the ship sank through the ice and was gone. It was a huge loss, but no one felt the disappointment more deeply than Shackleton. He knew all too well that the ship's disappearance was the end of a venture on which he had staked not only enormous energy and other resources, but also great personal ambition. "With a war under way at home," as writer Caroline Alexander has pointed out, "it was unlikely that [Shackleton] would have another opportunity of returning to the south anytime soon; this was his last shot." As the leader surveyed the vast, icy landscape that stretched out endlessly in every direction, he saw the end of his dream of walking across Antarctica and achieving enduring fame.

Nonetheless, he was completely committed to his new mission: bring his men safely back to civilization. With historical perspective, we can see that once conditions changed unexpectedly and irrevocably, Shackleton jettisoned one objective, to walk across the continent, and embraced another, to save his crew. This is an important lesson that all leaders operating in great turbulence must learn: how to let go of former goals and embrace new ones, even dramatically different objectives, as circumstances demand.

Shackleton had no idea how he was going to get his men home. There was much he couldn't control, and many times he couldn't make visible progress toward his goal—all he and his men could do was wait. This frustrated him to no end. "Put footstep of courage into stirrup of patience," reads a diary entry from around this time. On another page, Shackleton scribbled only, "Waiting Waiting Waiting." And on a third, "Patience Patience Patience."

The commander did his best to shield his men from his own anxiety and exasperation. This exacted a heavy toll. In early December, for example, he suffered intermittent bouts of what he labeled "sciatica"—a painful condition resulting from the compression of spinal nerves. At times, he was in so much agony he could not leave his sleeping bag. But even as he lay there, he debated how to maintain the crew's productive energy. James, who shared a tent with the Boss, recalled that despite poor health and limited mobility during these weeks, Shackleton was "constantly on the watch for any break in morale, or any discontent, so that he could deal with it at once."

Everyone was keenly interested in their location. Using instruments salvaged from the *Endurance*, Worsley gauged the crew's location and predicted the path of the ice floe. The men hoped that winds and currents would carry them north and west toward Snow Hill Island. But in mid-December, calculations revealed that the floe was drifting alternately northwest and then east, *away* from land. To counteract the drift and the idleness that he sensed was beginning to settle over his team, Shackleton decided to attempt a second march. The leader estimated that the end of the pack ice—and therefore an opportunity to launch the lifeboats into open water—lay about 150 miles to the west.

When the Boss announced his decision, the men's reactions were mixed. Some, such as Macklin, were excited to be doing something; others worried that in slightly warmer temperatures, the ice would be too soft to traverse. Shackleton decided the group would travel at night when the temperature was lower, and the ice more solid underfoot. On December 22, 1915, he ordered an early Christmas celebration, allowing the men to eat as much as they wished (Greenstreet observed that after the meal, the men each felt "full as a tick"). Early the next morning, the party set out from Ocean Camp with two lifeboats and all the stores they could carry.

Once again, the march was exhausting and discouraging. Men in harnesses pulled two of the boats on sledges over slushy, uneven ice for hours at a time. Dog teams carried other loads between Ocean Camp and the changing location of the front of the line. But as with the first attempt at marching overland, the party covered little ground. By the fourth day, they had moved about six miles. Given the wet conditions and rough terrain, an extended trek seemed impossible.

But this time, Shackleton did not issue any change in orders. On the fifth day, he and Wild set out ahead to search for a workable route across the ice; when they returned, McNish announced he would no longer march. Angry, exhausted, and in physical pain, the carpenter had openly challenged Worsley, whom the Boss had left in charge. Now the carpenter took on Shackleton himself, arguing that his duty to follow the commander's orders had officially ended when the *Endurance* sank. Without a word, the leader walked away and returned with a copy of the Ship's Articles. Then he called the men together and reviewed the clauses aloud, making one critical change: he declared (speciously) that one of these ensured that the

Articles hadn't been terminated when the ship was lost. This meant that the men's wages wouldn't cease when the *Endurance* sank. It also meant that the men owed their loyalty to their commander. The Boss promised to pay every man until they reached port.

This extemporaneous revision of maritime law accomplished two critical things. First, it isolated McNish, whose insubordination, if unchecked, could have led to widespread defiance. Second, as Huntford has written, "it lifted the worry that had been gnawing [at the men] since the ship went down" that they wouldn't be paid. "It removed the cause of discontent."

Still, McNish's challenge had given voice to what each member of the team was thinking: in the prevailing conditions, it was pointless to continue marching. Indeed, two days later, Shackleton halted the trek on the grounds that the party had covered few miles and rations were short. Then, he resolved, as he noted in his diary, "to camp once more on the floe and to possess our souls with what patience we could till conditions appeared more favourable for a renewal of the attempt to escape." The Boss called their new location Patience Camp.

As the New Year 1916 dawned, all Shackleton could hope for was that currents would carry the floe toward Paulet Island, north of Snow Hill Island; in either place, he believed the men would find cached stores. In the meantime, the leader was concerned about food supplies, particularly when the men found few penguins and seals to hunt. In mid-January, he ordered most of the dogs shot to conserve food; the animals required a seal a day while the same amount of meat could feed the men for three. Dog meat could also be made into stew for the team. The men had long known that the dogs could not travel with them in any kind of open-boat journey and had thus foreseen their companions' end. But the men had also become emotionally attached to the animals and were deeply grieved by their deaths. "Hail to thee old leader Shakespeare," Hurley wrote in tribute to his favorite dog. "I shall ever remember thee—fearless, faithful & diligent."

In early February, Shackleton authorized Wild to take eighteen men back to Ocean Camp to retrieve the third lifeboat they had left behind. The leader met his men returning with the vessel about a mile out of Patience Camp. With him was "a sledge with a hoosh pot full of tea," James remembered, "the most welcome tea I ever had." Captain Worsley was greatly relieved to have the third lifeboat at hand. Twenty-eight men would need all three crafts when open water appeared and they sailed for help.

With the rescue of the remaining lifeboat, there was little left to do. The men passed the time hunting when penguins and seals appeared, walking around the floe for exercise, and reading the few books they had salvaged from the ship. At times, harsh weather confined them to the tents during the day. But getting any kind of rest was difficult in the frayed, thinning structures. Their sleeping bags were often wet by day and frozen at night.

The Boss ordered the men to sleep fully clothed so they would be ready to take to the boats quickly if the ice broke up. The leader's plan offered the men hope that at any moment they might make a move toward safety. But the ice did not loosen, and the crew became frustrated; some grew depressed. In early March, Worsley let loose in his diary, longing for a way forward, "however little to aid our escape from this white interminable prison where the minds energies & abilities of all are atrophying & where we are rusting & wasting our lives away, while the whole world is at War & we know nothing of how it goes."

Shackleton and Wild worked to maintain morale under the strain. The second-in-command was patient and modest; the commander was more active, explaining his decisions to the team, watching for ways to make the men's food more satisfying even as stores ran down, visiting each tent after dinner to recite poetry or play cards, and never losing an opportunity to maintain as much normalcy as he could. For example, one day, in honor of the leap year 1916, he ordered three full meals and hot beverages with each. "We all feel well fed & happy tonight," Worsley wrote. Not only did such orders bolster the men's spirits, they also communicated Shackleton's concern for their welfare.

Time after time, the Boss used calculated offerings of food and hot drinks as a leadership tool. For millennia, women have understood that food does much more than provide sustenance. And they have used it to lead their families and other networks: to hush a crying baby, soothe a cranky partner, bring people together, or show affection for loved ones. Shackleton understood that one important way to a man's well-being was through his stomach and consistently acted on this understanding. From a historian's perspective, these actions look almost maternal and thus tinged with irony in the intensely masculine world of polar expeditions. But the crew members saw nothing strange or questionable about what their leader was doing. Food and hot drink nourished and, at times, comforted them. It brought them together as a group. It reestablished stability amid pervasive disruption. The literal feeding and watering of his men was one of the most powerful things that Shackleton did.

CHAPTER SIX

Journey to Dry Land

In March 1916, the pack began to change. The men felt the ocean swell beneath the floe; the Boss paced the ice relentlessly looking for leads to open water. At one point, the floe opened, but then it quickly closed again. It was an anxious time. Food supplies were dwindling. Autumn was approaching. Tempers were short. The men were keen to launch the lifeboats and sail for land, no matter how dangerous the prevailing currents and movements of the surrounding icebergs.

As the floe continued to heave and crack, Shackleton carefully considered his next move. He was as eager to act as his men—perhaps more so. But, as Huntford has written, even then "he did not lose the gift of separating emotion and judgment." The leader realized that if they set sail without a viable lead to open water, the lifeboats might be crushed by the pack. On March 23, the men spotted Paulet Island, some forty miles west. Still, Shackleton waited. Without open water in which to launch the boats, he could not give the order to set sail.

Then, at daybreak on April 7, the Boss and several men spotted Clarence Island, some sixty miles northwest of Patience Camp. Observing the ice and the ocean's movement, Shackleton was certain they were close to open water. He knew that their long-awaited boat journey was about to begin and described the moment:

> I feel sure that we are at the verge of the floe-ice. One strong gale followed by a calm would scatter the pack, I think, and then we

could push through. I have been thinking much of our prospects. The appearance of Clarence Island after our long drift seems, somehow, to convey an ultimatum. The island is the last outpost of the south and our final chance of a landing-place. Beyond it lies the broad Atlantic. Our little boats may be compelled any day now to sail unsheltered over the open sea, with a thousand leagues of ocean separating them from land to the north and east. It seems vital that we should land on Clarence Island or its neighbour, Elephant Island.

On April 9, Shackleton gave the order to launch the lifeboats and sail for land. He would command the *James Caird*. He appointed Worsley to lead the *Dudley Docker* and officer Hubert Hudson to steer the smallest boat, the *Stancomb Wills*. Sailor William Bakewell remembered that first day at sea as "one of the coldest and most dangerous of the expedition. The ice was running riot. It was a hard race to keep our boats in the open leads. . . . [W]e had many narrow escapes from being crushed when the larger masses of the pack would come together."

The first night brought more turbulence. The team camped on a floe, only to be rocked awake in the middle of the night as an ocean swell cracked open the ice beneath them and tossed seaman Ernest Holness, still encased in his sleeping bag, into the freezing waters. Shackleton immediately reached into the sea, grabbed the bag, and heaved it onto the ice with Holness inside. "A few seconds later," the leader remembered, "the ice-edges came together again with a tremendous force." The unfortunate sailor was wet and very cold, yet otherwise unharmed. But there would be no more rest that evening. Shackleton ordered hot milk and a small ration of food all round; the crew spent the remainder of the night huddled near the blubber-fired stove, listening to the calls of killer whales and watching for the possibility of another crack in the ice.

The days that followed in the open boats were just as difficult. Heavy waves, snow squalls, and shifting icebergs all threatened to capsize the small vessels. On the second night, moving pack ice came close to trapping the boats. From that point, Shackleton decided, they would not make camp again. As nighttime temperatures fell to -7°

Fahrenheit (-22° Celsius), sleep in the open boats became virtually impossible.

After several days, the weather cleared sufficiently for Worsley to attempt a reading of their position using a sextant (an instrument that measures the angle between the sun or another celestial object, and the horizon). Once he had these measurements and made some calculations, the captain could gauge the lifeboats' coordinates and thus their location. Shackleton estimated they had traveled more than thirty miles toward their target, but the sextant reading delivered what Worsley privately called "a terrible disapp[ointmen]t"· far from progressing northwest toward Clarence Island, the three boats had actually drifted thirty miles east and eleven miles south of their departure point. They were farther from their destination than when they had left Patience Camp.

For the rest of that day, the boats tossed about in choppy waters strewn with large chunks of ice. The high winds continued into the evening, and Shackleton ordered the three boats tied up stern-to-stern. The men assigned to keep watch kept their eyes peeled for icebergs as best they could through constant snow showers, rowing as necessary to keep the boats from colliding with hunks of the floating pack. The others did their best to sleep in the heaving, crowded vessels; the crew lay in one another's arms for warmth. "We clung motionless," the leader remembered, "whispering each to his companion our hopes and thoughts."

When dawn came, the men could see that the ice had formed a thick plating on each boat. Drawing the vessels alongside each other, crew members hacked the ice away as best they could. Meanwhile, Shackleton took measure of his team. "Most of the men were now looking seriously worn and strained," he observed. "Their lips were cracked and their eyes and eyelids showed red in their salt-encrusted faces." Some were seasick; many were suffering from diarrhea, which resulted from gnawing on frozen dog pemmican (a mixture of meat and fat). Every man was thirsty; the boats had launched into open water so quickly to avoid getting locked in the pack that the team had forgotten to bring plenty of freshwater ice. Seriously worried about his men's condition, Shackleton decided he must make land quickly. Calculating that Elephant Island was closer than Clarence Island, he decided to sail for the former, which was located about 550 miles south of Cape Horn, the southernmost point of South America.

As the boats turned toward Elephant Island, Shackleton could see hopelessness creeping across his men's faces. Fearing the crew was losing confidence that the boats would reach dry land, the commander stood up in the stern of the *James Caird* as a symbol of assurance. He remained there through the day and night, keeping what Orde-Lees called an "incessant vigil" over his crew. When the Boss noticed that Frank Hurley had lost his mittens, Shackleton

> at once divested himself of his own, and in spite of the fact that he was standing up in the most exposed position all the while he insisted upon Hurley's acceptance of the mitts, and on the latter's protesting Sir Ernest was on the point of throwing them overboard rather than wear them when one of his subordinates had to go without; as a consequence Sir Ernest had one finger rather severely frostbitten.

On April 15, 1916, after two more grueling days and nights, the party landed the boats on Elephant Island. The men were thrilled and relieved to be on solid ground. "We did not know, until it was released," Reginald James wrote in his diary, "what a strain the last few days had been. We took childish joy in looking at the black rocks and picking up the stones for we had stepped on no land since Dec. 5, 1914." The crew made camp, feasted on freshly killed seal, and then slept. "How delicious to wake in one's sleep and listen to the chanting of the penguins mingling with the music of the sea," Hurley wrote. "To fall asleep and awaken again and feel this is real. We have reached the land!!"

Shackleton's relief at getting all his men to terra firma alive was short-lived. He knew they wouldn't be rescued on Elephant Island. The small, uninhabited spit of land wasn't on any recognized shipping route. As important, their new home offered little shelter from the huge waves, powerful winds, and winter weather. "The icy fingers of the gale searched every cranny of our beach," the commander remembered, "and pushed relentlessly through our worn garments and tattered tents."

It was clear to Shackleton that his crew couldn't remain long on Elephant Island, and he began planning his next move. After consulting with Wild and Worsley, he decided to go for help. Looking back, Shackleton explained his choice of destination:

> The nearest port where assistance could certainly be secured was Port Stanley, in the Falkland Islands, 540 miles away, but we could scarcely hope to beat up against the prevailing north-westerly wind in a frail and weakened boat with a small sail area. South Georgia [Island] was over 800 miles away [to the northeast] but lay in the area of west winds [meaning the island was navigable with these winds blowing behind the boat]. . . . [This] must be our objective.

Once the Boss had announced his decision to sail for South Georgia, he selected the men who would accompany him. Worsley, the captain, was essential because he was the best qualified to pilot the small boat through the stormy southern Atlantic while trying to locate the hundred-mile-long island. The leader also chose Tom Crean because he was tough, McNish for his abilities as a carpenter, and Timothy McCarthy and John Vincent because they were good sailors. Another important consideration in choosing McNish and Vincent was that both men could be difficult; Shackleton did not want them sowing dissent among those remaining on Elephant Island.

In preparation for the journey, McNish and others began readying the twenty-two-foot lifeboat, the *James Caird*. Using wood from packing cases and a sled, the carpenter built a framework for a deck that he covered in canvas. He reinforced the boat's keel with the mast from the *Stancomb Wills* and caulked the seams of the boat with lamp wick, oil paints, and seal blood. Other crew members loaded the bottom of the vessel with bags of shingle and loose stones to provide ballast in the churning waters. The crew packed a month's worth of food for the six men: sledging rations, biscuits, powdered milk, nut food, Bovril cubes, 250 pounds of ice, and two casks of freshwater they had melted from glacial ice. They also took matches, sleeping bags, a Primus stove, candles, a sextant, binoculars, Worsley's navigational charts, a compass, and a sea anchor.

While some of the team readied the *James Caird*, others made a more permanent camp on the island. The twenty-two men remaining would need the best protection they could devise from blizzards and falling temperatures. The other two lifeboats were upended to create a roof for a rudimentary shelter, and two four-foot walls were made of stones from the beach. When the primitive hut was completed, it was dark and cramped, measuring about nineteen feet by ten. When all the men were lying down inside, Hurley wrote, the hut was "a catacomb like scene of objects resembling mummies. These objects are us in reindeer sleeping bags mingling our snores with the roar of the blizzard."

Before setting out, Shackleton put Wild in charge of the crew members remaining on Elephant Island and left him written instructions. The leader explained:

> In the event of my not surviving the boat journey to South Georgia, you will do your best for the rescue of the party. You are in full command from the time the boat leaves this island, and all hands are under your orders. On your return to England, you are to communicate with the [Royal Geographical Society] Committee. I wish you, [Orde-]Lees & Hurley to write the book. You watch my interests. . . . I have every confidence in you and always have had. May God prosper your work and your life. You can convey my love to my people and say I tried my best.

On April 24, 1916, the *James Caird*, with Shackleton and his five-man crew, set out from Elephant Island. The weather on the first day of the trip was fair, and they traveled forty-five miles. By the second afternoon, however, the sailors faced gale-force winds and huge waves; these conditions prevailed day after day. "We fought the seas and the winds and at the same time had a daily struggle to keep ourselves alive," the leader remembered.

> At times we were in dire peril. Generally we were upheld by the knowledge that we were making progress towards the land where

we [wanted to] be, but there were days and nights when we lay hove to [with the helm and sail in fixed positions so that the boat did not have to be actively steered], drifting across the storm-whitened seas and watching with eyes interested rather than apprehensive the uprearing masses of water, flung to and fro by Nature in the pride of her strength. Deep seemed the valleys when we lay between the reeling seas. High were the hills when we perched momentarily on the tops of giant combers [long, curling waves]. Nearly always there were gales. So small was our boat and so great were the seas that often our sail flapped idly in the calm between the crests of two waves. Then we would climb the next slope and catch the full fury of the gale where the wool-like whiteness of the breaking water surged around us.

Early in the journey, Shackleton divided the crew into two teams that would alternate four-hour shifts of standing watch and resting. "The routine was," recalled Worsley, "three men in bags deluding themselves that they were sleeping, and three men 'on deck'; that is one man steering for an hour, while the other two [were] pumping, baling [sic] or handling sails." The man stationed at the helm had the most difficult job, bracing himself against giant, icy waves that hit the ship. The other two on watch were not better off since the boat required pumping. The frigid air left the brass pump so cold that it numbed a man's (gloved) hands within five minutes; this meant that those not steering had to change places frequently.

Even for the men who were purportedly resting, every hour was painful. The sleeping bags were arranged in a cramped five-by-seven-foot space in the bow of the vessel, accessible only by slithering on hands, knees, and stomach over the layer of rocks used as the boat's ballast. Conditions were extremely uncomfortable. "When we had slept for an hour or so we would wake up half-smothered," Worsley recalled. "More than once when I woke suddenly I was unable to collect my thoughts or realise where I was, and had the ghastly fear that I was buried alive."

By the third day, the *James Caird* had traveled 128 miles. But Worsley was not sure they were on course, and staying so was critical.

If the boat veered even a small way off and missed South Georgia, it would be carried into three thousand miles of open sea. The captain used a sextant to calculate their position; this instrument measured the angle between the sun and the horizon, but the former was rarely visible because of nearly constant cloud cover. The crew also had a primitive compass to help guide the boat. Still, at night, Worsley could check it only one or two times because there were few candles and matches to spare. He and his companions steered into the darkness by the feel of the wind and by observing the angle of the pennant that flew from the masthead.

On April 29, the fifth day, the crew had traveled 238 miles—almost a third of the total distance—toward South Georgia and were feeling the effects of continual exposure to the elements. Their skin was rubbed raw by wet clothes; they had developed boils; their hands burned from frostbite; and some of the men's legs had swelled from immersion in salt water as they bailed the vessel. To counter the cold and collective fatigue, Shackleton gave his team two hot meals a day cooked on the Primus stove in the tiny quarters "below-decks." Some of the food had originally been created for the overland crossing—"composition cakes," made of beef protein, fat, oats, sugar, and salt, that were heated with water into a kind of stew. Along with each half-pound serving of this mixture, the Boss added a sledging biscuit, four lumps of sugar, and the sweet nougat of nut food. Between meals, hot milk was served.

The leader carefully monitored each of his men. "Two of the party at least were very close to death," Worsley recalled. "Indeed, it might be said that [Shackleton] kept a finger on each man's pulse. Whenever he noticed that a man seemed extra cold and shivered, he would immediately order another hot drink of milk to be prepared and served to all. He never let the man know that [the milk serving] was on his account, lest he become nervous about himself, and while we all participated, it was the coldest, naturally, who got the greatest advantage."

Early in the morning on the seventh day, the crew realized that the *James Caird* was sitting low in the water; it was iced over and threatening to capsize. The men began chipping away the ice—almost a foot thick in places—balancing themselves on the deck's slick surface. Worsley remembered, "I saw Vincent slide right across the icy sheathing of the canvas, and horror-stricken, I threw myself forward instinctively to help him, only to find that he was beyond my reach. Fortunately he managed to grasp the mast just as he was going overboard."

But the most harrowing moment of the voyage was yet to come. Toward midnight on May 5, Shackleton was at the tiller. He looked up

and suddenly noticed a line of clear sky between the south and south-west. I called to the other men that the sky was clearing, and then a moment later I realized that what I had seen was not a rift in the clouds but the white crest of an enormous wave. During twenty-six years' experience of the ocean in all its moods I had not encountered a wave so gigantic. It was a mighty upheaval of the ocean, a thing quite apart from the white-capped seas that had been our tireless enemies for many days. I shouted, "For God's sake, hold on! It's got us." Then came a moment of suspense that seemed drawn out into hours. White surged the foam of the breaking sea around us. We felt our boat lifted and flung forward like a cork in breaking surf. We were in a seething chaos of tortured water; but somehow the boat lived through it, half full of water, sagging to the dead weight and shuddering under the blow. We baled [sic] with the energy of men fighting for life, flinging the water over the sides with every receptacle that came to our hands, and after ten minutes of uncertainty we felt the boat renew her life beneath us.

Two weeks after leaving Elephant Island, the crew had traveled seven hundred nautical miles, and Worsley estimated that the men were within ninety miles of South Georgia. (During the entire journey, he had been able to take only three measurements of their position using the sextant.) Shackleton recognized the need to land as quickly as possible. They had run out of drinking water. Their mouths were so parched that swallowing had become painful, and they were unable to eat. The crew's ultimate destination had been the whaling station on the east coast of South Georgia. But given the rough seas and the men's weakening condition, the commander doubted they could make it round the island to the station. He ordered the *James Caird* to land on the uninhabited west coast.

Before they could do this, however, they had to survive a hurricane that had developed and was buffeting the *James Caird* from all directions. Steering the vessel was nearly impossible, but Worsley, with assistance from the other five, persisted. On May 10, 1916, after five attempts, they sailed into a narrow cove. As the men stumbled ashore, the leader remembered, "we heard a gurgling sound that was sweet music in our ears, and, peering around, found a stream of fresh water almost at our feet. A moment later we were down on our knees drinking the pure, ice-cold water in long draughts that put new life into us. It was a splendid moment."

CHAPTER SEVEN

Saving His Men

The men had sailed across eight hundred nautical miles of the world's most turbulent waters. (The same hurricane through which they had navigated sank a five-hundred-ton steamer in the vicinity.) But at the moment they landed, as Caroline Alexander has written, the team "could hardly have known—or cared—that in the carefully weighted judgment of authorities yet to come, the voyage of the *James Caird* would be ranked as one of the greatest boat journeys ever accomplished."

What mattered to Shackleton and his five men—in early May 1916—when they came ashore was that help lay on the *opposite* side of the mountainous, uncharted island. Their lifeboat was too damaged and the currents were too strong for them to travel by sea to the whaling station. This meant that some of the crew would have to make the journey overland on foot. Shackleton was impatient to set out, but he knew his men were tired, hungry, and weak and had to rest. For four days, all six feasted on freshly killed albatross, kept warm by driftwood fires, and slept on the grass underneath a sheltering cliff.

Shackleton decided to take Worsley and Crean with him on the trek to the whaling station, leaving McNish, Vincent, and McCarthy behind to be rescued once he'd obtained help. Winter had arrived; Shackleton knew his only hope of safely crossing the island's interior was to wait for decent weather and then walk without stopping in an effort to beat the storms. The three men packed two compasses, binoculars, a small stove, a large coil of rope, and an ice ax. To improve the hikers' traction when climbing, McNish fitted their boots with makeshift crampons fashioned from boat screws.

Early in the morning on May 19, Shackleton, Worsley, and Crean set out. Within an hour, they were trudging uphill through soft, ankle-deep snow. When a dense fog set in, the men tethered themselves together with rope. The going was difficult, so they developed a system of taking a short rest every fifteen minutes and eating small hot meals every four hours to combat exhaustion.

After thirteen hours and several unsuccessful attempts to cross a mountain range, Shackleton, Worsley, and Crean were worn-out. But the leader sensed that his men would persevere as long as he kept moving. Then, as the team ascended to search for a passage through the mountains, another heavy fog rolled in. The men could see almost nothing below, and Shackleton realized they were in trouble. Without shelter, they would die in the cold at this altitude. They had to get down quickly. The three began cutting steps in the ice, but made scant progress. Seeing no other way to escape nightfall and freezing temperatures, Shackleton announced, "It's a devil of a risk, but we've got to take it. We'll slide." Using the coiled rope as an improvised sled, the three men braced themselves in a row and shot down the mountain, descending fifteen hundred feet in just minutes. They slowed to a halt in a snowbank, stood up, and solemnly shook hands.

The men ate another quick meal and continued marching. After midnight, they believed they were getting close to the whaling station, but soon discovered that in their fatigue they had taken a wrong turn and were off course. Once more, they retraced their steps, resetting themselves in the proper direction. Tired and dehydrated, they continued on.

Just before dawn, after twenty-four hours of trekking with no rest save for brief meals, Shackleton decided they must stop briefly. A large rock provided some shelter, and almost immediately, Crean and Worsley fell into a deep sleep. The leader, however, did not dare close his eyes. "I realized," he wrote, "that it would be disastrous if we all slumbered together, for sleep under such conditions merges into death." He watched his colleagues for five minutes before rousing them, saying they had been asleep for half an hour and it was time to start again. At sunrise, the men came over a slope and saw the outlines of Stromness Bay, site of the whaling station. They estimated they were about twelve miles away.

Nine hours later, at 4:00 p.m. on May 20, 1916, Shackleton, Worsley, and Crean reached the outpost. They had traveled thirty-two hours without sleep or shelter, but they had—at last—arrived at civilization. The appearance of the three foul-smelling men dressed in rags with overgrown beards and grime-covered faces surprised many of the sailors there. Some knew that the *Endurance* had left South Georgia eighteen months earlier. But the whalers had had no news of the expedition, and most had given the crew up for lost. The Norwegian station manager, whom Shackleton had met before, did not recognize the explorer. But as soon as the Boss made his identity known, the manager took the three men in and fed them generously. When they had eaten their fill, the leader and his comrades set about scrubbing away months' worth of dirt and grease. "I don't think I have ever appreciated anything so much as that hot bath," Worsley recalled. Later that day, a ship was dispatched to bring back McNish, Vincent, and McCarthy from the other side of the island; those crew members were soon on their way home to Britain.

When he had arrived at the whaling station, Shackleton's first question to the manager concerned the war that had begun almost two years earlier when the *Endurance* departed Britain:

"Tell me, when was the war over?"

"The war is not over," the manager answered. "Millions are being killed. Europe is mad. The world is mad."

Shackleton wasted no time trying to rescue the remaining twenty-two crew members on Elephant Island. Three days after his arrival at Stromness Bay, he borrowed the *Southern Sky*, a whaling ship, and the vessel departed South Georgia with Shackleton, Worsley, Crean, and its crew on board. About seventy miles from South Georgia, severe pack ice forced the *Southern Sky* to turn back; Shackleton realized he would need a stronger ship for the next attempt.

Frustrated, Shackleton sailed the ship five hundred miles northwest to Port Stanley, in the Falkland Islands. There he cabled London, informing family members and officials that he was alive and in urgent need of a rescue vessel. The news that the explorer had survived caused great popular excitement, and congratulatory messages poured in. Even King George V sent a telegram rejoicing that Shackleton was safe. But World War I was on, and the British Admiralty did not have a ship available. The government offered the *Discovery*, on which Scott and Shackleton had sailed during the 1901–4 Antarctic expedition; the ship would be ready by late September, but it wouldn't reach the southern hemisphere before October.

Shackleton couldn't wait that long. The leader knew the men couldn't subsist indefinitely on the barren, inhospitable terrain of Elephant Island; to delay the relief effort several months would threaten their lives. He appealed to several South American governments for a ship that was strong enough to travel through pack ice. On June 16, Shackleton, Worsley, Crean, and a crew set out from Port Stanley on a vessel loaned by Uruguay. This time, the ship sailed to within twenty miles of its destination, only to be stopped by solid pack ice. As he ordered the ship to turn back to the Falklands, the explorer was nearly heartbroken. Worsley remembered the return journey:

> It was a dreadful experience to get within so short a distance of our marooned shipmates and then fail to reach them. At one time we were actually facing the camp, and had it not been for a white low-lying mist they would have seen us. With each mile that we put between the island and ourselves [as the ship steamed back to the Falklands] our spirits sank lower, and we were not altogether sorry when a gale sprang up and took our minds from the waiting men.

His anxiety rising, Shackleton then traveled to Punta Arenas, Chile, where he told a group of British expatriates the story of his rescue efforts. Within days, the leader had raised £1,500 (about $153,000 today), with which he chartered a vessel named the *Emma*. Shackleton, Worsley, Crean, and another crew of sailors set out in mid-July. But when the ship came to within one hundred miles of Elephant

Island, winter conditions, including pack ice, proved too severe for her to continue, and the men were forced to turn back.

The commander grew frantic. He was worried that as winter lengthened, his men would starve. "The wear and tear of this period was dreadful," Worsley recalled. "To Shackleton it was little less than maddening. Lines scored themselves on his face more deeply day by day; his thick, dark, wavy hair was becoming silver. He had not had a grey hair when we had started out to rescue our men the first time. Now, on the third return journey, he was grey-headed." The captain also noticed that Shackleton had begun to drink, something he had never known the Boss to do before.

The leader next approached Chilean government officials to ask for assistance. They obliged, furnishing him with a small steamer called the *Yelcho*. No one, least of all Shackleton, knew whether the vessel was strong enough to make the round-trip journey to Elephant Island. But on August 25, the expedition leader, Crean, Worsley, and a crew of naval volunteers departed Punta Arenas for a fourth attempt at rescuing the men of the *Endurance*.

On August 30, 1916, four months and six days after the *James Caird* set sail for South Georgia, the *Yelcho* pulled within view of Shackleton's men on Elephant Island. During the months of waiting, the twenty-two crew members had lived on the few remaining rations and seal meat until the animals stopped appearing on the island. By mid-August, the specter of starvation loomed close, and meager nourishment, heavy winds, and winter weather had taken a serious physical and mental toll. Several men suffered from badly infected wounds. Others had frostbite. The men on the island no longer held out hope that Shackleton would rescue them; they had decided that when the weather allowed, a party would set out in the *Dudley Docker* to try to intercept one of the whaling ships that occasionally sailed off the tip of the Antarctic Peninsula.

Midday on August 30, most of the crew on Elephant Island were in their improvised hut, eating a stew made from seal bones. Frank Hurley and George Marston, the expedition's artist, remained outside shelling limpets (snails); then, as the photographer remembered, "I called Marston's attention to a curious piece of ice on the horizon, which bore a striking resemblance to a ship. Whilst we were so engaged a ship rounded the [point]! We immediately called out Ship O, which was instantly followed by a general exodus of cheering & semi hysterical . . . inmates."

As the *Yelcho* approached the island, Shackleton stood on deck, looking through his binoculars and counting the men onshore. When he reached the number twenty-two, Worsley recalled, "He put his glasses back in their case and turned to me, his face showing more emotion than I had ever known it show before. Crean had joined us, and we were all unable to speak. Then Shackleton galvanised into life. It sounds trite, but years literally seemed to drop from him as he stood before us." The Boss climbed into the *Yelcho*'s lifeboat with some of the Chilean sailors and headed for shore. He later described the moment of rescue: "I called out, 'Are you all well?' and [Wild] answered, 'We are all well, boss,' and then I heard three cheers. As I drew close to the rock I flung packets of cigarettes ashore; they fell on them like hungry tigers, for well I know that for months tobacco was dreamed of and talk[ed] of."

Shackleton hurried to get his crew aboard the *Yelcho* and out of the shifting pack ice. Within an hour, the ship was fully loaded and bound for civilization. Four days later, on September 3, 1916, the leader and his men steamed into port at Punta Arenas, Chile. The explorer dashed off a letter to his wife, Emily: "I have done it. Damn the Admiralty. . . . Not a life lost and we have been through Hell."

CHAPTER EIGHT

Homeward Bound

Shackleton's last duty as captain of the expedition was to organize a rescue of the Ross Sea party, which had sailed a ship named *Aurora* to the Australian side of Antarctica in late 1914. Some of these men had been responsible for laying food depots along the second half of the route that Shackleton and five others from the *Endurance* planned to take across the continent.

After unloading most of its crew at McMurdo Sound along the Ross Sea in early 1915, the *Aurora* was torn from its moorings by a severe gale and swept out to sea. Once there, she was locked in pack ice and drifted northward, leaving the rest of the Ross Sea party stranded at base camp on the Antarctic coast. (Eventually, the ship broke free of the ice and made her way to New Zealand, arriving in April 1916.) During the next two summers, the men at base camp traveled south to cache food supplies for Shackleton and the rest of the transcontinental party, who were expected to arrive in early 1916. But unbeknownst to them, the *Endurance* had never reached land on the other side of the continent. During their second trek south in 1916, three of the Ross Sea party perished. By August 1916, the seven surviving men were back at base camp without any means of communication or escape.

After returning to civilization in the fall of 1916, Shackleton received news that the *Aurora* had made it to New Zealand with only a few of its men. He immediately made plans to sail for Antarctica to rescue the remaining members of the expedition. In December, he and others sailed south from New Zealand, bound for McMurdo Sound. Once there, Shackleton learned that three of the Ross Sea party had died. He and his colleagues brought the remaining seven men back to Britain in the spring of 1917.

Shackleton and his team returned to a very different world from the one they'd left more than two years earlier. (True to his word, Shackleton paid his crew members through the time they arrived home in Britain.) Fighting had engulfed Europe. Millions had died. The heroes of the day were not individual explorers, but men who had fallen on the battlefield. Orde-Lees was struck by this shift: "People think nothing of being killed, nowadays it is looked on as an honour. Opinions have changed on all sorts of subjects. They call it the Roll of Honour now instead of the casualty list. . . . Maybe one or two of us congratulated ourselves on our luck in still being in time to do our bit." At least fifteen of the twenty-eight men on the *Endurance*, including Shackleton, served in the armed forces. In September 1916, just three weeks after returning to Britain, Timothy McCarthy died behind his gun; not long after, a German torpedo killed former third officer Alfred Cheetham.

When Shackleton came back to Britain, he sought a commission in the British military, although at age forty-two he was legally exempt from service. After much wrangling, he found a post related to arctic transport in northern Russia. (Some writers have suggested that Shackleton enlisted because he knew his future reputation would be dependent on a record of patriotic service in the war.)

In 1918, when the war ended, Shackleton turned his full attention to repaying the loans he had taken out to fund the *Endurance* expedition. He had raised some money for this purpose in 1917 during a short lecture tour in the United States, and in 1919, the explorer published a popular memoir. (He never saw any profits from its sales, however; a benefactor's heirs demanded restitution for the family's investment in the failed journey, and the author signed over the book rights to settle the debt.) That same year, Hurley released *In the Grip of the Polar Pack*, a film about the Antarctic and the *Endurance*; it was well received, and some of its revenues went toward paying off

Shackleton's creditors. The commander continued to lecture on the *Endurance* voyage, but public interest in the story soon waned.

By 1920, the Boss was hungry for another adventure. The world had ceased to be fascinated by polar exploration, but Shackleton never lost his passion for the ice. Without a definite plan, he convinced an old friend to fund another Antarctic trip aboard a ship called the *Quest*. Hearing from their former commander that a new expedition was in the offing, eight of the *Endurance* crew—Worsley, Wild, Green, McIlroy, Hussey, Macklin, McLeod, and Kerr—returned to Britain from the corners of the world to which they had dispersed, eager to embark on another journey with their leader. In September 1921, the *Quest* left London with Shackleton and his team aboard.

When the ship stopped in Rio de Janeiro to take on supplies, the commander suffered a heart attack. He recovered, waving away any suggestion that he seek medical attention, and ordered his ship to continue. On January 4, 1922, the party arrived at the whaling station on South Georgia Island. Then early the next morning, in his cabin aboard the docked *Quest*, Shackleton suffered a second, and fatal, heart attack. He was forty-seven. At the request of his wife, Emily, crew members buried him on South Georgia. Remembering the leader, Worsley later wrote:

> He was not only a great explorer; he was also a great man. Twenty-two years of his life he had devoted to Polar work—work which had brought him fame and had earned him a knighthood. He had forced his way to within ninety-seven miles of the South Pole and had returned with all his men. He had discovered the Beardmore Glacier and added two hundred miles of Antarctic coastline to the map. He had conquered scurvy—the scourge of all explorers till his time—and had never lost a man who was under his protection. He had been the means of enabling the Magnetic South Pole to be located.
>
> And what of him as a man? I recalled the way in which he had led his party across the ice-floes after the *Endurance* had been lost; how, by his genius for leadership he had kept us all in health; how, by the sheer force of his personality he had kept our spirits up;

and how, by his magnificent example, he had enabled us to win through when the dice of the elements were loaded most heavily against us. . . .

He was a proud and dauntless spirit, a spirit that made one glad he was an Englishman. Surely there is no end with such a man as Shackleton: something of his spirit must still live on with us; something of his greatness must surely be a legacy to his countrymen. . . . "He had a way of compelling loyalty," writes one who sailed with him. "We would have gone anywhere without question just on his order."

CHAPTER NINE

The World after Ernest Shackleton

When Shackleton returned home in May 1917, it was to a nation at war. The imperial age of Antarctic exploration, with its emphasis on patriotic discovery, had abruptly ended, obliterated by the carnage of the First World War, in which more than 28 million people had been killed or wounded. He was briefly hailed as a hero for saving the lives of twenty-seven men against virtually impossible odds. But in the aftermath of the global conflict, Shackleton's achievement was eclipsed by a collective cynicism about individual heroes and nationalistic conquest.

By the late 1920s, the British public had rediscovered Robert Falcon Scott and his failed attempt to return from the South Pole in 1912. Hailed for his courage, sacrifice, and patriotic service, Scott became widely known in the United Kingdom. Monuments were erected in his honor; books were written; schoolchildren learned the story of his last expedition; Scott's diary was deemed a national treasure and housed in the British Library. In contrast, Shackleton and the voyage of the *Endurance* slipped into relative obscurity, largely outshone by general interest in Scott.

But in the 1960s, Shackleton began attracting more attention in both Britain and the United States. A series of books about the *Endurance* expedition appeared during the next twenty years. At the same time, historians, most prominently Roland Huntford, reevaluated Scott's leadership in a much more critical light. By the late 1990s, the tables of public interest and acclaim had completely turned; Scott's popularity faded, while Shackleton's soared. As the twenty-first century opened, a spate of books, films, television programs, and exhibitions both reflected and fueled a groundswell of interest in the commander of the *Endurance*. Businesses and educational institutions followed popular attention, embracing Shackleton's story as a case study in crisis leadership, empathic authority, and individual agency in the face of enormous obstacles. (Indeed, my own interest in Shackleton began in 2003, when I decided to write a case about him for the Harvard Business School.)

What accounts for our contemporary fascination with Shackleton, and how is this phenomenon related to his lasting impact? Undoubtedly the story of the *Endurance* is a gripping narrative set in the harshness of untamed nature. Equally compelling is the flexibility Shackleton demonstrated as he tried to keep his men alive—he was willing to pursue any avenue, play any card, use every trick he had to get his crew safely home. With the advantage of historical hindsight, however, we also know that, at times, he doubted he could actually achieve his mission. This is where Shackleton's story becomes even more interesting, because the explorer never let his men know their leader was afraid. A century after the *Endurance* expedition, we can take important insights from Shackleton's consistent emotional control, and how important this was to saving his men.

The explorer's claim on our attention follows from other aspects of his leadership and management. One of these was the responsibility that Shackleton assumed for his crew once the ship was locked in the ice. He likely realized his own hurry to leave South Georgia in the face of the whalers' warnings about pack ice played a role in the expedition's fate. He left no record of such thoughts, but whether or not he acknowledged his own culpability, he was prepared from the onset of the crisis to take full responsibility for the outcome of the enterprise.

A second aspect of Shackleton's authority was his consistent ability to face forward. Again and again, he refused to become mired in what had already happened: what had not worked, what had been missed, or who was to blame for the most recent setback or disappointment. With Shackleton, as with other effective leaders, his forward orientation was not an excuse for sloppy execution, willful blindness, or personal denial. He was a smart student of what had gone before, learning quickly from mistakes and constantly adjusting his behavior as he took in new information. The explorer knew that focusing on the myriad factors that had led to the *Endurance*'s being lost could only diminish team morale and cohesion, thus injuring his men's will to survive. It takes reserves of emotional awareness and discipline for leaders to balance attention on the path ahead with knowledge gleaned from the past. Shackleton cultivated both as he struggled to bring his men back to safety.

Another important attribute of his leadership was the way he managed his crew's energy. He understood this was a critical determinant in the ultimate fate of the expedition. He also realized that he could affect this in a range of subtle but powerful ways—from isolating the men he knew were "doubting Thomases" to using food rations to boost physical and emotional energy to institutionalizing social hours after dinner. During the fifteen months after the ship became locked in pack ice, Shackleton kept a sharp eye on his men, working to discern the present well-being of each and then responding as needed. He did this without the men's even realizing it. It was an extraordinary exercise in the application of empathy harnessed to the starkest of objectives: bring the men home alive.

The final aspect of Shackleton's leadership that demands our attention today is the humanity with which he exercised his authority. We catch glimpses of this in how he fed and watered his men: dispensing hot milk as he walked round the tents, reciting a poem to an enlisted man over a makeshift stove, and arranging dogsled races. We see it as well in the anxiety he suffered in mid-1916 trying to find a vessel that could get through the pack ice to rescue his team. Shackleton literally went gray with worry during the four months between reaching South Georgia in the lifeboat and returning to Elephant Island on the *Yelcho*. Perhaps the most powerful view of this leader's unmistakable humanity is that in the face of the mistakes he made in rushing south in 1914, of ongoing financial problems, and of the narcissistic quest for fame that drove him to Antarctica the first three times—in the face of these and other faults—he proved capable, indeed, he *made* himself capable, of doing an extraordinary thing.

PART TWO

Save and Transform the Nation

ABRAHAM LINCOLN'S CHALLENGE

CHAPTER TEN

His Last Card

By midsummer 1862, Abraham Lincoln's back was up against the wall. The second year of the Civil War had opened with Union victories at Shiloh, Tennessee, in New Orleans, and in the West. But the momentum of Northern forces soon stalled, and the ensuing months brought a series of stalemates and federal retreats. In late June, near Richmond, Virginia, Confederate forces under the command of General Robert E. Lee ferociously attacked government troops under General George McClellan. The intense fighting—six bloody encounters within a week that became known as the Seven Days' Battles—resulted in heavy casualties: sixteen thousand Union soldiers killed, wounded, or captured. Rebel forces lost even more men: twenty thousand killed, wounded, or captured. Despite these numbers, the outcome of the fighting was widely regarded as a Confederate victory.

In early July, when news of McClellan's retreat reached the North, public morale plummeted. Newspapers and politicians assailed the president for incompetence. Investors on Wall Street reacted by selling stocks and the newly created greenback dollar, and the value of each tumbled. Meanwhile, abolitionists, such as the former slave Frederick Douglass, who had, since the beginning of the war, urged Lincoln to move aggressively against slavery, grew increasingly frustrated with the administration. One government official described the Fourth of July as "the gloomiest since the birth of this republic. Never was the country so low, and after such sacrifices of blood, of time, and of money."

All of this bore down on Lincoln. He worried constantly. He lost weight because he was too anxious to eat. Since the beginning of the war, he'd had insomnia; now it grew worse. When he couldn't sleep, he often worked in his office on the second floor of the White House (or the Executive Mansion as it was then known). If a battle was raging, he walked to the telegraph office in the nearby War Department to get the latest news. At times, he passed the hours after midnight slowly pacing the hallway that connected his office with the family living quarters and the rooms assigned to his secretaries, John Hay and John Nicolay. If the young men were awake, Lincoln would swap stories or talk shop with them. Occasionally, the president would sing a bawdy tune. Anything to momentarily lessen the load he carried, to relieve the stress.

As the months passed, Lincoln appeared more careworn, and his wife, Mary, and friends feared for his health. When Orville Browning, a US senator and former colleague from Illinois, expressed concern about the toll that the war was taking on the president, Lincoln took his friend's hand, "pressed it, and said in a very tender and touching tone—'Browning, I must die sometime.'"

Lincoln pushed on, logging long hours as commander in chief. In public, he worked to maintain an air of calm as he issued military instructions, consulted with his cabinet, and met the endless stream of citizens who lined up at the White House each weekday to see him. In between his daily commitments and the unscheduled press of people, Lincoln tried to make sense of the astounding conflict that had torn the country in two.

He had always been an autodidact; since childhood, he had taught himself what he needed to know when he needed to know it: surveying, politics, the law, public speaking, Euclid's geometry, and Shakespeare. Now, at the center of a perfect storm of difficulty and in charge of a flagging Union army, Lincoln began teaching himself military strategy. He borrowed books from the Library of Congress and studied them. We can see him in his office, reading by gas lamp late into the night. During these long hours of darkness when the

White House was quiet, what did he make of the worsening conflict? How did he puzzle out the bloody contest unfolding around him?

In mid-1862, one thing was clear: the war continued to confound Lincoln's expectations. Confederate officers were better strategists than he (and many other Northerners) had predicted. Rebel soldiers and Southern civilians were more determined and resourceful at making war than the president had initially believed. In the North, public opinion was more incendiary than even Lincoln had foreseen. This last aspect meant that virtually any move the leader made ignited a firestorm of reaction.

Facing intense personal criticism sapped his energy and chipped away at his emotional well-being. When a group of congressmen visited the White House to complain about Lincoln's conduct of the war that year, a representative said many Republican leaders wanted the chief executive to know that they "would be glad to hear some morning that you had been found hanging from the post of a lamp at the door of the White House." Depressed and subdued, the president responded, "You need not be surprised to find that that suggestion has been executed any morning. The violent preliminaries to such an event would not surprise me."

Lincoln grasped the animosity coming at him as the war and the challenges of leading it continued to unfold in new, thorny ways. For one thing, despite his constant urging, George McClellan, commander of the Army of the Potomac, refused to aggressively attack Confederate forces. When Lincoln turned to other military officials, he found that many lacked the will to prosecute a complicated war. For another thing, the federal government had run out of money; revenues from tariff and excise taxes could not come close to meeting the war's escalating costs. In the early months of the conflict, the government had borrowed funds from various banks. But these sources were now tapped out. Rather than take out loans from European banks at exorbitant interest rates, Lincoln and Treasury Secretary Salmon Chase decided to petition Congress to issue paper money (greenback dollars). The president questioned the constitutionality of this action. But he saw no other practicable way to pay for the war.

Adding to Lincoln's burdens was the threat that Britain and France would enter the contest on the side of the Confederacy. Both nations wanted to maintain the steady supply of cotton that was critical to their respective textile industries and indicated they were prepared to come to the aid of the rebellious states. This possibility threatened the long-term existence of the Union.

Then there was the actual fighting. When the conflict broke out in April 1861, Americans on both sides predicted a short, decisive contest; "done and settled by Christmas" was a popular assessment. But more than a year and some eighty thousand casualties later, it was becoming increasingly clear that the Civil War would be much longer and more savage than anyone could have imagined. For example, at the battle of Shiloh, which took place in April 1862, more than twenty-three thousand men were killed or wounded. When the fighting ended, Union general Ulysses S. Grant surveyed the battlefield. The corpses were so numerous, he said, "It would have been possible to walk across the clearing in any direction stepping on dead bodies without a foot touching the ground."

The more ghastly the fighting became, the greater the stakes the war assumed. The most important of these, by far, was slavery. Lincoln had long opposed the expansion of the institution because it violated the rights of all people to life, liberty, and the pursuit of happiness as set forth in the Declaration of Independence. But when he entered office in March 1861, he'd done so committed to preserving the Union, including upholding slavery where it legally existed. Once the war broke out, Lincoln publicly kept to this position, explaining that saving the country was more important than attacking slavery head-on.

Several factors governed his thinking. He worried that he lacked lawful authority for bold action against an institution protected by the Constitution. Strategically, he was nervous about alienating supporters of slavery in the Border States of Delaware, Kentucky, Missouri, and Maryland, as well as the possibility that these states might leave the Union and join the Confederacy. Lincoln was also uncertain what to do with the thousands of slaves who were fleeing to the Union army as a path to freedom. Were these men and women private property that had to be returned to their legal owners? Or were escaping slaves contraband of war, as some Northern military officers asserted, and thus justly seized by government troops? If so, were these fugitive slaves entitled to their freedom?

During the first year of the war, Lincoln dealt cautiously with all questions related to slavery. As a political candidate in the 1850s, he'd cultivated the ability to detach himself from his immediate surroundings in order to mentally walk around a particular issue so he could see it from all relevant angles. Now, he leaned heavily on these powers of detachment as he faced the growing military, political, and moral difficulties that arose concerning slavery. Uncertain about what to do about the institution, attacked by critics across the political spectrum, and strained to manage the war, Lincoln hoped for military victories.

When McClellan and his huge army met defeat in the Seven Days' Battles, these hopes were dashed. For Lincoln, this military loss was almost unbearable. In the aftermath, he described himself as "nearly inconsolable as I could be and live." Personally, the death of his eleven-year-old son, Willie, five months earlier still weighed heavily on both the president and his wife.

Despite his despondency, Lincoln did not give way to his darkest fears. His resilience and commitment to preserve the Union helped sustain him. The ability to experience negative emotions without falling through the floorboards of doubt is a vital lesson for today's leaders. Even in the face of great obstacles, individuals must learn to maintain their equanimity while trying to advance their cause. This is true for chief executives trying to transform a struggling company, entrepreneurs dealing with the ups and downs of starting a business, and mothers caring for sick children. If a leader falters and can't recover, his or her mission is most likely doomed. As Lincoln explained to a senator who reproached him for telling a funny story right after the Seven Days' Battles:

> Senator, do you think that this situation weighs more heavily upon you than it does upon me? If the cause goes against us, not only will the country be lost, but I shall be disgraced to all time. But what would happen if I appeared upon the streets of Washington

to-day with such a countenance as yours? The news would spread throughout the country that the President's very demeanor is an admission that defeat is inevitable.

Now, surrounded by difficulties, Lincoln decided to make a bigger, bolder move against slavery. His earlier concerns with protecting the legality of the institution, preserving Border State loyalty, and moving cautiously as he gauged Northern political sentiment had all been overridden by exigency. "Things had gone from bad to worse," the president later recalled, "until I felt we had reached the end of our rope on the plan of operations we had been pursuing; that we had about played our last card, and must change our tactics or lose the game!" Like Shackleton, Lincoln understood that he had to shape his methods to changing circumstances without giving up his ultimate goal; he then had to move forward into the consequences of these choices.

In early July 1862, the president began drafting what would become the Emancipation Proclamation. Initially, he worked in secret, telling almost no one what he was doing. But by the third week of the month, he was ready to present the draft to his cabinet. On July 22, he told the assembled group that he had "resolved upon this step, and had not called them together to ask their advice," but rather "to lay the subject-matter of a proclamation before them." He had decided that, as of January 1, 1863, all people held as slaves in states in rebellion against the US government would be declared forever free. This action, as historian Eric Foner has written, "went well beyond anything Congress or Lincoln had previously envisioned." The president, Foner continued, "audaciously proposed to extend wartime emancipation to all the slaves in most of the places where the institution existed. Abolition would be immediate and without compensation. Whether the owner was loyal to the Union or a rebel would make no difference."

The cabinet was divided over the proposed action. Some members were supportive. But one worried that the proclamation would cost the administration the midterm elections that fall; another disliked emancipation by presidential decree. A third objected to freeing slaves in any way. The president listened carefully to his colleagues. But he'd put a great deal of thought into his proclamation and was unlikely to be dissuaded from it. Nothing was said during the meeting, Lincoln remembered, "that I had not already fully anticipated and settled in my own mind, until Secretary [of State William] Seward spoke." The cabinet member suggested the president wait for a Union victory before publicly issuing the decree, lest the action seem "the last measure of an exhausted government, a cry for help." The leader was impressed with Seward's advice. "It was an aspect of the case," Lincoln recalled, "that in all my thought upon the subject, I had entirely overlooked." He decided to put the proclamation aside until the North won a big battle.

He waited two months. On September 22, 1862, after a bloody triumph at Antietam, Maryland, in which more than twenty thousand Union and Confederate soldiers were killed or wounded, the president announced the Emancipation Proclamation to the American people.

Practically, it would free none of the more than 3.5 million slaves held in the Confederacy, where it could not be enforced. It also made no claims to liberate slaves in the Border States that were not in rebellion against the government, and it did not free slaves held in those parts of the Confederacy occupied by Union forces. Nonetheless, as Lincoln understood, the proclamation was a radical act. In declaring most slaves free by virtue of military necessity, it transformed the purpose and nature of the Civil War. What had started as a conflict to save the Union as it had existed since the 1787 Constitutional Convention had become a contest to save a different kind of United States—one in which slavery was on its way to being permanently abolished.

The decree was bound to be controversial in both the North and the South. Lincoln knew this, but he didn't waver. By mid-July 1862, he was as certain as he needed to be that, on balance, Northern public opinion supported his action and that such support was critical to prosecuting the war. As the casualty numbers mounted, he understood as well that he'd need more manpower, and the Emancipation Proclamation held out the likelihood of African-Americans playing a much bigger part in the conflict. As important, the decree promised to reduce the possibility of Great Britain or France coming to the aid of the Confederacy, since in both nations popular interest in abolition was strong enough to overwhelm political concern with cotton production. Finally, Lincoln believed slavery was wrong and should be ended. Now, some fifteen months into a terrible contest, larger circumstances, including the force of exigency, had combined to offer a way forward to emancipation. For all the risks involved in issuing the decree—and there were many—Lincoln saw his action as the best course.

Going forward, he realized he would *have to lead* from the path forged by the Emancipation Proclamation. Come what may. This would mean directing the war and governing the country in accordance with the promise he had made to abolish slavery. As the conflict stretched on and its terrible costs mounted, Lincoln would draw again and again on his commitment to the proclamation. He did not become president in 1861 with the intention of eradicating slavery, but in the midst of a grave crisis, his mission changed. And his steadfast dedication to this new, broader purpose would prove critical to its achievement.

CHAPTER ELEVEN

Growing Up

Abraham Lincoln was born on February 12, 1809, near Hodgen-ville, Kentucky, in the middle of the state. He was the second child of Thomas and Nancy Hanks Lincoln; a daughter, Sarah, had been born two years earlier. Thomas Lincoln was a farmer who owned some three hundred acres. While her husband tilled the land, Nancy kept house in a sixteen-by-eighteen-foot log cabin. Abe grew into boyhood bringing in wood and water, running errands, weeding his mother's garden, and playing in the woods. Thomas Lincoln could not read; it is possible his wife was literate, but she did not know how to write. Still, Sarah and Abe briefly went to a one-room schoolhouse, located about two miles away. The children learned the rudiments of reading, writing, and arithmetic.

In late 1816, when Abe was seven, his family moved west across the Ohio River to Pigeon Creek in southwestern Indiana. When the Lincolns arrived, this area was remote, heavily wooded, and virtually unpopulated. Conditions were harsh, and the family hacked their livelihood out of the terrain with their own hands. Thomas built a one-room log cabin, and he and his son cleared a small plot in which to plant crops, such as corn and oats. They also tended a few head of livestock. Game was plentiful, and the family ate what Thomas killed. Abe learned to hunt, and just before his eighth birthday, he downed a wild turkey. Killing the bird upset him, however, and he vowed not to do it again. Remembering the incident in a third-person autobiography decades later, he wrote, "He has never since pulled a trigger on any larger game."

Not long after the Lincolns arrived in Indiana, Nancy's aunt and uncle, Elizabeth and Thomas Sparrow, joined them from Kentucky. The Sparrows brought Nancy's eighteen-year-old cousin, Dennis Hanks, with them. Sarah and Abe, who had known Dennis in their former home, were glad to be reunited with their cheerful friend.

But in the autumn of 1818, tragedy struck. Elizabeth and Thomas came down with milk sickness, a dreaded ailment that resulted from drinking the milk of cows that had eaten the poisonous snakeroot plant. (Today, the condition is known as brucellosis, a bacterial infection.) The symptoms, which included fever, nausea, irregular breathing, and joint pain, came quickly and usually ended in death.

Nancy nursed the couple, but within days, both husband and wife succumbed. As Thomas Lincoln was making their coffins, Nancy herself became ill. For the next several days, she grew weaker and sicker. Before she fell into a coma, she called her children to her bedside, telling them "to be good & kind to their father—to one an other [sic] and to the world." She died on October 5, 1818. Thomas made another coffin, this time with Abe whittling the wooden pegs that held its slats together. They laid Nancy's body to rest on a knoll near the family's home.

The historical record is virtually silent on how nine-year-old Abe experienced his mother's sudden death. In later years, Lincoln said little about his mother, but there can be little doubt that the boy was devastated by her passing. During the Civil War, Lincoln wrote a letter of condolence to the daughter of an Illinois colleague who'd been killed in battle; after expressing sadness at the young girl's grief, the president revealed something of his own early loss:

> In this sad world of ours, sorrow comes to all; and, to the young, it comes with bitterest agony, because it takes them unawares. The older have learned to ever expect it. . . . You can not now realize that you will ever feel better. Is not this so? And yet it is a mistake. You are sure to be happy again. To know this, which is certainly true, will make you some less miserable now. I have had experience enough to know what I say.

During his adult life, Lincoln suffered from frequent bouts of depression, or melancholy, as it was known at the time. Friends and colleagues often commented on his tendency to slip into dispirited gloom, and his longtime law partner, William Herndon, once said that Lincoln's "melancholy dript [sic] from him as he walked." Since the early death of a parent is often associated with depression later in life, it seems likely that Lincoln's was related to the profound loss he suffered when his mother died.

After Nancy's passing, Thomas Lincoln decided that life on the frontier with two young children demanded a wife. In late 1819, he went back to Kentucky to find a bride, leaving Sarah, Abe, and Dennis Hanks to fend for themselves. When Thomas returned to Indiana, he brought his new wife, Sarah Johnston, a widow, and her three young children.

Almost immediately, she made a big, positive difference. She was gentle, organized, and hardworking, and she set about improving the Lincolns' primitive household. Sarah had her husband lay a floor in the cabin, cut a window, build a real door, and construct a sleeping loft for Abe, Dennis Hanks, and her son, John D. She replaced the rags that Abe and his sister had been wearing with garments she had brought from Kentucky and cooked for her newly enlarged brood: corn bread, pork, chicken, squirrels, wild turkey, mush, and, on special occasions, gingerbread. Her kindly industry brought order and comfort to the Lincoln children, both of whom had spent a miserable year since their mother died.

Although their stepmother's practical contributions were important, her emotional gifts were even more so. She had the ability, historian David Donald has written, "to blend the two families harmoniously and without jealousy." Sarah grew especially fond of Abe. Years later, she remembered that her stepson "never gave me a cross word or look and never refused in fact, or Even in appearance, to do any thing I requested him." Abe drank in her love and returned it, calling her Mama. As an adult, he spoke highly of the encouragement she so consistently gave him. Like many other effective leaders, the young Lincoln benefited from the emotional support of a caring adult. Sarah's love for and interest in Abe helped him develop a core sense of self-worth and strength that he'd draw on again and again.

Thomas's new wife was illiterate, but she thought the children should be educated. During the next several years, Abe attended three nearby schools, staying for a few months at each. He was a good student and worked hard. As his stepmother remembered:

> Abe read all the books he could lay his hands on—and when he came across a passage that Struck him he would write it down on boards if he had no paper or no slate and when the board would get too black he would shave it off with a drawing knife and go on again.

Abe cut something of an unusual figure among the other school-children. He was taller than his peers—standing over six feet as an adolescent—and he wore a coonskin cap and leather breeches that were always too short for his long legs. But his peers respected him as a first-rate storyteller, gathering round as he spun yarns or told jokes. From an early age, Abe refined his public-speaking abilities: telling tales in the schoolyard, reciting church sermons to anyone who would listen, or, if he was alone, repeating book passages from memory into the surrounding woods and farmland.

When he was fifteen, Abe's formal schooling ended. Years later, he calculated that the total time he had spent in school amounted to less than a year. This seems remarkable when we consider Lincoln's achievements as a lawyer, politician, and president. How did he come to know all that he did? The answer is that Lincoln educated himself. He did this in a direct, focused—what today we might call surgical-strike—manner, obtaining the resources he needed to learn about a particular subject, absorbing what he discovered, and then honing his newfound understanding, first for himself and then in practice. Whether he was learning grammar to improve his speaking and writing, land surveying to make a living, or legal precedents to train for the Illinois bar, Lincoln was both teacher and student.

As Abe entered his teens, he and his father grew apart. Although Thomas Lincoln had encouraged his son to go to school, Thomas himself was not interested in the world of ideas. Focused on supporting a family of eight, he needed his son to help farm the land, tend the livestock, and work for neighbors who paid the older Lincoln for the boy's time.

Abe hated the hardscrabble farming to which his father was devoted and resented the physical labor Thomas exacted from him. The more confidence the son gained in his intellectual abilities, the less interested he became in his father's way of life. "I don't always intend to delve, grub, shuck corn, split rails, and the like," Abe told a friend. He wanted a profession, he said, in which he could excel relative to his peers.

In the fall 1828, his older sister, Sarah, who had married two years earlier and lived nearby with her husband, died in childbirth. Abe was heartbroken. A neighbor recalled that Abe, on hearing the news of her death, "sat down, burying his face in his hands. The tears trickled through his large fingers, and sobs shook his frame. From then on he was alone in the world." With his sister gone, Abe's urge to get away from his father and all that he represented increased.

In early 1830, Thomas Lincoln moved his family west to Decatur, Illinois, in the middle of the neighboring state. Abe helped his family get settled, staying with them for about a year. This was the last time Lincoln would devote energy to his father. In later years, he had virtually nothing good to say about the older man and, on more than one occasion, criticized his lack of education and ambition. When, in early 1851, Lincoln learned that Thomas was near death, the son chose not to make the three-day journey from Springfield, Illinois, to the eastern part of the state where his father and stepmother lived.

At the time, Abe had a heavy workload, and his wife had just given birth to another child. No doubt these factors weighed on his decision. But something else was going on. "Say to him," Abe wrote his stepbrother who had entreated him to come see his father, "that if we could meet now, it is doubtful whether it would not be more painful than pleasant." Thomas Lincoln died shortly thereafter. His son did not attend the funeral.

CHAPTER TWELVE

On His Own

In mid-1831, Lincoln was twenty-two years old and no longer under legal obligation to remain with his family, and he left. With the promise of a job in a small general store, he moved to New Salem, Illinois, a village located some twenty miles northwest of Springfield along the Sangamon River. At the time Lincoln arrived, about twenty-five families were living there. Most of these people farmed some acreage, and many kept livestock. But New Salem was primarily organized around commerce and was home to a blacksmith, two doctors, several general stores, a tavern, and a leather tannery.

New Salem expanded Lincoln's horizons. It was the largest, busiest place he had lived in. The men and women there hailed from a variety of places, and many of the town's lawyers and merchants had direct connections to the growing economy of central Illinois—an economy powered by canals, railroads, and commercial development. Despite the differences in their backgrounds, the residents of New Salem generally banded together to support one another, maintaining an informal but palpable social unity, where hierarchy counted for little. For a young man with virtually no cash or connections, it was an ideal place to make a start in life.

In September 1831, Lincoln began work—for $15 a month—as a clerk in Denton Offutt's general store. Abe sold coffee, tobacco, gunpowder, calico, and other goods, performing his duties with diligence. When he overcharged a woman for a dress, for example,

Lincoln swiftly refunded the difference. On another occasion, when he accidentally weighed out half a pound of tea rather than the full one for which he had charged a customer, he immediately took another half pound to the woman's home. These and other actions soon earned him the nickname Honest Abe.

It wasn't only the newcomer's work that impressed people around him. They enjoyed his stories and wit, both of which he punctuated with telling details, skilled mimicry, and emphatic gestures. When Lincoln told a tale or lewd joke, a neighbor remembered, "his countenance would brighten. . . . [And] his eyes would Sparkle, all terminating in an unrestrained Laugh in which every one present willing or unwilling were compelled to take part."

For all his humor and bonhomie, however, he could also display flashes of anger and impatience. When a customer in Offutt's store ignored Lincoln's warning to stop using profanity in front of women, for example, Abe grabbed the man and threw him on the ground outside. "I am going to rub the lesson in so that you will not forget again," Lincoln said, stuffing weeds into the offender's mouth.

Lincoln was physically strong. Standing six feet four inches and weighing about 215 pounds, he was sinewy from years of manual labor. That said, he looked nothing like what we think of today as a graceful, well-proportioned athlete. His chest was thin and his shoulders narrow; his limbs were long and his movements gawky. Still, he was fast on his feet, coordinated, and vigorous in sport. According to those who knew him, he could easily lift four hundred pounds. He could also grab two axes by the ends of their handles and, with his elbows locked, lift them straight over his head.

All his life, Lincoln's bodily strength was an important asset. In New Salem, it earned him the respect of others. Years later, as a lawyer, his physical sturdiness impressed juries. As president, this same strength helped him persevere through the grueling demands of the Civil War.

Soon after he started work in the New Salem general store, his employer bet another shopkeeper that Abe could outwrestle any man. A gang of young men from the nearby village of Clary's Grove took the wager, putting forward their strongest member, Jack Armstrong.

Lincoln was reluctant to fight. But he knew that if he did not accept the challenge, he risked being labeled a coward, a damning characterization for anyone on the frontier.

The match took place in front of a large crowd. Armstrong was an experienced wrestler, but Lincoln's height and reach made the contest close. Accounts of what happened vary, but most indicate that Armstrong used an illegal hold to throw Lincoln. A larger brawl threatened to break out. However, when Lincoln said he would take on all the members of the Clary's Grove gang—wrestling them one at a time—tensions cooled, and the fighting subsided.

The match had no clear winner; but Lincoln had scored an important victory. His neighbors admired the newcomer's strength and courage. Others were impressed that he was not obviously angry about his opponent's breaking the rules—perhaps no one more so than Armstrong and his friends. From that day forward, these men became some of Lincoln's most devoted admirers, inviting him to referee their horse races and supporting him as his career in public life took shape.

We do not know what Lincoln made of this moment. Certainly, he understood he had won the respect of a wide circle of people. No doubt he also recognized that keeping his emotions in check and allowing his rivals some latitude to alter their actions was a useful strategy. Less obviously, the young man realized he could improve himself by virtue of his everyday experiences. Although biographers and historians have long recognized Lincoln's capacity for growth during his presidency, much less attention has been paid to the work he did on himself during his twenties. In New Salem, Lincoln came to understand that life itself was the best classroom, and that failures, obstacles, and disappointments provided important opportunities to hone emotional awareness and behavior.

Lincoln discovered other resources for self-improvement in the village. For example, the schoolmaster gave him a book on English grammar, and the young man set about teaching himself its contents. He worked on this whenever he could, walking around the village with a book up to his face and studying when business was slow at Offutt's store.

Intent on improving his reasoning as well, Lincoln joined the New Salem Literary and Debating Society. The group met regularly to discuss political and economic issues including temperance, railroad policy, and the future of freed slaves. Society members were impressed with Lincoln. He "pursued the question," one recalled, "with reason and argument so pithy and forcible that all were amazed."

The young man discovered still more people in New Salem from whom he could learn. Jack Kelso had memorized a great deal of Shakespeare and the poetry of Robert Burns and shared his zeal for both writers with the newcomer. After Lincoln's first exposure to Shakespeare, he read particular plays over and over, learning stanzas in *Macbeth*, *Richard III*, and *Hamlet* well enough to recite them aloud. He also absorbed verses from Burns, Lord Byron, William Knox, and Oliver Wendell Holmes; all his life he would return to these passages. The four poets, along with the Bard and the King James Version of the Bible, became his literary staples.

During his first year in New Salem, Lincoln became friends with Bowling Green, the justice of the peace, who encouraged him to study law. Before long, village residents were asking Lincoln to write up deeds and contracts, which he did without accepting payment. He was intrigued by the possibility of becoming a lawyer, but worried that he lacked sufficient formal education, and so put thoughts of a legal career aside.

In early 1832, Green and others urged Lincoln to run for the Illinois state legislature, and this challenge he accepted. In March, he announced his candidacy, running as a member of the Whig Party, which was still in its infancy. Established to oppose President Andrew Jackson's Democratic Party, the Whigs championed active government, economic development, and protective tariffs. In an open letter to the voters of his legislative district, Sangamon County, Lincoln endorsed internal improvements, such as railroads and canals, and stressed the importance of education. He ended the letter with an appeal to voters based on his modest beginnings and larger purpose:

Every man is said to have his peculiar ambition. Whether it be true or not, I can say for one that I have no other so great as that of being

truly esteemed of my fellow men, by rendering myself worthy of
their esteem. How far I shall succeed in gratifying this ambition, is
yet to be developed. I am young and unknown to many of you. . . .
I have no wealthy or popular relations to recommend me. My case
is thrown exclusively upon the independent voters of this county,
and if elected they will have conferred a favor upon me, for which
I shall be unremitting in my labors to compensate.

For a young man who had arrived in New Salem nine months
earlier with only the clothes on his back, the decision to run for state
office was bold. Lincoln's ambition had been piqued—he had found
access to his own "supreme self-confidence," as David Donald has
written, "his belief that he was at least the equal, if not the superior,
of any man he ever met."

During the summer of 1832, Lincoln spent several weeks campaigning around Sangamon County. But when the votes were counted
in August, he was defeated, polling eighth of thirteen candidates, of
which the top four were elected. Lincoln was disappointed; still, he
resolved to run again—in two years—at the next election for the
state legislature.

In the interim, he had to earn a living. Denton Offutt's store had
gone bankrupt in the spring, leaving Lincoln out of work, and that
April he enlisted as a militiaman to fight in the Black Hawk War. The
conflict, one of many between Native Americans and white settlers
on the nineteenth-century frontier, had broken out over land rights.
In 1832, the work of the Illinois militia was to push members of the
Black Hawk tribe out of the state, west across the Mississippi River.
Although he saw no fighting, Lincoln was elected captain of his com-
pany and took great satisfaction in serving as a leader of his peers.
His service in the Black Hawk War was also important financially.
At a time when he had no other income, the State of Illinois paid
him more than $100 for his service.

Furloughed out in the summer 1832, he returned to New Salem
and began looking for work. Before long, he and William Berry, a
member of his militia company, decided to buy one of the remaining
general stores in the village, paying for the business on credit. From

the beginning, sales were slow, and in early 1833, the store went bankrupt. The two proprietors had taken out large loans to buy the store, and in 1835, Berry died, leaving Lincoln with a total indebtedness of about $1,100. For Lincoln, who earned less than $100 a year, this was a staggering amount. But he was determined to repay every note of what he called the "national debt." Some colleagues estimated it took him more than a decade to do this, but eventually he did.

During the next several years, Lincoln tried on a number of jobs. He performed them willingly, but none came close to satisfying his thirst for advancement and public recognition. Lincoln, like many other leaders, didn't blaze onto the larger stage at a young age. And even in the 1840s, when he began to build a legal and political career, his path was marked by as many failures as successes. The making of courageous leaders is rarely swift and smooth. Indeed, as the stories here illustrate, the setbacks and the times that each of these people spent *not* being able to gratify their ambitions were important ingredients in the wisdom, resilience, and empathy that they nurtured and then used so successfully.

In May 1833, Lincoln was appointed postmaster of New Salem. He also learned to be a surveyor, traveling throughout Sangamon County measuring land for homes, towns, roads, and schools. In many quarters he became known for his kindness. For instance, one winter day, Lincoln met a boy in bare feet chopping wood and asked him how much he was being paid and what he was going to do with the money. The boy answered that he expected to earn $1 and hoped to buy a pair of shoes. Lincoln sent the boy indoors to get warm, finishing the job himself. On another occasion, Charles Chandler, who was trying to buy acreage abutting his property in central Illinois, had to race to the Springfield land office to preempt another settler interested in the same parcel. Chandler took off on horseback, encountering Lincoln on the way. When Chandler explained why he was in such a hurry, Lincoln offered to swap his fresh steed for the tired animal the other man was riding. Chandler demurred, saying he would get to Springfield in time on his own mount. But he was impressed with the offer. "I became a Lincoln man then," he remembered.

Lincoln's reputation became particularly important in the spring of 1834, when he again ran for state legislature. During the campaign, he went from village to village and farm to farm, introducing himself to residents. When he met a group of men harvesting grain, for example, some said they could not support a man who could not work a field. Without missing a beat, Lincoln grabbed a scythe and started swinging, saying, "Boys, if that is all, I am [sure] of your votes." A nearby homeowner remembered that Lincoln did not lose a vote among the crowd.

The candidate was equally comfortable knocking on doors. He talked as much about crops, livestock, and a family's hopes as he did about politics, and this made many feel, recalled a New Salem resident, that "they had met a friend—one near as a brother." Lincoln also made time for small children on the campaign trail. He brought them candy or nuts, telling funny stories, playing tricks, or asking them about their animals. As biographer Michael Burlingame has written, Lincoln was "folksy and congenial, and he made people feel he was one of them—clearly, a smarter version of them, but one of them nonetheless." Virtually all effective leaders work from a place of familiarity with and respect for the people they want to influence. Like Shackleton and Lincoln, they don't stand aloof.

In the August 1834 election, Lincoln earned the second-highest vote total among the twelve candidates, becoming one of four men elected to the state legislature. Three years earlier, he had compared his arrival in New Salem to "a piece of floating driftwood" that had come down the river and accidentally lodged in the village. Now, at age twenty-five, he was about to take his place on the field of public affairs. Even for Lincoln, with his outsize ambition, this was a big step forward.

But he knew there was more to be done. He needed a career that would feed his growing interest in politics while helping him improve his lot, and he returned to the idea of studying law. John Todd Stuart, whom he had met in the Black Hawk War, was an accomplished attorney and state legislator from Sangamon County. Now, Stuart encouraged his younger colleague to become a lawyer.

Lincoln decided this was the right course and began borrowing Stuart's law books. He studied by himself, starting with the eighteenth-century treatise on common law, Blackstone's *Commentaries on the Laws of England*. "The more I read," Lincoln wrote later, "the more intensely interested I became. Never in my whole life was my mind so thoroughly absorbed. I read until I devoured [the *Commentaries*]." When he finished Blackstone, Lincoln dug into other books. He became fixated on his studies. Lincoln the law student, a neighbor remembered, "would go day after day for weeks and sit under an oak tree on [a] hill . . . and read." When the sun moved, the neighbor continued, Lincoln "moved round [the] tree to keep in [the] shade . . . [he] was so absorbed that people said he was crazy. Sometimes [he] did not notice people when he met them." Years later, Lincoln advised a young man who was considering a legal career:

> If you are resolutely determined to make a lawyer of yourself, the thing is more than half done already. It is but a small matter whether you read *with* any body or not. I did not read with any one. Get the books, and read and study them till, you understand them in their principal features; and that is the main thing. It is of no consequence to be in a large town while you are reading. I read at New-Salem, which never had three hundred people living in it. The *books*, and your *capacity* for understanding them, are just the same in all places. . . . Always bear in mind that your own resolution to succeed, is more important than any other one thing.

We do not know exactly how Lincoln sustained his determination to succeed. What we *do* know is that from an early age he practiced great discipline in relation to the things that mattered. Some of the discipline was focused on practical ends: toward preparing himself to be a lawyer or bettering himself intellectually. Some of it was directed at managing his emotions. As his prospects expanded, he worked to comport himself with greater dignity and forbearance.

In November 1834, Lincoln headed off to the state capital of Vandalia, located about seventy-five miles southeast of Springfield, to begin work as a state legislator. During the ten-week term, Lincoln watched and learned. As he grew more comfortable with the business of legislation, he helped colleagues draw up bills, and on two occasions he briefly took the floor. In mid-February 1835, when the legislative session ended, Lincoln returned to New Salem.

In 1836, he successfully ran again. During his second term, he emerged as a Whig leader, helping his fellow legislators organize support for two important issues: moving the state capital from Vandalia to Springfield, and launching a large-scale plan to bring railroads, canals, and roads to various parts of Illinois. Both of these measures passed, the second with mixed consequences. (The enormous cost of funding this infrastructure would burden Illinois taxpayers for years.) When this action-packed session ended in early 1837, Lincoln had absorbed a great deal about the hands-on work of state politics. The twenty-seven-year-old, as Burlingame has written, had become "an adept partisan, renowned for logrolling and scourging [the opposition]."

When the Illinois General Assembly was not in session, Lincoln delivered mail in New Salem, studied law, took on surveying and other jobs, and socialized. Most of his ongoing interactions were with men, married women, and children. Lincoln liked and respected women, but was generally shy around those his own age. Some of his diffidence may have resulted from his lack of social polish or his sense that he was homely, which he occasionally joked about. (For example, during the 1858 contest for the US Senate seat from Illinois, Lincoln's opponent, Stephen Douglas, accused him of being two-faced. Lincoln reportedly shot back, "If I had another face, do you think I'd wear this one?")

An even more likely reason behind Lincoln's reticence around single women was a fear of intimacy. The deaths of his mother and sister had been searing and seemed to have cast long shadows across his life, fueling both his frequent depressions and the emotional circumspection he practiced in his personal relationships. Given this, perhaps he was frightened of exposing himself to another, particularly his vulnerabilities. Whatever the root cause of Lincoln's hesitancy toward close relationships, he was bashful around eligible women. The wives of several friends tried to make a match for him, but their efforts came to naught.

In 1835, however, Lincoln may have fallen in love with Ann

Rutledge, whose father owned the New Salem tavern. At age twenty-two, Ann was four years younger than Lincoln. She was kind, intelligent, and pretty, standing about five feet three inches tall and weighing about 120 pounds. She had caught the eye of several men in New Salem, including Lincoln. During the spring and summer of 1835, he and Ann began spending time together, strolling along New Salem's main street and poring over grammar books as Ann tried to improve her grasp of the subject. They may have come to an understanding that they would eventually marry, but there is no written record that they were romantically involved. Lincoln never mentioned Ann in any of his correspondence, and no letter from her to him is known to exist. What evidence historians do have about Lincoln's relationship with Ann consists of recollections of New Salem residents gathered after his death.

In August 1835, Ann fell ill, possibly with typhoid fever. During the ensuing weeks, she grew steadily worse. But she wanted to see Lincoln, and he went to her. Ann's sister remembered that when he left Ann's room, both were crying. A few days later, on August 25, 1835, she died. Lincoln was overwhelmed with grief, sinking into a deep depression. His sadness was so intense that some friends feared for his emotional well-being. They were compelled, one remembered, "to keep watch and ward over Mr. Lincoln" because he was "from the sudden shock somewhat temporarily deranged." Another New Salem resident, John Hill, recalled that Lincoln was so distraught that he may have considered suicide. If Lincoln did harbor thoughts of killing himself, it may not have been the first time. It would not be the last.

In the weeks following Ann's death, Lincoln sought comfort from his friend Bowling Green and his wife, Nancy, staying with them while he tried to regain his emotional composure. By the autumn of 1835, he was sufficiently recovered to return to surveying and other work. Late in the year, he took his seat in the state legislature when it met for the winter 1835–36 session.

Finding the internal stability to resume his duties was not easy. Ann's death had catapulted Lincoln deep into the canyon of what he labeled "the hypo," and it required a lot of hard, serious labor to climb up and out of this emotional place. But Lincoln found the will to face his suffering, endure it, and go on. And he found this strength not only in 1835, but also, as writer Joshua Wolf Shenk has argued, at other moments of great sadness and doubt, including several during his presidency.

What did Lincoln learn from his experience with depression? How, if at all, did it influence his leadership? The sixteenth president left little evidence of his inner life: no diaries, no journals, and only a handful of intimate letters. This means that scholars and biographers trying to understand Lincoln's inner life are working on ground that includes patches of speculation. From many years of research on Lincoln, I am convinced that dealing with chronic depression—including facing it and moving through it without giving up—helped strengthen his core muscles of endurance. Each episode of melancholy through which he navigated was difficult; each was unique in some aspects, similar in others; and as his experience with these moments accumulated, so, too, did his ability to persevere through to the next one. The knowledge that he had battled his emotional demons on many occasions and come out whole on the other side nurtured a subtle, deep-seated confidence that helped sustain his faith in himself and his mission as president.

Lincoln's ability to deal with melancholy enriched his leadership in other ways. It forced him to reflect deeply on his life and its purpose. In the midst of debilitating thoughts, thoughts so despairing that he once told a friend "he never dare carry a knife in his pocket," he was forced to find some kind of reason to carry on. For Lincoln, this meant accomplishing something that would earn the esteem of his fellow men and that would, as Shenk has noted, connect his name with the great events of his generation. Lincoln had articulated this goal in his 1832 letter to voters announcing his first political campaign, and he would come back to this resolve during the next twenty years.

In April 1837, Lincoln left New Salem for good. He'd earned his license to practice law, and his mentor John Stuart invited him to become a junior partner in his Springfield law practice. Lincoln left no record of what his time in New Salem had meant. But with the benefit of hindsight, we can see how far he'd come in the preceding six years. He'd sampled several careers and chosen one. He'd been elected to state office, discovered the thrill of politics, and begun to make a mark on the stage of public affairs. He'd won the respect and trust of a broad swath of people, many of whom considered him a friend. He'd met a woman to whom he'd been strongly attracted and perhaps tasted romance. Even more important, he'd worked to improve himself and had seen those efforts bear fruit. He was a better thinker, writer, and speaker than when he first arrived in New Salem, and his possibilities had greatly expanded. He'd put some real distance between his adult life and the one he'd led as Thomas Lincoln's son.

CHAPTER THIRTEEN

Putting Down Roots

In April 1837, when Lincoln arrived in Springfield, the state's new capital of fifteen hundred residents was fast becoming the center of Illinois politics outside of Chicago and St. Louis. Springfield was home to a Whig newspaper, the *Sangamon Journal*, and before long a Democratic-leaning periodical, the *Illinois Republican*.

Lincoln was determined to make the most of his move to the capital. As in New Salem, neighbors, associates, and friends eased his way. A colleague from the state legislature offered the newcomer free meals at his Springfield home, and for five years Lincoln ate there without charge. He found lodgings through the kindness of another resident. Shortly after arriving, the newcomer went into a general store to buy a mattress for a bedstead. When he asked what it cost, the proprietor, Joshua Speed, said $17. The lawyer replied that he did not have the money and was not sure his legal work would turn out well enough for him to repay the debt. The merchant asked him whether he had found a place to live, and when Lincoln said no, Speed suggested the two share the large room above the store. "Without saying a word," the clerk remembered, Lincoln "took his saddle-bags on his arm, went up stairs, set them down on the floor, came down again, and with a face beaming with pleasure and smiles exclaimed, 'Well, Speed, I'm moved.'"

It was common for men living on the frontier to share sleeping space; two other men, including Lincoln's future law partner William Herndon, who was a clerk in the store, also roomed with Speed. While privacy was limited, conversation and humor were plentiful. On many evenings, a group of single men gathered in Speed's store and talked poetry, politics, legal issues, and current events.

During the next several years, Speed and Lincoln grew to be close friends. Speed was five years younger than Lincoln and came from a prosperous, slaveholding Kentucky family; he was well educated and well groomed. The young men's backgrounds were different, but they discovered they had a great deal in common. Both were ambitious: Speed wanted wealth, Lincoln, political power and fame. As they came to know each other, they shared ideas about different subjects and people, including the women with whom each would become involved. Speed was the only close friend Lincoln ever had.

Lincoln's first law partner, John Stuart, was as well connected in political circles as Speed. Stuart's practice was busy, so Lincoln had plenty of work. The firm of Stuart and Lincoln handled libel, trespass, assault, larceny, divorce, and other cases. Most of these were small and quickly resolved. For example, Lincoln's caseload included reclaiming a debt of $3 for a hog, seeking title to land that had been swapped in a handshake, collecting compensation for damages to a stove, and seeking payment on a debt to Speed's store.

During his early years as a lawyer, Lincoln learned as he went. In 1838 and again in 1840, Stuart was elected to the US House of Representatives and was thus frequently absent from the practice. This left the junior partner largely on his own to prepare briefs, research case law, speak with clients, and observe judges and other lawyers as they went about their business. He taught himself what he needed to know case by case, often cramming his preparation into the day or two before a particular court date. When he was trying to master a legal issue, he used the same intense concentration he had relied on when he began studying law. In these moments, a colleague remembered, Lincoln would "study twenty-four hours without food or sleep . . . often walking unconscious, his head on one side, thinking and talking, to himself." Lincoln enjoyed such focused research. "When I have a particular case in hand," he told another lawyer,

"I . . . love to dig up the question by the roots and hold it up and dry it before the fires of the mind."

In addition to handing off most of his caseload, Stuart also put Lincoln in charge of the firm's finances. Here, the young man proved less engaged and adept. Neither partner was a careful bookkeeper, so documents, bills, and other papers were stored in desk drawers, on tabletops, and in Lincoln's stovepipe hat. On occasion, the partners lost deeds and other records. (In later years, when Lincoln was practicing law in his own firm, he and his partner were even more disorganized. One of the many piles of paper in the office had a note on top of it that said, in Lincoln's hand, "When you can't find it anywhere else, look in this.")

Stuart and Lincoln charged $5 or $10 for most cases; federal cases cost more. The partners split fees equally, and revenues mounted. During the four years Lincoln worked with Stuart, the younger lawyer's yearly income averaged about $1,000. Later, when he worked with another senior partner, Stephen Logan, Lincoln received only one-third of the firm's fees. But this still translated into an annual income of $1,500. By the late 1850s, he would take home between $4,000 and $5,000 a year from his own practice.

Set against his peers in Springfield, as historian Michael Burlingame has pointed out, Lincoln was never a particularly affluent attorney. (Ranked by assets, he was twelfth of seventeen lawyers in town, according to the 1860 census.) Certainly, Lincoln could have earned more than he did. But for much of the time he practiced law, he charged low—and often, *very* low—fees. At times, clients were astonished that after winning a large judgment on their behalf, Lincoln would ask for $15 or $25. In one instance, he collected $2,000 in an unpaid debt for a client, charging him $2.

Lincoln's legal career is one of the least studied aspects of his life, and we don't know exactly why he kept his fees so low. He wasn't at all financially naïve; he understood money and could see its impact. He also knew what his colleagues charged. With his own clients, he was careful to collect the money owed him and, when all else failed, sued those who hadn't paid.

But Lincoln was never motivated primarily by money. Measured against his father's livelihood, the son made a good living. Lincoln was also consistently careful about his reputation. He may have wanted to avoid any hint of impropriety associated with charging high prices—either to poor clients who couldn't afford them or to wealthier ones to whom he might feel beholden. Lincoln might also have wanted people to remember him as a lawyer who underpromised and overdelivered. This strategy was good for building a legal practice. It was also useful for one interested in electoral politics. In the 1860 presidential election, for example, Lincoln's small fees would be held up as evidence of his good character.

Regardless of what Springfield lawyers charged, Lincoln and his contemporaries could not make a living practicing only in town. The Circuit Court for Sangamon County was based there, as was the Illinois Supreme Court. But both courts met for only brief terms each year. At other times, justice came to the people in the form of a traveling court. For most of his legal career, Lincoln rode the Eighth Judicial Circuit all around central Illinois. In the early 1840s, the circuit spanned fifteen counties and encompassed a geographic area of more than a thousand square miles. Judges and lawyers traveled by horseback or buggy from county seat to county seat, where they dealt with whatever litigation local residents brought before them.

Life on the circuit was often difficult. In the spring, mud frequently made the roads impassable; at times, streams flowed so high that the traveling band had to swim across them. Accommodations were usually primitive, and on many nights, lawyers bunked on a tavern or farmhouse floor. The food was no better. "Hardly fit for the stomach of a horse" was how Judge David Davis described a particularly bad meal. During the warmer months, bedbugs and mosquitoes plagued the men, who did business in whatever structure was available: a courthouse in some towns, a tavern or hotel in others.

For all its hardships, legal work on the road had its advantages. It was an important source of income for many lawyers, including Lincoln. And most of the attorneys found riding the circuit more interesting than life in the office. Each week, remembered Henry Whitney, who rode the Eighth Circuit with Lincoln, brought "new and diverse juries to entertain, cajole or convince; new and distinct

PUTTING DOWN ROOTS 109

conditions of chaos, to evoke order from." The lawyers and presiding judge also became friends. When the men were not working, they ate together, played cards, and told stories. Frequently, Lincoln was at the center of the group, his anecdotes and jokes entertaining those around him. But at other moments he dropped out of conversation or simply left. One evening in Danville, for example, he disappeared after supper without notice. He returned several hours later, telling the other men he had been to a nearby show for schoolchildren that featured a magic lantern, electrical machine, and other small wonders.

For Lincoln, riding the circuit also gave him exposure to scores—and later, hundreds—of people in central Illinois. He met them, heard their concerns, learned to work with them, and saw the possibilities the changing regional economy offered them. Equally important, these same people came to know Lincoln. Some met him as a lawyer who helped them with a specific issue; others encountered him as he told a story around a tavern fire. Still others fed him or sold him a place to sleep. As in New Salem, most of Lincoln's acquaintances remembered him. And he, with a keen memory, did the same. All of this was important grist for the mill of Lincoln's political ambitions.

At the same time, he earned a reputation as an attorney who was skilled before a jury. Not because he mastered the laws of evidence or finer points of precedents; he did neither. Instead, this reputation rested on his ability to concentrate a jury's attention on the few essential points of a case while conceding the less important issues to his opponent. Carrying these critical points with the jury maximized Lincoln's chances of winning the case. The strategy had the added advantage of disarming the other side. As his colleague Leonard Swett explained:

[Lincoln] was wise as a serpent in the trial of a cause, but I have had too many scares from his blows to certify that he was harmless as a dove. When the whole thing was unravelled [sic], the adversary would begin to see that what [Lincoln] was so blandly giving away was simply what he couldn't get and keep. By giving away six points and carrying the seventh he carried his case, and the whole case hanging on the seventh, he traded away everything which would give him the least aid in carrying that. Any man who took Lincoln for a simple-minded man would very soon wake up with his back in a ditch.

Lincoln's ability to relate to juries provides a useful lesson about *discernment*. Leaders trying to accomplish a worthy mission have to cultivate the ability to identify the one, two, or three essential issues facing them at a given moment. It is never five or ten. It is always one or two—maybe three—issues that really matter. Having indentified these, leaders must let the remaining concerns go, either by giving themselves permission to turn their attention away from all that is not central to their purpose or by handing peripheral issues to others, including an adversary. Being able to do this—to concentrate on the most important issues while relinquishing the rest—depends on a leader's willingness to recognize two things: first, he or she cannot do it all, and second, by saying no to that which is not mission critical, one is actually saying yes to that which is.

Aside from a two-year interruption when he was elected to the US Congress in the late 1840s, Lincoln practiced law from early 1837 until he became president in 1861. During this time, he worked with three different partners. From 1837 to 1841, he was the junior partner to John Stuart. From 1841 until 1844, he worked as the junior partner to Stephen Logan, another busy, highly competent Springfield attorney. Nine years older than Lincoln, Logan taught him the importance of procedures, case law, and carefully written pleadings. By modeling more dignified conduct in court, Logan also helped the junior partner temper his propensity to lash out against opponents.

Lincoln's last and most important legal partnership began in 1844, when he established his own firm and invited William "Billy" Herndon to join him as the junior partner. Herndon was nine years younger than Lincoln and well connected in Whig political circles. He was also loyal and kept the practice operating in Springfield when Lincoln was riding the circuit. From the beginning, the two men split legal fees down the center.

During his career as a lawyer, Lincoln was involved in almost four thousand known cases. Through this experience, as historian Brian

Dirck has pointed out, he gained an abiding respect for the law, which would play an important role in many of the decisions he made as president. He also acquired a sense of how quickly or slowly public opinion could change. He learned as well how to resolve conflicts and preserve order among members of a community. For all his skill in front of a jury, Lincoln always tried to settle disputes without going to trial. "Discourage litigation," he advised in a note composed for a law lecture. "Persuade your neighbors to compromise whenever you can. Point out to them how the nominal winner is often a real loser—in fees, expenses, and waste of time. As a peacemaker the lawyer has a superior opportunity of being a good man. There will still be business enough."

During his thirties, Lincoln worked hard at being a lawyer and politician. In 1838 and then again in 1840, he was elected to two additional terms in the state legislature. When Lincoln was not riding the circuit or attending to state business, he and Joshua Speed were often guests at parties hosted by Ninian and Elizabeth Edwards. Ninian Edwards was the son of a former Illinois governor and an ambitious politician in his own right. His wife Elizabeth Todd Edwards was an attractive, well-educated woman from a prominent family in Lexington, Kentucky. Together, the couple managed their position at the top of Springfield's social hierarchy.

On Sundays, they frequently opened their home to well-connected men from central Illinois, who came to socialize, conduct political business, and intermingle with the single women who were regular attendees. All these women were attractive, but virtually no one outshone Mrs. Edwards's younger sister, Mary Todd.

In the summer of 1839, Mary had come for an extended stay with her older sister. Age twenty, she stood five feet two inches and had luminous skin, chestnut hair, and brilliant blue eyes. She was bright, vivacious, and, more often than not, determined to have her own way. Family members knew she had a quick tongue and, at times, a temper to match.

Mary and Elizabeth's father, Robert Todd, was a successful Lexington businessman who owned slaves, entertained public figures such as US senator Henry Clay, and encouraged his sons and daughters in their education. By the time she was eighteen, Mary had had ten years of formal schooling (by contemporary standards, this was a remarkable amount for a woman). When she arrived in Springfield, Mary was fluent in French and possessed an impressive knowledge of literature, history, and astronomy. She was also keenly interested in politics. Mary Todd understood power: its uses, its ebbs and flows, and the men who attained and lost it.

Small wonder she turned heads at Springfield gatherings. William Herndon, who came to intensely dislike her, remembered that she "soon became one of the belles, leading the young men of the town [on] a merry dance." Mary was "the very creature of excitement," according to Springfield lawyer James Conkling. Ninian Edwards was more direct: "Mary could make a bishop forget his prayers." Stephen Douglas, the leading Democrat in Illinois, was one of the men who noticed her. In 1839, Douglas was a savvy, accomplished politician who was on his way to a national career. Known as the Little Giant for his small stature—he was five feet four inches tall—and expanding influence, Douglas enjoyed flirting with the witty woman from Kentucky.

Lincoln also took note of Mary Todd. The two probably met in late 1839, and from the beginning, they were a study in contrasts. He towered over her by more than a foot. He was plain and, at age thirty, still largely unschooled in social graces; she was ten years younger, pretty, and elegant. Lincoln's natural energy was slow, and he was often silent and moody. Mary was all quickness and action. He was largely self-taught, and while confident of his intellectual abilities, he was also aware of his lack of formal schooling. She was well educated and comfortable displaying her knowledge.

Despite these differences, Lincoln was attracted to Mary and took to calling on her at the Edwards home. The couple sat together on the parlor sofa. "Mary led the conversation," her sister recalled. "Lincoln would listen and gaze on her as if drawn by some superior power." He was "fascinated with her quick sagacity—her will—her nature—and culture." This was more than infatuation; Lincoln had met a woman with whom he could share important aspects of himself. For one thing, Mary cared about intellectual issues and enjoyed discussing books and ideas. She loved poetry, particularly Robert Burns, and the couple often read aloud to each other. For another, Mary was passionate and knowledgeable about politics, and many of the couple's conversations centered on the Springfield political scene. For Lincoln, whose churning ambition was focused on elected office, this was a powerful connection.

Both Lincoln and Mary were committed Whigs. Both were from Kentucky. Both had lost their mothers unexpectedly when they were young: Lincoln at age nine, Mary at age six, when her mother died from complications of childbirth. He suffered from depression; it seems likely she did as well. Certainly, she endured periods of debilitating sadness (and migraines) throughout her life. Perhaps most important, Mary reveled in Lincoln's wish to rise. Back home, she had joked that she intended to marry a man who would be president. In Lincoln, she found a suitor who was highly intelligent, honest, considerate, and, as her relatives remembered, free "from the pretty flatteries and the conventional gallantries of the men in her social set." There is no evidence that in 1839 and 1840 Lincoln harbored—much less voiced—presidential aspirations. But, undoubtedly, he could sense Mary's belief in him.

We have little historical evidence about Lincoln's feelings for her when they were courting. A very private man, he rarely revealed his deepest emotions. But it seems probable that Mary's admiration for Lincoln, including her faith in his prospects, was a strong source of attraction. As countless women have for men, Mary Todd held out the possibility of shoring up his confidence and helping him climb the ladder of success. Lincoln was too self-aware and too deft not to have recognized this.

By late 1840, the couple reached an informal agreement to marry. There was no announcement or ring. Still, friends and family knew of their understanding, and some supported it. Others worried that Lincoln and Mary were too different to make a successful marriage. What role, if any, these opinions played in subsequent events is unclear. But sometime in very late 1840 or early 1841, the engagement fell apart.

Since Lincoln's death, biographers and scholars have devoted enormous attention to his early involvement with Mary Todd. Despite this scrutiny, we do not know exactly why the engagement ended. Perhaps Mary called it off because she sensed Lincoln was not fully committed, or because she was worried about the couple's compatibility. It is also possible that Lincoln had become romantically interested in someone else, or maybe, as David Donald has speculated, he simply got cold feet. Perhaps he was anxious about his ability to support a wife and a family. He was a relatively inexperienced attorney, and in 1840, his political fortunes in the state legislature were not what they had once been.

Regardless of the precise causes of the breakup, Lincoln was devastated. By January 1841, he was mired in guilt, shame, and unhappiness. He grew seriously depressed, taking to his bed for a week, missing roll calls in the general assembly and refusing contact with anyone but Speed and a doctor, Anson Henry. Many years later, the longtime friend remembered removing razors from Abe's room for fear he would hurt himself. Late in the month when Lincoln returned to government business, he was emaciated and weak. "I am now the most miserable man living," he wrote John Stuart. "If what I feel were equally distributed to the whole human family, there would not be one cheerful face on the earth. Whether I shall ever be better I cannot tell; I awfully forebode I shall not. To remain as I am is impossible; I must die or be better, it appears to me."

During the spring of 1841, Lincoln slowly climbed out of his depression. Henry treated him, most likely relying on leeches, mustard rubs, and cold baths, all standard nineteenth-century remedies for melancholy. As Lincoln found his emotional footing, he focused on his legal work and avoided the Edwardses' social circle, including Mary Todd and many of his friends.

During the summer, he traveled to Kentucky to visit Speed, who had moved back to his family's elegant home. In this restorative trip, Lincoln soaked up the attention that Speed's brother, half sister, and mother paid him and enjoyed the luxury of the mansion, where Lincoln had his own house slave. He also took long walks with his friend, the two men talking about Mary Todd and Fanny Henning, to whom Speed had recently become engaged.

During the next year, Lincoln and Speed shared their hopes and fears about marriage in a series of intimate letters. Speed was married in early 1842; Lincoln was exuberant when his friend wrote that he was far happier than he had expected to be. "I am not going beyond the truth," Lincoln quickly replied, "when I tell you, that the short space it took me to read your last letter, gave me more pleasure, than the total sum of all I have enjoyed since that fatal first of Jany, '41."

Later in 1842, Lincoln and Mary Todd began seeing each other again. They met secretly at a friend's home. Reprising their conversations from more than a year ago, they took up literature and, of course, politics. Still nervous about making a long-term commitment, Lincoln consulted Speed. "You have now been the husband of a lovely woman nearly eight months," Lincoln wrote him. "Are you now in *feeling* as well as *judgement* [sic], glad you are married as you are?" Speed swiftly responded in the affirmative, advising his friend not to doubt that he would find happiness with Mary Todd.

Not long after this exchange, Lincoln proposed to Mary, and she accepted. On November 4, 1842, the couple announced to the Edwardses they intended to wed that very day. Years later, Mary explained why the couple kept their relationship quiet until the last minute: "Woman & man were uncertain & slippery . . . it was best to keep the secret Courtship from all Eyes & Ears." A private ceremony was hastily arranged at the Edwards home, and that evening, in the presence of Mary's family and several friends, an Episcopalian minister married the couple. A week after the ceremony, Lincoln mentioned his wedding to a fellow lawyer, writing, "Nothing new here, except my marrying, which to me, is matter of profound wonder."

Before long, Mary was pregnant, and on August 1, 1843, a son was born. The proud parents named him Robert Todd Lincoln after Mary's father and began looking for bigger living quarters. That autumn, the Lincolns rented a small house in Springfield, but they would not be there long. In May 1844, with financial help from Mary's father, the couple bought a five-room house at the corner of Eighth and Jackson Streets, a short walk from the courthouse square and Lincoln's law office. (In the mid-1850s, they improved the house, adding a second story.) This would be their home for the next seventeen years, until the family left for Washington in 1861.

Married life was a big adjustment for Lincoln and Mary. He was used to a bachelor's existence, which meant coming and going as he pleased. As a husband, however, he was responsible for a family, with the financial, social, and emotional obligations that this involved. For her part, Mary found herself living in more straitened circumstances. In Kentucky, she had grown up in luxury, surrounded by domestic slaves. In Springfield, she had lived for three years in the Edwardses' mansion with their hired servants.

But as a wife whose husband was still building a career, Mary had to manage a tight family budget. She worried a great deal about money, trying to be frugal about groceries, food, and clothing. For example, Lincoln had his suits made by Springfield tailors, but Mary sewed her own garments. At times, she could afford a girl to help her at home; at others, she kept house alone. Even when she had another pair of hands, Mary worked hard, cooking meals, cleaning the house, hauling water from the pump, and on occasion entertaining her husband's colleagues.

As husband and wife, the Lincolns also came face-to-face with the stark differences in their personalities. She was a social creature, eager to be noticed and known for her graceful manners. He cared little for such niceties. For example, he once greeted a caller looking for his wife by saying, "She will be down as soon as she has all her trotting harness on." At the end of a day, he liked to sprawl on the parlor rug and read, often ignoring Mary's requests to make conversation or tend the fire. He was used to plenty of time alone and slipping out of conversation in the presence of others. These habits often hurt or angered his wife.

Marital discord has been a common theme in scores of books written about the sixteenth president. Many of these authors have blamed Mary for this friction, portraying her as selfish, neurotic, and highly unstable—and thus a poor choice for Lincoln to have made in a wife. But others, such as historians David Donald and Jean Harvey Baker, who has written a biography of Mary Lincoln, suggest that throughout their marriage, husband and wife were devoted to each other. Undoubtedly, Lincoln and Mary had their differences, as all married couples have, and at various junctures these strained the bonds between them. But the two remained consistently respectful and affectionate toward each other during a twenty-three-year marriage that saw great turbulence and terrible grief. Each consistently believed in the other while trying to understand the burdens that his or her partner carried.

More important than their differences, however, was what they shared. Mary used her political knowledge to remain actively involved in her husband's career. She believed deeply in Lincoln's prospects for being elected to national office and in his ability to excel in this role. Her faith in him never wavered, and she supported him in all kinds of ways: critiquing his speeches, advising him on how to deal with colleagues, and encouraging him when his own confidence flagged.

Within the context of nineteenth-century social roles, Mary's involvement in her husband's career was unusual. Married women were expected to stay out of the larger world of politics, power, and money, confining their energies to mothering and domestic tasks. Mary ignored these unwritten rules (indeed, some of the criticism Lincoln's associates leveled at her after he died may have stemmed from the outsize influence she had on him). Again and again, she used her sharp intelligence, high energy, and abiding love for her husband to keep him and his career moving forward.

Between 1843 and 1853, Mary gave birth to four sons: Robert Todd in 1843, Edward Baker in 1846, William Wallace in 1850, and Thomas, or "Tad," in 1853. Before their first two sons were very old, both parents adopted a style of child rearing that was lax by the standards of the time. They continued this approach with Willie and Tad, allowing them great latitude in their behavior and, more often than not, refusing to discipline them. As a result, the boys were frequently unruly. Lincoln's law partner William Herndon remembered Willie and Tad wreaking havoc in the partners' office: turning over inkstands, pulling books off shelves, and firing spitballs everywhere. In the White House, the younger sons often barged into cabinet meetings dressed as soldiers, paraded a menagerie of animals through the halls, and tried to extract tolls from constituents lined up outside the president's office. If Herndon and others saw the Lincoln children as "brats," their parents believed they were "free, happy and unrestrained by parental tyranny." "Love is the chain," Lincoln said to his wife, "whereby to bind a child to its parents."

Lincoln and Mary grieved intensely when, in 1850, their second son, Eddie, died at the age of three. They grieved again in 1862, when their third son, Willie, died at age eleven. Despite the loss of two children, Lincoln drew strength and resilience from his family, and some of his success as a leader rested on this foundation. We tend to think of Abraham Lincoln as a solitary figure, alone in the White House, lost in thought, and preoccupied by the burdens of the Civil War. We forget that he was a family man, who, in spite of a predisposition to create distance between himself and others, learned to deeply love and depend on his wife and boys.

CHAPTER FOURTEEN

Embrace the Cause

In 1842, Lincoln's fourth term as a state legislator ended. His position in the general assembly was not as strong as it had once been, and he did not seek reelection. But he did not relinquish his aspirations to higher office. "That man who thinks Lincoln calmly sat down," Herndon once remarked, "and gathered his robes about him, waiting for the people to call him, has a very erroneous knowledge of Lincoln. He was always calculating, and always planning ahead. His ambition was a little engine that knew no rest."

In the mid-1840s, he set his eye on the US Congress. His former colleague John Stuart announced he was going to vacate his seat, and Illinois Whig Party leaders decided that in 1846 it would be Lincoln's turn to run for it. During the campaign, Herndon remembered, Lincoln "was active and alert, speaking everywhere, and abandoning his share of business in the law office entirely." When the votes were counted that August, Lincoln was elected to the US House of Representatives by a large majority.

In December 1847, he took his seat in the Thirtieth Congress. During his first year in Washington, Lincoln devoted most of his attention to attacking Democratic president James Polk's prosecution of the Mexican War. The conflict, which had erupted in 1846 between American and Mexican troops partly in response to the annexation of Texas by the United States a year earlier, was almost over when Lincoln arrived in the nation's capital. In January 1848, he made a speech assailing the president for trying to rationalize the war and for requesting federal funds to consolidate the Western territories claimed as spoils of victory. (This land, some five hundred thousand square miles, encompassed the present-day states of California, Nevada, and Utah, as well as parts of Arizona and New Mexico.)

Lincoln hoped his speech would be well received, but it was not. Within Washington, his words were lost in a larger Whig assault on Polk, and back home in Illinois, colleagues accused Lincoln of being unpatriotic. Even Herndon thought his law partner had made a mistake in lashing out at the president and the Mexican War. Lincoln wrote a detailed response to his critics, but he couldn't erase some damage to his reputation.

The Thirtieth Congress also took up the issue of slavery. Most of these discussions centered on the Wilmot Proviso, an initiative introduced to ban slavery from the territory recently acquired from Mexico. The setting for the debate was ironic given that in Washington, DC, slavery was legal; of the city's total population of fifty-two thousand people, almost four thousand were slaves. Indeed, one of the nation's biggest slave markets was located just seven blocks from the Capitol.

In 1849, a group of antislavery congressmen set out to outlaw the institution in the District. Lincoln tried to stay away from the controversy, voting against—or to table—most of these initiatives. He was one of a tiny Northern minority to do this.

Then, in a surprising about-face, Lincoln began preparing his own initiative to end slavery in the city. His plan called for a local referendum, which, if passed, would make all black children born after January 1, 1850, free. For owners who chose to voluntarily emancipate their slaves, the federal government would pay them the full cash value of their human chattel. To make his program more appealing to Southern congressmen, Lincoln pledged that city authorities would vigorously pursue fugitive slaves. He shared his initiative with antislavery legislators, all of whom approved of it.

Before Lincoln could officially introduce his bill, however, support for it evaporated. Abolitionists, such as Wendell Phillips of Massachusetts, objected to the fugitive-slave provisions. Other antislavery spokesmen protested that monetary compensation for slaveholders recognized the legitimacy of an unjust institution. Discouraged by these defections, Lincoln tabled his plan.

In March 1849, his term in office ended, and he returned to Springfield. There, he discovered that his political stock was lower than when he had left. The Whigs had failed to elect their candidate to the congressional seat that Lincoln was vacating, and many of his supporters blamed him and his unpopular position on the Mexican War for the defeat.

Lincoln fell into a depression. After years of planning and campaigning, he had obtained national office. But in Congress, his actions had been met with general indifference at best, and partisan scorn at worst. Now, back in the place where he had so carefully constructed his base, Lincoln saw few prospects for his political future. For a man who lived and breathed the possibility of higher office, this was a demoralizing moment. We get a sense of his pessimism in an early-1849 response he sent to an autograph seeker: "If you collect the signatures of all persons who are no less distinguished than I, you will have a very undistinguishing mass of names."

During the early 1850s, Lincoln focused on his law practice. But he did not completely abandon politics. He stumped for allies when they ran for office and stayed informed about national events, reading newspapers and copies of congressional debates. As he surveyed the political scene, Lincoln saw that long-simmering tensions about slavery were rising. Responding to growing discord between free states and slave states, Congress passed the Compromise of 1850; this set of measures attempted to balance concessions to opponents of slavery with concessions to those who supported the institution.

Under the terms of the legislation, California was admitted as a free state, and the slave trade was abolished in the District of Columbia. As an offset to these provisions, slaveholding states obtained the Fugitive Slave Act of 1850. This new law required private citizens to assist in the recovery of escaped slaves, denied suspected fugitives the right to a trial by jury, and established special commissioners to locate them. Northern abolitionists such as William Lloyd Garrison and Frederick Douglass spoke out strongly against the law. Despite these and other objections, many Americans hoped the Compromise of 1850 would alleviate the increasing hostility between North and South.

But this did not happen. In May 1854, Congress passed the Kansas-Nebraska Act, and the landscape of American politics was marred by new flare-ups of discord. Sponsored by Stephen Douglas, the Democratic senator from Illinois, the law provided that a huge territory (which later became the states of Kansas, Nebraska, North Dakota, South Dakota, Montana, and parts of Wyoming and Colorado) would be organized into two tracts, Kansas and Nebraska, that would be open to settlement. The legislation also stipulated that residents in these territories would determine the legality of slavery by plebiscite. This meant that popular sovereignty—not Congress, which since the nation's founding had held jurisdiction over the legal status (and thus the geography) of slavery—would determine its fate. The Kansas-Nebraska Act also repealed the Missouri Compromise of 1820, which had outlawed slavery in all lands north of the latitude 36°30', except for the state of Missouri, which had entered the Union as a slave state.

Almost immediately, the 1854 act unleashed a firestorm. Northern politicians, journalists, and ordinary citizens launched a war of words against the new law, denouncing it as a triumph of Southern efforts to expand the institution. Some opponents attacked the legislation as an attempt to exclude small farmers and other free laborers from the Western territories in favor of large slaveholders and the rigid social hierarchy of a plantation economy. Other opponents were enraged that congressional authority had been usurped by the concept of popular sovereignty. Still other detractors predicted (quite accurately) that the act would unleash a violent struggle between anti- and pro-slavery forces to control the new lands. Collective anger against Stephen Douglas as the sponsor of the law was so intense that the Illinois senator joked that he could "travel from Boston to Chicago by the light of my own [burning] effigies."

In the wake of the Kansas-Nebraska Act, antislavery sentiment erupted all over the North. The Fugitive Slave Act of 1850 had seeded some of this ground. So, too, had the 1852 publication of Harriet

Beecher Stowe's novel *Uncle Tom's Cabin*, which exposed countless readers to the horrors of slavery. (A smash hit, the book sold three hundred thousand copies in its first year, equivalent to about 3 million copies in our time.)

The political reverberations of the Kansas-Nebraska Act were equally important. The legislation, and the larger issues it raised concerning slavery, sowed division among Democrats. One group thought the legislation did not go far enough in allowing slavery's expansion; a second group, represented by Northern Democrats, supported the act; a third coalition, concerned about the institution's extension in any form, began to look for another political home. The other national political party, the Whigs, were already fractured from within over slavery and now began to unravel. During the next two years, many Northern Whigs, including Lincoln, would join the newly formed Republican Party, and the Whigs would cease to exist. Seemingly overnight, American politics had become very fluid.

Lincoln understood that the country had arrived at a critical juncture and that the political confusion presented an important opportunity for him. The Kansas-Nebraska Act, including the repeal of the Missouri Compromise, he wrote years later in a third-person autobiography, "aroused him as he had never been before." In hindsight, it seems clear that Lincoln realized in 1854 that slavery had become *the* defining issue of his time, and that his political future was necessarily bound up with it. That summer, he decided to publicly respond to Stephen Douglas and his Kansas-Nebraska Act. He intended to challenge the US senator during one of his many appearances in Illinois; on October 16, the men shared a platform in Peoria.

This was Lincoln's first major speech on slavery, and he prepared carefully for it. He began by outlining the history of the institution in the United States, arguing that the founding fathers had objected to slavery on principle and therefore intended to restrict its spread and put it on a path to ultimate extinction. Because the institution had existed for more than a century when the country was established, Lincoln contended, the framers accepted slavery in certain states, legalizing it in those places and protecting slaveholders' rights in the Constitution. "The plain unmistakable spirit of that age, towards slavery," Lincoln explained, "was hostility to the PRINCIPLE, and toleration, ONLY BY NECESSITY."

This same spirit, he continued, formed the basis of the Missouri Compromise, which, when it was passed in 1820, had recognized slavery in the states where it was legal, allowed it in the new state of Missouri, and prohibited it north of the parallel 36°30'. The recent repeal of this legislation by the Kansas-Nebraska Act, Lincoln asserted, had disastrous consequences. By potentially extending slavery, the new law compromised the nation's integrity:

> This *declared* indifference, but as I must think, covert *real* zeal for the spread of slavery, I can not but hate. I hate it because of the monstrous injustice of slavery itself. I hate it because it deprives our republican example of its just influence in the world [and] enables the enemies of free institutions, with plausibility, to taunt us as hypocrites [and] causes the real friends of freedom to doubt our sincerity, and especially because it forces so many really good men amongst ourselves into an open war with the very fundamental principles of civil liberty—criticising [*sic*] the Declaration of Independence, and insisting that there is no right principle of action but *self-interest*.

Lincoln also attacked the new law's reliance on popular sovereignty as a means of deciding slavery's fate in the Western territories. He acknowledged the importance of self-government, but he argued that, in certain circumstances, this must be limited. Voters in Virginia, for example, could make laws about oyster fishing just as Indiana voters could decide about cranberry laws. These were issues, Lincoln asserted, that communities should be allowed to determine by local ballot. But when it came to the most fundamental matters, such as whether people were legally allowed to enslave other people, the federal government could not remain morally neutral and leave such choices to local referenda. In Lincoln's view, no local majority should be able to decide the legality of an institution that robbed millions of Americans of their inalienable rights to life, liberty, and the pursuit of happiness.

At the same time that Lincoln acknowledged slavery was unjust, he also insisted that the constitutional rights of slaveholders had to be upheld. These included the right to own slaves in states where the institution was legal, the right to count each slave as three-fifths of a person for purposes of congressional representation and the Electoral College, and—because the Constitution contained a fugitive-slave clause—the right to legal redress if slaves escaped. "Now all this is manifestly unfair," Lincoln admitted. But "it is in the constitution; and I do not, for that cause, or any other cause, propose to destroy, or alter, or disregard the constitution."

For three hours, Lincoln held his listeners' attention with clear language and sturdy logic. As he reached the denouement of the speech, he invoked biblical imagery:

> Our republican robe is soiled, and trailed in the dust. Let us repurify it. Let us turn and wash it white, in the spirit, if not the blood, of the Revolution. Let us turn slavery from its claims of "moral right," back upon its existing legal rights, and its arguments of "necessity." Let us return it to the position our fathers gave it; and there let it rest in peace. Let us re-adopt the Declaration of Independence. . . . If we do this, we shall not only have saved the Union; but we shall have so saved it, as to make, and to keep it, forever worthy of the saving.

Afterward, Lincoln knew the speech had been a success and sent it to an Illinois Whig newspaper for publication. It took seven issues to print the remarks, which were read throughout the state. During the ensuing weeks, Lincoln made a series of speeches in towns across Illinois. By the end of the year, historian Eric Foner has written, Lincoln had "emerged as his state's most eloquent opponent of the expansion of slavery." He, like many other individuals who become courageous leaders, had discovered a cause that demanded his time, energy, and gifts. In 1854, he was ready to embrace this, and—in A. G. Lafley's words—"get in the game."

CHAPTER FIFTEEN

Quest for National Office

Late that year Lincoln challenged the Democrat incumbent James
Shields for his US Senate seat; Stephen Douglas held the other
seat. Although the Whig Party was fast losing its cohesion, Lincoln
had no choice but to run as a candidate from that party. He knew it
would be a tight race in the Illinois state legislature (until adoption
of the Seventeenth Amendment in 1913, US senators were elected
by their state assemblies). He also realized the contest would be a
referendum on the Kansas-Nebraska Act.

In February 1855, balloting for the Senate seat began in the general
assembly. Four candidates emerged, and during early voting, Lincoln's
prospects appeared strong. However, as the roll calls continued without a clear winner, his position deteriorated, and he became fearful
that a candidate who supported the Kansas-Nebraska Act would
ultimately win. After the ninth ballot, Lincoln ordered his supporters
to turn their votes over to Lyman Trumbull, a Democrat who opposed
the legislation, and on the next ballot the assembly elected him. This
was a victory for opponents of the Kansas-Nebraska Act. But it was
a bitter defeat for Lincoln, and he sank into melancholy. He told an
old friend he "would never strive for office again."

But as the Whig Party continued to disintegrate, Lincoln found
the allure of politics irresistible and set about helping to organize the
young Republican Party in Illinois. As the political coalition began to
take shape nationally, it encompassed a variety of interests located

primarily in the North, all of which opposed the Kansas-Nebraska Act. These included radical abolitionists, former Whigs, antislavery Democrats, and "Free-Soilers," who wanted Western lands left open to white labor. The diversity of the party's membership meant Republican leaders had to craft a platform capable of uniting a range of groups. The central element of this platform was opposition to slavery's extension and acceptance of its legality where it already existed.

Within Illinois, Lincoln became a leading spokesman for this position. Beginning in early 1856, he took to the stump, speaking at political meetings and publishing editorials. One of his main lines of attack on slavery's expansion was the danger it posed to *all* Americans. If slavery's supporters were ready to steal the bread a black man made, Lincoln asked, what was to stop them from restricting freedom for other citizens? "Our progress in degeneracy appears to me to be pretty rapid," he wrote Joshua Speed.

> As a nation, we began by declaring that *"all men are created equal."* We now practically read it "all men are created equal, *except negroes.*" When the Know-Nothings [a political party based on antagonism toward immigrants, Catholics, and African-Americans] get control, it will read "all men are created equal, except negroes, *and foreigners, and catholics* [sic]." When it comes to this I should prefer emigrating to some country where they make no pretence of loving liberty—to Russia, for instance, where despotism can be taken pure, and without the base alloy of hypocrasy [sic].

In June 1856, the Republican Party met in Philadelphia for its first national convention. The assembled delegates nominated the former California politician John Frémont for president. In early balloting for the vice-presidential nominee, Lincoln received 110 votes to front-runner William Dayton's 253. The delegates ultimately chose Dayton, a former Whig senator from New Jersey. But support for Lincoln demonstrated his growing reputation. When news of the voting reached him on the legal circuit in Urbana, Illinois, he said, "I reckon that ain't me; there's another great man in Massachusetts named Lincoln, and I reckon it's him."

Perhaps he spoke those words during one of his gloomy spells. Perhaps they were a result of calculated humility or false modesty, as David Donald has suggested. Whatever Lincoln's public reaction to the vice-presidential balloting, he was inwardly pleased and threw himself into the 1856 campaign, rallying support for the Republican ticket. But in the end, the Democratic candidate, James Buchanan, won the Electoral College and became the nation's fifteenth president.

On March 6, 1857, just days after Buchanan's inauguration, the Supreme Court handed down the Dred Scott decision. The case concerned an African-American slave, Dred Scott, who had in 1833 been moved from Missouri, a slave state, to Illinois, a state in which slavery was prohibited. Scott's owner then took him to Wisconsin Territory, where slavery was also illegal. The slave was then brought back to Missouri, and when his owner died, Scott unsuccessfully attempted to purchase his freedom from the white man's widow. In 1846, the slave petitioned the Missouri state courts for his emancipation on the grounds that he had lived for several years in free lands. In late 1856, his case finally reached the Supreme Court.

Writing for a 7–2 majority, Chief Justice Roger Taney ruled that Scott was not entitled to seek justice in the courts because, as a Negro, he was not a citizen. At the time of the country's founding, Taney wrote, "the class of persons imported as slaves . . . [were] regarded as beings of an inferior order, and altogether unfit to associate with the white race, either in social or political relations; and so far inferior that they had no rights which the white man was bound to respect." Taney ruled that the Fifth Amendment denied Congress the right to deprive persons of their property without due process of law, and therefore the Missouri Compromise, which prohibited slavery north of the 36°30' line, was unconstitutional.

Throughout the North, antislavery groups were incensed. The *New-York Tribune* labeled the Supreme Court's decision "wicked" and "abominable." A Chicago newspaper predicted dire consequences, including the possibility of slavery coming to its home city, complete with open-air slave markets. According to William Lloyd Garrison's abolitionist newspaper, the *Liberator*, the court's judgment was "to the last degree, infamous and tyrannical."

Lincoln took this all in and waited. Then in June 1857, he reacted to the Supreme Court's ruling. In a speech given in the Illinois State House, Lincoln argued that the majority of justices were wrong in stating that Negroes were not entitled to essential civil liberties. The Declaration of Independence, Lincoln asserted, included the whole human family, blacks as well as whites, and the first principle of that document—all men are created equal—stipulated every American's right to life, liberty, and the pursuit of happiness. Lincoln accused Chief Justice Taney and Stephen Douglas, who supported the Dred Scott decision, of conspiring with other Democrats to expand and perpetuate slavery. In doing this, Lincoln contended, they were making the already oppressed Negro even more oppressed:

All the powers of earth seem rapidly combining against [the Negro]. . . . They have him in his prison house; they have searched his person, and left no prying instrument with him. One after another they have closed the heavy iron doors upon him, and now they have him, as it were, bolted in with a lock of a hundred keys, which can never be unlocked without the concurrence of every key; the keys in the hands of a hundred different men, and they scattered to a hundred different and distant places; and they stand musing as to what invention, in all the dominions of mind and matter, can be produced to make the impossibility of his escape more complete than it is.

For the remainder of 1857, Lincoln made plans to challenge the Democratic incumbent, Stephen Douglas, for his US Senate seat in 1858. Lincoln prepared for the upcoming election by mobilizing supporters, keeping close tabs on important precincts, and urging party members to help elect state legislators who would vote for him. Conscious not to draw outward attention, he counseled his allies, "Let all be so quiet that the [adversary] shall not be notified."

Meanwhile, the country continued to seethe over slavery. Since 1854, a series of violent confrontations between pro- and antislavery forces had erupted in Western lands. In 1856, armed conflict and mayhem exploded in parts of Kansas Territory and Missouri. Individuals were kidnapped and—in an eerie replay of colonial protests against the British crown—tarred and feathered. At times, the fighting turned deadly, and men from both sides were killed. In May, pro-slavery forces entered Lawrence, Kansas, torching a hotel, destroying newspaper offices, and ransacking other buildings. In retaliation, Northern abolitionist John Brown and several followers brutally killed five pro-slavery men. The murders, known as the Pottawatomie Massacre, ignited three months of bloody raids and reprisals in which another twenty-nine people were killed.

During the next two years, the turbulence in the Western territories continued. In the midst of this, Lincoln and his Republican supporters redoubled their efforts to elect him to the US Senate. On June 16, 1858, Lincoln gave a speech in the Illinois State House that he knew would be widely reported as his opening salvo in the contest against the nationally famous incumbent, Stephen Douglas. The Republican candidate began with a biblical image:

"A house divided against itself cannot stand."

I believe this government cannot endure, permanently half *slave* and half *free*.

I do not expect the Union to be *dissolved*—I do not expect the house to *fall*—but I *do* expect it will cease to be divided.

It will become *all* one thing, or *all* the other.

Either the *opponents* of slavery, will arrest the further spread of it, and place it where the public mind shall rest in the belief that it is in course of ultimate extinction; or its *advocates* will push it forward, till it shall become alike lawful in *all* the States, *old* as well as *new*—*North* as well as *South*.

Have we no *tendency* to the latter condition?

The last sentence, in the form of a question, was deliberately ominous, paving the way for the main thrust of Lincoln's remarks. He hoped to demonstrate that the country's highest-ranking leaders were conspiring to extend slavery throughout the United States. As evidence, Lincoln pointed first to the Kansas-Nebraska Act, which had opened great tracts of land to the possibility of slavery. He next turned to the Dred Scott decision; by declaring the Missouri Compromise unconstitutional and ruling that slavery couldn't be excluded from any territory, Lincoln argued, the Supreme Court had created the potential for slaveholders to lawfully bring their slaves into free states. To defeat such a conspiracy, Lincoln urged citizens to join hands with the Republican Party, which stood firmly against the spread of slavery.

In struggling to make sense of American slavery and the politics surrounding it, Lincoln didn't work as an academic or formal theorist might—from an overarching frame or a grand design. He aspired to be and then became *a leader*. This meant that he built the structure of his thinking brick by brick, responding to the volatility of larger events, the political opportunities and exigencies that he faced, *and* changes within himself. As conditions shifted and he evolved, he amended his judgment—at times discarding previously important aspects and incorporating new ones. All the while, he was observing, reflecting, and, ultimately, trying to get right with himself about the meaning of slavery and what he should do in regard to this momentous issue.

This is not to say Lincoln got it right from the beginning—far from it. For example, today we find his commitment to respecting the legality of slavery where it already existed shameful and strange coming from a leader many think of as the Great Emancipator. And as historians have noted, Lincoln's reading of the founding fathers' attitudes toward slavery was highly selective.

Like the other individuals in this book, Lincoln made plenty of mistakes and exhibited many flaws. From our perspective, it seems he catered to the prejudice that most of his white contemporaries harbored toward blacks. Certainly, as we shall see in his debates with Stephen Douglas during the 1858 Senate race, Lincoln was often at pains to disavow any kind of social equality between the races. Like Frederick Douglass, who frequently criticized him, we view Lincoln's position on slavery in the 1850s as weak, even cowardly.

We can see all this when we step back to consider Lincoln not as a looming figure in marble or as a national martyr, but instead as a *human being* who grew—emotionally, intellectually, and morally—as he advanced along his journey. This growth was not a result of happenstance or fate. Rather it flowed from Lincoln's ongoing commitment to better himself—inside as well as out. After 1854, his development as a leader was also a result of what he did to construct a cohesive, politically viable, and ethically grounded position on slavery.

His persistence in trying to address the transcendent issue of his time and to do so with integrity is a defining aspect of courageous leaders. Once such men and women embrace a cause, they don't give up working to understand it (and their own relationship to the mission); they keep on revising their own tools and means for accomplishing the goal; they continually work to improve how they communicate the cause to those around them; and perhaps most important, these leaders are constantly looking inward, "checking in with themselves," to make sure they're both nurturing the inner assets they need to achieve their mission and serving a just end.

During the 1858 Senate campaign, Abraham Lincoln and Stephen Douglas made scores of speeches across Illinois. In late July, Lincoln challenged the incumbent to a series of debates, and Douglas agreed. From the start, these attracted national interest. This was due in part to Douglas's fame, and also because Illinois was regarded as a battleground state—not only in skirmishes between Democrats and Republicans, but also between supporters and opponents of slavery. Eastern newspapers, including the *New York Herald* and the *New York Times*, sent reporters to cover the debates. This was some of the first close-on national coverage of any political contest in the country's history.

Many journalists commented on the differences in style between the two candidates. Douglas was always well dressed and traveled with his beautiful second wife, Adele Cutts, the grandniece of Dolley Madison. The couple moved between campaign stops in a private railroad car, in which they entertained local dignitaries. Lincoln, as David Donald has written, "deliberately cultivated a different image." The Republican candidate rode the regular rails and wore his usual clothes, which were often old and ill fitting. When Carl Schurz, the German revolutionary who went on to become a general in the Union army and a US senator, first encountered Lincoln before the sixth debate in Quincy, Illinois, he was surprised:

[Lincoln] wore a somewhat battered "stove-pipe hat." . . . [His] ungainly body was clad in a rusty black frock-coat with sleeves that should have been longer. . . . His black trousers, too, permitted a very full view of his large feet. On his left arm he carried a gray woolen shawl, which evidently served him for an overcoat in chilly weather. His left hand held a cotton umbrella of the bulging kind, and also a black satchel that bore the marks of long and hard usage. His right hand he had kept free for hand-shaking, of which there was no end until everybody in the [railroad] car seemed to be satisfied. I had seen, in Washington and in the West, several public men of rough appearance, but none whose looks seemed quite so uncouth, not to say grotesque, as Lincoln's.

The Lincoln-Douglas debates began in late August and ended in mid-October. All told, tens of thousands of men, women, and children attended, with each debate taking on the excitement of a major regional event. "We were fed on politics in those days," remembered a woman who, as a child, had been at the second encounter. "My twin sister and I would not have missed the debate for all the things in the world." The siblings, like everyone else, had come to see two skilled orators face off on slavery, the burning issue of the day.

During the seven debates, Douglas and Lincoln each covered ground they had been over before: the history and future of slavery, the founding fathers' intentions toward the institution, the Dred Scott decision, and the status of black Americans. What was new was the breadth and quality of the *public* discussion that the confrontations inspired. As the individual debates were happening, Americans of all rank and file talked about the issues the two opponents raised. And they did so at a deeply informed level, one almost inconceivable in our own age of sound bites and the media's search for the salacious story.

From the start, the debates had the feel of a verbal chess match, with each man trying to outmaneuver the other. The pawns, the rooks, and the queen were the issues surrounding slavery; the chessboard was the American political landscape of the 1850s. Logic and political calculation formed the basis of the debates, but they were not the speakers' only tools. Each also used pointed humor, direct appeals to the audience, and his own interpretation of history to try to strengthen his position and weaken his opponent's. Neither candidate was above insulting the other. In their second meeting, for example, Douglas said that Lincoln had racked his brain so much in devising a specific response that he "had not strength enough to invent the others." In their sixth encounter, Lincoln mocked Douglas's doctrine of popular sovereignty as being so thin it was "the homeopathic soup that was made by boiling the shadow of a pigeon that had starved to death." The men also set traps for each other. During the second debate in Freeport, for example, Lincoln lured Douglas into a position in which he was forced to repudiate either popular sovereignty or support of the Dred Scott decision.

The quality of discussion—the caliber of play—was not consistently high. For example, during the third debate, held in Jonesboro, in the very southern part of Illinois, neither Lincoln nor Douglas was particularly forceful or well reasoned. They were both undignified, making baseless accusations against each other. They also used political maneuvering, irrelevant lines of argument, and what would today be called racial slurs. The third debate was grubby street fighting, with each candidate snatching all the chess pieces he could to defeat his adversary, and with each man, at times, descending to insult and innuendo. For Lincoln the politician, Lincoln the trial lawyer, and Lincoln the frontier wrestler, this was all in a day's work.

At various points during the first three debates, Douglas held the advantage, attacking Lincoln by saying he was trying to create an "abolition party" under the name of the Republican Party. Douglas also accused his opponent of supporting full equality between the races. Worried that these charges were making their candidate appear too radical, Lincoln's advisers urged him to tackle the allegations head-on. At the fourth debate, held in mid-September in Charleston in central Illinois, Lincoln acted on their counsel. He opened by laying out his view on the relative position of whites and blacks:

> I will say then that I am not, nor ever have been in favor of bringing
> about in any way the social and political equality of the white and
> black races,—that I am not nor ever have been in favor of making

voters or jurors of negroes, nor of qualifying them to hold office, nor to intermarry with white people; and I will say in addition to this that there is a physical difference between the white and black races which I believe will for ever forbid the two races living together on terms of social and political equality. And inasmuch as they cannot so live, while they do remain together there must be the position of superior and inferior, and I as much as any other man am in favor of having the superior position assigned to the white race.

Lincoln hurried on to qualify these remarks. "I do not perceive that because the white man is to have the superior position the negro should be denied everything. . . . Because I do not want a negro woman for a slave," he said, does not mean "I must necessarily want her for a wife. My understanding is that I can just let her alone."

During the final three encounters, the debates' momentum shifted, and Lincoln gained the advantage. The fifth meeting took place in early October at Knox College in Galesburg, in the northwestern part of the state. Heavy winds on the day of the event forced organizers to move the speakers' platform to abut a campus building. To reach the dais, Lincoln and Douglas had to climb through a window. "Well, at last I have gone through college," Lincoln said as he emerged onto the platform.

The most important points that Lincoln raised in this encounter dealt with differences between the Republicans, and Douglas and his supporters, including the two groups' views on the morality of slavery. Republicans, Lincoln argued, believed slavery was unjust, while "every sentiment [Douglas] utters disregards the idea that there is anything wrong in Slavery." Lincoln continued, "Now, I confess myself as belonging to that class in the country who contemplate slavery as a moral, social and political evil, having due regard for its actual existence among us . . . but, nevertheless, desire a policy that looks to the prevention of it as a wrong, and looks hopefully to the time when as a wrong it may come to an end."

In the seventh and final debate, Lincoln closed his remarks by returning to the morality of slavery:

That is the real issue. That is the issue that will continue in this country when these poor tongues of Judge Douglas and myself shall be silent. It is the eternal struggle between these two principles—right and wrong—throughout the world. They are the two principles that have stood face to face from the beginning of time; and will ever continue to struggle. The one is the common right of humanity and the other the divine right of kings. It is the same principle in whatever shape it develops itself. It is the same spirit that says, "You work and toil and earn bread, and I'll eat it." No matter in what shape it comes, whether from the mouth of a king who seeks to bestride the people of his own nation and live by the fruit of their labor, or from one race of men as an apology for enslaving another race, it is the same tyrannical principle.

After a brief rejoinder by Douglas, the debates ended. During their seven encounters, the candidates had faced each other for a total of twenty-one hours. The aim of the candidates' roughly 130,000 words had been to engage and influence their audience—not only those present, but also citizens across the country reading newspaper accounts of the confrontations.

But more was going on during the debates than political sparring, as compelling as this often was. Beneath the words that the candidates exchanged were two fundamentally different views on the meaning of America. For Douglas, as political scientist Michael Sandel has pointed out, the defining aspect of democracy was popular sovereignty, voters exercising their collective will. In contrast, Lincoln saw the essence of democracy, particularly American democracy, as principle. Slavery was morally wrong, and it was a democratic government's responsibility to treat the institution as such. This meant preventing its extension to the Western territories or any other new place.

After the final debate, two weeks remained until the election on November 4. When the votes were counted in Illinois, Republican candidates won several state offices; in the legislature, however, the Democratic Party maintained control, winning 53 percent of the seats. On January 5, 1859, when these newly elected Illinois representatives voted for their next US senator, Stephen Douglas received fifty-four ballots to Lincoln's forty-six.

Lincoln was deeply disappointed. Once again, he'd given an election everything he had, and once again, he'd lost. In early January, after the general assembly ballots had been counted, Henry Whitney, a colleague, went to see him in his Springfield law office. He found the defeated candidate alone, dejected, and certain that his life had been "an abject and lamentable failure." "I never saw any man so radically and thoroughly depressed," recalled Whitney, "so completely steeped in the bitter waters of hopeless despair." Certain his political career was over, Lincoln predicted that the only thing he could count on was the loyalty of his longtime law partner. "I expect everyone to desert me except Billy [Herndon]," he said.

Still, Lincoln did not succumb to his negative feelings. Perhaps he recognized his supporters were also upset about the outcome. These people, many of whom had invested time and energy in his candidacy, were looking to their leader to make sense of the defeat and carry on. Perhaps Lincoln was also buoyed by the impact his candidacy had made. He may have taken heart, too, from his position on the large issues at stake in 1858. "I am glad I made the late race," he wrote his old Springfield friend Dr. Anson Henry several weeks after the election. "It gave me a hearing on the great and durable question of the age, which I could have had in no other way; and though I now sink out of view, and shall be forgotten, I believe I have made some marks which will tell for the cause of civil liberty long after I am gone."

CHAPTER SIXTEEN

Road to the White House

After his Senate defeat, Lincoln went back to practicing law, but he could not keep himself out of the political fray. His debates with Douglas had attracted great interest, and Lincoln was asked to give scores of speeches, many of which he did. Late in 1859, several Illinois newspapers and national publications, including the *New York Herald*, mentioned Lincoln as a potential presidential candidate in the 1860 election. He resisted such a possibility, saying, "I do not think myself fit for the Presidency."

When Lincoln surveyed the field of candidates for the Republican Party nomination, he saw a group of men who were more educated and successful than he. William Seward, a US senator from New York, was widely regarded as the front-runner. Republican governor Salmon Chase of Ohio was a well-known abolitionist who also wanted to win the nomination. Edward Bates of Missouri was a former congressman who had the support of Horace Greeley, the powerful editor of the *New-York Tribune*. Pennsylvania senator Simon Cameron, who had made a fortune speculating in railroads and banking, was a possible candidate. Other men, such as John Frémont, the Republican Party's nominee in 1856, were also known to be interested.

Stacked up against these men, Lincoln wrote a supporter, he could not be the "*first* choice of a very great many." He had little formal schooling, no administrative track record, and few relationships with Eastern politicians. But he knew that each of the major contenders also had weaknesses. Many voters, for example, viewed Seward as an extremist; Chase was a clumsy tactician. In his late sixties, Bates was considered old, and allegations of financial impropriety swirled around Cameron. If Republican Party leaders grew concerned about these vulnerabilities, Lincoln reasoned, he might emerge as a dark-horse candidate. "Our policy," he explained to a colleague, "is to give no offence to others—leave them in a mood to come to us, if they shall be compelled to give up their first love."

Lincoln decided to test the waters outside Illinois. Early in 1860, he arranged with an Ohio publisher to release a printed version of his debates with Stephen Douglas, and the book quickly became a bestseller. Lincoln also put together a brief autobiography. "There is not much of it," he wrote, forwarding the piece to a newspaper editor, "for the reason, I suppose, that there is not much of me."

In late 1859, Republican Party officials invited Lincoln to come East to give a lecture in Brooklyn, New York, early the next year, and he quickly accepted. He knew an urbane, influential audience would be assessing him in relation to the leading presidential candidates. He decided to speak about slavery and the history of the federal government's action toward it.

In late February, Lincoln set out for New York City. When he arrived, he learned that the venue for the speech had changed—from Brooklyn to the Cooper Institute (known more commonly as Cooper Union) in Manhattan. On February 27, 1860, about thirteen hundred people, including newspaper editors Horace Greeley and William Cullen Bryant of the *New York Evening Post*, filed into Cooper Union's Great Hall to hear Lincoln's address.

Many in the crowd were discomfited by the Illinois lawyer and politician as he began to speak. "The first impression of the man from the West," one audience member recalled, "did nothing to contradict the expectation of something weird, rough, and uncultivated. . . . The long, gaunt head capped by a shock of hair that seemed not to have been thoroughly brushed out made a picture which did not fit in with New York's conception of a finished statesman." Lincoln's speaking style did little to reassure the audience. He had a high, sometimes squeaky voice. And when he spoke, a journalist remembered, he "used singularly awkward, almost absurd, up-and-down and sidewise movements of his body to give emphasis to his arguments."

But once he warmed to his subject, Lincoln held the crowd's attention. As Lincoln expert Harold Holzer has written, the speech was a "laboriously researched, studiously legalistic, and dispassionately restrained antislavery treatise that hearkened back to the will of the founding fathers, preached political moderation and sectional harmony, yet at the same time bristled with barely contained indignation over the moral outrage of human slavery."

Lincoln made three important points. The first was that the founding fathers intended the federal government to regulate slavery, and that toward this end, most of the framers wanted to limit its spread. The second was that the Republicans sought only to restrict slavery's expansion—not to tamper with it where it already existed. The third was that the Republican Party should not abandon the position that slavery was morally wrong and should therefore not be allowed in Western lands.

In framing his remarks, Lincoln had several objectives. He wanted to present himself as a thinker who was as sophisticated as his Eastern counterparts. He also hoped to appear a moderate with respect to slavery and thus a viable alternative to the outspoken abolitionist William Seward. Once again, Lincoln tried to demolish the credibility of the Democratic Party's faith in popular sovereignty. He ended his ninety-minute address by laying down what he saw as the Republican gauntlet regarding slavery:

> Neither let us be slandered from our duty by false accusations against us, nor frightened from it by menaces of destruction to the Government nor of dungeons to ourselves. LET US HAVE FAITH THAT RIGHT MAKES MIGHT, AND IN THAT FAITH, LET US, TO THE END, DARE TO DO OUR DUTY AS WE UNDERSTAND IT.

The audience was enthralled, interrupting the speaker several times with applause and standing to cheer when he finished. "Mr. Lincoln is one of Nature's orators," Horace Greeley wrote, "using his rare powers solely to elucidate and convince, though their inevitable effect is to delight and electrify as well." In the days after his performance, the speech was widely reprinted, and as acclaim for Lincoln's remarks circulated, the event's organizers were exuberant. When one of these men sent Lincoln his $200 honorarium, he wrote, "Would that it were $200,000 for you are worthy of it."

The only assessment that Lincoln offered of his performance came in a letter he wrote to Mary several days later: "The speech at New York, being within my calculation before I started, went off passably well, and gave me no trouble whatever." Despite this modest self-appraisal, Lincoln knew that he'd become nationally known, and when he returned to Springfield, he authorized his advisers to begin working toward the Republican presidential nomination. He continued to think his chances were slim, but the more Lincoln considered the possibility, the more interesting it became. When his former political rival Lyman Trumbull asked him how he felt about the nomination, Lincoln replied, "I will be entirely frank. The taste *is* in my mouth a little."

In May 1860, the Republican Convention opened in Chicago. Although the Democrats had held their national meeting a month earlier, the delegates had been unable to agree on the front-runner Stephen Douglas as their nominee, and the party planned to reconvene in early June. This meant that Republican delegates assembled to pick their candidate did not know whom they would face in the November election. Lincoln and his advisers' strategy was straightforward: to try to make their man the nominee if the leading candidate, William Seward, did not obtain enough votes on the first ballot.

Judge David Davis, Lincoln's old friend and legal colleague from central Illinois, managed political operations on the ground at the convention. Davis's aim was to win one hundred votes for Lincoln on the first roll call to demonstrate his credibility should Seward not win the nomination right away. The strategy worked. In the first ballot, Seward received 174 votes, and Lincoln 102, the second-highest tally. In the next round, Seward's total climbed to 185 votes, and Lincoln's to 181. On the third ballot, on May 18, Lincoln won 364 of 466 possible votes, becoming the Republican nominee for president.

The convention chose Hannibal Hamlin, a former US senator from Maine, as the vice-presidential nominee.

The candidate himself wasn't in Chicago. But from the Springfield telegraph office, Lincoln kept close tabs on the voting. When he found out he'd won the nomination, his neighbors and supporters crowded into the room to congratulate him. He shook hands all around and then excused himself to go home, saying, "There is a lady over yonder who is deeply interested in this news; I will carry it to her."

During the six months before the election, Lincoln remained in Springfield, meeting scores of people who came to see him, responding to hundreds of requests for information about his life, and following the larger campaign. By late summer, the presidential contest had become a four-man race. In May, representatives from the young Constitutional Union Party, largely made up of Southern Democrats who did not support possible secession, had nominated John Bell, a former US senator from Tennessee. A month later, the Democrats had met again to try to select a nominee. This time, party delegates split, with Northern members backing Stephen Douglas and Southern delegates supporting John Breckinridge, who was then the vice president under James Buchanan. This three-way split of the Democrats greatly increased the odds of a Republican victory in the general election.

On November 6, election day, Lincoln and his supporters waited in the Springfield telegraph office for the returns. Slowly, news trickled in of the Republican Party's victories in Pennsylvania and other states, and at about two in the morning, Lincoln learned that he'd been elected president. According to the final ballot counts, he won about 40 percent of the popular vote, taking 180 Electoral College votes of a total of 303 (Breckinridge won 72 of these votes, Bell 39, and Douglas 12). The son of Thomas Lincoln, who had grown up on the frontier and clawed his way out, had ridden his unyielding ambition, keen intelligence, and emotional discernment all the way to the White House.

It had been an extraordinary triumph. Yet, as he walked back home in the wee hours of November 7, Lincoln did not exult. Recalling the moment two years later, he said he slept little before dawn. "I then felt, as I never had before, the responsibility that was upon me."

Lincoln's election precipitated a national crisis. Convinced that the president-elect would try to abolish slavery, many Southern leaders believed the only way to protect the institution—and the way of life that rested on it—was to leave the United States and establish their own country. On December 20, 1860, South Carolina seceded; Mississippi, Florida, Alabama, Georgia, Louisiana, and Texas soon followed. In early February 1861, representatives of the seceded states met in Montgomery, Alabama, to form a new nation, the Confederate States of America, and adopt a constitution. The delegates also elected a president, Jefferson Davis, who, until secession, had been a US senator from Mississippi. As the Southern states left the Union, newly formed Confederate militias began seizing federal arsenals, forts, and post offices in the South; these civilian troops even took the US Mint in New Orleans.

During the winter of 1860–61, President James Buchanan, who held office until Inauguration Day on March 4, urged Congress to find a solution to the unfolding crisis. But discussions among senators and representatives about how to keep the country intact came to naught. So, too, did an attempted peace conference initiated by the Virginia General Assembly. (A few days after the outbreak of war in mid-April 1861, Virginia would leave the Union to join the Confederacy; Arkansas, Tennessee, and North Carolina would secede in May.)

Watching events from Springfield, the president-elect kept silent. When journalists and politicians urged him to speak out, Lincoln demurred. He had good reason to remain quiet. He was not legally president until the votes from the Electoral College were counted on February 13, 1861, so he had no legitimate authority before then. (Also, in the wake of secession, Lincoln and others worried that electors might not be able to safely assemble.) The president-elect was also conscious that any effort to conciliate the South risked increasing confusion and anxiety in the North.

During the four months between his election and his inauguration on March 4, 1861 (not until 1937 was Inauguration Day changed to January 20), Lincoln worked long days, meeting countless politicians, journalists, and office seekers. He also started assembling his cabinet.

In doing this, as writer Doris Kearns Goodwin has explained, Lincoln purposely chose a group of men who were more experienced and greater in stature than he. Several of the men he selected, such as William Seward, who became secretary of state, Salmon Chase, whom Lincoln made head of the Treasury, and Edward Bates, who became attorney general, had been rivals for the Republican nomination; even Simon Cameron, whom Lincoln appointed secretary of war, had sought the position Lincoln now held. That the president-elect created a cabinet including former opponents was a testament to his self-confidence. And it was a credit to his political dexterity that, with rare exception, he held the group together, using their expertise and political connections to help him lead during his presidency.

In the months before his inauguration, Lincoln couldn't see the specific challenges that he and his colleagues would face. What he did know was that the Republican Party represented diverse interests—from radical abolitionists to former Democrats who hated black Americans. As president, Lincoln would have to maintain cohesion among these factions, and he used his cabinet choices toward this end. For example, he balanced the antislavery Seward with the conservative Bates. The president-elect also recognized that he would need specific skills and political capital he himself lacked, and thus, he chose men who would bring these assets to the work of governing.

In early 1861, the Lincolns prepared to leave Springfield for the nation's capital. The president-elect rented his family's home to a railroad executive, and he and Mary sold the furniture, china, chamber sets, and other household items that they could not take to Washington. Lincoln also sold his horse, Old Bob, and, over protests from Willie and Tad, gave the family's dog, an ebullient midsize mongrel named Fido, to a neighboring family who promised to love him (Lincoln also sent along Fido's favorite bed—a horsehair sofa). On February 6, the Lincolns hosted a "farewell soirée" in their home. In later years, guests remembered that hundreds of people came to bid good-bye to Springfield's most famous man and his family.

But the most important and difficult leave-takings that Lincoln had to make were private. In late January, he set out for Coles County in eastern Illinois to visit his stepmother, Sarah Lincoln. Accompanied by his cousin Dennis Hanks, Lincoln reunited with the woman who had done so much to love and encourage him. The three spent a quiet evening reminiscing, and during his visit, Lincoln went to his father's nearby grave, promising his stepmother he would send money to erect a headstone (this promise was never kept). When it was time for Lincoln to go, he and his stepmother hugged each other. Sarah broke into tears, saying she was afraid he would be killed in office. "No, no, Mama," Lincoln reassured her. "Trust in the Lord and all will be well. We will See each other—again."

On February 10, Lincoln walked to his office to do some final legal work and say good-bye to Billy Herndon. The two men ran through their case files, discussing outstanding business. Then, as the younger man remembered, Lincoln commented that in sixteen years of working together, they had never exchanged a cross word. After staring at the Lincoln-Herndon signboard at the foot of the stairs, the older partner said, "Let it hang there undisturbed. . . . Give our clients to understand that the election of a President makes no change in the firm. . . . If I live I'm coming back some time, and then we'll go right on practising [sic] law as if nothing had ever happened."

The next morning, Lincoln boarded a train for Washington. Mary, Willie, and Tad would meet him later. The weather was cold; drizzling rain fell. A crowd had gathered to send him off. Standing on the platform of the last passenger car, Lincoln doffed his hat and asked for silence. Speaking without notes in a voice that cracked with emotion, the Springfield lawyer parted from his neighbors:

> My friends—No one, not in my situation, can appreciate my feeling of sadness at this parting. To this place, and the kindness of these people, I owe every thing. Here I have lived a quarter of a century, and have passed from a young to an old man. Here my children have been born, and one is buried. I now leave, not knowing when, or whether ever, I may return, with a task before me greater than that which rested upon Washington. Without the assistance of that Divine Being, who ever attended him, I cannot succeed. With that assistance I cannot fail. Trusting in Him, who can go with me, and remain with you and be every where for good, let us confidently

hope that all will yet be well. To His care commending you, as I hope in your prayers you will commend me, I bid you an affectionate farewell.

On March 4, 1861, before a crowd of fifty thousand, Lincoln delivered his inaugural address on the steps of the US Capitol. He knew the fate of the upper Southern states of Virginia, Arkansas, Tennessee, and North Carolina, which had not yet seceded, might depend on what he said, and he took pains to reassure Southerners that he would leave slavery alone in the states where it already existed. He also vowed to uphold the Fugitive Slave Act. At the same time, however, Lincoln made it clear that the Union was inviolate, and that a minority of citizens had no legal right to secede from the government because that minority did not agree with the will of the majority. "Plainly, the central idea of secession, is the essence of anarchy," he stated. "A majority, held in restraint by constitutional checks, and limitations, and always changing easily, with deliberate changes of popular opinions and sentiments, is the only true sovereign of a free people."

Pledging to maintain the Union, the president said he would use his office to enforce federal laws, furnish the mails, and "hold, occupy, and possess the property, and places belonging to the government." In doing this, Lincoln explained, "there needs to be no bloodshed or violence; and there shall be none, unless it be forced upon the national authority." The only substantial dispute between the South and the North, he continued, is that "one section of our country believes slavery is *right*, and ought to be extended, while the other believes it is *wrong*, and ought not to be extended."

As he came to the final paragraphs, Lincoln put the responsibility for armed conflict on the seceding states: "In *your* hands, my dissatisfied fellow countrymen, and not in *mine*, is the momentous issue of civil war." He continued, "The government will not assail *you*. You can have no conflict, without being yourselves the aggressors. *You* have no oath registered in Heaven to destroy the government, while *I* shall have the most solemn one to 'preserve, protect and defend' it." He ended with a plea for national unity:

I am loth to close. We are not enemies, but friends. We must not be enemies. Though passion may have strained, it must not break our bonds of affection. The mystic chords of memory, stretching from every battle-field, and patriot grave, to every living heart and hearthstone, all over this broad land, will yet swell the chorus of the Union, when again touched, as surely they will be, by the better angels of our nature.

In spite of Lincoln's efforts, tensions between North and South escalated. These came to a head with the president's decision on Fort Sumter, a federal garrison in the harbor of Charleston, South Carolina. Government soldiers inside the fort were running out of food. But sending provisions into what was now hostile territory risked Confederate attack. For weeks, Lincoln agonized over what to do. He did not want his administration to appear weak by not resupplying the fort and thus effectively surrendering it. But he also did not want to initiate open warfare.

After many sleepless nights and conversations with his cabinet, Lincoln ordered government forces to sail for Charleston Harbor with food. Wanting to avoid Northern responsibility for a war that now seemed imminent, Lincoln also decided to notify the governor of South Carolina that if the expedition encountered no resistance, it would make no attempt to bring arms or ammunition to Fort Sumter. On April 12, 1861, with the federal fleet nearby, Confederates bombarded the garrison with shells and gunfire. Within thirty-six hours, the commanding officer of the fort, Major Robert Anderson, surrendered to Southern forces. The Civil War had begun.

CHAPTER SEVENTEEN

The War Came

Lincoln's leadership during the war encompassed two sets of responsibilities. On one hand, as president and commander in chief, he had to hold the nation together while prosecuting the conflict. On the other, he had to define what the war meant and why it was being fought; he then had to communicate this to the American people and the larger world. Both sets of obligations took hold within the larger environment of a national crisis characterized by rapid—almost constant—change, high stakes, and collective anxiety.

The two sets of obligations were interrelated. Lincoln could not direct a civil war and hold the country together without clearly articulating a credible purpose. The war would have no meaning, no viable purpose, if the nation fell apart while fighting it. This could happen if public sentiment gave way to panic, Northern political elites lost faith in the president, or the machinery of the federal government stopped functioning.

Although it was not obvious in early 1861, Lincoln's ability to discharge both sets of responsibilities was dependent on the larger fortunes of the Union army. When the pendulum of military advantage swung toward the North, the president had greater latitude to prosecute the war and more political cohesion behind his leadership. When Confederate armies held the balance of power, as they did at many important junctures, Lincoln had fewer options, and the probability of losing the whole game—the war, its purpose, and the Union—greatly increased.

If we step back to think about these two kinds of obligations, we can see that they were not unique to Abraham Lincoln, even if the extraordinary challenges that he faced were. In the midst of a crisis, every leader has to shoulder the two sets of burdens that Lincoln did. He or she has to manage the turbulence itself—fight the war, turn the company around, or save the teenager who has turned to drugs. At the same time, he or she has to define what the crisis means and why it is worth navigating, solving, or reversing—first for him- or herself, and then for all the other people involved. Lincoln and the other four leaders in this book understood this. They all worked to steer through a larger crisis while struggling to understand its meaning for themselves and those they led. As they did, they also remained supple enough to evolve in ways that enabled them to achieve their missions.

Lincoln did not think about his presidency in these terms (the language of crisis leadership is a late-twentieth-century phenomenon). Instead, he realized that he had to save the Union and that this entailed fighting a bloody civil war. As the conflict became longer, more complicated, and more violent than anyone had expected, discerning its meaning and purpose, and then communicating this to the American people, became more important.

From the perspective of hindsight, we can see Lincoln's leadership in both these contexts: as president, politician, and commander in chief working to keep the country unified during wartime, and as president and guide focused on understanding what the conflict meant, why it was being fought, and how to convey this. The majority of research on Lincoln has focused on the first set of responsibilities: his work as politician and commander in chief. This is a critical framework. But as a historian of leadership, I have been interested in Lincoln in terms of his second set of obligations. In my view, his commitment to make sense of the crisis in which he found himself, to keep trying to understand its ultimate purpose, and to express this to others—including politicians, military officers, the American public, and other countries—offers a powerful lens into his development as a leader.

During the first eighteen months of the war, Lincoln was careful to frame the contest as one to save the country. During a July 1861 address to a special session of Congress, the president articulated what he saw as the central issue of the war. The conflict, he said,

> presents to the whole family of man, the question, whether a constitutional republic, or democracy—a government of the people, by the same people—can, or cannot, maintain its territorial integrity, against its own domestic foes. . . . It forces us to ask: "Is there, in all republics, this inherent, and fatal weakness?" "Must a government, of necessity, be too *strong* for the liberties of its own people, or too *weak* to maintain its own existence?"

Lincoln knew full well that the chief motive of the rebellious states was to maintain and expand slavery. But during the war's early months, he was convinced that the conflict could not be prosecuted to abolish slavery. Several factors underlay his thinking. Legally, the president believed he had no credible grounds to attack slavery because it was protected by the Constitution. Politically, he knew public opinion in the North was sharply divided over the institution. He recognized that collective support for abolition had grown tremendously during recent years, but he also understood that many Northerners feared and hated black Americans. Even his own party had split over slavery: conservative and moderate factions favored leaving it alone, while radical Republicans wanted the war fought for immediate emancipation.

Strategically, Lincoln believed he could not afford to alienate slaveholders in the Border States of Kentucky, Missouri, Maryland, and Delaware. Keeping these states in the Union was critical to winning the war. Together, Kentucky, Missouri, and Maryland could have added 45 percent to the military manpower of the Confederacy, 80 percent to its manufacturing capabilities, and more than 30 percent to its supply of mules and horses. These three states also occupied critical ground: Kentucky contained the Ohio, Cumberland, and Tennessee Rivers; Missouri served as a gateway to the Western territories; and Maryland enclosed Washington, DC, on three sides.

In mid-1861, these three states had not seceded. Each remained in the Union, and each was deeply divided. (Senator John Crittenden of Kentucky, for example, saw one of his sons join the Union army, another the Confederacy. Mary Todd Lincoln, also from Kentucky, was a staunch Unionist; she lost three half brothers in the Civil War, all of whom fought for the Confederacy.) Each of the Border States had a committed secessionist minority with the potential to tip that state's balance toward the South. No one understood the importance of the Border States better than Lincoln. "I hope to have God on my side," he reportedly said early in the conflict, "but I must have Kentucky."

From the start, the Civil War defied Americans' expectations. In the aftermath of Fort Sumter, for example, many Northerners and Southerners believed that victory was imminent for their respective side, and that few lives would be lost. But after the Battle of Bull Run near Manassas, Virginia, in July 1861, in which almost five thousand government and Confederate troops were killed or wounded, it became clear that the war would be longer and bloodier than most had anticipated. Bull Run was a terrible Union defeat, and the day after the battle, Lincoln called for five hundred thousand volunteers; within days, Congress authorized an additional half million troops. The national legislature also approved a measure known as the Confiscation Act, which allowed the government to seize any Confederate property used for military purposes, including slaves. Lincoln was reluctant to sign the bill. But confronted with overwhelming Republican congressional support for it, he did.

Lincoln's hesitation about signing the act, which would bring some slaves under the Union army's control, stemmed from his desire to keep slavery out of the national conversation about the war's purpose. But unfolding events soon made this impossible. In August 1861, for example, Union general John Frémont proclaimed martial law in Missouri, announcing that all slaves held by persons supporting the rebellion would be freed. Lincoln was furious. He worried the general's actions would jeopardize the Border States' loyalty to the Union. Lincoln was also angry because he wanted to restrict government authority to act on slavery to the office of the president, and thus he could not countenance military officers in the field effectively making local or national policy. The president ordered Frémont to rescind his proclamation. This met with harsh criticism from antislavery elements across the North. "To fight against slaveholders, without fighting against slavery," Frederick Douglass wrote, "is but a half-hearted business, and paralyzes the hands engaged in it."

As the year came to a close, slavery was very much on Lincoln's mind, and he was making plans for dealing with it. He proposed a program of compensated emancipation, in which state governments would use federal funds to purchase slaves' freedom from their owners. Once freed, blacks would be encouraged to relocate to a homeland outside the United States in an initiative that became known as "colonization." From the president's perspective, this program had several advantages. It was constitutional because it did not seize property without just payment. It could be accomplished *with* the consent of slaveholders. And it would be gradual, allowing blacks and whites, Lincoln explained, to "live themselves out of their old relation to each other, and both come out better prepared for the new."

The president hoped that if he could elicit slaveholder support for his plan, particularly in the Border States, it might hasten the war's end. But militarily, there was little cause for optimism. In late 1861, the Union initiative was stalled in the East, where the new general-in-chief, George McClellan, had reorganized troops around Washington, but then refused to move them south to attack Confederate forces. His Army of the Potomac—some 120,000-men strong—remained in and near the capital without seeing any kind of real action. The first year of the war thus passed without a major Union victory. Northerners grew impatient with McClellan and the president.

Worried about the general's inaction, Lincoln began visiting McClellan at home during the evenings. On November 13, the president and one of his secretaries, John Hay, called at the general's house. McClellan was not in, and the two decided to wait. When the general arrived an hour later, he hurried upstairs, ignoring his visitors. The president and his secretary remained where they were for thirty minutes before Lincoln sent word up that he was still downstairs. McClellan sent his own message back, saying he had gone to bed. Hay was appalled at the general's insolence, voicing this to the president as they walked back to the White House. "It was better at this time," Lincoln responded, "not to be making points of etiquette & personal dignity." As he and the other leaders in this book came to understand, not all issues—including personal slights and insults—that came before them were of equal importance. Lincoln realized he had to keep his eye (not to mention his emotional energy) on what was central to his mission and not become distracted by what we would today label "sweating the small stuff." Still, the president paid no more visits to McClellan's home.

By late 1861, the Lincolns had settled into life in the White House. They spent most of their time on the second floor, where the president's office, his secretaries' space, and the family living quarters were located. The president's days usually began at 6:00 or 7:00 a.m.; if a battle was raging, he was up even earlier. He started in his office, reading and writing before stopping for breakfast with Mary and the children. He had always eaten simply, and he continued this habit in the White House: an egg and black coffee for breakfast, an apple and biscuit for lunch, and soup, meat, and potatoes for dinner. He loved apple pie and often ate it for dessert. Lincoln almost never drank alcohol, so Mary ordered water served with family meals, reserving wine and spirits for official functions or dinner parties with friends.

After breakfast, the president dealt with government business, including military reports, important correspondence, and political memorandums. He worked with his two devoted secretaries, John Nicolay, age twenty-nine in 1861, and John Hay, age twenty-three. Both men had come with Lincoln from Illinois and now lived in rooms across the corridor from the president's office. (The two were certain their boss was destined to be a great president and resolved to write a book about his leadership. Behind his back, they called him "the Ancient" or "the Tycoon.") Lincoln trusted his secretaries implicitly and relied heavily on their unflagging support.

Most mornings, Lincoln visited the War Department to check on news from the fronts and confer with military personnel. Once back at the White House, he spent three hours receiving visitors: office seekers, those requesting clemency for soldiers who had deserted, inventors with new guns to market, and anyone else who wanted access to the nation's chief executive. On any given weekday, more than a hundred people lined up to see the president; the queue often stretched down the stairs to the first floor, out the White House door, and along the driveway. As soon as Lincoln ordered the main doors opened, a crowd rushed up to the second floor. Some who sought the president, Hay remembered, wanted "merely to shake hands, to wish him God-speed; their errand was soon done." But others hoped to "unfold their schemes for their own advantage or their neighbor's hurt."

Nicolay and Hay worked diligently to keep order among the swarms of visitors, every one of whom, the latter recalled, "took something from [the president] in the way of wasted nervous force." Both secretaries thought Lincoln should curtail the time he spent seeing individual citizens, but he continued to hold office hours throughout his presidency. Labeling the visits "public opinion baths," Lincoln viewed them as an important means to gauge popular sentiment about the war and his policies.

On Tuesday and Friday afternoons, the chief executive met the cabinet in his office. He spent the rest of the afternoons going back to the War Department or meeting military officials and politicians. Worried for his health, Mary urged him to get fresh air, so some afternoons he would take a carriage ride with her or—less frequently—go for a ride on his horse. (Lincoln generally did these things without escort or official security detail. The Secret Service wasn't established until shortly after Lincoln was assassinated, and at the time its work was to combat counterfeit money. The force didn't assume full-time responsibility for protecting the chief executive until 1902, a year after President William McKinley was shot. Lincoln received many death threats as president, but he often refused to have a bodyguard, telling his family and advisers that if someone wanted to kill him, he reckoned the person would find a way whether Lincoln had protection or not.)

At six or seven in the evening, the Lincolns sat down to dinner. On occasion, old friends joined them, and their discussions stretched on into the evening. "His happiest moments," historian Allan Nevins has written, were "when a few intimates gathered after dinner in his office and he relaxed in . . . political gossip and general talk, telling stories and giving his humor free scope. In such a group, he would talk of critical military and political affairs with complete candor, stating his opinion of men and events in plain prairie language."

If a battle was underway, the president returned to the War Department after dinner; sometimes, he spent the night there. Otherwise, he went back to his office for several hours. His youngest son, Tad, often joined him in the large room, falling asleep on the sofa while his father worked. When Lincoln was finished for the night, he met Mary for a bit of conversation. "I consider myself fortunate," she wrote a friend, "if at eleven o'clock, I once more find myself [in the sitting room] & very especially, if my tired & weary Husband, is *there*, resting in the lounge to receive me—to chat over the occurrences of the day."

Robert, the Lincolns' oldest son, had enrolled at Harvard College in the fall of 1860, and was away from Washington for most of his father's presidency. The two younger children, Willie and Tad, who were eleven and eight in 1861, loved the chaos of the busy residence. Because the nation's capital was frequently in danger of invasion, federal soldiers were stationed in and near the Executive Mansion throughout the conflict. The enlisted men were a source of great amusement for the boys, who followed the troops around, drilling in formation behind them as they marched, begging for stories, and clamoring to see battle scars and weapons.

The president enjoyed the boys' commotion and, whenever possible, took time away from his duties to play with them. One day, for example, Julia Taft, the daughter of a lawyer in the Patent Office and the sister of playmates of Willie and Tad's, walked into the second-floor sitting room and saw the commander in chief lying on the floor. Willie and Julia's brother held Lincoln's arms, while Tad and her sister pinned down his legs. "Julie, come quick," Tad yelled, "and sit on his stomach." The president beamed. At other, quieter times, Lincoln read to his children or told them stories, balancing a boy on each knee.

But the war was never far away. As 1862 opened, McClellan refused to attack the Confederacy. Politicians, journalists, and even the attorney general, Edward Bates, blamed Lincoln for the stalled war effort. The chief executive, Bates said privately, "is an excellent man, and, in the main wise; but he lacks *will* and *purpose*, and, I greatly fear, he, has not *the power to command*." Disgruntled Republicans in Congress formed a Committee on the Conduct of the War in an effort to wrest control of military strategy away from the president. At the same time, allegations of significant corruption in the War Department surfaced.

In response to these charges, Lincoln removed Secretary of War Simon Cameron and, in his place, appointed Edwin Stanton, a scrupulously honest, highly successful lawyer who was a Democrat and had served in Buchanan's administration. Stanton had first met Lincoln in 1855 during a trial in Ohio, dismissing the homespun Illinois attorney as a crude, ignorant "long-armed ape." Never one to hold a grudge, in 1862 Lincoln chose Stanton for his integrity and practicability. As time passed, the two men grew to like and respect each other, forging one of the strongest administrative partnerships in US history. Impressed with his new cabinet member's remarkable reserves of energy, Lincoln once compared him to a Methodist minister whose sermons were so high-spirited that congregation members wanted to put bricks in his pockets to hold him down. "We may be obliged to serve Stanton the same way," Lincoln told a congressman, "but I guess we'll just let him jump a while first."

In early 1862, frustrated with Union commander George McClellan and his refusal to fight, Lincoln issued a direct order for the army and the navy to move against rebel forces. (This was known as General War Order Number One.) The president also began to teach himself military strategy, borrowing textbooks from the Library of Congress, poring over field reports, and conferring with military officers. As he did this, it became clear to him that a Union victory depended on the North's ability to exploit its greater resources—human and economic—in a series of interrelated attacks on the Confederacy. The president could see what must be done to win the war and save the nation. But how could he make his generals execute this strategy? McClellan effectively ignored Lincoln's war order. Other commanders, often acting without top-level coordination, followed their own plans or simply waited.

In February, tragedy struck. Willie and Tad fell ill with "bilious fever" (probably typhoid fever). Both parents sat up each night with their children. As Willie grew worse, Lincoln and Mary became more and more anxious. The president's grueling work rhythms slowed. For two weeks, both parents nursed their sick children. For a short time, it appeared Willie was improving, but late in the month, he took a sharp turn for the worse. In the early afternoon of February 20, 1862, he died.

A White House servant was with Lincoln at his son's bedside. "I never saw a man so bowed down with grief," she remembered. "He came to the bed, lifted the cover from the face of his child, gazed at it long and earnestly." Speaking aloud, the president said, "My poor boy, he was too good for this earth. God has called him home. I know that he is much better off in heaven, but then we loved him so. It is hard, hard to have him die!"

In the days following Willie's death, Lincoln took some comfort in caring for Tad, who gradually recovered. But sadness continued to press down on the president, interrupting his already fitful sleep and driving him into melancholy. When the pain became unbearable, he shut himself in Willie's bedroom to weep. He dreamed of his son being alive, only to awaken to his absence. The president once told an army officer that every day he caught himself involuntarily talking to his departed son.

Mary Lincoln was even more grief stricken. This was the second child the couple had lost; in 1850, three-year-old Eddie Lincoln had succumbed to a fatal illness. In the wake of Willie's death, Mary was unable to leave her room even to attend the funeral service. For weeks, she sobbed continuously. She was so unnerved that Lincoln led her to a window, pointed to an insane asylum in the distance, and said, "Mother, do you see that large white building on the hill yonder? Try and control your grief, or it will drive you mad, and we may have to send you there."

After Willie's death Mary Lincoln wanted to support her husband, and he her. But the tragedy dealt another blow to the Lincolns' marriage, which had frayed since the couple arrived in Washington. Several things had pulled the two apart. The most important was the war; almost immediately, the crisis claimed a huge share of Lincoln's attention, leaving less for his family. Another factor was Mary's position in the capital city. Her family was Southern, so questions circulated about her loyalty to the Union, and this created a subtle rift between husband and wife. A third issue was Mary's insecurity about her role. She had hoped to help make her husband's presidency a success by being a gracious, refined companion and White House hostess. (Indeed, the term *first lady* was coined with reference to Mary Lincoln.) But she had few trustworthy guides and often stumbled badly. These mistakes presented additional difficulties for Lincoln in the first eighteen months of his presidency. It was often easier to avoid dealing directly with such complications, and this resulted in his spending less time with his wife.

Like the other four leaders here, Lincoln was often lonely. Some of his loneliness flowed from the authority and responsibility he carried. The president knew that saving the Union rested critically on his shoulders—on *his* ability to simultaneously lead on many fronts against many obstacles. This heavy realization isolated Lincoln from family, friends, and colleagues. Not only could these people not fully grasp what he was dealing with; not only did he have to be careful about entrusting his thoughts and feelings to others; but Lincoln also understood that no one else could travel the *internal* path he was taking as a leader. None could see the things he was discovering about himself and his impact, see the ways he was changing as the war stretched on, or, finally, experience his doubts and fears. These were essential aspects of his leadership, and they were his alone. They made for cold company.

Virtually every leader will know real loneliness. This is intrinsic to the work; it can rarely be avoided or wiped away by specific action. Instead, effective leaders learn to accept such moments of isolation, using them in service to their larger mission by keeping their own counsel, reflecting carefully on a particular issue, or grappling with their thoughts and feelings.

CHAPTER EIGHTEEN

Emerging Vision

Following the intense period of grief that followed Willie's death, Lincoln returned to his duties and the larger military situation. In mid-February, Union general Ulysses S. Grant's forces had captured the Confederate stronghold of Fort Donelson near the border between Tennessee and Kentucky, taking more than twelve thousand Southern soldiers prisoner. This major Northern victory followed another triumph for Grant earlier in the month: the capture of the smaller Fort Henry on the Tennessee River. Together, the two successes helped ensure that Kentucky would remain in the Union; the capture of both forts also opened up both the Tennessee and Cumberland Rivers to federal control. Northerners were ebullient; many were confident the war would soon be over.

But then little happened. McClellan did not advance with the Army of the Potomac. Big federal victories did not come. The conflict dragged on, and the public grew restive. Radical Republicans and abolitionists urged the president to take action against slavery. As *Chicago Tribune* editor Joseph Medill wrote the president, "For God's sake and your country's sake, rise to the realization of our awful national evil. You, I and the Country know that this is a Slave holders rebellion."

Lincoln responded by trying to promote his policy of compensated emancipation. In early March, he introduced a resolution to this effect in Congress. The legislature endorsed the proposal, as did several cabinet members, abolitionists, and Northern newspapers. But some antislavery spokesmen criticized Lincoln for not taking a bolder stand. Frederick Douglass lambasted the idea of establishing former slaves in a colony of their own. Lincoln's plan, he said, "expresses merely the desire to get rid of them, and reminds one of the politeness with which a man might try to bow out of his house some troublesome creditor." Other critics thought the program too expensive. Perhaps most important, representatives of the Border States of Kentucky, Missouri, and Maryland, where Lincoln hoped to enact compensated emancipation first, rejected the proposal virtually out of hand. Without these states' agreement, the president's plans were, for all practical purposes, dead.

Lincoln was greatly disappointed. As he considered this failure, he learned a critical lesson: he had no silver bullets to save the Union. This was difficult to accept. But he was beginning to understand that the complexity of the conflict and the magnitude of its stakes made a single, clear-cut way to end it virtually impossible.

This is an insight for today's leaders. We are under pressure to move fast, leap tall buildings in a single bound, and make a big impact. But the reality of trying to accomplish something real and good gives lie to the seductive notion that there is one simple solution. Almost anything along our life journeys that is worth investing in, worth fighting for, and worth summoning our best selves for has no silver bullet. The bigger the issue, the less likely it is that a leader can resolve it in one or two swift strokes. Understanding this means abandoning the quest for *the single definitive answer*. Letting go of this quest frees leaders—emotionally and practically—to focus on the many possible approaches and actions needed to make a meaningful difference.

In April 1862, Lincoln signed a bill to enact compensated emancipation in the nation's capital, where thirty-one hundred black men, women, and children were held in bondage. The bill also appropriated $100,000 to freed slaves who wanted to emigrate from the nation's capital. A law with such limited application was not what the president had wanted; he intended a much bigger policy aimed at gradually ending slavery nationwide. But in the current circumstances, compensated emancipation in the District of Columbia was all he had.

Now, he hoped for military victories. However, as spring turned to summer, there were only Union losses. The most dramatic of these were the defeats during the Seven Days' Battles that General George McClellan and the Army of the Potomac suffered in late June and early July. With his back up against the wall, Lincoln began drafting the Emancipation Proclamation. He decided to hold off publicly announcing it until the North scored a military victory.

It was a difficult wait. In late August, Northern troops were defeated at the Second Battle of Bull Run in Virginia. Some fourteen thousand Union soldiers were killed, wounded, captured, or missing; Confederate armies suffered almost nine thousand casualties. Lincoln became deeply depressed. At a cabinet meeting after the battle, the president "seemed wrung by the bitterest anguish," the attorney general noted, adding that Lincoln said he felt "almost ready to hang himself."

But the president did not act on such feelings. Instead, he found the strength to carry on. We cannot be certain how he did this. But we know that he kept trying to make sense of the war. Not only what it meant politically and practically, but also what it might mean on a higher plane. In the midst of the bullets, bloodshed, and a thousand material concerns, perhaps, he reasoned, a larger power was at work. In language that seemed to emanate from a soul in distress, Lincoln wrote the following private reflection:

> The will of God prevails. In great contests each party claims to act in accordance with the will of God. Both *may* be, and one *must* be wrong. God can not be *for*, and *against* the same thing at the same time. In the present civil war it is quite possible that God's purpose is something different from the purpose of either party— and yet the human instrumentalities, working just as they do, are of the best adaptation to effect His purpose. I am almost ready to say this is probably true—that God wills this contest, and wills that it shall not end yet. By his mere quiet power, on the minds of the now contestants, He could have either *saved* or *destroyed* the Union without a human contest. Yet the contest began. And having begun He could give the final victory to either side any day. Yet the contest proceeds.

Finally, in mid-September 1862, Union forces under the command of George McClellan won a victory at Antietam. This gave Lincoln the opportunity to promulgate his Emancipation Proclamation, and on September 22, he did. Public reaction was divided. Northern antislavery interests applauded the proclamation. "The skies are brighter and the air is purer," exulted Massachusetts senator Charles Sumner, "now that Slavery has been handed over to judgment." "We shout for joy," wrote Frederick Douglass, "that we live to record this righteous decree." The abolitionist predicted that Lincoln's action would "disarm all purpose on the part of European Government[s] to intervene in favor of the rebels and thus cast off at a blow one source of rebel power."

Conservative Northerners, including Democrats and Republicans who opposed fighting a war to end slavery, lambasted the proclamation. Some were sure it would diminish Union support in the Border States. Others thought white soldiers would refuse to fight to liberate black Americans. Still others were convinced that the decree would incite violent slave rebellions. In November 1862, reaction to the Emancipation Proclamation, the government's deteriorating military fortunes, and the war's enormous casualties combined to hand the Republican Party major reversals in the midterm elections.

In early December, Lincoln delivered his annual message to Congress. After reporting on a range of issues—from foreign affairs to the creation of the Department of Agriculture—he turned to the Civil War. As the conflict entered its third year, with the Emancipation Proclamation about to become law, he realized the nation had crossed the Rubicon. Beyond it lay important, but unknown, territory. He closed his address by explaining what this brand-new moment demanded of all Americans:

> The dogmas of the quiet past, are inadequate to the stormy present. The occasion is piled high with difficulty, and we must rise with the occasion. As our case is new, so we must think anew, and act anew. We must disenthrall ourselves, and then we shall save our country.
>
> Fellow-citizens, *we* cannot escape history. We of this Congress and this administration, will be remembered in spite of ourselves.

No personal significance, or insignificance, can spare one or another of us. The fiery trial through which we pass, will light us down, in honor or dishonor, to the latest generation. . . . In *giving* freedom to the *slave*, we *assure* freedom to the *free*—honorable alike in what we give, and what we preserve. We shall nobly save, or meanly lose, the last best, hope of earth.

The year ended badly for the North. In December, the Army of the Potomac, now under the leadership of General Ambrose Burnside (Lincoln had removed McClellan from command in November 1862), suffered a terrible defeat at Fredericksburg, Virginia. When the four-day battle ended, more than thirteen thousand federal soldiers were dead, wounded, or missing. Confederate general Robert E. Lee's Army of Northern Virginia endured losses of forty-six hundred men. When Northerners learned about the battle's outcome, they once again attacked Lincoln and his administration. "The fact is that the country is done for unless something is done at once," observed US senator Zachariah Chandler of Michigan. The president "is a weak man, too weak for the occasion," he added, "and those fool or traitor generals are wasting time and yet more precious blood in indecisive battles and delays."

As Lincoln absorbed the defeat at Fredericksburg, he sank into despair. "If there is a worse place than hell I am in it," he told a military official. When Pennsylvania governor Andrew Curtin, who had been to the battlefield, described what he called the "slaughter-pen" to the president, Lincoln became visibly upset, pacing the room, wringing his hands, and asking, "What has God put me in this place for?"

Those who visited the president were struck by the toll the war had taken on him. Noah Brooks, a reporter who had met Lincoln six years earlier, was aghast:

The President and his wife are both in deep mourning for their son, who died last Spring, and his Excellency has grievously altered from the happy-faced Springfield lawyer of 1856. . . . His hair is grizzled, his gait more stooping, his countenance sallow, and there is a sunken, deathly look about the large, cavernous eyes, which is saddening to those who see there the marks of care and anxiety, such as no President of the United States has ever before known. It is a lesson for human ambition to look upon that anxious and careworn face, prematurely aged by public labors and private griefs, and to remember that with the fleeting glory of his term of office have come responsibilities which make his life one long series of harassing care.

Lincoln was indeed tired. He was physically weary, partly because he did not sleep well. He also ate little. During his presidency, Lincoln lost some thirty pounds (when he died, he weighed about 155 pounds).

On New Year's Day, the Lincolns hosted the traditional White House reception, and hundreds filed into the Blue Room, where the receiving line was located. After three hours of greeting diplomats, politicians, and ordinary citizens, Lincoln went upstairs to his office to sign the final version of the Emancipation Proclamation. As he made ready, his arm trembled, the result of shaking so many hands earlier in the day. Worried that if his signature looked weak, future readers might think he had reservations about the decree, the president waited until he could sign it in a clear, strong hand. "I never in my life felt more certain that I was doing right than I do in signing this paper," he said to William Seward and his son Frederick, who were present.

The proclamation that became law that day was a dry, meticulously constructed document written in legal language. It contained none of the soaring rhetoric of the Declaration of Independence or the pre-amble to the Constitution. The decree, historian Richard Hofstadter has written, "had all the moral grandeur of a bill of lading" (used to confer title to a shipment of goods). The decree offered no indictment of slavery; emancipation was based entirely on military necessity. The proclamation applied only to slaves held in states in rebellion against the United States. It did not affect the almost five hundred thousand black Americans held in bondage in the Border States. It did not free the slaves in areas occupied by federal troops, including Tennessee, parts of southern Louisiana, and seven counties in Virginia.

Despite its limited application, the Emancipation Proclamation represented a critical inflection point. It altered the purpose and dimension of the Civil War. It marked an irrevocable break with the nation's past. The institution that had done so much to structure social and economic relations in both the North and the South, affect national politics, and provoke the ongoing conflict had been, in the stroke of a pen, put on a path to potential extinction.

By signing the document, Lincoln had effectively eliminated the possibility of a negotiated peace with the Confederacy. After January 1, 1863, as he clearly understood, if the North won the war, this victory would also include the death of slavery. This would, in turn, give rise to widespread social and economic transformation in the South and among millions of freed blacks, who would take their places among white Americans in the nation they shared.

The proclamation was also a watershed moment for Lincoln's leadership. In signing it, he left behind his own carefully nurtured plans for a gradual, peaceful end to slavery. He walked away from the position he had upheld since first entering national politics in 1854: a solution to the problem of slavery that opposed its extension while recognizing its constitutional legality.

More important, the new law gave the president a mightier purpose than that he had assumed when he took office. In early 1863, Lincoln realized that his work had become bigger than saving the Union, as essential as this was. His responsibility now encompassed *transforming* the country—even as he tried to preserve it—by aligning it more closely with the United States' original reason for being: freedom for all. In the aftermath of signing the Emancipation Proclamation, he could not see exactly what this larger, more radical mission would entail.

More practically, the new law included another important change in government policy: the decree provided that black soldiers could serve and fight in the military. Six months earlier, Lincoln had opposed enlisting black troops because he was worried about resistance in the Border States and that white troops might refuse to fight alongside Negro soldiers. But by early 1863, events had once again overtaken him.

For one thing, the war demanded soldiers in unprecedented numbers. By the time the conflict ended in 1865, roughly 2 million men—

about 9 percent of the North's total population—would fight for the Union. Many of these Americans volunteered. But as the conflict dragged on and casualty counts from disease and battle continued to climb, Lincoln, Stanton, and military leaders realized they needed more men than they could recruit through calls for white volunteers. In March 1863, Congress passed the Civil War Military Draft Act, which required the enrollment of every male citizen between the ages of twenty and forty-five. The legislation was controversial, and its enforcement sparked large riots in New York City in July 1863.

For another thing, Congress had already opened the door to enlisting black soldiers in mid-1862 when it passed the Militia Act. Well aware that Confederate armies were using slaves for manual labor, Northern legislators had authorized the president "to receive into the service of the United States, for the purpose of . . . labor, or any military or naval service for which they may be found competent, persons of African descent." Lincoln had initially responded to the congressional action by approving the use of blacks in support roles to the Union army; but he had declined to allow the same men to fight. In the last months of 1862, however, he changed his position, revising the final version of the Emancipation Proclamation to include provisions for black soldiers.

Once the president made this decision, he committed whole-heartedly to it. Shortly after signing the decree, Lincoln authorized Massachusetts governor John Andrew to create a regiment of black soldiers. Commanded by a white man, Robert Gould Shaw, this regiment, the Fifty-Fourth Massachusetts, enlisted blacks from across the North. (In July 1863, Shaw and half his men were killed in an assault on the Confederate stronghold of Fort Wagner in Charleston, South Carolina—a sacrifice immortalized in the 1989 film *Glory*.) In March 1863, the president ordered Stanton to begin recruiting black soldiers in the Mississippi Valley. At the same time, the president encouraged the military governor of Tennessee, Andrew Johnson, to bring blacks into the army. "The colored population," Lincoln wrote, "is the great *available* and yet *unavailed* of, force for restoring the Union. The bare sight of fifty thousand armed, and drilled black soldiers on the banks of the Mississippi, would end the rebellion at once. And who doubts that we can present that sight, if we but take hold in earnest?"

Once the Emancipation Proclamation became law, thousands and thousands of black Americans joined the Union struggle. On battlefields such as Fort Wagner and at Port Hudson and Milliken's Bend in Louisiana, they fought courageously, quickly demonstrating to white officers and soldiers how vital their contribution was. In August, for example, responding to the president's call to raise one hundred thousand black troops, General Ulysses S. Grant wrote, "I have given the subject of arming the negro my hearty support. This with the emancipation of the negro, is the heavyest [sic] blow yet given the Confederacy." Some months later, Stanton wrote Lincoln that the black soldiers who fought in Louisiana "have proved themselves among the bravest of the brave in fighting for the Union, performing deeds of daring and shedding their blood with a heroism unsurpassed by soldiers of any other race."

As Lincoln watched black men go bravely into battle, he knew that a government victory would bring about unprecedented possibilities and challenges. The most important of these was that slavery would cease to exist, and African-Americans would play new roles and assume new positions in the American polity.

As we consider the making of Abraham Lincoln, we need to remember that for most of his life, until he came to live in the White House, he had had limited contact with black Americans. He had grown up among other whites who, at worst, hated Negroes, and at best, tolerated them. Not surprisingly, Lincoln absorbed and reflected these prejudices, even as he expressed antipathy toward slavery. But as president at the center of the Civil War, his attitude toward African-Americans seemed to change. Historian Eric Foner has attributed this shift to the respect Lincoln accorded black soldiers and to his experience with African-American leaders, such as Frederick Douglass, whom Lincoln met during his time in the White House.

This is not to say that the president overcame all his racial prejudices. In private, Lincoln continued to tell stories about "darkies," and he never came to see Native Americans as having a legitimate place in the country. But as chief executive, some of his long-held beliefs gave way to new and—in some cases—more enlightened ones. After meeting Douglass a second time, for example, he told a military staffer that given the conditions from which the black abolitionist had come, he was "one of the most meritorious men in America."

Lincoln altered his perspective on people and events because he was *willing* to learn from his experience and then assimilate this learning. As the leader's attitudes toward black Americans shifted, he worked from this enlarged view, using it as he mapped out a future path for the country. In an 1863 speech, for instance, he spoke publicly about blacks' exceptional courage on the battlefield and what this meant for the government's postwar obligations to Negroes; eighteen months later, as the war drew to a close, Lincoln was working on economic and educational programs for black Americans.

CHAPTER NINETEEN

Frame the Stakes

To aggressively prosecute the war, the president needed public and congressional support. But by early 1863, popular opposition to the conflict had erupted once again; Union military defeats and the human and financial costs of the war had also increased antagonism among elites in Congress and state legislatures. Lincoln realized that these political opponents—also known as Peace Democrats or Copperheads—posed a serious threat to his war policy. Massachusetts senator Charles Sumner remembered the president saying he feared for this "fire in the rear" as much as for the government's military chances.

The "fire in the rear" gathered momentum. The president's prosecution of the conflict was so unpopular in the West that some commentators predicted the imminent secession of other states. If this happened, one Illinois Democrat warned the president, some of the Midwestern states that left the Union might join the Confederacy. Many Republicans, including Illinois congressman Elihu Washburne, were frightened by what they witnessed. "All confidence is lost in the administration," wrote one of Washburne's constituents. Another federal defeat, the Illinois resident added, "will disintegrate this whole country. Treason is everywhere, bold, defiant, and active, *with impunity.*"

In early May, disastrous news arrived. Confederate forces commanded by Generals Robert E. Lee and Stonewall Jackson battered

Union troops fighting under General Joseph Hooker in Chancellors-
ville, Virginia. During the battle, government forces lost seventeen
thousand men; Southern troops suffered thirteen thousand casualties.
On the afternoon of May 6, when Lincoln learned of Hooker's defeat
by telegraph, he handed the dispatch to his friend Dr. Anson Henry
and the reporter Noah Brooks, both of whom were with him in the
White House. "Read it—news from the army," the president said,
his face ashen. "My God! My God!" he despaired. "What will the
country say! What will the country say!"

Two months later, the pendulum of military advantage swung
toward the government. In early July 1863, the Army of the Potomac,
now under the leadership of General George Meade, won a decisive
battle in Gettysburg, Pennsylvania, repulsing Lee's Army of Northern
Virginia as it attempted to invade the North. It was a critical victory.
The Confederates' "best army is routed," proclaimed New York
attorney George Templeton Strong, and "the charm of Robert Lee's
invincibility [is] broken. . . . Government is strengthened four-fold
at home and abroad." Opponents of the war, Strong continued, "are
palsied and dumb for the moment at least."

But Meade's success at Gettysburg had come at a fearsome cost.
At the opening of the confrontation, a total of 160,000 troops from
both sides had poured into the Pennsylvania hamlet. When the smoke
cleared three days later, 51,000 Americans were dead, wounded, or
missing; 23,000 of these men were federal soldiers, 28,000 were
Confederates.

On July 4, just as news from Gettysburg reached Northern cities,
Union general Ulysses S. Grant and his Army of the Tennessee, which
had, for months, laid siege to Vicksburg, Mississippi, captured the city.
The Confederate surrender gave the government control of the Mississippi River. Northerners were jubilant. "I wanted to hug the army
of the Potomac," Henry Adams wrote his brother Charles. "I wanted
to get the whole of the army of Vicksburg drunk at my own expense.
I wanted to fight some small man and lick him."

The president and many other Union supporters hoped that the
victories at Gettysburg and Vicksburg would spell the end of the
Confederacy. But in some quarters, including Lincoln's home state

of Illinois, this possibility served only to increase public interest in a negotiated peace. Appalled by the human carnage, many Northerners thought the government should stop fighting and seek a settlement with the rebel states, one that recognized the legality of slavery.

Lincoln refused to consider this option. Opening peace discussions in mid-1863 would have meant repealing the Emancipation Proclamation and ending the recruitment of black soldiers. The president was certain that the best way forward was to prosecute the conflict as vigorously as possible. The Confederacy, he told his secretary John Hay, "will break to pieces if we only stand firm now." The commander in chief also refused to receive the vice president of the Confederacy, Alexander Stephens, who sought permission under a flag of truce to come to Washington, ostensibly to discuss an exchange of prisoners.

Nonetheless, the president knew that he had to deal with growing calls for peace. In late summer he decided to accept an invitation from his old friend James Conkling to address a large meeting of Union supporters in Springfield, Illinois. As the speech grew closer, however, pressing responsibilities prevented the president from leaving Washington. So instead of returning to his hometown, he wrote a letter for Conkling to present at the gathering. The letter, which was published in newspapers across the country, laid out the principal arguments of the peace faction and Lincoln's careful response to these.

On September 3, Conkling read the president's letter in Springfield to a crowd estimated at fifty thousand. The most important sections dealt with the Emancipation Proclamation and the enlistment of black soldiers. Both measures, the president asserted, were critical to saving the Union. "But, to be plain," Lincoln wrote, addressing his opponents, "you are dissatisfied with me about the negro. Quite likely there is a difference of opinion between you and myself upon that subject. I certainly wish that all men could be free, while I suppose you do not. Yet I have neither adopted, nor proposed any measure, which is not consistent with even your view, provided you are for the Union." After reiterating the military rationale for the Emancipation Proclamation, Lincoln turned to the important contributions of black soldiers:

I know as fully as one can know the opinions of others, that some of
the commanders of our armies in the field who have given us our most
important successes, believe the emancipation policy, and the use of
colored troops, constitute the heaviest blow yet dealt to the rebellion;
and that, at least one of those important successes, could not have been
achieved when it was, but for the aid of black soldiers.

Toward the end of the letter, the president took up the pledge of
permanent emancipation contained in his decision to recruit black
troops. He also contrasted these soldiers' patriotism with that of his
detractors and intimated his determination to lead the war to what
he now saw as its just conclusion:

But negroes, like other people, act upon motives. Why should they
do any thing for us, if we will do nothing for them? If they stake
their lives for us, they must be prompted by the strongest motive—
even the promise of freedom. And the promise being made, must
be kept. . . .

   Peace does not appear so distant as it did. I hope it will come
soon, and come to stay; and so come as to be worth the keeping
in all future time. It will then have been proved that, among free
men, there can be no successful appeal from the ballot to the bullet; and that they who take such appeal are sure to lose their case,
and pay the cost.

Looking back, we can see that Lincoln was doing more than
making the case for his policies. As any serious leader engaged in
large-scale change must, he was also trying to keep the relevant lines
of communication open. He understood that widespread transformation always unleashes waves of collective fear, discontent, and
doubt—emotions that often translate into vocal, and potentially more
destructive, opposition. He also knew that if left unacknowledged,
adversaries have the power to derail even the worthiest attempts at
reform, and thus it is a leader's responsibility to identify and, when
necessary, neutralize his or her most powerful critics.

   But how is the person at the center of the change to do this without appearing weak, creating additional enemies, or potentially legitimating the very attacks he or she is trying to mitigate? These are complicated issues, so it is not surprising that leaders often avoid head-on engagement with their challengers, hoping instead that the rallying cry of the mission and the enthusiasm of supporters will overwhelm naysayers.

But this is a risky strategy, especially when the stakes are high. It was to Lincoln's credit that during the summer of 1863 he understood the power of Northern elites, who did not want to fight a war to end slavery. The president also realized that to defuse the "fire in the rear," he had to speak directly to the American public, and he had to do this by addressing the specific arguments his opponents were making against him. Finally, he had to explain his actions in terms of his larger purpose. Lincoln did all of this in the speech for James Conkling. Seen from the perspective of a change leader effectively communicating with relevant stakeholders and trying to alleviate serious threats to the broader transformation, the president's letter was a tour de force.

In September, Union armies under the command of General William Rosecrans suffered a big defeat fighting along the Chickamauga Creek on the border between Tennessee and Georgia. More than sixteen thousand federal troops were killed, wounded, or went missing during the two-day battle; Confederate losses numbered more than eighteen thousand. But in late November, Union armies under the command of generals Ulysses S. Grant, William Tecumseh Sherman, Joseph Hooker, and George Thomas successfully counterattacked, greatly strengthening the Union position in Tennessee and northwest Georgia, and creating the possibility of a federal invasion of the Deep South.

At about the same time, Lincoln proclaimed the fourth Thursday in November a national Thanksgiving Day. He urged Americans to ask God's help to heal the nation and restore "peace, harmony, tranquility and Union." Despite this call, peace did not come. The war raged on—with seemingly no end in sight. Why, the president asked himself, could he not bring the conflict to a close? Why was it proving so violent? As he thought about these questions, his mind went back to the Battle of Gettysburg, an important inflection point.

If only Union general George Meade had attacked Lee and the Army of Northern Virginia as they retreated south after the battle, Lincoln reasoned, the war would have ended. But this had not happened, and the bloodshed went on.

In early November, when he received an invitation to deliver "a few appropriate remarks" at the dedication of a new national cemetery at Gettysburg, Lincoln saw an opportunity to give voice to the larger issues he'd been wrestling with. He accepted the invitation and, during the ensuing weeks, thought long and hard about what to say. By the time he left for Pennsylvania, he'd written about half the speech. He had the rest clearly in mind, but as he told a friend, he was struggling with the ending.

On the evening of November 18, Lincoln and his party arrived at Gettysburg; early the following morning, the president finished his remarks, copying them onto two sheets of paper. The dedication ceremony began at noon that day, November 19, opening with a speech by the statesman Edward Everett. For almost two hours, the former secretary of state and former governor of Massachusetts addressed the crowd of fifteen thousand, offering a detailed explanation of the battle. When he finished, Ward Hill Lamon, US marshal of the District of Columbia, introduced the president. Lincoln took the platform and began to speak. His remarks totaled only 272 words. It took him less than three minutes to deliver them:

> Four score and seven years ago our fathers brought forth on this continent, a new nation, conceived in Liberty, and dedicated to the proposition that all men are created equal.
>
> Now we are engaged in a great civil war, testing whether that nation, or any nation so conceived and so dedicated, can long endure. We are met on a great battle-field of that war. We have come to dedicate a portion of that field, as a final resting place for those who here gave their lives that that nation might live. It is altogether fitting and proper that we should do this.
>
> But, in a larger sense, we can not dedicate—we can not consecrate—we can not hallow—this ground. The brave men, living and dead, who struggled here, have consecrated it, far above

our poor power to add or detract. The world will little note, nor long remember what we say here, but it can never forget what they did here. It is for us the living, rather, to be dedicated here to the unfinished work which they who fought here have thus far so nobly advanced. It is rather for us to be here dedicated to the great task remaining before us—that from these honored dead we take increased devotion to that cause for which they gave the last full measure of devotion—that we here highly resolve that these dead shall not have died in vain—that this nation, under God, shall have a new birth of freedom—and that government of the people, by the people, for the people, shall not perish from the earth.

In the aftermath of the speech, many commentators recognized the power of Lincoln's words. The president's remarks, the *Chicago Tribune* noted, "will live among the annals of man." According to the Massachusetts-based *Springfield Republican*, the president's speech was "a perfect gem; deep in feeling, compact in thought and expression, and tasteful and elegant in every word and comma." "I should be glad, if I could flatter myself," Edward Everett wrote Lincoln, "that I came as near to the central idea of the occasion, in two hours, as you did in two minutes."

Critics were equally swift to attack the speech. The *New York World*, for example, accused Lincoln of "gross ignorance or willful misstatement," reminding readers that the United States was not the result of the Declaration of Independence but had instead come about from "the ratification of a compact known as the Constitution," which said absolutely nothing about equality. The *Chicago Times* also assaulted the president's understanding of the nation's founding, noting that several clauses of the Constitution recognized the legality of slavery. "Do these provisions," the newspaper asked, "dedicate the nation to 'the proposition that all men are created equal'?" The president, the editorial continued, "occupies his present position by virtue of this constitution, and is sworn to the maintenance and enforcement of these provisions. . . . How [dare] he, then, standing on [soldiers'] graves, misstate the cause for which they died, and libel the statesmen who founded the government?"

Lincoln did not set out to insult the framers of the Constitution. But perhaps he did intend, as writer Garry Wills has suggested, to subordinate this founding document to the Declaration of Independence. It was the document signed on July 4, 1776—four score and seven years before Lincoln delivered the Gettysburg Address—which the president believed was the more important because it set forth the nation's reason for being. Now, at the end of almost three years of terrible civil war, Lincoln was ready to commit the nation to the ideal laid out in the Declaration of Independence. He was prepared, as he explained at Gettysburg, to prosecute the conflict with the avowed purpose of saving *and* transforming the Union—to restore the promise of America, a country founded on the principle that all men are created equal.

In this context, Lincoln's speech is a first-rate example of a leader framing the stakes of the change. In hindsight, we can see that he used the dedication ceremony to connect the continuing turbulence—the Civil War—with the history and mission of the enterprise—the American polity and its central proposition. He then led his audience to the present moment, relating their action to "the unfinished work" in which they and all other Americans were involved. He laid down the gauntlet for every citizen who supported the Union: "it is rather for us to be here dedicated to the great task remaining before us—that from these honored dead we take increased devotion to that cause for which they gave the last full measure of devotion."

In saying this, Lincoln presented the trade-offs of committing to the mission: a great civil war, a testing struggle, and thousands of deaths. He concluded by stating that as formidable as these costs were, they were the price of a mighty end, one with lasting significance: "that this nation, under God, shall have a new birth of freedom—and that government of the people, by the people, for the people, shall not perish from the earth."

Every modern leader navigating through a crisis can learn from the Gettysburg Address. We are unlikely to approach the eloquence and power of Lincoln's language. But we can take from his leadership the critical importance of framing the stakes of a particular moment. This means connecting current change efforts to the history and future of the enterprise, locating these efforts in the arc of ongoing events, explaining each stakeholder's role in the process, identifying the specific trade-offs of making the change, and understanding these costs in relation to the ultimate goal. The more turbulent the world becomes in the early twenty-first century, the more vital it is for leaders to interpret and frame this volatility in relation to a worthy purpose.

CHAPTER TWENTY

Hold the Line

Lincoln returned from Pennsylvania with a mild form of smallpox. (Laid up in bed, he said that, at last, he had a solution to the endless requests of office seekers. "Now," he reportedly joked, "I have something that I can give to everybody.") But the president had little time to convalesce. At the end of 1863, he realized that everything he was working for, including holding on to the presidency for a second term and thus seeing the war and his larger mission through to completion, depended on Union victories.

But none were to be had. In the East, the Army of the Potomac and the Army of Northern Virginia were locked in a long stalemate. In the West, federal troops were largely inactive. Meanwhile, illness and desertion sapped the strength of Union forces. Exhausted by the conflict and intimidated by mounting casualty counts, few Northerners volunteered. In the early months of 1864, Lincoln issued draft orders for seven hundred thousand additional soldiers.

He also appointed Ulysses S. Grant commander of all Northern armies. By late April 1864, the general intended to move the Army of the Potomac south in a massive overland assault on Robert E. Lee's forces in Virginia. At the same time, Union general William Tecumseh Sherman would lead his men toward Atlanta to try to take that city. In a series of other coordinated attacks, Union generals would advance on Mobile, Alabama, and Petersburg, Virginia. The logic of the strategy was similar to that Lincoln had recommended to George McClellan two years earlier: attack and keep attacking the Confederate army's entire line to exploit the Union forces' numerical superiority.

In May 1864, generals Grant and George Meade, along with one hundred thousand men of the Army of the Potomac, headed south toward Richmond, the Confederate capital. Within a few days, Union troops attacked Lee's smaller forces west of Fredericksburg, Virginia, in what became known as the Battle of the Wilderness. During two days of ferocious fighting, government troops suffered more than eighteen thousand casualties; Confederate forces lost more than eleven thousand men. (Almost two hundred wounded Union soldiers who lay waiting for help were burned alive when the leaves in which they had fallen caught fire from rifle sparks; both armies could hear their screams.)

Undeterred, Grant immediately turned his army southeast toward nearby Spotsylvania Court House, Virginia. On May 8, federal troops assaulted Lee's army a second time. For twelve days, Union soldiers tried to break the Confederate line. Grant's forces came close to cutting the opposing army in two, but Southern counterattacks closed the gap, and the battle continued for more than twenty hours. It was some of the fiercest combat of the war. "Nothing can describe the confusion, the savage blood-curdling yells, the murderous faces, the awful curses, and the grisly horror of the melee," remembered one veteran. The battle, said another, was a "seething, bubbling, roaring hell of hate and murder."

When the fighting subsided, neither side could claim victory. But the costs had been enormous: eighteen thousand Union soldiers killed, wounded, or missing, and more than twelve thousand Confederate soldiers lost. During the first three weeks of his overland campaign, Grant had suffered more than thirty-five thousand casualties. Northerners were appalled. Lincoln's critics pounced on the military failures. The president himself was almost sick with anxiety. Speaker of the House Schuyler Colfax, visiting the president in his office, watched him pace up and down the room, asking, "Why do we suffer reverses after reverses! Could we have avoided this terrible, bloody war! Was it not forced upon us! Is it ever to end!"

Grant continued his campaign south. In early June, the Army of the Potomac attacked Confederate forces at Cold Harbor, Virginia, ten miles northeast of Richmond. When the worst of the fighting ended, Southern forces had successfully repulsed the Union advance; the federals suffered seven thousand casualties to the Confederates' fifteen hundred. Grant later said he regretted ordering the attack at Cold Harbor. But at the time, he had entertained no thoughts of retreat. "I propose to fight it out on this line if it takes all summer," he had written Secretary of War Edwin Stanton in May.

The general's determination was indicative of the war's new rhythm. Gone was the cadence that had defined the conflict for its first three years: big battles followed by retreat and then rest and recuperation for each of the opposing armies. In the spring and early summer of 1864, by contrast, both sides were engaged, historian James McPherson has explained, in "a new kind of relentless, ceaseless warfare."

Both Grant and Lee had good reasons to continue the pace and intensity. Confident in superior numbers, the Union commander hoped to batter Southern forces into submission through constant attack. For his part, Lee knew that the Army of the Potomac was losing almost two men to every one lost by his Army of Northern Virginia. If he could maintain this shocking arithmetic and hold Southern defenses without Grant's scoring a major victory, Lee reasoned, Northern voters might reject Lincoln in November and instead choose a candidate who would sue for a negotiated peace.

In June, Grant turned his army south to Petersburg, Virginia, hoping to take the city and, from there, launch an assault on Richmond. At the same time, the nation began preparing for a presidential election. On June 7, Republicans convened in Baltimore, nominating Lincoln for a second term. They also adopted a platform calling for vigorous prosecution of the war and a constitutional amendment to end slavery. The delegates nominated Andrew Johnson, military governor of Tennessee, for vice president.

Meanwhile, many Northern Democrats called for peace talks with the Confederacy. In late summer, this faction controlled the party's national convention in Chicago; delegates there nominated the former Union general George McClellan for president. The party platform declared the war a failure, promised to preserve "the rights of States unimpaired," and demanded that "immediate efforts be made for a cessation of hostilities." Southerners rejoiced at the Democratic plat-form and its nominee. McClellan's election, the *Charleston Mercury* wrote, "must lead to peace and our independence," provided that "for the next two months *we hold our own and prevent military success by our foes.*"

Everything now rested on the tally of military victories and defeats. As summer stretched on, Union armies made scant progress. Grant's assault on Petersburg was stalled outside the heavily defended city. Both federal and Confederate troops—a combined total of more than one hundred thousand men—dug in for a long engagement. They fought from trench lines that snaked around the city, foreshadowing combat in World War I. From Tennessee, William Tecumseh Sherman moved slowly toward Atlanta, seemingly unable to break through Confederate forces that stood between his army and the city. In the Shenandoah Valley, Union troops made few advances.

At the same time, wounded Union soldiers poured into hospitals throughout the North, including Washington, DC. Outside the city's infirmaries—some of which were housed in government structures such as the Patent Office Building—piles of amputated limbs de-composed in the stifling heat. At every turn, residents in the capital city confronted the terrible costs of the war. Watching a train of ambulances go by his carriage one evening, Lincoln said to a friend, "Look yonder at those poor fellows. I cannot bear it. This suffering, this loss of life is dreadful."

The poet Walt Whitman, who served as a nurse during the war, described the situation in one city hospital: "Things are going pretty badly with the wounded," he wrote his mother. "They are crowded here in Washington in immense numbers, and all those that come up from the Wilderness [campaign] and that region, arrived here so neglected, and in such plight, it was awful. . . . We receive them here with their wounds full of worms—some all swelled and inflamed. Many of the amputations have to be done over again. One new feature is that many of the poor afflicted young men are crazy. Every ward has some in it that are wandering. They have suffered too much, and it is perhaps a privilege that they are out of their senses."

As the summer 1864 wore on, Northern morale collapsed. Politicians and journalists called for an immediate end to the war, with many predicting that Lincoln would lose the election. "The people are wild for Peace," said New York politician Thurlow Weed. They won't support the president, he added, because they are told he "will only listen to terms of peace on condition [that] slavery be abandoned." Henry Raymond, editor of the *New York Times* and chairman of the Republican National Committee, told Lincoln that the "tide is setting sharply against us." The editor said his sources predicted that Illinois, Indiana, Pennsylvania, and New York would go against the president in the upcoming election. He went on to urge Lincoln to initiate peace talks with Confederate president Jefferson Davis "on the sole Condition of acknowledging the supremacy of the Constitution,—all other questions to be settled in a convention of the people of all the States."

By late August, Lincoln faced a crisis as great as any other he had confronted. Northern political support had turned strongly against him. The chief executive understood what this meant. "You think I don't know I am going to be beaten," he remarked to a visitor in late summer, "but I do, and unless some great change takes place, *badly beaten.*" If McClellan was elected, Lincoln realized, the likelihood was strong that the war would end with the South becoming an independent nation—one that would keep slavery intact.

The president was racked with worry. He knew he could not relinquish universal emancipation as a condition of ending the war. He could not send black soldiers who had bravely fought for the Union back to their masters. "I should be damned in time & in eternity for so doing," he explained to two government officials. "The world shall know that I will keep my faith to friends & enemies, come what will."

But as the military stalemate continued, the pressure on the president to seek settlement terms with the Confederacy increased. This pressure, James McPherson has written, became "almost irresistible." And the commander in chief began to waver. Perhaps, he told himself as he paced the White House hallway late at night, he should enter into peace talks with Southern leaders. On August 19, he drafted a potentially momentous letter to a Democratic politician

and newspaper editor, ending the communication with this proposition: "If Jefferson Davis wishes . . . to know what I would do if he
were to offer peace and re-union, saying nothing about slavery, let
him try me."

Having written these words, Lincoln paused. He did not send the
letter; instead, he stored it in his desk while he thought about what
to do. Two days later, when Frederick Douglass visited Lincoln at
the White House to discuss recruiting slaves into the Union army,
the president read the letter aloud to him. The black activist strongly
urged the chief executive to keep it to himself. If he sent it, Douglass
said, the missive would be interpreted "as a complete surrender of
your anti-slavery policy, and do you serious damage."

Lincoln took the advice. He returned the letter to his files. With
renewed confidence, the president decided emancipation would remain
an essential condition of any negotiations with the Confederacy. For
a few days during the long, hot summer of 1864, Lincoln had considered backing away from his mission. But in the end—at the moment
it really mattered—he did not. He held the line. First, he moved
slowly enough *not* to send a letter that might have initiated peace
talks with rebel leaders. Second, he sought input from individuals
such as Frederick Douglass, who Lincoln surely knew would advise
against sending the communication. Third, he stayed the course by
accessing his commitment to the larger purpose.

Historians and biographers have pointed to a number of Lincoln's strengths and their role in his leadership. But one of the most
significant of these strengths is not often mentioned, and this is that
Lincoln simply kept going. Once he made a crucial decision, he saw it
through, even when virtually everything around him seemed stacked
against such a commitment. This adherence was not the result of
stubbornness or self-righteousness. Rather, it came from the care that
Lincoln exercised in making choices, including the slowness with
which he acted when the stakes were high; from his growing depth
as a moral actor; and from his sheer will to get up each morning and
do what he could in service of his mission.

In early September, Union forces scored a critical military victory.
After six weeks of laying siege to Atlanta, Sherman's troops succeeded

in cutting all major supply lines to the city, and on September 1, Confederate forces under the command of General John Bell Hood evacuated the area. The next day, Sherman's army marched in, raising the American flag over city hall. The Union general cabled Washington, "Atlanta is ours and fairly won."

The balance of the war had shifted again and, with it, Lincoln's possibilities for a second term. On November 8, 1864, the president carried the election, winning every Northern state except for New Jersey, Delaware, and Kentucky. The same groups that had elected him four years earlier supported the party now: native-born farmers, New Englanders, and urban professional men. Federal soldiers, voting from battlefields across the country, overwhelmingly chose Lincoln.

During the next few months, the war moved swiftly to a close. In the autumn, Union general Philip Sheridan led his men through the Shenandoah Valley, attacking Confederate forces, burning farms, slaughtering livestock, and stealing provisions. In late December, after a three-hundred-mile march to the sea, Sherman and his army captured Savannah, Georgia. (The Union general wrote the president a telegram on December 22: "I beg to present you, as a Christmas gift, the city of Savannah, with 150 heavy guns and plenty of ammunition, and also about 25,000 bales of cotton.") On April 3, 1865, Union forces under Grant's command finally captured the Confederate capital of Richmond.

An important military prize, Richmond had been hard won. In the wake of its fall, events unfolded that would have been inconceivable two years earlier—symbols of the enormous changes the war had wrought. For example, some of the first government soldiers to enter the former Confederate capital were members of the all-black Twenty-Fifth Corps. Taking their cue from these troops, emancipated slaves quickly poured into city streets, singing, shouting, and dancing. The pens in the Richmond slave market were thrown open; black men, women, and children swept out of the enclosures, praising God and the president.

Watching all this, white residents were shocked by the reception that black Americans gave Union troops and then Lincoln when he visited Richmond on April 4. Crowds of freed blacks surrounded the commander in chief as he walked through the streets. Some knelt; many tried to touch him; virtually all acknowledged his role in ending slavery. "I know that I am free," said one older black woman, "for I have seen Father Abraham and felt him."

A few days later on April 9, Robert E. Lee surrendered his army to Ulysses S. Grant at Appomattox Court House, Virginia, effectively ending the Civil War. The Union general, acting under instructions from the president, offered generous terms of surrender. "I want no one punished," Lincoln had told Grant, "treat them liberally all round. We want those people to return to their allegiance to the Union and submit to the laws." The terms that Grant presented Lee paroled Confederate officers and enlisted men, provided they agreed to not take up arms against the government; required them to relinquish military equipment; and allowed them to keep their horses and personal possessions. When the Confederate general told Grant that his men were hungry, the Northern commander arranged for twenty-five thousand rations to be sent to the defeated army.

CHAPTER TWENTY-ONE

A New Birth of Freedom

Before it was clear that Union armies would triumph, Lincoln had been thinking about the future of a reunited nation: How should the federal government deal with the former Confederate states when they were readmitted to the Union? What provisions—political, economic, and social—should be made for freed black Americans? In his annual message to Congress in December 1864, the president had urged legislators to support a constitutional amendment to abolish slavery everywhere in the United States. The proposed amendment had passed the Senate eight months earlier, but had failed to secure the necessary two-thirds majority in the House. At the end of 1864, Lincoln asked lame-duck representatives to vote again on the amendment before the Thirty-Eighth Congress adjourned in March 1865.

In the final weeks of 1864 and the early weeks of the new year, Lincoln worked hard to secure passage of the amendment. He met with individual legislators, urging loyal politicians to lobby others to vote for it. Some evidence suggests that the president dispensed patronage to specific members in exchange for their support. Certainly, Secretary of State William Seward had jobs to offer lame-duck Democrats who pledged to back the amendment. The historical record is silent on other actions that Lincoln may have taken behind the scenes to procure the needed votes. Years later, remembering the president's role in the legislative struggle, the abolitionist and congressman Thaddeus Stevens said, "The greatest measure of the nineteenth century was passed by corruption, aided and abetted by the purest man in America."

On January 31, 1865, before a packed spectators' gallery, the House voted 119–56 to pass the Thirteenth Amendment to the Constitution. The majority was slightly more than the two-thirds required. When the final vote tally was read aloud, applause exploded among Republicans and other supporters on the floor. The *Congressional Globe* reported that in the gallery viewers jumped from their seats; men waved their hats in the air and "cheered loud and long, while the ladies, hundreds of whom were present . . . waved their handkerchiefs, participating in and adding to the general excitement and intense interest of the scene. This lasted for several minutes."

Once the House approved the amendment, it was sent to the individual states for ratification. Illinois, Lincoln's adopted home, was the first to ratify. Rhode Island, Michigan, Maryland, New York, Pennsylvania, and West Virginia followed. In early December 1865, Georgia and North Carolina became the last states of the three-fourths needed to ratify the constitutional provision that permanently outlawed slavery and involuntary servitude.

In early 1865 as the war wound to a close, Lincoln also devoted a great deal of attention to Reconstruction. His thinking on the subject was based on his efforts to establish loyal governments in Southern states that were occupied by Union troops. In Louisiana, for example, which had been held by federal forces since 1862, the president sought to bring white Unionists together to work toward emancipation and reunification.

What economic and social provisions would be made for black Americans, including whether they would be granted the right to vote, were open questions as the war sped to its conclusion. Abolitionists strongly urged Lincoln to support black suffrage. But conservative Republicans, Democrats, and other Northerners opposed this possibility, as did the majority of white Southerners. The president understood he would have to manage all of these factions as he tried to reunite the country. In his last public speech in early spring 1865, Lincoln said he favored giving the vote to intelligent black men and "those who serve our cause as soldiers." Seen from a modern perspective, such advocacy hardly seems courageous. But, as Eric Foner has pointed out, it was a remarkable statement; no other US president had ever before publicly supported black suffrage.

As Lincoln considered the future, he returned once again to the meaning of the war. Now that it was virtually over, how was the nation to make sense of this tragedy? How could he and his fellow citizens explain the undeniable immorality of slavery and its long life in the American polity? In the face of these issues, how was the country to move forward as one people dedicated to democratic ideals?

Lincoln took up these questions in his Second Inaugural Address, which he delivered on March 4, 1865, roughly a month before General Robert E. Lee would surrender at the Appomattox Court House. The day dawned cold, windy, and rainy. A crowd of more than thirty thousand gathered near the east front of the Capitol. Shortly after noon, the president stepped forward on the platform, and as he did, the sun burst through the clouds, flooding the scene with light. Some onlookers saw the sudden change as an auspicious omen, a sign of the "dispersion of the clouds of war," one government official said, "and the restoration of the clear sun light of prosperous peace."

The president held only a few sheets of paper. At just over seven hundred words, the address was one of the shortest inaugurals in American history. Lincoln opened with a brief account of the war's beginning. But he did not offer a careful analysis of the outbreak of hostilities. He did not revisit his own past attempts to keep the seceding states in the Union. He did not mention any specific battle or other incident. Instead, he simply said, "Both parties deprecated war; but one of them would *make* war rather than let the nation survive; and the other would *accept* war rather than let it perish. And the war came." This astounding understatement purposely avoided placing blame for the war on any one group of Americans.

Lincoln had a larger agenda. And he turned to it in his third paragraph, where he took up the momentous issue of slavery—its role in the war, its historical intractability in both the North and the South, and its place in the larger moral order. As the president explained it, slavery was not only the cause of the war, but also an institution that owed its existence to both the North and the South. It was "American

Slavery," not "Southern Slavery," that was at the center of this terrible war, a war that had touched virtually every citizen. God, Lincoln asserted, had meted out a punishment of blood "drawn with the sword" to atone for the dreadful, inescapable wrong of "blood drawn with the lash." This punishment applied equally to all Americans, whether they were Northerners or Southerners, whether they wore the blue or the gray. The sin of American slavery, Lincoln stated, accounted for the awfulness of the conflict. This meant, the president said, that the shock and awe of a war that defied human understanding was ultimately the work of a true, righteous (and judging) God.

Some historians have interpreted this part of the speech as indicative of Lincoln's deepening religious devotion. Certainly, there is good evidence that as president he became more interested in a powerful divinity. Lincoln had read the Bible all his life, but he had never attended church regularly or talked publicly about sustaining any kind of spiritual faith. Once he was in the White House and found himself at the center of a perfect storm, however, he referred at various moments to God and His purposes, hoping, he said, to discern and lead in accordance with these ends.

My own research suggests that more is going on in the Second Inaugural than the president's increased devotion. Like any other person who has been through a life-changing calamity, Lincoln had struggled to make sense of this experience. He had also tried to mitigate the tragedy even as he staggered under its effects, giving everything he had to these efforts. But like many others who endure great misfortune, he came to realize that all of his attempts to right the ship of events had fallen short. His intelligence, actions, and will were simply not enough, and he was forced—against his rational judgment—to consider the possibility that larger forces were at work. Despite all the human effort the war had entailed, the president asserted, God and Providence had had their way. For Lincoln—as for all individuals who forgo bitterness and instead vow to find redemption in the wreckage of tragedy—these forces were those of goodness. The war was ultimately, he concluded, the result of divine purpose, a purpose that he and the nation had to recognize.

All courageous leaders confront the limitations of their own agency. They then confront an important choice: whether to embrace the possibilities of decency and hope or those of baseness and despair. All five of the individuals in this book faced this choice. All five decided to move forward, humbled in their newfound understanding of what was beyond their control and, at the same time, resolute in their embrace of an honorable purpose.

Now, it was left to mortals to learn from the conflict, transcend the collective thirst for vengeance, and carry on with forgiveness. Lincoln closed his speech by calling citizens to their higher selves:

> With malice toward none; with charity for all; with firmness in the right, as God gives us to see the right, let us strive on to finish the work we are in; to bind up the nation's wounds; to care for him who shall have borne the battle, and for his widow, and his orphan—to do all which may achieve and cherish a just, and a lasting peace, among ourselves, and with all nations.

Some journalists and politicians were puzzled by the president's address. Lincoln was not surprised. "I believe it is not immediately popular," he wrote a colleague. "Men are not flattered by being shown that there has been a difference of purpose between the Almighty and them." Still, the president continued, "it is a truth which I thought needed to be told; and as whatever of humiliation there is in it, falls most directly on myself, I thought others might afford me to tell it." Such modesty did not prevent Lincoln from beaming when Frederick Douglass complimented the speech at the White House reception following the inauguration ceremony. "I am glad you liked it!" the chief executive called out as the abolitionist moved down the receiving line.

Lincoln was deeply tired, and he rested in bed for several days, before returning to the grueling schedule that had characterized his first term. Now that the war was ending, a new series of challenges confronted the country. These involved Reconstruction, the final terms of surrender for the Confederacy, the ratification of the Thirteenth Amendment, and planning for the end of slavery across the United States. The president approached all these issues with greater confidence and public support than he had known during the past four years. In March 1865, for example, he signed the Freedmen's Bureau Act, which established a government agency within the War Department to aid former slaves in making the transition to freedom. The bureau's responsibilities included providing food, clothing, and fuel to freed slaves and destitute white refugees, introducing a free labor system, overseeing schools for African-Americans, resolving disputes between white landowners and black workers, and ensuring that blacks were served justice in state courts.

The president also spent time managing the last stages of the war, meeting with Grant, Sherman, and his cabinet during the early weeks of his second term. During a visit to Grant's headquarters at City Point, Virginia, in early April, Lincoln spent a day touring the Field Depot Hospital. With ten thousand beds, the infirmary was the largest of four army hospitals at Union headquarters, and the commander in chief wanted to meet the wounded Union and Confederate troops housed there. He shook hands with the soldiers who could walk, and he went from bed to bed to greet others. An attendant remembered that the men were "pleased . . . beyond measure" to see the president, and that Lincoln "took almost as much pleasure in honoring the boy[s], as the boys did in receiving the honor from him." That day, the leader shook hands with six thousand patients and yet showed no sign of fatigue. When a doctor noted that the president's arm must be tired from the strain, Lincoln picked up an ax with his right hand, extended his arm horizontally, and, without a tremor, began chopping wood. (After he departed, several soldiers tried unsuccessfully to repeat this show of strength.)

In between the press of business, the president recovered his energy by seeing old friends. Joshua Speed came by the White House; so, too, did Illinois governor Richard Oglesby. As always, Lincoln relaxed in the company of trusted companions, telling stories, reciting Shakespeare, and reading humorous verse. The president also took pleasure in going to the theater and the opera.

As warmer weather returned to Washington, he and Mary made time for carriage rides, which they both enjoyed. After the Confederate surrender at Appomattox, the couple began to talk about what they would do when Lincoln's second term ended. They hoped to travel;

he wanted to see California, and perhaps the Holy Land. During an open-air buggy ride on April 14, Mary remarked to her husband that he seemed in such good spirits that "you almost startle me by your great cheerfulness." "And well I may feel so, Mary," Lincoln replied. "I consider *this day*, the war, has come to a close. . . . We must *both*, be more cheerful in the future—between the war & the loss of our darling Willie—we have both, been very miserable."

That evening, Abraham Lincoln was shot at Ford's Theatre in Washington, DC. He died the next morning, April 15, 1865.

CHAPTER TWENTY-TWO

The World after Abraham Lincoln

Harshly criticized in life, Abraham Lincoln was lionized in death. He was the first president to be killed in office, and he became the stuff of legend almost as soon as his body was laid in state. In the days following his assassination on Good Friday, tens of thousands of mourners in Washington, DC, paid their respects—first at the White House, and then inside the Capitol rotunda. During the ensuing weeks, many more Americans took part in memorial services held in the cities where the president's funeral train stopped along its journey to Illinois. Everywhere the train went, huge crowds of men, women, and children gathered to try to see Lincoln's coffin.

By May 4, 1865, when the president's body was laid to rest in Oak Ridge Cemetery in Springfield, Illinois, more than a million Americans had seen the leader's casket or witnessed the funeral procession's carefully orchestrated progress. Among them was six-year-old Teddy Roosevelt, who looked down from a second-floor window as Lincoln's cortege moved slowly down Broadway through Manhattan. When the early-twentieth-century leader became president himself many years later, he called Lincoln "my great hero" and said that he meant "more to me than any other of our public men." Roosevelt had the sixteenth president's portrait hung on the wall of his White House office, explaining to visitors and colleagues, "I look up to that picture, and I do as I believe Lincoln would have done."

In the decades following Lincoln's assassination, people from all walks of life shared a version of Roosevelt's sentiments. The slain president was revered as a martyr to the cause of freedom; he was lauded as a man of the people who had risen to the highest pinnacle of national power. Biographers praised him as an exemplary states- man whose wisdom and military leadership had saved the nation at its most important juncture. Countless Americans, black and white, saw Lincoln as the Great Emancipator, who had ended slavery and restored the fundamental promise of the United States.

But among some citizens—particularly in the South—popular opinion of Lincoln was far less enthusiastic. During his life and after his death, he was vilified as a hypocrite, a weak president, and the chief instigator of the Civil War. As historian Don Fehrenbacher has written, an anti-Lincoln tradition continued to flourish well into the late twentieth century. Revisionist historians and other writers have taken the sixteenth president to task for political manipulation, tyrannical designs, and malignant passions they allege culminated in his willingness to start and maintain a bloody war.

Such negative assessments have not dampened past or current interest in this leader, however, including conjecture about what might have happened if he had lived. Beginning in the late nineteenth century and continuing intermittently into our own time, some scholars have theorized that had Lincoln completed his second term, the unification of the country—including the development of race relations in the United States—would have followed a much less divisive and de- structive trajectory than it did under President Andrew Johnson and his contemporaries. This is interesting speculation, especially given the importance that Lincoln accorded Reconstruction during the last eighteen months of his presidency and the evolution of his own views on black Americans. But the simple truth is that the sixteenth president did not live long enough to articulate, much less execute, a comprehensive plan for reuniting the country after the war. We continue to long for his leadership beyond Appomattox.

By the time Lincoln's face was being carved into the granite wall of Mount Rushmore in the late 1930s and early 1940s, popular conceptions of the leader had ascended into a kind of rarefied ether, and the sixteenth president had become a modern-day saint. Such conceptions were far removed from the self-perception of the man who once told an Ohio regiment, "I happen temporarily to occupy this big White House. I am a living witness that any one of your children may look to come here as my father's child has."

But recent work on Lincoln, including a spate of biographies published to commemorate the bicentennial of his birth and director Steven Spielberg's feature film, has attempted to chip away at his marbled presence and find the man beneath. Beginning in about 2000, books appeared on Lincoln's chronic depression, pragmatism, use of language, moral purpose, purported homosexuality, and even the Soldiers' Home, where he and his family spent some summer months.

Many of these works have greatly expanded our collective understanding of Abraham Lincoln, *the person*. But they have often done so by focusing on a single aspect of this complicated, fascinating, and enigmatic individual without reference to the larger context in which he lived. Lincoln was no more defined by one attribute or element of his life than are any of the rest of us; nor did he work in a vacuum. We owe it to ourselves as well as the historical record to remain mindful of the various components of his humanity—including his flaws and blunders—and the bigger stage on which he worked as we look to him for guidance in our own turbulent moment.

The Civil War ended more than 150 years ago. But we, it seems, are not finished with the man who led the country through it. Not by a long shot. At a time when public faith in political officials has all but disappeared, we would do well to take careful stock of Lincoln's leadership during a particularly perilous era. His was not a story of superhuman heroism. Lincoln's journey was one of learning by doing, ongoing commitment to bettering himself, keen intelligence harnessed to equally acute emotional awareness, and the moral seriousness into which he grew as he attained immense power. It was also an all-too-human path marked by setbacks, derailments, and disappointments.

Abraham Lincoln *was made into an effective leader*—first from the inside out and then from the outside in—as he developed and changed throughout his life. That, as president, he refused to ignore the larger consequences of his actions on men and women who had little or no agency, that he saw beyond the immediate moment and owned the responsibility of affecting a vast future, and that he rejected an ethical callousness about the choices he made are demonstrations of leadership that we yearn for today. "For anyone trying to understand America's past or shape its future," as Fehrenbacher has noted, Lincoln "is a force to be reckoned with." May all who aspire to lead with worth and dignity learn from the life and leadership of Abraham Lincoln.

PART THREE

End Slavery Forever

FREDERICK DOUGLASS'S CHALLENGE

CHAPTER TWENTY-THREE

Return to the Struggle

On April 15, 1847, the twenty-nine-year-old abolitionist Frederick Douglass stood on a Liverpool wharf and looked out over the Atlantic. He was bound for Boston aboard the *Cambria*—the same steamship that had ferried him across the Atlantic eighteen months earlier. He had arrived in Britain as a fugitive slave, orator, and author.

Three months before sailing to the United Kingdom in 1845, Douglass had published his autobiography, *Narrative of the Life of Frederick Douglass, an American Slave*. A gripping account of his twenty years in bondage and his 1838 escape from slavery, the book had attracted widespread attention in the United States. Abolitionists took notice, as did politicians, ministers, and journalists. Readers clamored to know more about the angry and articulate young man; almost overnight, he had become famous.

Douglass's sudden notoriety extended to Maryland, where he had been a slave and his master, Hugh Auld, still lived. Incensed by the book's portrayal of him, Auld vowed to "spare no pains or expense in order to regain possession" of the black man. Worried for his safety, Douglass's supporters, including the well-known antislavery activist William Lloyd Garrison, quickly arranged a lecture tour for the black author in the United Kingdom.

These people hoped that Douglass's book and his formidable speaking skills would increase British support for their cause. Britain had abolished slavery more than seventy years earlier, but during the

early nineteenth century, reformers there turned their focus to countries where it still existed—particularly the United States—working
to end it from afar. In August 1845, Douglass left his family behind
in Boston and set sail, not knowing what he would find or how long
he would be gone.

Once in Britain, the abolitionist discovered a whole new life. He
traveled widely, speaking to large, enthusiastic crowds who roared
their approval. Thousands of men and women came, Douglass
wrote Garrison, "to hear the cruel wrongs of my down-trodden and
long-enslaved fellow country-men portrayed" and evinced "strong
abhorrence of the slaveholder." The press was no less appreciative,
praising the fugitive's book and oratorical skills. The black man had
experienced popular acclaim in the Northern United States, but he
had not known unqualified admiration on this scale.

This was not the only thing that was different about lecturing in the
United Kingdom. His speeches in the United States had occasionally
been interrupted by violence. During an 1843 meeting in Indiana, for
example, he and other abolitionists had been physically attacked, and
Douglass suffered permanent damage to his right hand. American
reporters and politicians had also accused him of being an impostor;
no escaped slave, critics charged, could possibly speak so intelligently
and persuasively. The black reformer had written his life story partly
in response to these accusations. He understood that to make a big
difference in the fight against slavery—whether as a witness to the
institution, a spokesperson against it, or a symbol of the potential
and promise of African-Americans—people had to believe in him.
In the United Kingdom they did; here no physical threats or charges
of trickery dogged him.

As important, for the first time in his life, Douglass did not experience racial discrimination. This contrasted sharply with what he had
known in the United States, where after he had escaped from slavery,
he had frequently been refused admission to hotels and restaurants,
thrown out of train compartments, denied access to churches, and
shut out from steamboat cabins. By comparison, in England, Ireland,
and Scotland, he lived and moved as whites did—without affront or
reprisal. "I gaze around in vain for one who will question my equal

humanity," Douglass observed, or "claim me as his slave, or offer me an insult."

Life in the United Kingdom had still other appealing aspects. Douglass liked English manners and enjoyed meeting prominent authors and politicians. He also made good friends, building relationships with other abolitionists, many of whom wanted to help advance his career. Within a year of arriving, he began to consider the possibility of settling permanently in Britain. Colleagues there urged him to stay, assuring the activist that he would earn enough money as a speaker and writer to support himself, his wife, Anna, and the couple's four young children.

This possibility took hold of Douglass. Like Lincoln and Shackleton, he hungered for public recognition, and he had found this in full measure in Britain. He also discovered a group of like-minded men and women, who believed in him and thought he could make a big difference working in their country to end slavery in America. Douglass also believed his children would have economic and educational opportunities that simply did not exist for blacks in the United States.

As he took stock of his new life in Great Britain, the black reformer found himself at an important juncture. One road forward was to remain in Britain and, from there, help lead the struggle to end American slavery. The other was to return to his home and resume his abolition work. Douglass knew all too well that going back meant subjecting himself to the threat of arrest as a fugitive slave. Supporters in Massachusetts might claim him as a celebrated author, but legal precedent suggested that the courts wouldn't protect him from recapture by his master. "Do you think it would be safe for me to come home this fall?" he wrote a friend in July 1846. "Would master Hugh [Auld] stand much chance in Mass[achusetts]? Think he could take me from the old Bay State? The old fellow is evidently anxious to get Hold of me."

Douglass thought long and hard, turning the two possibilities over in his mind. As he did this, he also wrote home, broaching the possibility of resettling in England with his wife, Anna. There is no record of her refusal, but existing correspondence among family members suggests that she wanted to stay in Massachusetts. Because her husband traveled so much, Anna took care of her children and home largely on her own, and she was deeply connected to both.

Family, economic, and practical considerations were significant. But as Douglass debated with himself, he could not get away from the big picture of slavery and what he might accomplish as an abolitionist working in either country. The more he thought about the divergent paths ahead, the clearer it became to him that he could not do what he believed he must from the safety of the United Kingdom. For all the seductive appeal of life in that nation, Douglass understood that the hardest, most important part of the struggle against slavery had to unfold in the United States, and that he needed to be at the center of it. Like other leaders in the midst of conflict, he believed he *had* to be in the thick of the contest. No other course would allow him to be true to himself. After a great deal of internal debate, he decided to return to his native land. In a March 1847 speech to a British audience, he explained why:

> I do not go [back] to America to sit still, remain quiet, and enjoy ease and comfort. . . . I glory in the conflict, that I may hereafter exult in the victory. . . . I will go back, for the sake of my brethren. I go to suffer with them; to toil with them; to endure insult with them; to undergo outrage with them; to lift up my voice in their behalf . . . and struggle in their ranks for that emancipation which shall yet be achieved by the power of truth and of principle for that oppressed people.

Douglass's supporters in Britain were sad to see him go. Many also worried that he would be arrested and returned to his master, Hugh Auld. Without the black man's knowledge, a few English friends began raising money to buy his freedom. One initiated negotiations with Douglass's owner, and before the abolitionist left Britain, his manumission papers were filed in Baltimore. His freedom had been purchased for $711.66.

In debating whether to return to America, Douglass had crossed a critical threshold with himself. He had examined the larger moment and the purpose that had long animated him: to escape from the evils of slavery and then work to destroy it. Like the other leaders in this book—especially Dietrich Bonhoeffer, who, in 1939, faced a choice to leave the safety of the United States and return to Germany on the eve of war to try to overthrow Hitler—Douglass had to come to terms with *exactly what he would wager* in service to his mission. This personal reckoning was complicated and difficult; he not only had to determine what he was going to do, but also how much he would give up to do it.

Every leader will find him- or herself at a crossroads like the one Frederick Douglass confronted in 1846. Each will have to examine the larger stage—be it a pressing environmental problem, a company that has lost its way, or a political election in which no candidate will speak the truth—and work out whether and how he or she can make an appreciable difference. Then each leader has to determine which trade-offs he or she is willing to make to move forward. The more crucial the issue, the less certainty and security there is likely to be, and thus the more difficult the potential trade-offs.

By early 1847, Douglass had decided that he had to go back to America. He knew this meant fighting slavery where that was both dangerous and unpredictable. But this was the place and the role in which he could have the most impact, and he accepted the risks that came with his choice. As he sailed for Boston in early 1847, the black reformer was ready for the challenges ahead. He had put *the* definitive stake in the ground: his commitment to lead with everything he had.

CHAPTER TWENTY-FOUR

Born a Slave

Frederick Augustus Washington Bailey was born in early 1818 in Talbot County, Maryland, near the Chesapeake Bay. (After he escaped from slavery as an adult, Frederick Bailey changed his name to Frederick Douglass.) His mother, Harriet, was a slave, and this meant Frederick was also a slave because by law the children of female slaves became slaves at birth. Frederick never knew who his father was, but he was certain he was white; it was largely assumed that the man was Harriet's owner, a plantation manager named Aaron Anthony.

When Frederick was still an infant, Anthony separated him from his mother, sending Harriet back to the fields, where she helped cultivate wheat and other crops. Slaves were commonly separated from their children; slaveholders often moved their human chattel as if they were pieces of equipment, shifting them around to extract their highest value.

Frederick was left in the care of his grandparents Betsy Bailey, another of Anthony's slaves, and her husband, a free black man named Isaac Bailey. When Frederick came to live with the couple, they resided in a one-room log cabin located on a farm belonging to Anthony. At forty-six, Betsy was considered too old for field labor; instead, she served as midwife and surrogate mother for many of the slave children who belonged to Anthony. Most of these boys and girls stayed with Betsy until they were six or seven, when they began work as domestic servants in Anthony's home or were leased out to other households.

In 1818, the year Frederick was born, more than 1.5 million black men, women, and children lived in bondage in the United States. This meant that, in a total population of 9.5 million, one in six Americans was a slave. The vast majority of slaves lived in the South, with the highest concentrations in Virginia, Maryland, Georgia, Kentucky, and North and South Carolina. During the ensuing decades, as the nation acquired vast tracts of territory, slavery moved south and southwest into many of these lands, including the young states of Alabama, Louisiana, Mississippi, and Arkansas.

During the first half of the nineteenth century, slaves lived in many different situations. Some worked as domestic servants. Some labored in their owners' small businesses: making barrels, building ships, milling flour, and shoeing horses. Most, however, worked in agricultural settings, particularly on large plantations that produced staple crops such as cotton, rice, tobacco, and sugarcane; cotton was, by far, the most important of the cash crops grown in the antebellum South.

In the early 1800s, the cultivation of cotton across the South boomed as textile production in New England, Great Britain, and France rapidly expanded. (In 1801, for example, annual production of the commodity was 1 million pounds; by 1860, it had climbed to more than 1.5 billion.) From the mid-1830s until the outbreak of the Civil War in 1861, cotton accounted for at least half of the total value of US exports. As cotton production rose, so, too, did the demand for slaves.

During his early childhood, Frederick knew nothing of cotton or plantations. He spent his days playing with the other children who lived with Isaac and Betsy, and helping his grandmother catch shad and herring in a nearby creek and grow sweet potatoes in a small garden. "Grandmother and grandfather were the greatest people in the world to me," he remembered, "and being with them so snugly in their own little cabin . . . for a time there was nothing to disturb me."

In August 1824, when Frederick was six, his owner, Aaron Anthony, decided to separate the boy from his grandparents, ordering Betsy to deliver him to Wye Plantation, where the white man lived.

Once Betsy had walked her grandson the ten miles to Anthony's home, she left him there, heartbroken. Still, Frederick had no choice but to take up his duties as a house slave.

Living conditions for Anthony's slaves were harsh. The black children rarely had sufficient food, subsisting mainly on boiled cornmeal. They ate this out of a trough, racing one another, once the mush was poured, to gulp as much as possible before the mixture was gone. There was never enough. Years later, Douglass remembered feeling "so pinched with hunger" that he fought with Anthony's dog, Old Nep, for the scraps that fell from the kitchen table.

The black children were also poorly clothed. The master allowed each slave two coarse shirts per year, and they wore these day and night in every season. The winter months were particularly hard. The great difficulty, Douglass recalled,

> was to keep warm during the night. The pigs in the pen had leaves, and the horses in the stable had straw, but the children had no beds. They lodged anywhere in the ample kitchen. I slept generally in a little closet, without even a blanket to cover me. In very cold weather I sometimes got down the bag in which corn was carried to the mill, and crawled into that. Sleeping there with my head in and my feet out, I was partly protected, though never comfortable. My feet have been so cracked with the frost that the pen with which I am writing might be laid in the gashes.

For all the children suffered, some adult slaves endured much worse. One morning, for example, Frederick was awakened by the screams of a young woman named Esther. From the closet where he slept, the boy watched as Anthony dragged the slave, naked from neck to waist with her arms tied in front of her, into the kitchen. The white man then lifted her arms overhead, fastening them to a joist in the ceiling as he told her, "Now, you d——d b——h, I'll learn you how to disobey my orders!" Douglass remembered the scene:

> Behind her stood old master, with cowskin in hand, preparing his barbarous work with all manner of harsh, coarse, and tantalizing

epithets. The screams of his victim were most piercing. He was cru-
elly deliberate, and protracted the torture, as one who was delighted
with the scene. Again and again he drew the hateful whip through
his hand, adjusting it with a view of dealing the most pain-giving
blow. Poor Esther had never yet been severely whipped, and her
shoulders were plump and tender. Each blow, vigorously laid on,
brought screams as well as blood. *"Have mercy; Oh! have mercy"*
she cried; *"I won't do so no more;"* but her piercing cries seemed
only to increase his fury. . . . After laying on some thirty or forty
stripes, old master untied his suffering victim, and let her get down.
She could scarcely stand, when untied. From my heart I pitied her,
and—child though I was—the outrage kindled in me a feeling far
from peaceful; but I was hushed, terrified, stunned, and could do
nothing, and the fate of Esther might be mine next.

In addition to his own slaves, Aaron Anthony also helped manage
roughly one hundred African-Americans who belonged to Edward
Lloyd, a wealthy US senator and former Maryland governor. The
politician employed Anthony to oversee Wye Plantation, the Lloyd
family's ten-thousand-acre estate. At the center of this was Wye House,
where the senator lived. Located steps from Anthony's personal
residence, the mansion was a large Georgian structure with stately
columns, an expansive portico, and a long, sweeping driveway. Frederick was fascinated with the house, and although Anthony's slaves
were forbidden from entering, the boy managed to snatch glimpses
of life inside. He was amazed by the abundance he observed:

Immense wealth and its lavish expenditures filled the Great House
with all that could please the eye or tempt the taste. . . . Beef, veal,
mutton, and venison, of the most select kinds and quality, rolled
in bounteous profusion to this grand consumer. The teeming riches
of the Chesapeake Bay, its rock perch, drums, crocus, trout, oys-
ters, crabs, and terrapin were drawn hither to adorn the glittering
table. . . . Here were gathered figs, raisins, almonds, and grapes
from Spain, wines and brandies from France, teas of various flavor
from China, and rich, aromatic coffee from Java, all conspiring to

swell the tide of high life, where pride and indolence lounged in magnificence and satiety.

In 1826, when Frederick was about eight years old, Aaron Anthony left his position as manager of Wye Plantation, intending to take some of his slaves with him when he moved and hiring out the rest. But his daughter Lucretia had taken a special interest in Frederick and persuaded her father to send the boy to Baltimore to live with her brother-in-law, Hugh Auld, and his wife, Sophia. The white couple wanted a domestic servant and caretaker for their toddler son and agreed to take the young slave.

In convincing her father to part with Frederick, Lucretia likely wanted to give him a better life. She knew that if he continued in Anthony's possession, he was likely to be sold into the Deep South when he was an adolescent; there he would work as a field hand on a large plantation. In this region, known as the Cotton Belt, conditions for slaves were generally far worse, and escape was virtually impossible.

Anthony agreed to Lucretia's plan, and in the summer of 1826, Frederick boarded a vessel headed north to Baltimore. He had little idea of what lay in store for him, but he was excited. "On setting sail I walked aft and gave to Col. Lloyd's plantation what I hoped would be the last look I should give to it, or to any place like it," Douglass later remembered. He made his way to the bow, spending the rest of the journey looking ahead. "The broad bay opened like a shoreless ocean on my boyish vision, filling me with wonder and admiration."

After a day's journey, Frederick arrived at Hugh and Sophia Auld's home in Baltimore and was immediately struck by the warmth and comfort his new mistress offered him. From that first day, she made sure the slave boy had proper clothes and shoes, slept in a bed with sheets and blankets, and never went hungry. Frederick took his meals at the family table and helped himself to freshly baked bread whenever he wished.

The slave boy's responsibilities included running errands and helping Sophia look after her son, Tommy. Frederick was busy every day, but his experience with the Aulds was very different from working for Anthony. "I had been treated as a *pig* on the plantation," Douglass later recalled. "I was treated as a *child* now. . . . How could I hang down my head, and speak with bated breath, when there was no pride to scorn me, no coldness to repel me, and no hatred to inspire me with fear? I therefore soon learned to regard [Sophia] as something more akin to a mother, than a slaveholding mistress." She seemed to say, "Look up, child; don't be afraid; see, I am full of kindness and good will toward you."

This new life was soon interrupted. In October 1827, fourteen months after Frederick had arrived in Baltimore, Aaron Anthony died. His descendants—daughter Lucretia and her two brothers—ordered the slave returned to their father's home so that they could settle the estate. All of Anthony's property, including his slaves and farm animals, was to be divided among the three heirs. The value of men, women, and children was assessed alongside that of sheep, cattle, and swine. Each creature, Douglass later remembered, held "the same rank in the scale of being, and were all subjected to the same narrow examination." Frederick became part of Lucretia's inheritance, and she promptly returned him to Baltimore. He considered himself fortunate.

Back in the Maryland city, Frederick resumed helping Sophia. During the long days while her husband, Hugh, worked in a shipyard, she read the Scriptures aloud to her son Tommy and the black boy. This was the slave's first exposure to the written word, and he was fascinated. "The frequent hearing of my mistress reading the bible," he recalled, "soon awakened my curiosity in respect to this *mystery* of reading." He asked Sophia to teach him to read, and she obliged.

For slaves, this was highly unusual. In many slaveholding states, it was illegal to teach slaves to read on the grounds that literacy would make them more likely to rebel or escape. Even in states such as Maryland that had no such legal prohibitions, few slave owners taught their slaves to read, and most were illiterate.

Before long, Frederick had mastered the alphabet. Sophia, he later wrote, "seemed almost as proud of my progress, as if I had been her own child." Keen to share her success with her husband, one day she asked the boy to demonstrate his new learning. Auld was furious. "If you teach that nigger . . . how to read the bible," he warned, "there will be no keeping him." Such education, Hugh argued, "would for-ever unfit him for the duties of slave." As important, the white man explained, being able to read would stimulate the boy's ambition. Before you know it, Auld continued, "he'll want to know how to write; and, this accomplished, he'll be running away with himself."

Listening to his master's rant, Frederick experienced a painful and powerful revelation: the white man's power to keep the black man enslaved depended on maintaining his ignorance. It was now clear to him, Douglass later recalled, that "knowledge unfits a child to be a slave. I instinctively assented to [this] proposition; and from that moment I understood the direct pathway from slavery to freedom." He resolved to learn to read and write.

Auld's words also made a big impact on his wife. Sophia not only stopped teaching Frederick, she also kept her Bible and other reading materials from him. "I have had [my mistress] rush at me with a face made all up of fury," he remembered, "and snatch from me a newspaper, in a manner that fully revealed her apprehension." Looking back, Douglass blamed slavery for the change in Sophia's demeanor—an institution, he recognized, that damaged white masters as well as black slaves. "It was no easy matter," he explained,

> to induce [my mistress] to think and to feel that the curly-headed boy, who stood by her side, and even leaned on her lap; who was loved by little Tommy, and who loved little Tommy in turn; sustained to her only the relation of a chattel. I was *more* than that, and she felt me to be more than that. I could talk and sing; I could laugh and weep; I could reason and remember; I could love and hate. I was human, and she, dear lady, knew and felt me to be so. How could she, then, treat me as a brute, without a mighty struggle with all the noble powers of her own soul. That struggle came, and the will and power of the husband was victorious. Her noble soul was overthrown; but, he that overthrew it did not, himself, escape the consequences. He, not less than the other parties, was injured in his domestic peace by the fall.
>
> When I [first] went into their family . . . she had bread for the hungry, clothes for the naked, and comfort for every mourner that came within her reach. Slavery soon proved its ability to divest her of these excellent qualities, and her home of its early happiness.

After Auld's tirade, Frederick had a better understanding of slavery. He also had a challenge before him. The most important thing he could now do was to teach himself to read and write. In doing this, he knew he would have to find his own resources—out of sight of Hugh and Sophia Auld. The slave soon enlisted the help of some boys he had met while running errands on the Baltimore streets. Many were the sons of poor white laborers whom he could bribe with fresh bread from Sophia's kitchen. "For a single biscuit, any of my hungry little comrades would give me a lesson," he remembered.

Little by little, Frederick absorbed letters, words, and phrases. He also got his hands on a copy of the popular nineteenth-century *Noah Webster's American Spelling Book*, cracking it open whenever he was out of the Aulds' sight. Down at the harbor, the slave watched shipbuilders label piles of wood intended for the starboard and larboard sides of ships, and the forward and aft ends, using the letters: *S*, *L*, *F*, and *A*. Once he understood what the letters denoted, he practiced writing them. Then Frederick found a way to expand this ability:

> When I met with any boy who I knew could write, I would tell him I could write as well as he. The next word would be, "I don't believe you. Let me see you try it." I would then make the letters which I had been so fortunate as to learn, and ask him to beat that. In this way I got a good many lessons in writing, which it is quite possible I should never have gotten in any other way. During this time, my copy-book was the board fence, brick wall, and pavement; my pen and ink was a lump of chalk.

The slave boy devised other means of learning. When he was alone in the Auld house, for example, he stole away with workbooks that Tommy brought home from school, reproducing the boy's script in the margins. "The process was a tedious one, and I ran the risk of getting a flogging for marring the highly prized copy books of the oldest son," Douglass remembered. But Frederick stayed with it, often working at night when the family was asleep. He copied

Bible verses, Methodist hymns, and other writings on a barrel lid. Like the young Abraham Lincoln making his letters on firewood, he scraped the words off the lid when it was covered with marks and began again.

When the slave boy was thirteen, one of his rough-and-tumble crew introduced him to *The Columbian Orator*. Compiled in 1797 by Caleb Bingham, an educator and publisher, the book was a series of excerpts from famous speeches, sermons, and literature. It included orations by Socrates, the Roman consul Cicero, the British statesman William Pitt, and Napoléon Bonaparte, in addition to lessons on voice and gesture. The book taught students to write and speak in the style of well-known historical figures.

After hearing one of the boys deliver an address, Frederick took fifty cents he may have earned blacking boots and bought a copy of the book. It captivated him. "Alone, behind the shipyard wall," historian William S. McFeely has written, "Frederick . . . read aloud. Laboriously, studiously, at first, then fluently, melodically, he recited great speeches. . . . He had the whole world before him. He was Cato before the Roman senate, Pitt before Parliament defending American liberty . . . Washington bidding his officers farewell." As Frederick re-created such moments for himself, he developed an understanding of the power of oratory. He recognized that it was power for the men who wrote and gave the speeches. It was power for the ideas they espoused, and it was agency—in some cases, a direct call to action—for those who listened to the words.

Reading opened new doors for the teenager, but it also made him miserable. Being exposed to George Washington's first speech before Congress, for instance, brought into clear relief the misery of the slave's condition—*his* condition. Frederick could find no remedy, no ladder out of what he called "the horrible pit" of enslavement. At times, he despaired. "As I writhed under the sting and torment of this knowledge," he later wrote, "I almost envied my fellow slaves their stupid indifference." He wished himself "a beast, a bird, anything rather than a slave. I was wretched and gloomy beyond my ability to describe."

Even as Frederick despaired, he tried to learn more about slavery, gleaning information from newspapers, snatches of conversations, and public debate. As he did, he also became familiar with efforts to end the institution. In the 1830s, the abolition movement in Baltimore was gathering momentum. Two factors lay behind this shift. The first was the city's growing African-American population—slave and free. During the early nineteenth century, slaves came to Baltimore from rural areas when their owners hired them out to urban manufacturers. Free blacks also poured into the booming city, lured by the prospect of steady employment. By 1830, free blacks made up almost 12 percent of the city's population. The second factor stoking the local abolition movement was the presence of slave trading and the opposition it increasingly provoked. Baltimore was a major hub for buying, selling, and moving slaves. Between 1790 and the outbreak of the Civil War, more than a million slaves moved among regions in the South; about 70 percent of these people were bought and sold by traders, many of who operated in Baltimore.

Slave trading had always been controversial. For many years, the subject remained largely a private matter—lamented in personal discussion, criticized in letters, and mentioned in small political circles. But as the business of slave trading grew in Baltimore, so, too, did *public* antagonism toward it. During the 1830s, abolitionists such as the young William Lloyd Garrison protested the trafficking of human beings. Many city residents also voiced their distress at the sight of dealers marching African-Americans in chains through the streets. In response, traders took to moving their slaves in the middle of the night; Douglass remembered being awakened in the darkness by the "dead, heavy footsteps and the piteous cries of the chained gangs" headed for the docks.

Slave auctions usually took place near the harbor. Specific auction practices varied, but eyewitness accounts speak to their cruelty. A slave named William Anderson described his eight times on the auction block:

> The slaves are made to shave and wash in greasy pot liquor to make them look sleek and nice; their heads must be combed and their best clothes put on; and when called out to be examined they

are to stand in a row—the women and men apart—then they are picked out and taken into a room, and examined. See a large, rough slaveholder take a poor female slave into a room, make her strip, then feel of and examine her as though she were a pig, or a hen, or merchandise. O, how can a poor slave husband or father stand and see his wife, daughters and sons thus treated.

In slave auctions families were often forcibly separated. Husbands were divided from wives, mothers from children, brothers and sisters from one another. (The rupture of families was so commonplace that slave marriage vows often read "till death or distance do us part.") Josiah Henson, a preacher and former slave, remembered being parted from his mother and siblings when his family members were sold at auction:

My brothers and sisters were bid off first, and one by one, while my mother, paralyzed by grief, held me by the hand. Her turn came, and she was bought by Isaac Riley of Montgomery county [Maryland]. . . . My mother, half distracted with the thought of parting forever from all her children, pushed through the crowd while the bidding for me was going on, to the spot where Riley was standing. She fell at his feet and clung to his knees, entreating him in tones that a mother only could command to buy her *baby* as well as herself, and spare to her one, at least, of her little ones. Will it, can it, be believed that this man, thus appealed to, was capable not merely of turning a deaf ear to her supplication, but of disengaging himself from her with such violent blows and kicks as to reduce her to the necessity of creeping out of his reach and mingling the groan of bodily suffering with the sob of a breaking heart? . . . I must have been then between five and six years old. I seem to see and hear my poor weeping mother now.

Frederick was undoubtedly aware of Baltimore's slave auctions. As his knowledge of slavery increased, he discussed his own situation with a few trusted people. Some, Douglass recalled, "went so far as to tell me that I ought to run away, and go to the north; that

I should find friends there, and that I would be as free as anybody." The teenager held fast to what they said. "I . . . remembered their words and their advice," he later wrote, "and looked forward to an escape to the north, as a possible means of gaining the liberty for which my heart panted."

CHAPTER TWENTY-FIVE

A Man Is Made

In early 1832, when Frederick was fourteen and had lived with Hugh and Sophia Auld for seven years, his legal owner ordered his return. Since Aaron Anthony's death, the slave had been the property of Lucretia Anthony Auld, the daughter of his original master; but when she died in 1827, he became the property of her widower, Thomas Auld, the brother of Hugh. Thomas subsequently remarried, and he and his second wife, Rowena, decided they wanted Frederick to come work in their home, which was a short distance from where the slave had lived as a young child.

In March 1833, Frederick returned to rural Maryland. Living conditions under Thomas Auld's roof were a far cry from those Frederick had known in Baltimore. He and the several other slaves whom Thomas owned were each allocated eight quarts of cornmeal weekly—roughly four and a half cups per day—and little else. "It was not enough to subsist upon," Douglass remembered. "We were compelled either to beg, or to steal, and we did both."

During the first few months he lived with Thomas and Rowena, Frederick's relationship with his new master became acrimonious. Auld beat him many times for—among other things—accepting food from Rowena's parents, who lived nearby. When these punishments failed to produce the subservience that Thomas wanted, he concluded that life in Baltimore had ruined his slave. In December 1833, the white man decided to send Frederick away *to be broken*.

From the time slavery took hold in North America, masters employed a variety of tactics to keep their human property dutiful and productive. These included constant managerial oversight, physical and psychological intimidation, forced illiteracy, established hierarchies of slaves, and sophisticated reward systems for good behavior. Slave breaking, which relied on physical intimidation and emotional degradation, was one method for creating and maintaining slaves' submission to and respect for their white masters. Owners employed slave breaking for individuals they regarded as insubordinate or likely to flee. (Slave-breaking practices encompassed beating, sexual assault, and—infrequently—public murder of both men and women.)

On January 1, 1834, Auld sent Frederick to live with Edward Covey, a local farmer who had a reputation for successfully breaking recalcitrant young Negroes. A man of modest means, Covey rented a farm nearby, where he hired slaves to work the land, paying lower fees for those he agreed to break.

From the time Frederick arrived, Covey whipped him every week. The teenager's wounds had little time to heal before he was lashed again. But this was not the worst of it. Years later, Frederick remembered that punishing labor was a more powerful means of breaking his spirit than the switch that Covey wielded: "From the dawn of day in the morning, till the darkness was complete in the evening, I was kept hard at work. . . . At certain seasons of the year, we were all kept in the field till eleven and twelve o'clock at night. At these times, Covey would attend us . . . and urge us on with words or blows, as it seemed best to him."

Frederick sank into despondency. "I was somewhat unmanageable when I first went [to Covey's farm]," he remembered, "but a few months of this discipline tamed me. . . . I was broken in body, soul, and spirit. My natural elasticity was crushed, my intellect languished, the disposition to read departed, the cheerful spark that lingered about my eye died; the dark night of slavery closed in upon me; and behold a man transformed into a brute!" For six months, Frederick remained in a deep depression; at times, he considered suicide.

Then, one sweltering summer afternoon, an exchange with Covey kicked off a pivotal chain of events. Frederick was harvesting wheat and collapsed from exhaustion. He dragged himself into the shade, where the slave breaker found him and demanded to know what was going on. When the teenager explained that he had fallen from heatstroke, Covey kicked him and hit him with a hickory slat, telling him to rise. Unable to do so, the slave remained on the ground. At nightfall, the teenager walked the seven miles to Thomas Auld's house, seeking protection and telling his owner that Covey's savage treatment was likely to kill him. Auld dismissed this possibility outright and ordered him to return to the slave breaker the next morning.

At daybreak, Frederick walked back to Covey's farm. As soon as the white man caught sight of the slave, he lunged at him, whip in hand. But Frederick escaped into a nearby thicket. He remained there until the next morning, a Sunday, when the slave breaker, dressed for church, greeted him with uncharacteristic politeness.

On Monday, however, when Covey found the teenager on a barn ladder, the slave breaker tried to tie him up. Frederick evaded the white man by jumping down from the ladder, where he landed sprawled on the stable floor. "Mr. Covey seemed now to think he had me, and could do what he pleased," Douglass recalled. "But at this moment—from whence came the spirit I don't know—I resolved to fight; and, suiting my action to the resolution, I seized Covey hard by the throat; and as I did so, I rose."

The two began to struggle. The black teenager's strength surprised the white man, and Covey asked the slave if he intended to continue resisting. Frederick responded that he'd been used as a brute by the slave breaker for six months and would take no more. The brawl went on. Another slave arrived on the scene, and Covey ordered him to take hold of Frederick. But the black man refused, saying his owner had hired him to do farmwork, not to whip Covey's slaves. Drawn in by the commotion, another slave, a woman, entered the barn. She also refused to obey the white man's orders to help subdue Frederick, and the two slaves watched as the hand-to-hand combat entered its second hour.

Finally, the slave breaker relented, releasing his hold on Frederick. As the two untangled themselves, Covey declared he would not have fought so forcefully if the slave had not been so obstructive. But this, the teenager realized, was just the white man trying to save face. "The truth was," Douglass later wrote, "that he had not whipped me at all [during the struggle]. I considered him as getting entirely the worst end of the bargain; for he had drawn no blood from me, but I had from him." As Frederick understood, the fight with Covey had altered the balance of power between the white and the black man. Covey never again laid his hand on the slave.

In this turning point, in standing up to Edward Covey, Frederick regained his courage and sense of agency. He also stripped away the layers of self-doubt and depression that had piled on in the brutality of his life with the slave breaker. Underneath the coats of emotional varnish, Frederick discovered a stronger, more authentic part of himself. Years later, he recalled the importance of the event: "You have seen how a man was made a slave; you shall see how a slave was made a man."

Frederick's experience with Covey has a valuable lesson for today's leaders. This insight is about reclamation and its relationship to the fears and insecurities we all harbor. How do we move beyond the anxiety and doubts that hold us back, that keep us from being who we want to be, who we were meant to be?

Sometimes we do this through conscious, sustained effort; sometimes we do it through a choice we make in a flash. Frederick did not walk into Covey's barn that hot Monday morning with the intention of wrestling his own demons to the ground by taking on the white man; indeed, he had no idea what would happen when he next met the slave breaker. But when Covey tried to take hold of him, Frederick found something deep within himself—something he had lost access to during the past six months—that ultimately enabled him to move beyond his fear by first *moving into it*. In doing this, the young man regained whom he wanted to be: a braver and more powerful version of himself.

This was not a heroic act. In refusing to obey Covey, Frederick neither acquired superhuman powers nor physically dominated his opponent. Like Lincoln's fighting match with Jack Armstrong three years earlier in New Salem, the bondsman's struggle with the slave breaker ended in a draw. But for Frederick, as for Lincoln, a draw was more than good enough; a draw was, in fact, a victory. The slave had outlasted the self-doubts and self-defeat that he associated with the white man's treatment of him.

Every leader will come face-to-face with his or her darkest doubts. In these moments, the way forward is to move directly into one's fear—to do the thing, address the person, or seek out the information that seems so terrifying. When such a moment has passed—as it did for Frederick when the fight with Covey ended—a leader realizes not only that he or she is still standing, but also that beneath (or beyond) the fear is a more resilient, more courageous self that is waiting to be claimed. Shackleton learned this lesson during the *Endurance* expedition. So, too, we shall see, did Dietrich Bonhoeffer when he was incarcerated in a Gestapo prison. Neither could have done what he did without access to his core strength—the power that lies beyond self-doubt and insecurity.

In late 1834, Frederick's time with Covey ended, and Thomas Auld hired his slave out to a nearby farmer named William Freeland. Conditions at his farm were relatively good. Frederick and the other hands had plenty to eat, and the teenager was never beaten.

Comparing the circumstances at Covey's farm with his current situation, Frederick was struck by how material circumstances shaped the way slaves thought about themselves. "Beat and cuff your slave, keep him hungry and spiritless," Douglass later wrote, "and he will follow the chain of his master like a dog; but, feed and clothe him well,—work him moderately—surround him with physical comfort,—and dreams of freedom intrude. Give him a *bad* master, and he aspires to a *good* master; give him a good master, and he wishes to become his *own* master."

Within a year of arriving at Freeland's farm, Frederick was making plans to run away to the North. He shared his idea with five other slaves, and even though they recognized that huge obstacles lay ahead, all of the men were ready to join him. One hurdle was that they had no reliable information about where they could safely settle. "We had heard of Canada, the real Canaan of the American bondmen,"

Douglass recalled, "simply as a country to which the wild goose and the swan repaired at the end of winter . . . but not as the home of man." They knew little about the geography of Northern states as well. Even Frederick, the best read of the group, had never heard of Massachusetts; he was aware Pennsylvania was a free state, but had no idea how to get there.

A second challenge was making their way through unfamiliar terrain. Carrying little more than a few provisions, the men planned to paddle a stolen canoe seventy miles north to the head of the Chesapeake Bay and then walk to a free state, following the North Star. They realized that fatigue, bad weather, and bounty hunters could all besiege them as they made their way.

The practical difficulties were daunting enough. But the slaves experienced an even greater emotional challenge: intense fear. As they considered their journey north, Douglass recalled, "We saw grim death assuming a variety of horrid shapes." Starvation beckoned in an apparition so severe that, in it, the slaves were forced to eat their own flesh. Other fantasies in the form of stinging scorpions, biting snakes, and attacking wild beasts disturbed their thoughts. Finally, they faced the specter of hired kidnappers finding them, killing some, and capturing the rest. More than once, the men's collective dread became so acute that they considered giving up all plans to flee.

As the proposed day of escape drew near, the anxiety of the would-be fugitives increased, and one slave decided he could not go through with it. The remaining five intended to go, but they never got the chance. On April 1, 1836, several constables, who had been tipped off, rounded up the slaves and marched them at gunpoint fifteen miles to jail.

All five were interrogated. None disclosed the details of their plan, but Frederick stood out as the group's ringleader. Within days, his four companions were released to their owners. But the plan's architect lingered in jail for a week, considering his fate. With no word from Thomas Auld, the slave feared his owner would sell him into the Deep South. "A life of living death, beset with the innumerable horrors of the cotton field and the sugar plantation, seemed to be my doom," he remembered.

Frederick's worst nightmare was well founded; the logical decision for his owner was to sell the insubordinate eighteen-year-old
south. But Thomas Auld did not do this; instead, the white man sent
him back to Baltimore to live again with Hugh and Sophia Auld.
Thomas also promised his slave that he would set him free when he
was twenty-five.

This was the third time that the Auld family had chosen to spare
Frederick the harshness, anonymity, and virtual impossibility of escape
that constituted a slave's life on a large cotton plantation. Three times,
they moved him to Baltimore: first, in 1826, when Lucretia convinced
her father, Aaron Anthony, to send the boy to the city; second, a year
later, when after inheriting Frederick on her father's death, Lucretia
returned the slave to her in-laws in the urban center; and third, in
1836, when Thomas Auld sent him back after his attempted escape.

Given this, it is hard to avoid the conclusion that Thomas Auld,
like his first wife, Lucretia, felt something for the black man whom
he owned. This is not to say that Auld treated his slave well. He did
not. Nonetheless, his choice, like the two preceding it, had a huge
impact on Frederick's life.

Interestingly, the man who became Frederick Douglass, who rose
to fame by telling his life story as a slave, never publicly acknowledged the significance of these three decisions. He also did not talk
extensively about how the experience of slavery varied across different
settings. Being a house servant on a rural plantation was not the same
as being an errand boy in a city. Picking cotton was vastly different
from making shoes in a Georgia village. Slavery had distinct faces,
and all were unjust and immoral, as Douglass said time and time
again. But in his life (and in many others), the finer distinctions of
these experiences—including three seemingly small choices by members of one family—mattered a great deal. It is hard to imagine that
Frederick Douglass would have become one of the most important
leaders of the nineteenth century if he had been born on or sold to
a large plantation in the Deep South.

CHAPTER TWENTY-SIX

Escape to Freedom

In the spring of 1836, Frederick returned to Baltimore. He was older, physically stronger, and more prepossessing than when he had left three years earlier. He was also a quick study, and Hugh Auld found him a job as a caulker's apprentice in a local shipyard. The white man would collect all of the wages the slave earned.

Frederick soon noticed that most of the employees in the shipyard—slaves, free blacks, and whites—worked in relative harmony. But within a few months, this rough compatibility started to disintegrate. Concerned that their bosses wanted to reduce wages or push them out of their jobs to hire slaves or free blacks at lower pay, white workers grew hostile. One day, four white men wielding handspikes, sticks, and rocks attacked Frederick. A crowd of white dockworkers looked on as the group beat the slave until he lay prostrate on the ground. One of the assailants hit him in the head with such force, Douglass remembered, he was certain his eye had burst.

Hugh Auld was outraged, quickly arranging for his slave to work in another shipyard. During the next year, the slave learned to caulk, and each week he turned over his wages—$7.50 to $9—to Auld. In May 1838, the twenty-year-old asked Auld to allow him to move out of the white man's home and into his own lodgings. Under the terms of Frederick's proposal, Auld would save living expenses for the slave; in exchange, the white man would allow him to keep some of his income. At the time, many masters and slaves in Baltimore had similar arrangements. By keeping some of the money he earned, Frederick hoped to save enough to finance a successful escape.

During this time, Frederick met his future wife, Anna Murray. Born in 1813 in Denton, Maryland, near the Delaware border, to parents who had recently been manumitted, she was the eighth of twelve children and the first to be born free. Anna never learned to read, but as a girl, she had developed strong domestic skills; when she moved to Baltimore at age seventeen, she found work as a laundress and housekeeper.

Handsome and statuesque, she caught Frederick's attention in the spring of 1838. Perhaps the two met along the city docks or through mutual friends. However they encountered each other, the couple spent time together that summer and then became engaged. They hoped to have children, a possibility that made it more important that Frederick obtain his freedom—either by Thomas Auld's promised emancipation in what would now be five years, or sooner, by escape. If he chose the latter course, Anna could help. She earned a relatively good income and knew a number of free blacks in Baltimore.

In August 1838, an unexpected conflict with Hugh Auld forced the slave's hand. The confrontation arose when Frederick was two days late turning over his weekly wages to his master. The white man was furious, demanding that his slave come back to live at the Aulds' home and relinquish *all* of his income. "You shall hire your time no longer," Hugh said. "The next thing I shall hear of, will be your running away."

Frederick realized that more than his wages and mobility were now threatened. Going forward, the angry white man was likely to keep an even closer eye on him, and this meant that he had to escape as soon as possible. He and Anna agreed he would try to flee on September 3, 1838, using the money he had saved. According to family lore, Anna also sold her featherbed to help fund his journey. To make his way north, Frederick planned to rely on connections along the Underground Railroad, the informal networks of people, safe houses, small businesses, churches, and other groups dedicated to helping escaping slaves.

Frederick began plotting his trip. He would travel by train and ferry to Wilmington, Delaware, then by steamship to Philadelphia, then by train to New York City. Once he was safe in Manhattan, he would get word to Anna, and she would join him. From there, the couple would travel to Canada or New England.

The slave intended to travel by posing as a free black man; in Maryland and other states, this required documentation, known as free papers, which listed a person's age, height, scars, and other identifying marks. Escaping slaves often borrowed or bought such credentials from other African-Americans who were physically similar. This was a dangerous game: if a slave was caught with a free person's papers, both people would be severely punished. With Anna's help, Frederick obtained the needed documentation from a sailor. These credentials described a man with darker skin than Frederick's, but the slave decided to take his chances. If train conductors or other officials did not look too closely, he would slip by as a free man.

On the appointed morning, Frederick set out from the Aulds' home for the train station. He was dressed like a sailor, with a red shirt, tarpaulin hat, and black cravat around his neck. Fearful that buying a ticket in advance or lingering on the platform would invite attention, Frederick waited until the train was leaving the station to jump on board and take a seat in the "colored" car. As he sat down, he realized how frightened he was: "The heart of no fox or deer, with hungry hounds on his trail in full chase, could have beaten more anxiously or noisily than did mine from the time I left Baltimore till I reached Philadelphia."

Nearly an hour passed before an official asked to see Frederick's papers. "This was a critical moment in the drama," he recalled. "My whole future depended upon the decision of this conductor." The fugitive was careful to appear nonchalant as the white man approached. Rather than produce his papers unprompted as other passengers had, Frederick waited for the attendant to ask for them and then calmly handed them over. The agent took only a passing glance before moving on. The slave had to produce his documentation one more time when he boarded a steamship that ran between Wilmington and Philadelphia. But on this leg of the journey as well, the crewman gave the credentials only a cursory review. From Philadelphia,

Frederick took a train to New York City, arriving there early in the morning on September 4; his nerve-racking journey had taken less than twenty-four hours.

At last, Frederick was in a free state. "No man now had a right to call me his slave or assert mastery over me," he later wrote. "A new world had opened upon me. If life is more than breath and the 'quick round of blood,' I lived more in that one day than in a year of my slave life." The fugitive slave also took stock of the *internal* journey he had made:

> During ten or fifteen years I had been, as it were, dragging a heavy chain which no strength of mine could break; I was not only a slave, but a slave for life. . . . All efforts I had previously made to secure my freedom had not only failed, but had seemed only to rivet my fetters the more firmly, and to render my escape more difficult. Baffled, entangled, and discouraged, I had at times asked myself the question, May not my condition after all be God's work, and ordered for a wise purpose, and if so, Is not submission my duty? A contest had in fact been going on in my mind for a long time, be-tween the clear consciousness of right and the plausible make-shifts of theology and superstition. The one held me an abject slave—a prisoner for life, punished for some transgression in which I had no lot nor part; and the other counseled me to manly endeavor to secure my freedom. This contest was now ended; my chains were broken, and the victory brought me unspeakable joy.

As relieved as he was, Frederick knew he had to remain vigilant. Bounty hunters—black and white—prowled the city streets. He had the name and address of a black man, David Ruggles, who would provide assistance; but without a map of New York, the fugitive had no way to find him. Afraid to ask a stranger for help during his first day in the city, he wandered the streets, passing the night on a wharf. The next day, he was tired, hungry, and more anxious. Within hours, he approached a sailor he hoped was trustworthy. Luck was on the fugitive's side. The seaman invited him to stay the night and took him to meet Ruggles the next day.

From Ruggles's home, Frederick sent for Anna, who arrived a few days later. James W. C. Pennington, a black minister who was also an escaped slave, quickly married the two. The newlyweds decided that New York City was too dangerous a place to live, and they asked David Ruggles for advice. He suggested New Bedford, Massachusetts, a port city on the Atlantic Ocean about forty-five miles south of Boston.

Boasting a population of twelve thousand, New Bedford was known for its relative friendliness toward fugitive slaves. Frederick was likely to find work in one of the city's booming sectors: textiles, shoemaking, commerce, fishing, and, most important, whaling. Frederick and Anna decided to settle there, arriving in early September. They had spent all their money, but they soon met a free black couple, Nathan and Mary Johnson, who offered them a place to stay. Fearing Frederick might be caught, the newlyweds decided to change their surname. Nathan advised against choosing Johnson, as they had originally proposed, explaining that it was the most popular name assumed by runaway slaves in New Bedford. He suggested Douglas after a character from the Sir Walter Scott poem *The Lady of the Lake*. Frederick liked this suggestion, but chose an alternate spelling—Douglass.

As Frederick Douglass walked the streets of his New England home, he was struck by its affluence and refinement: "I had been taught that slavery was the bottom-fact of all wealth. With this foundation idea, I came naturally to the conclusion that poverty must be the general condition of the people of the free States." But this was not what Douglass saw when he surveyed the city's tidy streets, busy shops, and stately homes.

Not only was New Bedford not poor, it was more prosperous than rural Maryland, and even Baltimore. He attributed this difference to what today we call economic innovation—specifically, labor-saving technological change. A dearth of cheap labor, Douglass reasoned, created a need for efficiency; all that he observed about New Bedford industry suggested that business owners understood this. He noticed that everything—from the pumps used to draw water to the self-shutting gates that dotted fences in town—was done "with scrupulous regard to economy, both in regard to men and things, time and strength." This contrasted sharply with what he had experienced in Maryland. "Main strength, unassisted by skill," he observed, "is slavery's method of labor. An old ox, worth eighty dollars, was doing, in New Bedford, what would have required fifteen thousand dollars' worth of human bones and muscles to have performed in a southern port."

Douglass's keen observational skills and subsequent reflection are essential for leaders today. We are often moving so rapidly that we risk missing a great deal of what is going on around us. Some of what we overlook are small details, but these can be important. Some of what we fail to see is larger: a set of connections between seemingly disparate people, a different perspective on a given problem, or a specific occurrence that unlocks a previously hidden solution. The higher the stakes, the more critical it is that leaders slow down, take a deep breath, and scrutinize the bigger stage.

During the fall of 1838 and winter of 1839, Frederick picked up all the part-time work he could find to support himself and Anna, who was now pregnant. He chopped wood, shoveled coal, collected trash, and scrubbed ship cabins. In the spring of 1839, Frederick found a full-time job in a candle factory, and his work life and income became relatively stable. During the next three years, he migrated from the candle factory to a shipyard, then to a brass factory. Steady wages enabled him to provide for his growing family. In June 1839, a daughter, Rosetta, was born; a son, Lewis, followed one year later.

Whatever Douglass was doing, he made time and space for intellectual development. During long hours at the brass factory, for example, he often nailed a newspaper to the post near the bellows he operated so he could read while he pumped the heavy beams. Like Lincoln, who taught himself geometry, grammar, and military strategy, Douglass treated the improvement of his mind as an ongoing project. He did not know exactly how he would use what he was learning, but he was committed to making himself into all he could.

Part of this effort involved seeking out like-minded people. He began attending New Bedford's African Methodist Episcopal (AME) Zion chapel. Led by a fugitive slave, the Reverend Thomas James, the church welcomed black and white congregants alike. It also provided a forum for members to discuss political and social issues, including slavery and the abolition movement. James took a special interest in Douglass, inviting him to serve as a class leader and lay preacher. In both these roles, the fugitive slave honed the public-speaking skills he had begun to develop as a boy reciting speeches from *The Columbian Orator.*

Sometime in the spring of 1839, he got his hands on a copy of the *Liberator*, the antislavery newspaper published in Boston by William Lloyd Garrison. It was an important moment. "*The Liberator* was a paper after my own heart," Douglass remembered. "It detested slavery—exposed hypocrisy and wickedness in high places—made no truce with the traffickers in the bodies and souls of men; it preached human brotherhood, denounced oppression, and, with all the solemnity of God's word, demanded the complete emancipation of my race."

When Douglass began reading the newspaper, Garrison had been publishing it for almost a decade. In 1839, the white abolitionist was thirty-four and famous for his blazing antislavery rhetoric and persistent calls for both immediate manumission and black enfranchisement. In addition to running his newspaper, Garrison had helped establish the American Anti-Slavery Society and what became the Massachusetts Anti-Slavery Society. By the mid-1830s, the latter organization had scores of affiliated groups and thousands of members. Many of these were women, some of whom became nationally known activists in their own right. For example, Harriet Tubman, Elizabeth Cady Stanton, Lucretia Mott, and Susan B. Anthony all answered Garrison's call to work for immediate emancipation. Tubman also served as a conductor on the Underground Railroad and, like the other three, went on to fight for women's rights. They were a few of the thousands of women who played vital roles in the abolition movement—speaking out, writing pamphlets and newspapers, raising money, organizing petition drives, and recruiting new members.

Once Douglass became aware of the abolition movement, he began attending antislavery meetings in New Bedford. At a gathering in March 1839, for example, he spoke out against the colonization of American slaves, asserting that they shouldn't be sent to Africa and should instead be set free to build lives in the United States. The

Liberator took notice, reporting his name and the arguments he made. During the next two years, Douglass continued to attack slavery; he also met a number of influential reformers from around New England.

By early 1841, Frederick and Anna had begun to build an independent, middle-class life. They had come a long way since their first meeting in 1838, when Frederick was a slave and Anna a laundress. But Douglass yearned for more, and this created distance between him and his wife. While his public reputation began to grow, Anna immersed herself in her children and home. She attended church with Frederick, but she avoided the social engagements and political activity he thrived on. In hindsight, this was hardly unusual. Most nineteenth-century women dedicated the lion's share of their time and energy to the domestic realm.

But in this role, Anna Douglass made a vital contribution to her husband's leadership. She never learned to read, so she couldn't play a part in his writing. But she knew what he did. She believed in him and cared for him in the countless small, loving, and indispensable ways women do. As Frederick's career expanded, she made sure their house was a solid base: comfortable, welcoming, and dependable. She committed even more attention to making sure their children were well looked after. Taken together, Anna's efforts were essential to Frederick's ability to focus on achieving his mission, while putting other concerns aside. Courageous leaders determined to make a big, worthy impact are often single-minded. Many live and breathe the cause they've embraced. (Indeed, such investment is usually essential to fulfilling their purpose.) This means that leaders like Douglass—and as we shall see, Bonhoeffer and Carson—need people around them who can facilitate their single-mindedness.

We do not know whether Douglass acknowledged the importance of his wife's support. The scanty clues that remain suggest it is unlikely. But this doesn't diminish all that Anna did to help bring her husband's gifts and determination to the world. Someone as driven, angry, and committed as Frederick Douglass became could not have channeled this energy into fighting slavery as effectively as he did without the solid foundation provided by Anna Douglass.

CHAPTER TWENTY-SEVEN

A Voice Is Heard

In 1841, Douglass met the prominent abolitionist William C. Coffin. A friend of Garrison's, Coffin worked as a kind of scout for the Massachusetts Anti-Slavery Society, recruiting financial supporters and potential lecturers. After hearing Douglass speak at a New Bedford meeting, Coffin asked him to attend the group's annual convention on Nantucket Island.

In mid-August, Douglass traveled to Nantucket. Coffin greeted him, inviting him to address the assembly. The black man assented, and on the scheduled day, in front of a large crowd, he rose to speak. He began nervously, stammering out his first sentences. But soon he settled, and his strong, deep voice found its natural cadence as he told the story of his life.

No record has survived of precisely what Douglass said. But journalists who were present described an audience that was amazed by the narrative and the man who relayed it. Douglass "spoke with great power," an antislavery newspaper reported. "Flinty hearts were pierced, and cold ones melted by his eloquence. Our best pleaders for the slave held their breath for fear of interrupting him."

After he finished, Garrison took the podium, praising the speech and rallying the crowd into a cheer: "Have we been listening to a thing, a [personal] chattel, or a man?"

"A man! A man!" the group shouted back.

"Shall such a man be held a slave in a Christian land?"

"No! No! No!" the assembly yelled.

After the meeting, John Collins, executive director of the Massachusetts Anti-Slavery Society, approached Douglass and offered him a job as a traveling lecturer for the group. The full-time position, Collins explained, would pay $680 a year.

This was more than Douglass had ever earned, but he saw even greater potential benefits to the offer. As a black spokesman for the abolition movement, he would be on the front lines, meeting hundreds of people as he tried to build broad support for universal emancipation. The position would also give him a chance to lecture across the North, providing a much bigger platform than he had in New Bedford. Finally, becoming a lecturer for Garrison's organization would mean using his life story as an instrument of change, a weapon he could wield in the fight against slavery.

As appealing as the opportunity was, Douglass realized its serious risks. For one thing, he worried that his speaking skills might not be good enough; Garrison was mesmerizing before an audience, and other Anti-Slavery Society lecturers were also talented. For another, a larger public profile would put the fugitive in danger of recapture. (In 1841, Douglass was still a slave; his freedom would not be purchased and manumission papers filed until 1846.) Although Collins assured Douglass that his true identity would remain secret, no escaped slave had served in this capacity before. Of all that he had achieved since he came North, freedom was the one thing he could not afford to lose.

Even in the face of these hazards, he knew he could contribute to Garrison's efforts. Douglass and his story would refute the arguments made by proponents of slavery that African-Americans held in bondage were inherently suited to their lot and otherwise unable to support themselves. (These same apologists described white masters as benevolent and dedicated to the well-being of their slaves.) As important, abolition leaders needed a credible, moving account of slavery to win new converts, and no one currently on the Society's lecture circuit had such experience. Douglass decided to take the job.

He threw himself into his new role, traveling constantly and speaking before crowds gathered in churches, barns, and taverns across New England. Tall, handsome, and athletic, he cut a powerful figure on the podium. His eyes flashed as he spoke. His language was commanding. His energy was tightly coiled like that of a racehorse restive in the starting gate.

Audiences were captivated. "This is an extraordinary man," noted a New Hampshire newspaper editor. "He was cut out for a hero. . . . Let the South congratulate herself that he is a fugitive. It would not have been safe for her if he had remained about the plantation a year or two longer." Remembering Douglass's presence on the platform, the women's rights activist Elizabeth Cady Stanton likened him to "an African prince, majestic in his wrath," as he "graphically described the bitterness of slavery." How, she asked herself, had anyone

> ever tried to subjugate a being with such talents intensified with the love of liberty. Around him sat the great antislavery orators of the day, earnestly watching the effect of his eloquence on that immense audience, that laughed and wept by turns, completely carried away by the wondrous gifts of his pathos and humor. On this occasion, all the other speakers seemed tame after Frederick Douglass.

As Douglass told his story again and again, he also endorsed several of Garrison's central ideas. One of these was his embrace of moral suasion as the most effective weapon against slavery. Although Garrison and his followers hated the institution, they did not support the use of armed force to eradicate it. Instead, they were confident slavery could be peacefully abolished by persuading Americans to demand its end on ethical grounds. The winning of these hearts and minds, Garrison and his supporters believed, would come about by exposing as many people as possible to the widespread evils of slavery.

Another important idea championed by Garrison was his denunciation of the US Constitution as fundamentally pro-slavery. His argument rested on Article 1, Section 2—also known as the Three-Fifths Compromise—which counted the slave population as three-fifths of its actual total for the purpose of determining congressional representation and votes in the Electoral College. Garrison claimed that by counting black Americans as three-fifths of their total, this

clause effectively institutionalized slavery's legitimacy, safeguarded
it into perpetuity, and protected slaveholders' interests.

Garrison's rejection of the Constitution led him and his followers
to deprecate political activity as an avenue to abolishing slavery.
They asserted that all such action, because it unfolded within the
framework of a document they regarded as pro-slavery, was inherently corrupt. Some Garrisonians went so far as to argue that if the
Constitution could not be altered or abandoned, the Northern states
should give up on the Union, secede from it, and found their own
country untarnished by slavery.

After a few months on the lecture circuit, Douglass found himself wanting to move beyond his own story and discuss his broader
view of slavery. He understood that the long arm of the institution
stretched beyond the states where it was legal. Both Northerners
and Southerners, he argued, were entangled in the web of economic
and social relations that constituted the slave system. From New
England textile producers to Philadelphia merchants exporting
sugarcane to tobacco smokers all over the country, huge numbers
of Americans in the 1840s depended on the labor of 2.5 million
enslaved blacks. The majority of these men, women, and children
belonged to a small number of white Southerners who each owned
more than one hundred slaves on their respective plantations. Since
the country's founding, Douglass argued, these white Americans
and the larger slave system from which they and many other whites
benefited had exerted enormous political influence. He called this influence the Slave Power.

Douglass contended that this Power as well as slavery itself were
held in place by deep-seated racial discrimination. He spoke about
the prejudice he himself often encountered, including being refused
a well-paid job as a caulker in New Bedford because he was black
and being forcibly removed from a first-class train car in which he
had been traveling with a white colleague. People in Massachusetts,
Douglass explained to an audience,

> will say they like colored men as well as any other, *but in their
> proper place!* They assign us that place; they don't let us do it

for ourselves, nor will they allow us a voice in the decision. They will not allow that we have a head to think, and a heart to feel, and a soul to aspire. They treat us not as men, but as dogs. . . . That's the way we are liked. You degrade us, and then ask why we are degraded—you shut our mouths, and then ask why we don't speak—you close your colleges and seminaries against us, and then ask why we don't know more.

As the fugitive slave expanded his message, Massachusetts Anti-Slavery Society leaders became concerned. They could not deny that Douglass was attracting big crowds and broadening awareness of the organization, but officials worried he was speaking too brashly and perhaps too broadly. They feared that their popular speaker would alienate potential white supporters, who did not like thinking of themselves as prejudiced. "Give us the facts," Collins instructed him. "We will take care of the philosophy." Leaders also fretted that the black man appeared *too* intelligent and well spoken. "People won't believe you ever were a slave, Frederick, if you keep on this way," counseled another organizer. "Better have a little of the plantation speech than not," Collins added.

Douglass chose not to follow their advice. Perhaps his increasing confidence as a lecturer made it difficult for him to do what his older colleagues wanted. Perhaps he realized that ending slavery demanded a fuller exposition of its effects than his life story alone could offer. "New views of the subject were being presented to my mind," he remembered. "It did not entirely satisfy me to *narrate* wrongs; I felt like *denouncing* them. I could not always curb my moral indignation for the perpetrators of slave-holding villainy long enough for a circumstantial statement of the facts." Perhaps most important, as he later wrote, "I was growing and needed room."

Despite Douglass's certainty that he was doing the right thing for the cause, the fears of antislavery leaders soon became reality. Detractors accused the fugitive slave of being an impostor. Some critics claimed he was too smart to have been a bondman. Others pointed to his having refused to name his former master or the people who had helped him escape. By 1844, three years after Douglass began lecturing for the Massachusetts Anti-Slavery Society, doubt had spilled into nearly every venue in which he spoke.

Understanding that his credibility and potential impact were at risk, he decided to write an autobiography. He planned to include the places he had lived, the masters and overseers under whom he had served, and the singular details of the cruelties he had experienced and witnessed. "By such a revelation of facts as could not be made by any other than a genuine fugitive," Douglass explained, "I would dispel all doubt."

This was no small resolution. Publishing such a book jeopardized Douglass's and his family's safety, since his owner, Thomas Auld, could easily find him. The fugitive slave knew that after the autobiography came out, he would have to live as a hunted man. Despite these dangers, Douglass decided to go ahead. Between late 1844 and early 1845, he wrote the book, titling it *Narrative of the Life of Frederick Douglass, an American Slave.*

In 125 pages, the former bondman recounted the journey he had made since his birth in 1818 to the moment he took the podium at the Nantucket convention in August 1841. He told his readers about being permanently separated from his mother and grandmother, about wearing linen tow shirts during the dead of winter, and about gulping cornmeal mush out of a trough like a pig. He told them about Hugh and Sophia Auld, and his life in Baltimore. He wrote about Thomas Auld's sending him off to Edward Covey to be broken. He also sketched the outline of his escape, including the bits of luck and moments of dread. His chronicle of both human strength and man-made injustice has commanded widespread interest all the way into our own time. "Douglass's personal story," historian David Blight has written, "like American history itself, is both inspiring and terrible."

In May 1845, the Massachusetts Anti-Slavery Society published the *Narrative*. It quickly became a bestseller, greatly expanding its author's reputation at home and abroad. (By 1851, five years after publication, the book had sold more than thirty thousand copies in the United States.) When Thomas and Hugh Auld read the book, they were furious. One brother accused Douglass of lying; the other swore to recapture him and "place him in the cotton fields of the South."

Concerned for his safety, Douglass's supporters arranged for him to go on a speaking tour in Great Britain. They also hoped he could capitalize on British interest in the *Narrative* and on the country's long-standing antislavery movement.

Weeks after the book's publication, Douglass set sail for Liverpool, while Anna remained home with the children. Once the black orator arrived in the United Kingdom, he embarked on a hectic lecture schedule, speaking in Dublin, Belfast, Birmingham, London, Edinburgh, Glasgow, and other cities. Everywhere he went, British audiences flocked to see him; overnight, he became a celebrity. Douglass enjoyed his newfound fame, not only on the lecture circuit, but also in the scores of meetings he had with prominent figures. More than a few of these people urged him to break from Garrison and create his own antislavery platform, and some offered financial and logistical support. In 1846, for example, John Bright, a statesman and social reformer, donated money to help purchase Douglass's manumission from Thomas Auld.

Many of these supporters were white women. As in the United States, the abolition movement and the struggle for women's rights converged in the United Kingdom, with female leaders playing noteworthy roles in both. Among the women Douglass met in Britain was Ellen Richardson, a philanthropist who helped American fugitive slaves resettle in her country. He also came to know Ellen's sister-in-law, the writer Anna Richardson, who founded the Ladies Free Produce Association, which boycotted agricultural goods produced by slave labor. In late 1846, the Richardsons introduced Douglass to thirty-six-year-old Julia Griffiths. The daughter and sister of prominent abolitionists, Griffiths was intelligent, articulate, and energetic. She was impressed with Douglass, and he with her, sparking a friendship based on their shared commitment to ending slavery in America. Not long after their first meeting, Griffiths promised to do whatever she could to help him.

Practical assistance was not all that British abolitionists offered Douglass. Directly and indirectly, these men and women taught him three important lessons. First, unlike Garrison and his followers, these crusaders had worked within the British political system to overturn slavery. That activists had used Parliament, the courts, and churches to eradicate the institution had a lasting impact on Douglass. Second, his experience with British abolitionists drove home the power of voice—both written and spoken—in effecting political and social change. Everywhere he went, men and women praised the *Narrative*, not only as an excavation of the evils that Douglass had known, but also as a tool of disruption that American and British citizens could use in the fight to destroy slavery. Acclaim for his autobiography was so widespread that an Irish publisher brought out two editions of the book while its author was in the United Kingdom. (By 1851, the *Narrative* had gone through nine editions in that country.)

Finally, abolitionists and other British citizens treated Douglass as an equal. One of the most striking features of the United Kingdom, the black reformer wrote Garrison, "has been a total absence of all manifestations of prejudice against me, on account of my color." Douglass said that he moved in public places without experiencing the slightest hint "of that hateful and vulgar feeling against me. I find myself not treated as a *color*, but as a *man*—not as a thing, but as a child of the common Father of us all." In many circles, the American activist was accorded a deference that was new to him. He became known, historian Nathan Huggins has written, "as a man whose brilliance and imagination could reshape issues." Such experiences nourished Douglass's self-respect, and this, in turn, helped fuel the next stage of his journey.

CHAPTER TWENTY-EIGHT

The *North Star*

In April 1847, Douglass returned to America a free man. Garrison, his colleague Wendell Phillips, and other New England abolitionists greeted Douglass warmly. They were glad to have their emissary back from his successful tour, and within weeks he was back out on the lecture circuit. In contrast to his experience three years earlier, no one attacked him as an impostor. The former slave was now a well-known author; in places such as Philadelphia and Buffalo, crowds greeted him with applause and shouts of approval. At a May abolitionist meeting in New York, where he shared the podium with Garrison, the audience clamored to hear from the returning hero, interrupting the older man's speech, chanting, "Douglass, Douglass."

Within months of coming back to America, the black reformer decided to leave Garrison and the Massachusetts Anti-Slavery Society and strike out on his own. He intended to start a weekly antislavery newspaper, one that would also take up race, discrimination, and women's rights. The publication would be open, he declared, to "all measures and topics of a moral and humane character, which may serve to enlighten, improve, and elevate mankind." In addition to being a mouthpiece for his ideas, the newspaper would supply compelling evidence, Douglass explained, "that the Negro was too much of a man to be held a chattel."

When he told Garrison and Phillips about his plans, they advised against them. Publishing a newspaper, the two argued, was financially difficult. Indeed, in 1847, no antislavery publication earned enough revenue to cover production costs; each depended on donations to stay in business. The white activists also worried that Douglass's paper might dilute support for existing publications, including the *Liberator*. Finally, Garrison and Phillips claimed that Douglass would have less influence as an editor than he would as a traveling lecturer for their organization. In July 1847, Garrison took to his newspaper to voice his objections:

> With such powers of oratory, and so few lecturers in the field where so many are needed, it seems to us as clear as the noon-day sun, that it would be no gain, but rather a loss, to the anti-slavery cause, to have [Douglass] withdrawn . . . from the work of popular agitation, by assuming the cares, drudgery and perplexities of a publishing life.

Underneath the white abolitionist's concern that Douglass would build a rival organization lay Garrison's anger and hurt. The African-American he'd done so much to encourage was running away with himself and forging his own path. These actions, Garrison wrote his wife, were "impulsive, inconsiderate, and highly inconsistent." Douglass's conduct, the white man continued, "grieves me to the heart." From this point, the two men rarely spoke.

Many years later, the black abolitionist expressed regret that his decision had offended Garrison and his followers. No doubt Douglass appreciated their reasons for wanting him to remain within the fold of the Massachusetts Anti-Slavery Society. But he needed his independence, and this trumped everything else. Possibly this need was rooted in a quest for fame. Like Shackleton, Douglass enjoyed being known as a pathbreaker; perhaps he believed that he could only fully achieve the renown he sought by going it alone. Perhaps Douglass realized as well that to do as much as he could in the fight against slavery, he had to leave some predictability behind. He understood he would face financial, practical, and political obstacles as he tried to build his own abolitionist base, and he could not be sure that he and his enterprise would gain any momentum, let alone flourish. Despite such risks, Douglass took a leap of faith—from the security of well-known terrain onto uncharted, but potentially more fertile, ground.

To put some distance between himself and the Massachusetts Anti-Slavery Society, the activist moved to Rochester, New York. The city was home to a thriving abolitionist community; and Douglass had met some of its most prominent members; and in 1847, several of these men and women offered to help him. One couple, for example, invited him to stay with them until he found a permanent residence. Other antislavery leaders promised their assistance when he brought out the first issue of his paper.

On December 3, 1847, he did just that. He called the publication the *North Star* after the beacon that escaping slaves used to guide them to freedom. The weekly serial included antislavery speeches, news from recent meetings, advertisements, literary pieces, and editorials written primarily by Douglass.

The *North Star* was well received, but within months it ran into financial trouble. Operating costs exceeded subscription revenues, and the organization quickly used up all its start-up capital. To keep the newspaper going, Douglass took on paid speaking engagements. But these exhausted him and kept him from his writing. In February 1848, he bought a house for his family and moved Anna and the children to Rochester; shortly after, however, Douglass had to mortgage the property to raise money for the paper.

Two people came to his aid. One was Gerrit Smith, a white philanthropist and resident of nearby Peterboro, New York. Smith was a committed abolitionist who had spent some of his inheritance supporting the *Liberator* and a number of antislavery societies. (He'd also donated 120,000 acres of land near Lake Placid, New York, to a thousand black Americans in the hope they would establish a self-sufficient community there.) Impressed with early editions of the *North Star*, Smith reached out to Douglass, offering financial and other assistance.

The second supporter was Julia Griffiths, whom the black abolitionist had met in Britain. When Douglass wrote her about his paper's difficulties, she moved from England to Rochester to help; beginning in mid-1848, Griffiths assumed control of the *North Star*'s finances and administration. One of the first things she did was to raise money by contacting potential donors, organizing events, and launching postal campaigns. She also sold advertising and oversaw the newspaper's production schedule. Her efforts quickly made a difference. "In a single year by her energetic and effective management," Douglass wrote, Miss Griffiths "enabled me to extend the circulation of my paper from 2,000 to 4,000 copies, pay off the debts and lift the mortgage from my house. . . . She seemed to rise with every emergency, and her resources appeared inexhaustible."

Griffiths did more than keep the newspaper going. She also became a vital source of literary direction and personal support for Douglass during the seven years they worked together. As Huggins has written, Griffiths "helped him with grammar, syntax, and editorial work. While he had become a master of oratory, being self-taught he naturally remained unsure of written style [including spelling]. She gave him the assurance he needed. She guided his continuing education, often reading aloud to him from the classics and the canon of English literature." As Douglass came to rely more heavily on Griffiths's help, she also offered her friendship, encouraging him in moments of doubt and applauding his successes. "The image of Frederick Douglass as a strong, even arrogant, personality," David Blight has written, "who molded his own destiny has been hard for biographers to resist, but it must be tempered with the knowledge that during the crucial period of his emergence as an independent thinker (1848–1855) he leaned on Julia Griffiths, his highly skilled, fiercely loyal cohort."

By the early 1850s, Frederick Douglass was on solid ground. The *North Star* was financially and operationally viable. His domestic life was also stable. He and Anna now had five children—the last, Annie, had been born in 1849—and the family was settled into a comfortable nine-room, two-story brick house with a small yard. Their home was close to the newspaper office, and the children often joined their father at work, helping him with small chores. On summer evenings, the Douglasses gathered on their front lawn; Anna played the violin and Frederick led the children in rounds of hymns. When neighbors congregated to hear the music making, they called out requests, and the family obliged, offering up tunes such as "My Old Kentucky Home."

In the 1850s, Douglass continued to publish his newspaper and speak out against slavery. For months each year, he took to the lecture circuit, rallying crowds at abolition meetings, delivering speeches across the North, and sharing the podium with other reformers, including women's rights activists. (In 1848, for example, Douglass stood as the only male delegate to the first women's rights convention, held at Seneca Falls, New York.)

In addition to his writing and speaking, Douglass also helped the Underground Railroad. This series of local networks, safe houses, churches, and agents helped escaping slaves make their way northward to freedom. Both blacks and whites served as "agents" and "superintendents" along the network, guiding and protecting escaping slaves, providing information on the next "station," offering food and shelter, and alerting fugitives to the presence of slave patrols. When possible, fleeing slaves traveled in pairs, keeping to footpaths and byways. They often hid in cellars, remote farmhouses, or haylofts until it was safe for them to continue on. When they reached a Northern city, they sought out an agent on the Railroad—as Frederick Bailey had when he arrived in New York in 1838—who could help them resettle or move to another location.

During the thirty years before the Civil War, thousands of black Americans escaped from slavery. Modern-day estimates of how many are notoriously slippery; historian Eric Foner has put the number at between 30,000 and 150,000. Measured against a total slave population of 4 million in 1860, this was a small percentage. Still, the Underground Railroad stood as a powerful symbol of the spirit of freedom—as well as effective resistance—for both African-Americans and white abolitionists.

Rochester was the last stop along the Underground Railroad before Canada. From 1847, when Douglass arrived in the city, he devoted energy and time to assisting fugitive slaves. He and Anna provided them with food, clothes, and advice, offering many lodging in their home. In the morning, Frederick often arrived at work to find weary travelers waiting for him on his office doorstep. Historian Benjamin

Quarles has calculated that between 1847 and the end of the Civil War, Douglass helped more than four hundred slaves to freedom. "I can say I never did more congenial, attractive, fascinating, and satisfactory work," the abolitionist remembered. "True, as a means of destroying slavery, it was like an attempt to bail out the ocean with a teaspoon, but the thought that there was *one* less slave, and one more freeman . . . brought to my heart unspeakable joy."

Douglass's work on the Underground Railroad led directly into his protest against the Fugitive Slave Act. Enacted in 1850, the law was part of a larger legislative compromise that allowed California to enter the Union as a free state; in exchange, slaveholding states obtained a set of nationwide regulations that required private citizens to help recover fugitive slaves, established a rough bounty system to locate them, and denied these black Americans the right to a trial by jury.

Douglass and other abolitionists were enraged, asserting that the new law turned ordinary citizens into slave hunters and effectively made every state a slave state. "In glaring violation of justice," Douglass told an audience, "in shameless disregard of the forms of administering law, in cunning arrangement to entrap the defenceless [*sic*], and in diabolical intent this Fugitive Slave Law stands alone in the annals of tyrannical legislation." Some of his attacks were more aggressive. "The only way to make the Fugitive Slave Law a dead letter," Douglass declared in 1852, "is to make half a dozen or more dead kidnappers. . . . [This] would cool the ardor of Southern gentlemen, and keep their rapacity in check." Less publicly, the black activist worked to raise funds to support escaping slaves and defend private citizens accused of harboring them.

Douglass's response to the new law was part of a broader shift in his thinking about slavery. In the early 1850s, he knew that the institution was expanding geographically, and that the Slave Power was claiming greater authority in the nation's economy and politics. This realization led to another: moral suasion—a strategy that he, Garrison, and other abolition leaders had long endorsed—would not be nearly enough to eradicate slavery. Convincing white Americans in the South and the North to recognize the inherent immorality of human bondage, Douglass concluded, was no match for a system as entrenched as slavery had become. The time for ethical discourse had passed. Destroying the slave system was going to demand a bigger, more difficult, and potentially more violent struggle than he and many reformers had previously championed.

The black leader revised his thinking about other aspects of Garrison's platform as well, including the white abolitionist's condemnation of the Constitution. Perhaps, Douglass reasoned, the Constitution was not a fundamentally pro-slavery document, as his former mentor had long maintained. Perhaps, Douglass theorized, by not mentioning slavery—which the founding fathers understood was at odds with the principles of the republic—the authors of the Constitution intended to create what Douglass called a "permanent liberty document." It was, he determined after considerable reflection, ultimately antislavery.

By the early 1850s, the black leader had arrived at a critical juncture. Once he had decided that the Constitution was an antislavery document, several things became clear. One was that the fight to end slavery had to unfold within the *existing* political system as governed by that founding document. Legal action, legislation, and the electoral process, Douglass concluded, were all vital tools in this fight. Also evident was that the struggle had to involve the entire country—free *and* slave states. The black reformer, like virtually all effective leaders, nurtured a pragmatic streak. He never lost sight of the motivating idealism behind the struggle for universal emancipation. But he recognized that achieving such an end would demand every practical weapon and constituency that he and his supporters could mobilize. From this vantage point, the black abolitionist reasoned, the Northern states had no need to secede from the Union, as some of Garrison's followers claimed. The emergence of these views on the most effective ways to end slavery marked Douglass's definitive break from the famous white abolitionist.

The black reformer kept digging. Like Lincoln, who was also trying to make sense of slavery's expansion in the 1850s, Douglass looked back to the nation's history for understanding and guidance. How, in a country founded on ensuring every American's right to life, liberty, and the pursuit of happiness, had this institution—legalized human bondage—been allowed to exist? How had it been permitted to continue and expand? In an 1852 lecture, Douglass took up these questions. Invited by the Rochester Ladies Anti-Slavery Society to give an Independence Day oration, he attacked the duplicity that lay at the core of the American experiment. What, he asked, did the Fourth of July mean to the slave:

> I answer; a day that reveals to him, more than all other days in the year, the gross injustice and cruelty to which he is the constant victim. To him, your celebration is a sham; your boasted liberty, an unholy license; your national greatness, swelling vanity; your sounds of rejoicing are empty and heartless; your denunciation of tyrants, brass fronted impudence; your shouts of liberty and equality, hollow mockery; your prayers and hymns, your sermons and thanksgivings, with all your religious parade and solemnity, are, to Him, mere bombast, fraud, deception, impiety, and hypocrisy—a thin veil to cover up crimes which would disgrace a nation of savages. There is not a nation on earth guilty of practices more shocking and bloody than are the people of the United States, at this very hour.

Douglass's anger rippled throughout the speech. He railed against the growing slave trade, the Fugitive Slave Law, and churches across the country for allowing—and in some cases, supporting—slavery. He contrasted political and religious institutions in his home country with those in the United Kingdom. In the eyes of British citizens, American slavery was an ethical and political abomination. The existence of the institution, Douglass argued

> brands your republicanism as a sham, your humanity as a base pretense, and your Christianity as a lie. It destroys your moral power abroad: it corrupts your politicians at home. . . . It fetters your progress; it is the enemy of improvement; the deadly foe of education; it fosters pride; it breeds insolence . . . it is a curse to the earth that supports it; and yet you cling to it as if it were the sheet anchor of all your hopes.

As appalling as slavery was, Douglass declared, the fight to end it was ultimately winnable. But Americans must prepare themselves. This crusade would be difficult; it would demand tremendous popular momentum and the collective will to do what was necessary, no matter how disruptive. "For it is not light that is needed," he insisted,

> but fire; it is not the gentle shower, but thunder. We need the storm, the whirlwind, and the earthquake. The feeling of the nation must be quickened; the conscience of the nation must be roused; the propriety of the nation must be startled; the hypocrisy of the nation must be exposed; and its crimes against God and man must be proclaimed and denounced.

For Douglass, the way forward was clear. Slavery had to be extinguished—by any and all available means. Nothing short of this could restore the country to its original purpose. Almost ten years before Lincoln issued the Emancipation Proclamation and eleven years before he delivered the Gettysburg Address, the black leader understood that the battle to eliminate slavery was absolutely unavoidable and that it would define the nation's future.

Douglass spent the next fifteen years leading from the base he created in the early 1850s. In his intellectual foundation, the animating principles of the United States were antithetical to slavery; the institution's corrosive effects had to constantly be brought to the forefront of public consciousness; the contest to eradicate slavery had to occur within the existing political system; and he and other abolitionists had to lead the charge using any tools at their disposal.

Born of strategic practicality, keen vision, a burning sense of mission, and his experience as a narrator of slavery, this foundation was vital to Douglass's leadership. He intuitively understood, as we must today, that leaders need to construct a reinforced base to support all that they are going to do. What are the most important pillars of your thinking about a vital issue? Why are you invested in this particular problem? What do you hope to achieve as you delve into it, and what is your best guess about how you will do this? The answers to these questions are vital not only to your actions going forward, but also to how you sustain your commitment when you run into obstacles and setbacks.

Douglass recognized that to make a big impact, he had to create his own moral, intellectual, and emotional infrastructure. This was thorny, complicated work. We can imagine it as a series of conversations he had with himself as he considered how he might affect broader events. These internal discussions formed the cornerstone of Douglass's leadership, helping him make day-to-day choices, communicate his mission, and navigate through moments of doubt and despair. All individuals who aspire to lead effectively must build their own foundation.

CHAPTER TWENTY-NINE

All His Powers

As Douglass honed his ideas about slavery, the abolition movement in the United States was gathering force. This struggle was not new; it dated back to the mid-1600s, when slavery first took hold in the British colonies in North America. By the time of the Revolution, ministers, politicians, slaves, free blacks, and others were protesting the existence of bondage in a nation founded on individual liberty. Some of these efforts bore fruit: in the thirty years after the Declaration of Independence was signed, for example, several Northern states outlawed slavery.

Despite this progress, the institution grew rapidly during the early nineteenth century, and the antislavery struggle continued. This effort encompassed a range of people, including Elizabeth Margaret Chandler, a Philadelphia Quaker, who, in the 1820s, lobbied other women to oppose slavery, and the Virginia slave Nat Turner, who, in 1831, led an armed slave rebellion. These individuals and many others, as historian Manisha Sinha has written, helped set the stage for a larger, more powerful movement that arose in the three decades before the Civil War. The 1830s and 1840s, for instance, witnessed the emergence of a number of local, state, and national organizations committed to ending slavery. The majority of these were dedicated abolition groups, such as the American Anti-Slavery Society and the American and Foreign Anti-Slavery Society.

Committed activists, such as Garrison and Gerrit Smith, led many of these organizations. But the contest to end slavery also involved elite politicians, such as US senators William Seward of New York and Salmon Chase of Ohio; social reformers such as Henry Ward Beecher and his sister, the novelist Harriet Beecher Stowe; and perhaps most important, many African-American crusaders, including Sojourner Truth, an escaped slave and women's rights activist, and James W. C. Pennington, who fled slavery and became a minister, writer, and orator.

By 1850, abolitionists were better-organized, larger in numbers, and tactically more sophisticated than their predecessors, but they had not come close to achieving their goal. At the century's midpoint, slavery stretched from Maryland to Tennessee, from Florida to Texas; more than 3 million Americans belonged to other Americans. Between 1850 and 1860, the market price of men, women, and children held in bondage doubled, and the personal assets of slave owners rose accordingly. On the eve of the Civil War, slaves accounted for half of Southern wealth.

During the 1850s, a series of larger events effectively split the country in two—with pro-slavery sentiment dominating the South and antislavery opinion ruling the North. Amid mounting political tensions, abolitionists worked to advance their cause. Conveyed in speeches, books, and newspapers, their message played a pivotal role in shaping Northern public opinion. Douglass emerged as one of the leading abolitionists and the nation's most famous African-American.

In 1854, he was outraged by the Kansas-Nebraska Act. Approved by Congress in May, the law repealed the Missouri Compromise of 1820, which had outlawed slavery in all Western lands north of the latitude 36°30' (except for the slave state of Missouri). The 1854 legislation also mandated that a huge Western territory be organized into two tracts, Kansas and Nebraska, and that these lands be open to settlers who would determine the legality of slavery by local ballot.

Douglass spoke out against the new act, attacking the repeal of the Missouri Compromise and the notion that popular sovereignty was an honorable means of deciding the fate of black Americans in Western lands. "The only intelligible principle on which popular sovereignty is founded," Douglass told an audience in late 1854, is contained in the Declaration of Independence: "We hold these truths to be self-evident, that all men are created equal and are endowed by their Creator with the right of life, liberty and the pursuit of happiness." The right of each man to life, liberty, and the pursuit of happiness, he continued, "is the basis of all social and political right, and, therefore, how brass-fronted and shameless is that impudence, which while it aims to rob men of their liberty, and to deprive them of the right to the pursuit of happiness—screams itself hoarse to the words of popular sovereignty."

Douglass was far from alone in his anger. Northern reformers, newspaper editors, and ordinary citizens attacked the Kansas-Nebraska Act as a victory for Southern efforts to extend slavery across the country. Many critics of the legislation predicted—accurately—that violent conflict would break out in the Western territories between pro- and antislavery forces.

Simultaneously, the two major political parties, the Democrats and the Whigs, each fractured. The Democrats split into three groups, two of which supported slavery's expansion, and one of which condemned it. The Whig Party unraveled, within a few years, it would cease to exist.

Douglass welcomed the partisan upheaval, hoping that in the vacuum created by the political fallout of the Kansas-Nebraska Act, a party would arise that was dedicated to universal emancipation. But this did not come to pass; instead, Northern leaders from different ranks formed the Republican Party, a coalition organized to oppose slavery's expansion while recognizing its legality in the states where it existed.

Douglass was disappointed with the Republican Party's founding rationale. Challenging slavery's extension, he argued, was a weak response to a powerful institution. This position, Douglass continued, only served to

> keep the country in a constant commotion with Border Ruffian outrages, assassinations, incendiary-isms, conspiracies, civil wars, and all manner of sickening horrors. The only true remedy for the extension of slavery, is the immediate abolition of slavery. For while

the monster lives he will hunger and thirst, breathe, and expand. The true way is to put the knife into its quivering heart.

Even as he condemned the young coalition, Douglass endorsed its first national ticket in 1856: John C. Frémont for president and William Dayton for vice president. The black activist explained his action, saying that political consistency was less important than antislavery consistency; the latter demanded that he and other abolitionists use their votes to deliver the strongest possible blow against human bondage, and in 1856, the Republican Party represented that blow. Buoyed by support from abolitionists, former Whigs, and other groups, the Republicans carried eleven states (of thirty-one) in the November elections, winning almost 40 percent of the Electoral College votes. Despite this impressive showing, the Democrats took the White House, and in March 1857, James Buchanan became the fifteenth president.

During the next seven years, Douglass's attitude toward the Republican Party vacillated, depending on how optimistic or hopeless he felt about the prospects for ending slavery. At certain hopeful moments, he embraced the coalition as an important agent for change; at other, bleaker, times, he attacked it and its leaders for not moving quickly or aggressively against the institution. Other reformers criticized Douglass for his on-again, off-again allegiance to the Republicans— so much so that on the lecture circuit he took to joking about his reputation for political changeability.

Regardless of how Douglass felt about American politics, he worked tirelessly throughout the 1850s, as David Blight has written, "to help drive the cause of black liberation more and more to the center of national affairs." Douglass had several levers to pull. Elite politics was one; the lecture circuit was another; his writing provided a third. He continued to use his newspaper as a mouthpiece for abolition and for African-Americans' humanity.

In the mid-1850s, Douglass decided to write a second autobiography, and in 1855, it appeared under the title *My Bondage and My Freedom*. The book covered much of the same biographical ground as his first, but aspired to more. In relaying what he'd experienced as a slave and what he'd achieved since his escape, Douglass knew he was offering himself up as a role model for other African-Americans as well as a challenge to widespread assumptions of blacks' inferiority. "I have felt it to be a part of my mission," he wrote in the final chapter, "to impress my sable brothers in this country with the conviction that, not withstanding the ten thousand discouragements and the powerful hinderances [sic], which beset their existence . . . progress is yet possible, and bright skies shall yet shine upon their pathway." Douglass's ever-increasing reputation as well as the growing popular interest in slavery fueled sales of the book; it went through three editions in two years and sold more than twenty thousand copies by 1860.

In addition to writing and lecturing, Douglass remained connected with other well-known abolitionists, including the US senator from Massachusetts, Charles Sumner, and Harriet Beecher Stowe. In early March 1857, these and other reformers were incensed by the Supreme Court's Dred Scott decision. The case concerned an African-American slave, Dred Scott, who, in 1833, had been moved from Missouri, a slave state, to Illinois, a state where slavery was illegal, and then to Wisconsin, a territory in which it was also prohibited. In 1846, the black man petitioned the Missouri state courts, and ultimately the Supreme Court, for his freedom on the grounds that he'd lived for several years in free lands. Writing for a 7–2 majority, Chief Justice Roger Taney ruled that Scott wasn't entitled to seek justice in the courts because, as a Negro, he wasn't a citizen and not entitled to the same civil rights as a white man.

Across the North, antislavery leaders denounced the court's ruling. Some pointed to it as evidence of slaveholders' insidious power; others attacked the decision as racist. Douglass called the ruling a "judicial incarnation of wolfishness," but he also saw the seeds of positive change in it. The decision, he argued, might actually be the prelude to a chain of events that would result in the total eradication of the institution. "The American people have been called upon in a most striking manner," Douglass asserted, "to abolish and put away forever the system of slavery."

Exactly how widespread emancipation would actually take hold was a more open question for Douglass. If the ballot box failed, if legislators did not outlaw slavery, or if abolitionists did not find other peaceful means of extinguishing it, he saw several potentially violent outcomes. For example, the armed conflict between pro- and antislavery forces that had erupted in the Kansas territories might spread to other parts of the country. Another possibility was that slaves might rise up against their owners in large numbers. A third alternative—one more turbulent and deadly—was civil war.

Again and again, Douglass declared that the convulsion in which the country found itself in the 1850s wouldn't cease until slavery was eliminated. Indeed, he argued, the very turmoil created by the Dred Scott decision, the Kansas-Nebraska Act, and other such developments might be the best—the only—means of restoring the country to its original purpose: liberty for all. "Let me give you a word of the philosophy of reform," Douglass said in an 1857 speech.

> The whole history of the progress of human liberty shows that all concessions yet made to her august claims, have been born of earnest struggle. . . . If there is no struggle there is no progress. Those who profess to favor freedom and yet deprecate agitation, are men who want crops without plowing up the ground, they want rain without thunder and lightning. They want the ocean without the awful roar of its many waters.

As tensions escalated, Americans on both sides of the slavery question began to consider violence as a way of advancing their respective agendas. The most famous example of armed insurrection in service to the abolitionist cause was John Brown's attempt in October 1859 to seize the federal arsenal at Harpers Ferry, Virginia. The white abolitionist and his supporters intended to take control of enough weapons to arm thousands of slaves and free blacks, who, Brown was certain, would quickly join the growing revolt.

Douglass had first been introduced to Brown in the late 1840s. During the ensuing decade, the two met several times, and in 1857, the black leader learned of Brown's intention to lead a slave uprising. In principle, Douglass supported this idea, even going so far as to solicit donations on Brown's behalf. As the plans took concrete shape, however, it became clear to the former slave that the insurrection couldn't succeed, and shortly before the proposed date, Douglass told Brown that "he was going into a perfect steel-trap, and that once in he would never get out alive."

On the evening of October 16, 1859, Brown launched his attack. He and twenty-one men succeeded in taking roughly sixty people hostage in Harpers Ferry and seizing control of the armory. But the next morning, a gang of militiamen, shopkeepers, and farmers surrounded the building where Brown and some of his men had hunkered down; that afternoon, a platoon of US marines under the command of Colonel Robert E. Lee arrived to help put down the revolt. Brown refused to surrender, and a skirmish ensued. Lee's troops stormed the building, and by the morning of October 18, eight of Brown's followers and two of his sons, who were also part of the group, had been killed. Six civilians also died, including the town mayor, two slaves, and one free black man. Five of the radical abolitionists escaped, but their leader and six others were captured, convicted of treason, and hanged.

In the weeks after the attempted uprising, state and federal officials launched a nationwide manhunt for anyone suspected of working with Brown. When Douglass learned that authorities had found a note he'd written to the abolitionist, he knew he was at risk for arrest. The black reformer fled north from Rochester to Canada; fearful that US marshals would pursue him there; in November he sailed on to England. He reconnected with old friends and colleagues and resumed lecturing before audiences across the United Kingdom. Douglass wouldn't be in the country long, however. In March 1860, he was called home when his youngest child, Annie, died after a brief illness.

When he returned to the United States, the hunt for Brown's accomplices had ended. Douglass attributed this to two factors. The first, he wrote, was that "the men engaged in [the investigation] expected soon to be in rebellion themselves, and that, not a rebellion for liberty, like that of John Brown, but a rebellion for slavery." The second factor was the 1860 presidential election. That canvass consumed all the nation's attention, the black activist stated, and "had no parallel, involving as it did the question of peace or war, the integrity or the dismemberment of the Republic, and, I may add, the maintenance or destruction of slavery."

Years later, looking back on Brown's raid on Harpers Ferry, the black leader considered it an epic turning point. The insurrectionist, Douglass wrote, ignited the conflict that ultimately abolished slavery:

> If we look over the dates, places and men, for which this honor is claimed, we shall find that not Carolina, but Virginia—not Fort Sumter, but Harper's [sic] Ferry and the arsenal—not Col. Anderson [the commander of Fort Sumter], but John Brown, began the war that ended American slavery and made this a free Republic. Until this blow was struck, the prospect for freedom was dim, shadowy and uncertain. The irrepressible conflict was one of words, votes and compromises. When John Brown stretched forth his arm the sky was cleared. The time for compromises was gone—the armed hosts of freedom stood face to face over the chasm of a broken Union—and the clash of arms was at hand.

What are we to make of Douglass's involvement with Brown, the man who did so much to help start the Civil War? As David Blight has pointed out, Douglass never actively participated in or coordinated any slave revolt. This wasn't how he saw his role in helping lead the abolition movement. Nonetheless, the black activist could support armed rebellion if it had a good chance of success, and Douglass was always interested in what would work. The same realism that led him, in the end, to urge Brown to give up his scheme also fueled Douglass's interest in a *range* of instruments to wield against slavery—from moral suasion to political influence to violent revolt. When war came in early 1861, Douglass was ready to lead in service to the cause of black freedom on a much larger stage than the one on which he had begun his career.

Through the turmoil of the 1850s, as he considered different tools, different players, and different scenarios, Douglass never lost sight of a critical factor: how and under what circumstances he could make the greatest impact as a leader. For example, he knew he was never going to be a foot soldier in the guerrilla warfare envisioned by radical abolitionists such as John Brown. This wasn't because Douglass lacked physical courage; he had plenty of it. But he recognized that grabbing a rifle wasn't the most effective thing he could do for the cause. The best use of his talents and experience, as he understood, was to cast his voice, presence, and influence as far and wide as possible.

This is an essential lesson for anyone who yearns to lead. The temptation, especially in times of discouragement and failure, is to leap into the first opportunity that comes our way, to do something—*anything*—that may advance our mission. But this is not, as Douglass realized, right action for leaders. Right action requires taking a long pause and considering how one can do the most good. This always entails putting one's gifts and experience to their best use.

CHAPTER THIRTY

The Civil War and Beyond

In the 1860 presidential election, four political parties—the Democrats, Republicans, and two independent coalitions—fielded candidates. Douglass endorsed Abraham Lincoln, the Republican nominee. The black reformer continued to criticize the party's opposition to the extension of slavery as inadequate. But relative to the other three candidates, Douglass regarded Lincoln as the best choice.

After Lincoln's election in November, the abolitionist watched with keen interest as Southern states withdrew from the Union and began to form their own government. Douglass judged Southerners' actions excessive. Writing in his newspaper, he predicted that the president-elect and his administration would ultimately prove protectors of slavery:

> If Mr. Lincoln were really an Abolition President, which he is not . . . the dissolution of the Union might be the only effective mode of perpetuating slavery in the Southern States—since if it could succeed, it would place slavery beyond the power of the President and his Government. But the South has now no such cause for disunion. The present alarm and perturbation will cease; the Southern fire-eaters will be appeased, and will retrace their steps. . . . Whoever lives through the next four years will see Mr. Lincoln and his Administration attacked more bitterly for their pro-slavery truckling, than for doing any anti-slavery work.

With the outbreak of fighting at Fort Sumter in April 1861, Douglass became less skeptical of the new president. Lincoln, it seemed, was willing to prosecute a war that the black leader viewed as a contest about the future of slavery. Urging Northern audiences to see the war as he did, Douglass said in mid-1861, "Slavery is at the bottom of all mischief amongst us. . . . Not a slave should be left a slave in the returning footprints of the American army gone to put down this slaveholding rebellion."

As the war dragged on, Douglass's initial optimism waned, and he lost faith that Lincoln and his administration were seriously interested in fighting a war to eradicate slavery. By mid-1862, the president had been willing to take some action on the issue. He'd promoted a scheme for compensated emancipation and colonization, for example, and he'd outlawed slavery in Washington, DC. But in a concession to slaveholders in the Border States, Lincoln had also rescinded Union generals' orders to free slaves in areas of fighting.

From Douglass's perspective, the chief executive's actions were meager at best and reprehensible at worst. The reformer was heartened that slavery was now illegal in the nation's capital, but the government's war efforts, he asserted, still had to include universal abolition. As for compensated emancipation and colonization, Douglass was infuriated by both initiatives, arguing that they recognized the legitimacy of slavery and perpetrated another injustice against African-Americans by deporting them from their home country.

During the summer of 1862, Douglass grew intensely frustrated with the president. "Though elected as an anti-slavery man by Republican and abolition voters," the activist wrote, "Mr. Lincoln is quite a genuine representative of American prejudice and Negro hatred and far more concerned for the preservation of slavery, and the favor of the Border Slave States, than for any sentiment of magnanimity or principle of justice and humanity." Lincoln had said publicly that slavery was evil, Douglass conceded, but the president's actions belied this position. "Every step of [Lincoln's] career relating to slavery proves him active, decided, and brave for its support, and passive, cowardly, and treacherous to the very cause of liberty to which he owes his election."

Then, on September 22, 1862, Lincoln issued the Emancipation Proclamation. This "vast and startling" development, Douglass told a New York City audience, was "the greatest event of our nation's history if not the greatest event of the century" and represented a revolution in national politics. For more than sixty years, he noted, "the Federal Government has been little better than a stupendous engine of Slavery and oppression through which Slavery has ruled us, as with a rod of iron." But now, he said, the "doom of Slavery in all the States" has arrived. At long last, Douglass added, "the outspread wings of the American Eagle, afford shelter and protection to men of all colors, all countries, and all climes, and the long oppressed black man may honorably fall or gloriously flourish under the star-spangled banner."

The black reformer was deeply gratified by the Emancipation Proclamation and all that it portended. What was perhaps less obvious at the time was the essential role his own leadership had played in the president's decision to issue the executive order. Lincoln wouldn't have taken this unprecedented step if he didn't believe he had the necessary political support for it. That support—among the Northern public, press, and government officials—had been seeded, nurtured, and then galvanized by the abolition movement. For more than ten years, Douglass and other antislavery leaders had worked tirelessly to make eradication of slavery *the* central issue for the country. When the war broke out, these same leaders kept it at the forefront of the nation's consciousness. By the time Lincoln was ready to issue his proclamation, millions of people across the North believed that the war had to result in slavery's end. This represented a sea change from public opinion in 1850, when most white Northerners neither knew nor cared much about slavery.

Among the scores of important abolitionists, few were as visible, credible, and dedicated as Frederick Douglass. Virtually no other antislavery leader used so many different channels of influence, from exhorting the public to accessing political elites. And almost none could speak to the evils of slavery and the possibilities of African-Americans with the conviction and influence that Douglass could. All these aspects of his leadership were essential to the abolitionist cause during the 1850s and the Civil War. Indeed, it isn't too much to argue that without the black activist's determination, skills, and experience, the cause of ending slavery might have faltered. If it had, Abraham Lincoln could never have done what he did to transform the Union.

As Douglass realized, the Emancipation Proclamation was also important because it cleared the way for black soldiers to join the federal army. By late 1862, the conflict had become one to eradicate human bondage, and black men, the reformer declared, were needed and ready to fight in it. During the next two and a half years, he lobbied politicians, military officers, and the larger public to enlist black Americans and treat these soldiers on equal terms with whites. "We are striking the guilty rebels with our soft, white hand," Douglass said early in the war, "when we should be striking with the iron hand of the black man, which we keep chained behind us." Such is the pride, he asserted, "the stupid prejudice and folly that rules the hour."

Beyond the practical contributions black troops could make to the war effort, Douglass saw larger consequences. Fighting in the Union army would be a way for his black brothers to demonstrate their competence, devotion, and potential. Serving as soldiers was also a path to what Douglass called the elevation of his race. Once we let the "black man get upon his person the brass letters U.S.," the abolitionist wrote, "let him get an eagle on his button, and a musket on his shoulder, and bullets in his pocket . . . there is no power on the earth or under the earth which can deny that he has earned the right of citizenship in the United States."

Almost as soon as the Emancipation Proclamation became law on January 1, 1863, Douglass recruited more than a hundred young men for the country's first black regiment. This company was the Fifty-Fourth Massachusetts, and it was commanded by a white man, Colonel Robert Gould Shaw. Two of Douglass's sons, Lewis and Charles, joined the brigade. In the summer of 1863, Lewis was injured in the charge on Fort Wagner in Charleston, South Carolina, and was soon promoted to sergeant major, the highest military rank an African-American could then attain. Charles went on to enlist in the Fifth Massachusetts Cavalry, where he rose to sergeant.

By the time the war ended, more than 180,000 African-Americans had put on blue uniforms to fight for the United States. These men constituted almost a tenth of the federal army and more than a fifth of the country's adult male black population under age forty-five. Another 19,000 black Americans served in the navy. Other blacks moved the Union effort forward as cooks, laborers, steamboat pilots, surgeons, and guards. Black women weren't allowed to formally join the army. Nonetheless, many served as nurses, spies, and scouts. (The most famous of these was Harriet Tubman, who scouted for the Second South Carolina Volunteers during the conflict.) The majority of these men and women signed up of their own volition, motivated by the larger cause of black freedom.

However they came to serve, black Americans encountered prejudice. Many Union commanders refused to recruit and organize Negro troops. Some white soldiers protested fighting alongside their black countrymen. Enlisted black men were paid less than their white counterparts, and until the closing months of the war, blacks were not promoted to officers. Negro troops who were captured by Confederate forces confronted greater dangers than white soldiers. Most Southern military leaders didn't recognize black soldiers as prisoners of war. Some Confederate armies summarily executed blacks captured in battle; others shot African-Americans who attempted to escape.

Frederick Douglass was well aware of the obstacles black soldiers faced. By August 1863, he was angry and wanted to do more than discuss these issues in his newspaper and speeches; he decided to go to Washington, DC, to try to speak directly with the president and other government officials. When he set out for the nation's capital, he had no appointment at the White House and no assurance he would get one. But he hoped his reputation and the politicians he knew in Washington would afford him access to members of the administration. When he arrived, he ran into one of his contacts, Senator Samuel Pomeroy, from Kansas, who offered to try to get the abolitionist a meeting with Lincoln.

Douglass and the politician made their way to the White House, joining the throngs of people waiting to see the chief executive. The black leader took his place at the end of the long line, but within minutes, he and Pomeroy were summoned to Lincoln's office. As they hurried up the stairs to the second floor, Douglass overheard a white man say, "Damn it, I knew they would let the n—r through."

The two entered to find the president, as Douglass remembered, relaxing in a chair with his feet "in different parts of the room." The black leader and Lincoln were soon deep in conversation. Douglass pressed him on why it was taking so long to ensure the fair treatment of black soldiers, including equal pay. "The country needed talking up to [on] that point," the president replied, explaining that Northern opinion had to catch up to abolitionists' goals. The same reasoning, Lincoln continued, underlay his decision to issue the Emancipation Proclamation when he did. Had he issued the order to free the slaves too soon, he explained, the public would have been resistant; collective prejudice would have made matters worse and thus delayed the progress Douglass and other antislavery leaders sought.

The black leader wasn't convinced by Lincoln's explanation. But he understood the president's rationale. More than this, the reformer believed that Lincoln took him seriously. "By his silent listening not less than by his earnest reply to my words," Douglass recalled, the commander in chief "impressed me with the solid gravity of his character." As important, the activist noted, in Lincoln's presence, "I was never in any way reminded of my humble origin, or of my unpopular color."

For the remainder of the war, Douglass continued to speak out on the importance of black troops. But despite their impressive contributions, not until June 1864 would Congress grant African-American soldiers equal pay. The legislation was made retroactive to 1863 and also ensured black soldiers received the same rations and supplies as white troops, as well as comparable medical care.

In late summer 1864, Lincoln invited Douglass to the White House. The chief executive wanted to hear his thoughts on how to encourage slaves in Confederate states to escape to federal strongholds. Lincoln—who was almost certain he would be defeated in the upcoming presidential election by his Democratic opponent, George McClellan, who'd promised to bring the Southern states back into the Union with slavery intact—was worried about the fate of Southern slaves. Knowing the new president would quickly revoke the Emancipation Proclamation, Lincoln hoped to bring as many slaves as possible within government lines while he was still in office. The commander in chief sought Douglass's advice on recruiting agents who would travel through enemy territory helping slaves flee.

At this time, Union troops were stalled outside Richmond and Atlanta. Casualty counts had reached unprecedented numbers (since May, federal armies had suffered losses of roughly ninety thousand men), and Northern opposition to the war had reached a fever pitch. Everywhere Lincoln turned, politicians, newspaper editors, and others demanded that he sue for a negotiated peace—one that reunited the country by allowing Confederates to keep their slaves. Bowing to this intense pressure, Lincoln drafted a letter to a Wisconsin journalist implying that he would consider discussions with Confederate president Jefferson Davis that didn't insist on abolition as a condition of ending the war.

Having drafted the letter, Lincoln waited to send it. He shared the draft with several colleagues, and when Douglass appeared in his office on August 19, the president also showed it to him. The commander in chief asked the abolitionist whether he should send the letter on. "Certainly not," Douglass answered. "It would be given a broader meaning than you intend to convey; it would be taken as a complete surrender of your anti-slavery policy, and do you serious damage." After listening to the black leader's advice, Lincoln chose to not send the letter.

In early September, Union forces under the command of General William Tecumseh Sherman captured Atlanta. After taking the city, Sherman and his army marched south through Georgia and, in late December, seized Savannah. The tide of war had turned decisively in the government's favor. As it did, Douglass focused his attention on what kind of peace all citizens, black and white, would enjoy. He imagined an era of Reconstruction that would embrace full equality—not only for his race, but also for every American regardless of color or gender.

On March 4, 1865, the day of Lincoln's second inauguration, the black leader stood in the front row of the crowd gathered outside the

US Capitol to hear the president speak. After the ceremony, Douglass walked to the White House to join hundreds of other well-wishers at a reception. As he tried to enter the building, however, two policemen blocked his way, saying Negroes were not welcome. Douglass called to a passerby whom he recognized, asking the man to inform the president that he was outside. Before long, the abolitionist was admitted into the East Room, where he found Lincoln standing, "like a mountain pine high above all others . . . in his grand simplicity, and *home-like beauty*." Seeing the black man across the room, the president called out, "Here comes my friend Douglass." As the reformer reached the head of the receiving line, the chief executive took his hand and said, "I'm glad to see you." He asked Douglass what he thought of the inaugural address, adding, "There is no man in the country whose opinion I value more than yours." The speech was "a sacred effort," Douglass replied. It was the last time the two leaders saw each other.

In the months and years following the Civil War, Douglass continued to speak, write, and agitate on behalf of black Americans. He wanted the end of slavery to give rise to political, economic, and social equality and advocated full suffrage for African-Americans, as well as vocational colleges for blacks and the end of segregated schools. The leader concentrated much of his attention on suffrage—the fight for universal enfranchisement and federal protection of this right. It was not enough, he repeatedly argued, for blacks to win the right to vote state by state, since individual states could retract, circumvent, or dilute this right. What the nation needed, he asserted, was a constitutional amendment guaranteeing black Americans' right to vote. During the late 1860s, Douglass used all his influence and his outsize reputation to try to secure such a promise. On February 3, 1870, Congress ratified the Fifteenth Amendment, ensuring the voting rights of all male citizens, regardless of race.

During the next decade, Douglass held several government positions. In 1877, for example, President Rutherford Hayes appointed Douglass US marshal of the District of Columbia; it was the first time in American history that the US Senate had considered a black candidate for any kind of confirmation, and Douglass was confirmed.

Douglass also served as president of the Freedman's Savings and Trust Company, a bank chartered by Congress in 1865 to safeguard the savings of African-American veterans and former slaves.

The black leader continued to write and speak about specific issues, most notably women's rights. But by the end of the 1870s, Douglass had largely retired. In 1878, he purchased a twenty-room house on nine acres overlooking the US Capitol, calling his home Cedar Hill. He and his family enjoyed their spacious surroundings, entertaining in fine style. Douglass played the violin with his grandson Joseph, kept abreast of current politics, and in 1881 published his third and final autobiography, *The Life and Times of Frederick Douglass*.

In August 1882, Anna Douglass, who was nearly seventy, died after suffering a stroke. Anna's death hit Frederick hard. "When death comes into one's home—a home of four and forty years, it brings with it a lesson of thought, silence, humility and resignation," Douglass wrote a friend. "There is not much room for pride or self-importance in presence of this event." In the months after his wife's passing, Douglass slid into a deep depression, and in the summer of 1883, he seemed close to an emotional breakdown.

But then he recovered his strength and equanimity, and by 1884, he was vigorously working for women's suffrage. The same year, he married social activist Helen Pitts, a forty-six-year-old white woman, the daughter of an abolitionist. The newlyweds continued their reform work, punctuated by travel in the United States and Europe. On February 20, 1895, Douglass, age seventy-seven, died of a heart attack at Cedar Hill. He and Helen had just returned home from a meeting of the National Council of Women.

CHAPTER THIRTY-ONE

The World after Frederick Douglass

During his life, Frederick Douglass became the most famous African-American in the United States. As an abolitionist, an advocate for women's rights, and a spokesman for the cause of human freedom, he made an enormous impact on the defining issue of civil liberty and particularly on the momentous events of the 1850s and early 1860s, when slavery cleaved the nation in two and provoked the Civil War.

In our own time, the importance of Frederick Douglass's legacy and contributions is well recognized among African-Americans. But most white Americans know little about this ambitious, highly principled, and fiercely dedicated leader. Those who are familiar with the abolitionist are aware he was a fugitive slave, wrote an autobiography, and spoke out against slavery. But even *they* do not appreciate how penetrating his understanding of slavery was, including the role that racial prejudice and socioeconomic forces played in keeping it in place. Today, few Americans realize that this understanding helped Douglass to see—years before contemporaries such as Abraham Lincoln—that it was likely to require armed conflict to destroy such a powerful, entrenched institution.

During the middle decades of the nineteenth century, the black leader used this understanding to play a pivotal role in the struggle to end human bondage, urging ordinary citizens, other reformers, and politicians—particularly the president—to battle slavery with every available resource. As soon as the Civil War broke out, Douglass worked to define the conflict as one to eradicate slavery. Using his newspaper, the lecture circuit, and his political connections, he continued to push this perspective to the center of national debate. For almost two years, he doubted the Lincoln administration would embrace and act on what he saw as the animating purpose of the war. But in September 1862, when the president issued the Emancipation Proclamation, Douglass and many other abolitionists realized that they'd achieved a tremendously important victory: going forward, the war would be fought to extinguish slavery and transform the Union.

Douglass hoped this transformation would encompass full citizenship and equality for black Americans. Toward this end, he fought for black soldiers, lobbying government officials to enlist—and then pay and promote—them on the same terms as whites. When the conflict ended, the reformer worked to desegregate public schools, create economic opportunities for African-Americans, and secure the right to vote for blacks and women.

Through the lens of historical hindsight, we can see that Douglass relied on his keen vision, steadfast resolution, and moral judgment to articulate slavery as a terrible contradiction at the heart of the republic. He realized that slavery and the racial discrimination that underlay it contaminated whites as well as blacks and damaged the fabric of the nation. At an even deeper level, he recognized that Americans (or any other people) couldn't become all they might in the presence of widespread prejudice against their fellow citizens. In his consistent ability to frame the stakes of these issues, his leadership anticipated the work of Martin Luther King Jr., Nelson Mandela, Gloria Steinem, and other modern activists.

In the early twenty-first century, we continue to grapple with the reverberations of slavery, racial prejudice, and full citizenship for all Americans. We long for a leader like Frederick Douglass, who apprehended that the country could only achieve its full potential when Americans faced and righted a critical wrong. It's important to remember that the black abolitionist led from the lecture hall and the newspaper as much—or more—than he did from the offices of elite politicians. He believed that positive change began with ordinary citizens, and that his work as a leader was to help them affect the individuals who governed them. This is a vital lesson for our time. If we want to use it to change our country, we *must* understand the life and work of Frederick Douglass.

PART FOUR

Resist Nazi Evil

DIETRICH BONHOEFFER'S CHALLENGE

CHAPTER THIRTY-TWO

Crossing the Rubicon

In early June 1939, Dietrich Bonhoeffer left Europe for the United States aboard the SS *Bremen*. Three months earlier, Germany had occupied Czechoslovakia, and now Adolf Hitler was preparing to invade Poland. Europe was on the brink of war, and Bonhoeffer's friends wanted him on safer shores. After years of opposition to the Nazi-controlled state church and the Third Reich's persecution of Jews and others deemed enemies of the government, the thirty-three-year old pastor was at risk for arrest, imprisonment, and potentially far worse.

Bonhoeffer had long dreaded the coming of war and the possibility of conscription. "It seems to me conscientiously impossible," he wrote a colleague, "to join in a war under the present circumstances." All who enlisted were required to swear a personal oath of obedience and loyalty to the German state and Adolf Hitler. Making such a pledge ran counter to everything Bonhoeffer stood for.

Since January 1933, when Hitler and the National Socialists had come to power, Bonhoeffer had grappled with what it meant to be a committed Christian in a totalitarian state focused on excluding, isolating, and eliminating thousands—and eventually millions—of people. How is one to live responsibly when, as Bonhoeffer would write, the "great masquerade of evil has played havoc with all our ethical concepts?" What, if anything, did men and women who believed in the goodness of Christ's teachings owe to those who suffered at the hands of the Nazis, and how did these obligations translate into individual commitment and action?

These questions pressed in on Bonhoeffer during the 1930s, gaining force as Nazi aggression increased. Since 1933, he'd tried to effect change by appealing to the fundamental incompatibility between Christianity and National Socialism. Toward this end he took two paths. First, he worked within the international ecumenical movement, urging European church leaders to oppose Nazi influence on German ecclesiastical life and the Third Reich's growing attacks against Jews. Second, he helped found the Confessing Church as a Christian alternative to the Reichskirche, or state church. The Confessing Church proclaimed its adherence to the essential truth of the Gospel and denied the right of the government to dictate the Church's message, ideology, or decisions.

By 1939, this had become dangerous work. Bonhoeffer and other Confessing Church leaders had come under Nazi surveillance. Some had been arrested and imprisoned. Now, as Bonhoeffer faced conscription, he didn't want to refuse to serve. "I should cause a tremendous damage to my brethren," he wrote, "if I would make a stand on this point which would be regarded by the [Nazi] regime as typical of the hostility of our church toward the state." What to do, where to turn? For the fiercely independent young man, such uncertainty was unusual and discomfiting.

One option was to work in the United States. A decade earlier, Bonhoeffer had been a postdoctoral fellow at the Union Theological Seminary in New York City. Now, his colleagues there encouraged him to return as a teacher and minister. If Bonhoeffer accepted the yearlong post, he could legally leave Germany and avoid the draft. At first, he hesitated. But on May 22, 1939, he received notice to report for military service and realized he had no time to waste. Twelve days later, he boarded a steamship bound for the United States, arriving in New York on June 12.

Bonhoeffer had hoped the move to America would relieve his growing anxiety about what he should do next. But it did not. Within hours, he was besieged by doubt. Writing in his diary, he described his inner turmoil:

Since yesterday evening, my thoughts cannot get away from Germany. I would not have thought it possible that one at my age after so many years abroad can become so agonizingly homesick. . . . I would have liked to take the next ship. This inactivity, or rather activity spent on trivialities, is simply no longer bearable for us, thinking of the brothers [his like-minded friends in the Confessing Church] and the precious time. The full force of self-reproaches about a wrong decision comes back up and is almost suffocating. I was filled with despair.

The ensuing days brought no relief. Restless, Bonhoeffer wandered the city. He visited the World's Fair in Queens, attended services in Riverside Church, and read in the Union library. At night, he chain-smoked alone in his room, yearning for news from Germany. The wait, he wrote in his diary, "can hardly be endured."

This was not easy emotional terrain. For almost all of his adult life—first as a wunderkind academic at the University of Berlin, and later as an activist minister in the Confessing Church—he'd relied on deep reserves of self-control. But in June 1939, this internal discipline deserted him. As the world moved closer to war, he was unable to get right with himself about where he was meant to be. He scribbled in one of his notebooks:

No time is to be lost, and here I am losing days, perhaps weeks. In any case, that's how it looks at present. Then, on the other hand, I tell myself: it is cowardice and weakness to run away from here now. But will I ever really be able to do meaningful work here. . . . If turmoil now breaks out, I will definitely travel to Germany. I cannot be alone abroad. This is utterly clear to me.

On June 20, just over a week after he arrived, Bonhoeffer decided to sail home. He withdrew from his commitments at the seminary, explaining to his colleagues that he was "being pulled toward the brothers in struggle." In the privacy of his diary, Bonhoeffer admitted that he didn't understand why he'd come to the United States in the first place: "It is strange that in all my decisions, I am never completely clear about my motives. Is that a sign of lack of clarity, inner dishonesty, or is it a sign that we are *led* beyond that which we can discern, or is it both?"

Like many choices that leaders make when the stakes are high, Bonhoeffer's decision to return to Germany was an act of faith. He was wagering his personal safety on the chance that he could do right in a country ruled by men pursuing a barbaric agenda. In June 1939, Bonhoeffer couldn't see exactly *how* he would advance goodness, but he knew this was his mission. He also knew he couldn't stay in the United States. "To be here during a catastrophe," he wrote, "is simply unthinkable, unless it is meant to be. But to be guilty of this oneself, to have to reproach oneself for having gone abroad unnecessarily, is certainly crushing." Writing to a colleague at Union Theological Seminary, he laid out his situation:

> I have come to the conclusion that I have made a mistake in coming to America. I must live through this difficult period of our national history with the Christian people of Germany. I will have no right to participate in the reconstruction of Christian life [there], after the war if I do not share [in] the trials of this time with my people. . . . Christians in Germany will face the terrible alternative of either willing the defeat of their nation in order that Christian civilization may survive, or willing the victory of their nation and thereby destroying our civilization. I know which of these alternatives I must choose; but I cannot make that choice in security.

Bonhoeffer's eyes were fully open to the potential consequences of his decision. The young minister had long opposed the Führer and had been warned by Nazi authorities to limit his activities. He understood clearly the penalties for ignoring such warnings; he'd recently received news that one of his colleagues had been tortured to death in Buchenwald concentration camp. Writing in his notebook on June 20, 1939, Bonhoeffer acknowledged "how much personal concern, how much fear is contained in today's decision, as courageous as it may appear."

This was a defining moment for the thirty-three-year-old clergyman. It offers an important lesson for today's leaders. No matter the mission—whether it be fighting injustice, starting a company, or teaching a classroom of fifth graders—leaders have to put a stake in the ground acknowledging what they're doing and why. Each person must consciously decide for himself to embrace the larger purpose; he must also decide whether he is ready to walk onto the broader stage and lead.

Putting such stakes in the ground requires that leaders see not only the big picture, but also their impact on it. People who aspire to lead have to recognize what is at risk at a given juncture, what right action the moment demands, and what the consequences are of choosing one course over another. All five of the individuals in this book cultivated this perspective. They did so by looking widely, listening carefully, and reflecting constantly, often in conversation *with themselves* about what was going on around them and what it meant for their path.

In July 1939, in the midst of a personal crisis, Bonhoeffer was forced to consider the larger stage and his potential, while occupying it, to effect worthy change. As he did, he realized his impact would result not only from the *external* actions he would take in the struggle against Hitler, but also from the *internal* development he would undergo as he tried to accomplish his mission. On July 8, just after midnight, Bonhoeffer was once again aboard a ship in New York Harbor. The moonlight poured down behind the city skyline as he wrote in his diary:

> The journey is over. I am glad that I was there, and glad that I am on my way home again. I have perhaps learned more in this month than in the entire year nine years ago [when he was a visiting fellow at Union Theological Seminary]; at least I have come to realize important things for all future personal decisions. Probably this journey will have a great effect upon me.

For all of his resolve, the minister knew he was heading into danger. There was danger in the work he did for the Confessing Church, to be sure. But even greater hazard lay in the resistance work various members of his family were doing. Hans von Dohnanyi, the husband of Dietrich's sister Christine, was working within the Nazi government as part of a conspiracy to overthrow the regime. Since 1938,

Bonhoeffer had known of the conspiracy, and he and Dohnanyi had spoken often about it. Bonhoeffer hadn't been directly involved; but as he headed home, he considered whether he should be.

As he thought about his future, Bonhoeffer saw two distinct roads ahead. The first was to continue his work in the Confessing Church, spreading Christ's message during this dark moment in Germany. The alternative was to join his brother-in-law and others in their attempted coup d'état.

In the mid-1930s, Bonhoeffer had written of individuals who would hold fast to their faith even when threatened with violence; at the time, he'd emphasized the virtue of being willing to resist evil "to the point of shedding blood." In July 1939, as he sailed toward Europe, he himself crossed a metaphorical Rubicon. He could not foresee that his resistance work would lead to his imprisonment by the Gestapo, but he *did* know that the game had irrevocably changed. He'd found the resolve to take decisive action. Years later, a colleague from the Confessing Church recalled Bonhoeffer's unexpected arrival back in Germany that summer:

> I was immediately up in arms, blurting out how could he come back after it had cost so much trouble to get him into safety—safety for us, for our cause; here everything was lost anyway. He very calmly lit a cigarette. Then he said that he had made a mistake in going to America. He did not himself understand now why he had done it. . . . It is this fact—that he abandoned in all clarity many great possibilities for his own development in the free countries, that he returned to dismal slavery and a dark future, but also to his own reality—which gave to everything he told us then a strong and joyful firmness, such as only arises out of realized freedom. He knew he had taken a clear step, though the actualities before him were still quite unclear.

In the "realized freedom" that Bonhoeffer had found in returning to Germany, he was prepared to wager everything he had in pursuit of a big, daring mission.

CHAPTER THIRTY-THREE

Bonhoeffer's Early Years

Dietrich Bonhoeffer was born on February 4, 1906, in Breslau, Germany, into an illustrious family. His father, Karl Bonhoeffer, was a renowned psychiatrist and professor, who came from a long line of doctors, clergy, and lawyers. Dietrich's mother, Paula van Hase Bonhoeffer, was from an aristocratic family whose members included theologians, artists, and soldiers; for several years, her father had been court preacher to Kaiser Wilhelm II.

When Dietrich and his twin sister, Sabine, were born, Karl and Paula Bonhoeffer already had five young children: three sons and two daughters. Their last child, a girl, arrived three years after the twins. Eight children, all born within a decade, made for a busy household, but both parents enjoyed their large brood. "We feel that there are not too many of them," Karl Bonhoeffer wrote in 1909. "The house is roomy, the children have grown up normally, we parents are not too old yet, and are therefore concerned not to spoil them, but to make their youth a happy time." Happy it was. In the garden of the family's rambling house, the children climbed trees, erected tents, and learned to skate on the abandoned tennis court that Karl turned into an ice rink each winter. They also kept a menagerie of animals, including rabbits, guinea pigs, squirrels, lizards, snakes, and turtledoves.

Before she was married, Paula Bonhoeffer had earned a teaching certificate, and she schooled her children at home when they were young. She wanted them to learn with more freedom than the harsh, rigid methods German public schools allowed. (The Bonhoeffers were fond of quoting the saying "Germans have their backs broken twice in the course of their lives: first at school, and then during their military service.") Paula taught her children their basic lessons as well as poems, songs, and games, and they soaked it all up, excelling in public schools once they eventually enrolled.

As the daughter, granddaughter, and sister of theologians, Paula was a devoted Christian who wanted her children to learn the Scriptures. "She told us the Bible stories," her daughter Sabine remembered, "always in the biblical text, and [then] opened the large picture Bible. . . . We loved this." Paula did not often take her children to church—her goal was to teach them to believe in God rather than ceremony—but the Bonhoeffer children absorbed some Christian rituals. For example, they said grace before family meals and prayed at bedtime. Dietrich's twin sister remembered that before the two children went to sleep at night, they talked about eternal life.

Karl Bonhoeffer was less religious than his wife, but he shared the values she drew from her faith, namely generosity, selflessness, and helping others. Karl put great stock in self-control, thoughtfulness, and careful observation, passing these priorities on to his children. He also impressed on them the importance of listening well and choosing their words carefully. As Sabine remembered, her father had no patience for small talk. At family meals, Karl exerted his influence by speaking quietly and firmly:

> His rejection of the hollow phrase may have made us at times tongue-tied and uneasy, but as a result we could not abide any clichés, gossip, platitudes or pomposity when we grew up. . . . Sometimes our papa delighted in making us define concepts, or things, and if we managed to do so clearly, without being vague, he was happy.

Overall, the Bonhoeffer children grew up secure and protected. As an adult, Dietrich fretted that his sheltered upbringing had limited his exposure to those less fortunate than he. But there can be little doubt that the self-confidence he acquired as a child—raised in a caring family governed by principled, thoughtful parents who loved each other as much as their children—had a huge impact on him. Throughout his life, Dietrich Bonhoeffer drew on that sense of security and self-respect. Unlike Lincoln and Shackleton, who both consistently tried to outrun their early years, Bonhoeffer relied heavily on his family's support well into adulthood. This support helped power his development as a leader, enabling him to make big leaps—both inside and out.

As he grew older, Dietrich worked to distinguish himself from his older brothers. The eldest, Karl Friedrich, would go on to become a world-renowned chemist. The third son, Klaus, studied law and became the top legal counsel to the German airline Lufthansa (Walter, the second son, died on the battlefield in World War I). In 1920, when Dietrich was fourteen, he announced to his family that he intended to become a minister. Although his parents thought it an unusual choice, neither attempted to dissuade him. His siblings teased him, but Dietrich didn't waver.

Theology was a natural pursuit for a young man who gravitated toward contemplation and solitude. All his life, Bonhoeffer spent time in reflection. Some of this was spontaneous; some was deliberate. He used it to cultivate his self-awareness, puzzle out his relationships with others, and, as in New York in 1939, consider his journey and what to do next. Like several other leaders in this book, he used his time alone to detach himself from a particular moment and survey the larger scene from different angles.

In 1923, as Dietrich prepared to enter university, hyperinflation ravaged the national economy, devouring Germans' purchasing power. In 1922, the mark had been valued at seventy-five per US dollar; by August 1923, its value had plunged to 1 million per dollar, and by November, to 4 billion per dollar. In the midst of this economic turmoil, Adolf Hitler and his National Socialist Party tried to forcibly seize power. On November 8, 1923, two thousand Nazis marched to the center of Munich and confronted police, threatening nationwide rebellion. The Beer Hall Putsch, as it became known, failed, and Hitler received a prison sentence for treason. But the event brought him national publicity, and during the nine months he was incarcerated, he capitalized on this interest by working with his colleague Rudolf Hess to write *Mein Kampf*, which detailed Hitler's ideas on politics, nationalism, and anti-Semitism. (The book, which went on to sell 12 million copies during the Third Reich, became the political manifesto for National Socialism.)

Bonhoeffer kept abreast of these developments during his first year of university in Tübingen, Germany. As was custom in the Bonhoeffer family, he spent only a year at this institution, entering the University of Berlin in mid-1924 to pursue a PhD in theology. There, he studied under well-known theologians, including Swiss-born Karl Barth. At the time, Barth and other scholars were immersed in a series of theological debates about man's access to God, the nature of truth, and divine revelation. Bonhoeffer came of intellectual age in the ferment, absorbing contributions from different thinkers.

Drawing from these debates, Bonhoeffer decided to write his thesis on a big question: What is the church? In this work, he argued that the church exists not as an organization or historical entity, but rather as the embodiment of Christ on earth, what he called "Christ existing as church-community." This embodiment, he asserted, comprised a group of stumbling, sinful people who pray for one another, sacrifice for one another, and forgive one another. "Where one member is," Bonhoeffer stated, "there is the entire church-community. No one is alone, no one abandoned, no one homeless. The congregation is always there as well, in love, and that means in sacrifice." As he moved forward on his leadership journey, he would place growing importance on the power of communities that come together in the name of goodness—not only for spiritual reasons, but also to create positive change in the world.

In August 1927, his thesis was accepted for the PhD degree; a few months later, Bonhoeffer graduated summa cum laude. During the next twelve months, he served as a vicar in a German congregation in Barcelona. He then returned to the University of Berlin to lecture and complete a second thesis, which was required for his doctorate. During the preceding five years, he'd attended two universities, climbed to the top of his class in the second, finished one thesis and begun another, and ministered to an international congregation. Even for a person of Bonhoeffer's abundant energy, it had been an amazingly productive period.

What sustained Bonhoeffer's productivity was focus and discipline. All his life, he concentrated intently on what he was doing at a given moment, putting aside other thoughts, emotions, and calls on his attention. When he was listening to another person that was all he did. When he was grappling with an important issue or conversing with himself about his ambition or doubt, that was all he did. This focus was critical to Bonhoeffer's development. When he was a student, for example, it enabled him to invest in his own heart and mind. It enriched his relationships with others, and it gave rise to the key decisions he made about his life's journey. When the Nazis came to power, it helped him to grasp the big picture of German politics and how he should respond.

As important to Bonhoeffer as focus was the discipline he cultivated. Throughout his life, including his years as a Confessing Church minister and then later in prison, he ordered his days, devoting specific blocs of time to reading, thinking, praying, exercising, and more. These activities weren't pursued compulsively or with evident fussiness. But they did play to his stronger self and demanded consistent self-control.

Focus and discipline are essential tools for leaders in our own time. Attention spans are shrinking; many of us have trouble concentrating, listening well, and reflecting. Some of this difficulty is a result of nonstop connection to information and other people, and some is a function of trying to do several things at once. Many of us also have difficulty maintaining focus because we are living in several moments simultaneously: in what happened two hours ago, in what might happen later, and, almost as an afterthought, in what is actually unfolding right now. This constant careering among different "personal time zones" creates a vague underlying unease. Too often, this unease keeps us from being able to concentrate effectively on the most important work at hand. Like Bonhoeffer, leaders today must nurture a strong sense of self-discipline to direct their attention and energy toward what really matters.

In 1930, Bonhoeffer was twenty-four and a rising academic star. But he wasn't sure whether he should devote himself to the ministry or academics. As he debated, he wondered if he should study in a new environment and considered traveling to India to work with Mahatma Gandhi, but decided that would be too expensive. Soon after, he secured a fellowship at the Union Theological Seminary in New York City, planning to enroll that September.

Bonhoeffer was bowled over by New York when he arrived in the autumn of 1930. The skyscrapers and coursing energy on the street impressed him. So, too, did the struggles of the city's residents. In 1930, the United States was in the early throes of the Great Depression; businesses were failing, investment was declining, and national unemployment stood at 16 percent (by 1932, it would climb to almost 33 percent). Breadlines snaked down Manhattan streets as hundreds waited for food.

In America, Bonhoeffer also observed widespread racial discrimination, which he found disturbing. The conditions in which Negroes lived, he wrote his parents, "are really rather unbelievable. Not just separate railway cars, tramways and buses south of Washington [DC], but also, for example, when I wanted to eat in a small restaurant with a Negro [student], I was refused service." In a letter to his brother Karl Friedrich, who had also spent time in the United States, Bonhoeffer said he found the discrimination against Negroes "unnerving" in "a country with so inordinately many slogans about brotherhood, peace, and so on." Karl Friedrich agreed, writing back, "Our 'Jewish question' is a joke compared to [the discrimination in America]; only a few would still claim they are repressed here." Before long, however, both brothers would come to see frightening parallels between racial oppression in the United States and anti-Semitism at home.

As the academic year began, Bonhoeffer quickly judged American theology intellectually inferior to that in Germany. Seminary lectures often disappointed him, as did many conversations he had with peers. "One almost has to be cautious," he wrote to a church official in Germany, "lest the mutual visits and chatting take up too much time. For—these conversations almost never yield anything of substance. And that brings me to the sad part of the whole thing. There is no theology here. . . . [The students and professors] talk a blue streak without the slightest substantive foundation."

Despite these early assessments, Bonhoeffer learned a great deal during his time in New York. Three friends proved critical. One was Jean Lasserre, a French pacifist. From him, Bonhoeffer took the idea that all of the world's Christians were joined together in a set of beliefs and a way of peaceful living that superseded loyalty to any one national government. "Christendom is one great people," Bonhoeffer said in a 1930 sermon, "composed of peoples of every country, in concord in his faith and his love. . . . Above all differences of race, nationality, custom there is an invisible community of the children of God. Here, each one prays for the others, he might be American or German or African, here each one loves the others without reservation."

Frank Fisher, an African-American student, also played a pivotal role in Bonhoeffer's education. Fisher introduced him to the Abyssinian Baptist Church in Harlem. In 1930, this church, with its thirteen thousand members, was a vibrant center of Negro spirituality and politics led by the charismatic preacher Adam Clayton Powell Jr. The words, music, and energy Dietrich encountered at the church captivated him. He was also deeply moved by what he would later characterize as "the enormous intensity of [religious] feeling among the Negroes," which "repeatedly finds expression in their outcries and interrupting shouts." "The black Christ," he wrote in a summary of his year in America, "is preached with captivating passion and vividness." Powell's repeated calls from the pulpit to stamp out racism and alleviate social ills also impressed Dietrich.

The closest of Bonhoeffer's friends in New York was Paul Lehmann. A PhD candidate who spoke fluent German, Lehmann and his wife, Marion, opened their home to Dietrich, and the threesome spent evenings together debating politics, theology, and the difference between the Old and New Worlds. Lehmann regarded Bonhoeffer as very German in his theological training, exacting standards, and measured approach to solving problems. But the American also noted ways in which his friend defied stereotypes. "His aristocracy was unmistakable yet not obtrusive, chiefly, I think owing to his boundless curiosity about every new environment in which he found himself and to his irresistible and unfailing good humor," as well as his commitment to abiding friendship.

Bonhoeffer's instructors at Union Theological Seminary encouraged him to embrace the application of Christ's teachings in everyday life. "In making grace as transcendent as you do," wrote Professor Reinhold Niebuhr on one of the German student's essays, "I don't see how you can ascribe any ethical significance to it. Obedience to God's will may be a religious experience, but it is not an ethical one until it issues [forth] in actions, which can be socially valued." Outside the seminary, Bonhoeffer observed social workers and volunteers working in city settlement houses, night schools, and church organizations. In the classroom and on the streets, he gathered unmistakable evidence of the living gospel—the application of Christian faith to daily existence.

Despite his initial disdain for American theology, Bonhoeffer came to see his time in New York as important. With the benefit of hindsight, we can point to two powerful lessons he absorbed there. The first was the significance of assessing one's work in terms of its tangible consequences. He'd arrived in the United States an accomplished intellectual; he returned home concerned with what his theology and faith meant in the real world. As Germany's situation grew darker in the mid-1930s, this interest deepened. Bonhoeffer came to see his work—as minister, activist, and eventually political resister—in relation to its tangible impact. What lessons did Christianity offer to a nation controlled by the Third Reich? How was a follower of Christ to advance righteousness in the face of Nazi atrocities? The genesis of these questions dated directly to his year in New York.

The second lesson that Bonhoeffer took away from his time in America was the power of empathy. Through his experience in the black community, he discovered a world and a set of perspectives very different from his own. The more he learned about African-Americans, the more he understood what it meant to live on the margins of society. Bonhoeffer nourished this empathy, using it to try to understand the suffering of others—including victims of Nazi brutality. In late 1942, Bonhoeffer would define this empathy as "the view from below," the ability to see "the great events of world history . . . from the perspective of the outcast, the suspects, the maltreated, the powerless, the oppressed, the reviled—in short, from the perspective of those who suffer."

Some seventy years later, it is essential for leaders to understand the experience of those who are falling behind economically, socially, and politically. As wealth and income inequality surge, job growth stagnates, and certain regions boom while others bust, leaders have to reach across these divisions to connect with a broad spectrum of people. This means developing a sense of empathy and then using it to move one's mission forward. The more volatile the larger environment, the more crucial it is for hedge-fund managers, police officers, and others with significant authority to appreciate the experiences of those with less power and fewer options.

CHAPTER THIRTY-FOUR

A Christian in the World

In mid-1931, Bonhoeffer returned to Germany. For the next two years, he worked in three fields. He lectured in theology at the University of Berlin. He preached at a city church, where he also taught a confirmation class for working-class boys. And he was active in the European ecumenical movement, traveling and speaking on the role of the Christian church in modern society.

He made time and space for all of this. But teaching was his most important priority, and students found him captivating. Tall, broad-shouldered, and blond, Bonhoeffer was strikingly handsome, moving with an athlete's ease. Always impeccably dressed, he was also candid and confident. One of his students, Wolf-Dieter Zimmermann, remembered his first exposure to the University of Berlin professor in the fall of 1932:

> When I entered the classroom, there were about ten to fifteen students, a disheartening sight. For a moment I wondered whether I should retreat, but I stayed out of curiosity. A young lecturer stepped to the rostrum with a light, quick step, a man with very fair, rather thin hair, a broad face, rimless glasses with a golden bridge. After a few words of welcome he explained the meaning and structure of the lecture, in a firm, slightly throaty way of speaking. . . . I should have liked to write the whole lecture down, word for word. Every sentence went home; here was a concern for what troubled me, and

indeed all of us young people, what we asked and wanted to know. There was a lot of systematic theology in this lecture, as well as dogmatics and symbolics; but they served as occasions for dealing with the main question. And this was: what has God done? Where is he? How does he need us, and what does he expect from us?

Another student remembered Bonhoeffer as "an extremely inspiring personality" who was consumed by the material he was communicating. "We followed his words with such close attention that one could hear the flies humming. Sometimes, when we laid our pens down after a lecture, we were literally perspiring."

Many of these students sought out their teacher outside of lectures, and a group quickly formed around the young academic. Their conversations spilled into dormitory rooms, the Bonhoeffer family home, and the local *bierkeller* (pub), where Dietrich picked up the tab. These discussions were not wandering idylls; Bonhoeffer injected discipline into the conversations, directing his students toward important questions. One student remembered that their instructor encouraged "straight ways of thinking and to learn not to slink off into side-issues, or to be satisfied with premature cheap answers." This was a full-bodied experience, the student added. "Work and pleasure, objective discussion and heart-to-heart talk, everything had its proper place."

As Bonhoeffer lectured and attended to his clerical responsibilities, he remained anchored in his birth family, which now included the husbands and wives of his siblings. When they were together, the Bonhoeffer clan talked about the heavy clouds rolling in over Germany. "Great changes in the course of world history are before us," Bonhoeffer wrote in late 1931, referring to the deep depression battering his own country and many others. He speculated that the coming winter would see massive unemployment and as many as 20 million people going hungry, a third of his nation's total population. "Intelligent people in the field of economics have told me that things look as if we are being pushed at an enormous speed toward a destination that no one knows or could prevent," he wrote to a friend. "The omens are strange."

As 1931 ended, Germany was also engulfed in widespread political turmoil. Worsening economic conditions and popular frustration with the government's failure to deal with these had resulted in big gains for extremist parties, including the Communists and the National Socialists. In the late-1930 elections, for example, the latter coalition had won nearly 19 percent of the popular vote, a victory that made Hitler's party the second most powerful in the country.

By 1932, the German economy was coming apart at the seams. Unemployment reached 30 percent. Businesses went bankrupt, industrial production fell precipitously, and failing banks were put under government control. Millions of Germans were suddenly vulnerable. Crime escalated, as did suicide rates. As collective fear mounted, voters embraced the promises and rhetoric of the far right. In elections held in May 1932, the National Socialists became the largest party in the Reichstag (German parliament). During the next eight months, the Nazis consolidated their gains. The fragile multiparty coalition that had governed Germany since 1919 collapsed, effectively ending parliamentary democracy. On January 30, 1933, German president Paul von Hindenburg appointed Adolf Hitler chancellor of Germany. The Nazi onslaught had begun.

Bonhoeffer and his family were extremely alarmed. "I disliked and mistrusted Hitler," Karl Bonhoeffer remembered, "because of his demagogic propagandistic speeches . . . his choice of colleagues—with whose qualities, incidentally, we in Berlin were better acquainted than people elsewhere—and finally because of what I heard from professional colleagues about his psychopathic symptoms."

The Bonhoeffers' mistrust proved well founded. On February 27, 1933, the Reichstag building burned down. Nazi leaders attributed this to arson and a Communist attempt to overthrow the government, promptly issuing the Reichstag Fire Decree. This act suspended a host of civil liberties, including the right to assemble, freedom of speech, and freedom of the press. All restraints on police investigations were eliminated. The edict authorized "intervention in the privacy of post and telegraph and telephone . . . house searches and the confiscation and restriction of property beyond the hitherto legal limits." When the government decree went into effect, Bonhoeffer warned his friends outside the country that he could not write them freely because his letters were now subject to government censorship. Finally, the Reichstag Fire Decree enabled the operation of concentration camps.

On March 21, 1933, the Nazi government authorized the Malicious Practices Act. This act prohibited criticism of the national government and imposed restrictions on anyone unwilling to declare his or her loyalty to Germany. Citizens quickly felt its consequences. In April 1933, for example, when Bonhoeffer's American friends Paul and Marion Lehmann visited the family home in Berlin, they found it odd that Dietrich's brother Klaus kept getting up in the middle of their conversation and flinging open the door to see if anyone was listening behind it. A few days after the passage of the Malicious Practices Act, the Enabling Act gave Hitler the right to make laws without consulting the Reichstag (parliament), effectively making him dictator of Germany.

The Führer lost no time in imposing the anti-Semitic agenda he'd long espoused. On April 1, 1933, Hitler ordered a nationwide boycott of Jewish businesses. Storm troopers—members of Hitler's paramilitary organization, the SA (Sturmabteilung in German)—painted the Star of David on stores and other establishments owned by Jews, keeping guard outside them. They also splashed many of the windows with anti-Semitic slogans, such as "The Jews Are Our Misfortune."

Worse was to come for the six hundred thousand Jews in Germany. On April 7, 1933, the Law for the Restoration of the Professional Civil Service went into effect. The edict banned Jews from civil service and marked the Nazi government's first incorporation of an "Aryan Paragraph" into law. This regulation excluded Jews and other non-Aryans from certain professions, organizations, and other aspects of public life. During the same month, new national laws limited the number of Jewish students at German schools and universities and restricted "Jewish activity" in the legal and medical professions. Taken together, these edicts would form the basis for the Nuremberg Race Laws of 1935 that defined Jews by ancestral lineage rather than by religious activity and formalized their segregation from the so-called Aryan population.

The new laws went into effect almost immediately. Jewish civil servants, students, faculty members, and others were dismissed from

their positions. Other citizens were fired for not supporting government policies. Theologian Paul Tillich was let go from the University
of Frankfurt for getting into an argument with a government official
about the Jewish sources of Christianity. Another Frankfurt faculty
member, Peter Drucker, who was of Jewish descent, saw danger
coming and emigrated. In his memoir, *Adventures of a Bystander*,
he recalled his decision:

> The Nazis knew that control of Frankfurt University would mean
> control of German academia altogether. . . . Everybody knew that
> a trial of strength was at hand. . . .
>
> The new Nazi commissar wasted no time on the amenities. He
> immediately announced that Jews would be forbidden to enter
> university premises and would be dismissed without salary on
> March 15. . . . Then he launched into a tirade of abuse, filth, and
> four-letter words such as had rarely been heard even in the barracks
> and never before in academia. . . . Next the new boss pointed his
> finger at one department chairman after another and said: "You
> either do what I tell you or we'll put you into a concentration
> camp." There was dead silence when he finished. . . . I went out
> sick unto death—and I knew that I would leave Germany within
> forty-eight hours.

The effects of the Aryan Paragraph were not limited to citizens of
Jewish descent. In April 1933, Dietrich himself ran up against these
when his sister Sabine's father-in-law died, and the Bonhoeffers urged
the young pastor to conduct the funeral. Although Sabine's husband
Gerhard Leibholz had been baptized a Christian, his father was descended from a Jewish family. Worried that performing the funeral
rites might subject him to reprisal by state or church authorities,
Dietrich declined to take part. He quickly regretted the decision. As
he wrote to Sabine and his brother-in-law, "To be frank, I can't think
what made me behave as I did. How could I have been so horribly
afraid at the time? It must have seemed equally incomprehensible to
you both, and yet you said nothing. But it preys on my mind, because
it's the kind of thing one can never make up for."

Other alarming developments followed. In the spring of 1933, local governments were reorganized to bring them under tighter national control. The Gestapo, the official secret police of the Nazi government, was formed under the command of Hitler's longtime ally Hermann Göring. He, in turn, reported to Heinrich Himmler, who was head of the SS (Schutzstaffel in German), the police and military force that quashed dissent, served as political foot soldiers for Hitler, and carried out a range of Nazi intimidation measures. Some of these authorities were on hand the evening of May 10, 1933, in Berlin when twenty-five thousand books by authors viewed as enemies of the Third Reich were burned at ceremonial midnight rallies. The works of Albert Einstein, Thomas Mann, Sigmund Freud, Erich Maria Remarque, who'd written *All Quiet on the Western Front*, and others went up in flames as the writers' names were read aloud. That same month, Hitler banned all trade unions, and in July, the National Socialists declared themselves the only legal political party in Germany.

Of all the government actions, Bonhoeffer identified the Reich's attacks against the Jews as the most sinister. He knew that officials in many German churches were grappling with what the application of the Aryan Paragraph meant to their congregations. For example, did Nazi laws exclude those of Jewish blood—either those who had converted to Christianity or those who had Jewish relatives—from serving in the ministry? Did the same laws prevent baptized non-Aryans from being members of their churches? Protestant leaders, who made up two-thirds of German clerics, were divided on these issues. As 1933 wore on, they debated what their churches should do under the new, aggressive, and controlling government.

CHAPTER THIRTY-FIVE

Confronting Nazi Aggression

In the 1930s, the largest church in Germany was the German Evangelical Church. It incorporated Lutheranism and other major theological traditions that had emerged from the Reformation; most of the nation's 40 million Protestants were members. Historically, the German Evangelical Church had been loyal to the state. But as the National Socialists rose to power, an even more zealous patriotic movement emerged within it. Calling themselves the "German Christians," these members enthusiastically embraced Nazi ideology. As scholar Victoria Barnett has written, the group's leaders and lay members were "strongly anti-Semitic and supported the Nazi agenda as the political reflection of 'true' German Christianity. . . . The German people were seen as God's chosen instrument at a crucial historical moment, with Adolf Hitler as the man who would lead them out of the wilderness." By early 1933, German Christians hoped to create one national Reich (state) church; many also wanted to apply the Nazi edicts to church practices, forcing out members who were non-Aryan.

Against this backdrop, Bonhoeffer wrote an essay titled "The Church and the Jewish Question," focusing on the problems the Aryan Paragraph posed for the German Evangelical Church. What, Bonhoeffer asked, should church leaders do in the face of the Nazi government's actions against the Jews? He called for three responses. First, he wrote, the church should ask the state whether its actions were legitimate, thus "making the state responsible for what it does."

Second, Bonhoeffer asserted that the church had an unconditional obligation to care for and defend "the victims of any societal order, even if they do not belong to the Christian community." The third response, Bonhoeffer wrote, was to attack the origin of the suffering, which was the state itself, to stop such abuse. For most church officials in 1933, this was a radical, virtually unthinkable, position. "Bonhoeffer was almost alone in his opinions," theologian Heinz Eduard Tödt has written. He "was the only one who considered solidarity with the Jews . . . to be a matter of such importance as to obligate the Christian Churches to risk a massive conflict with the state—a risk which could threaten their very existence."

Bonhoeffer knew he was in a small minority, but he had to act. He was faced with a pressing ethical question that few had seen coming, and now many refused to acknowledge: What should one do in the face of overt, state-sanctioned racism? Long before many of his contemporaries, he grasped the seriousness of the Nazi government's attack on its enemies. He watched as government edicts stripped Jews of basic civil rights, and he feared Hitler and his supporters would do far worse. In Bonhoeffer's eyes, the Nazi actions were a violation of Christ's love and, particularly, of his commandments, which were to be applied to all, regardless of ancestry, race, or religion. Given this, Bonhoeffer couldn't remain silent. Deliberately or not, he'd drawn a line in the sand: Christianity and Nazism were at irreconcilable odds.

In writing "The Church and the Jewish Question," the young minister hoped to work together with leaders of the German Evangelical Church to confront Nazi laws and the state's increasing influence. Instead, his paper caused an uproar. Most clerics simply weren't prepared to go as far as Bonhoeffer in confronting the new government. Fearing that Hitler would try to intervene directly in church affairs, the majority of ecclesiastical leaders took the path of least resistance.

During the summer of 1933, the Nazi government consolidated its control of religious institutions, particularly the German Evangelical Church. In July, this body held elections for a new Reich bishop to lead it; Nazi officials threw their weight behind Ludwig Müller, a former military chaplain who'd known the Führer since the 1920s. Not surprisingly, when the votes were counted, Müller emerged victorious.

At about the same time, the Third Reich signed an agreement with the Vatican known as the Concordat. In exchange for guaranteeing the rights of German Catholics, the Holy See agreed that all bishops had to take an oath of loyalty to the head of the German government. The treaty also required all Catholic clergy to abstain from political activity. From this point, the majority of German churches came under state control.

All this was deeply disappointing for Bonhoeffer and other clerics who opposed Nazi ideology and state interference in the church. The dissident pastors decided to stop trying to change the German Evangelical Church—which had now effectively become the Reichskirche, or state church—and began building their own coalition to protest Nazi policies. Some of these reformers objected to the demands that the Third Reich was making of church leaders, including the requirement that ministers swear loyalty oaths to the Führer. Others disapproved of the German Christians' call to excise the Old Testament from the Bible because it was Jewish scripture. Still others, such as Bonhoeffer, believed that German Protestantism was fundamentally incompatible with Nazi ideology.

By late summer 1933, the twenty-seven-year-old pastor was gravely worried about the Nazis' ascendance to power. Some of his concern was related to the Reich's growing control over Christian institutions. Some of his worry was about the broader future: If the Nazis had so quickly begun robbing Jews of civil liberties, to what other lengths would they go? Bonhoeffer's anxiety also stemmed from inside information about the Nazi government that family members provided him. Among these was his brother-in-law Hans von Dohnanyi, the husband of his sister Christine. A fierce opponent of National Socialism, Dohnanyi worked as a lawyer in the Reich Ministry of Justice, serving as assistant to the chief minister there, Franz Gürtner. Like Dohnanyi, Gürtner had serious doubts about Hitler's totalitarian regime and often confided these to his assistant. Dohnanyi could see for himself how the Third Reich was constructing a system of political and legal authority based on growing intimidation, discrimination, and violence, and he shared what he learned with Bonhoeffer.

In 1933, did Bonhoeffer imagine the scope of brutality that was to come? There is no definitive evidence that he did. What there is, however—particularly in his letters, sermons, and other writings—is his dawning realization that Germany was playing with fire at the hands of Hitler. What was Bonhoeffer to do? How could he make a worthy difference? These were critical questions for the young minister.

Beginning in the spring of 1933, Bonhoeffer worked from a sense of urgency as he tried to turn the German Evangelical Church away from the Aryan Paragraph and force its leaders to address the inherent conflict between Christianity and Nazism. Bonhoeffer also became concerned about Hitler's military ambitions. For example, in October 1933, when Hitler pulled Germany out of the League of Nations, Bonhoeffer was greatly alarmed, confiding to a friend, "This has brought the danger of war very much closer." Few ministerial colleagues, including those who opposed the Aryan Paragraph, shared such concerns, and Bonhoeffer felt increasingly isolated. He described his situation in a letter to his former professor the theologian Karl Barth:

> I found myself in radical opposition to all my friends. . . . All this frightened me and shook my confidence, so that I began to fear that dogmatism might be leading me astray—since there seemed no particular reason why my own view in these matters should be any better, any more right, than the views of many really good and able pastors whom I sincerely respect. And so I thought it was about time to go into the wilderness for a spell. . . . At the time it seemed to me more dangerous to make a gesture than to retreat into silence.

The "wilderness" into which Bonhoeffer moved was London. There, in the autumn of 1933, he found work as a pastor for two German-speaking congregations and attempted to sort through his self-doubt and take stock of his path. "What he wanted," his biographer and close friend Eberhard Bethge has written, "was a period of seeking and testing in a small, quiet congregation."

Such a wish proved a pipe dream. In England, Bonhoeffer wrote his brother Karl Friedrich, "one is close enough to want to take part in everything [at home] and too far away for active participation. And during the past weeks this has made things exceptionally difficult for me." They would remain so throughout the eighteen months Bonhoeffer spent in London as he tried to influence the ongoing church struggle in Germany, fulfill his obligations in two city parishes, and remain active in the larger European ecumenical movement. The first and last of these commitments kept him in close contact with friends, colleagues, and church representatives, many of whom wanted his help and sought him out in London. Every few weeks, Bonhoeffer traveled back to Berlin. He also kept up a steady stream of letters, telegraphs, and telephone calls home. His phone bill was so large, his friends recalled, that the local British post office reduced it on the grounds that a foreign pastor should pay a more reasonable sum.

There were more demands on Bonhoeffer's time. While he was in London, he also worked with refugees, many of them Jewish émigrés from Germany, who needed assistance getting permission to work in England, finding a job, or otherwise putting down roots. As always, Bonhoeffer made time for friends, some of whom came to stay with him in his flat in southwest London. In the mornings, he and his guests read the *Times*, a more trusted source than many German newspapers. In the evenings, there was often music making, with Bonhoeffer playing the piano he'd brought with him from home.

In the nooks and crannies of this busy life, he also found time to see movies, rehearse his parish youth groups, and forge several new friendships, the most important of which was with George Bell, bishop of Chichester. The two men shared the same birthday and an abiding love of literature and music. Bonhoeffer admired Bell's integrity and graceful manners. Bell, in turn, respected the German's fine command of English, his trenchant observations about the Nazi regime, and his excellent listening skills. They each had a strong interest in the European ecumenical movement as a potential force against what was happening to the state church in Germany. Both men were also conscious, however, that the danger posed by the Third Reich couldn't be confronted by ecclesiastical action alone, and both became increasingly involved in political circles. In 1948, Bell remembered his experience with Bonhoeffer in England:

I knew him in London in the early days of the evil regime: and from him, more than from any other German, I learned the true character of the conflict. . . . I have no doubt that he did fine work with his German congregation[s]: but he taught many besides his fellow-countrymen while a pastor in England. He was crystal clear in his convictions; and young as he was, and humble-minded as he was, he saw the truth, and spoke it with a complete absence of fear. . . . Wherever he went, with whomever he was, with students, with those of his own age, or with his elders, he was undaunted, detached from himself, devoted to friends, to his home, to his country as God meant it to be, to his Church, to his Master.

During his time in London, Bonhoeffer stayed in touch with German church leaders who opposed the Reichskirche. In 1934, these clerics decided to establish their own church, naming it the Confessing Church. During organizational meetings held that year, the leaders of the new institution reached two important conclusions. First, the Confessing Church was the only true church in Germany, and thus it had no common faith with the German Evangelical Church. Second, as the only true church, the Confessing Church was entitled to establish its own seminaries, educate and ordain its own pastors, and create its own system of parish governance.

The ecclesiastical die was cast. Germany now had two Protestant churches: the Confessing Church, which included about seven thousand of a total of eighteen thousand pastors in Germany, and the larger Reichskirche, formed from the German Evangelical Church, which was under government control. Each of these institutions claimed to be the "true church." But critical theological, political, and practical issues separated the two, setting the stage for what historians have called the *Kirchenkampf*, or church struggle.

In the mid-1930s, Bonhoeffer devoted enormous effort to this contest, becoming a progressively more radical spokesman for the Confessing Church. Like his colleagues, he wanted this institution to resist state interference in ecclesiastical matters. He also hoped the alternative church would take a strong stand against National Socialism, particularly its racial discrimination. "It is also time for a final break with our theologically grounded reserve about whatever is being done by the state," he wrote his friend Edwin Sutz in 1934, "which really only comes down to fear. 'Speak out for those who cannot speak'—who in the church today still remembers that this is the very least the Bible asks of us in such times as these?"

During these years, Bonhoeffer was also very involved in the European ecumenical movement, in which he worked to mobilize support for the Confessing Church. He also called on European churches to leave behind what he saw as a misplaced patriotism and a threatening nationalism. He argued that churches in all countries must answer Christ's call to peace, which lies at the heart of the gospel.

At times, though, he sensed the limitations of the Confessing Church as an instrument for positive change. Ecclesiastical politics, he explained in a 1934 letter to a friend, had to ultimately give way to individual men and women deeply committed to the ethical imperatives of Christ's commandments:

> While I'm working with the church opposition with all my might, it's perfectly clear to me that *this* opposition is only a very temporary transitional phase on the way to opposition of a very different kind, and that very few of those involved in this preliminary skirmish are going to be there for that second struggle. I believe that all of Christendom should be praying with us for the coming of resistance "to the point of shedding blood" [a reference to Hebrews 12:4] and for the finding of people who can suffer it through. Simply suffering is what it will be about, not parries, blows, or thrusts such as may still be allowed and possible in the preliminary battles; the real struggle that perhaps lies ahead must be one of simply suffering through in faith.

At the time, Bonhoeffer could not see that "opposition of a very different kind" would ultimately lead him out of his ecclesiastical work and into active political resistance. But through unsparing self-examination, he knew that much more would be needed in the fight against the Third Reich.

CHAPTER THIRTY-SIX

Building Community

B y the mid-1930s, the Nazis had greatly consolidated their power. Some of this was accomplished by eliminating suspected enemies. In June 1934, for example, Hitler decided to take care of a host of people deemed threats to the regime. Under the direction of Gestapo founder Hermann Göring and Deputy Führer Rudolf Hess, as many as two hundred people were killed and over one thousand arrested as part of a three-day purge that became known as the Night of the Long Knives.

A day later, the Reich cabinet legalized the murders on the grounds that they were necessary to save the nation. As a quid pro quo for carrying out the killings, Hitler gave Heinrich Himmler and his SS troops additional authority. During the next six months, Himmler assumed control over the growing network of concentration camps. These were used then primarily to incarcerate Socialists, Communists, Gypsies, homosexuals, and other individuals accused of socially deviant behavior.

A month after the purge, on August 2, 1934, German president Paul von Hindenburg died. Hitler immediately merged the offices of president and chancellor, declaring himself *Führer* and *Reichskanzler*, "leader" and "chancellor." Two weeks later, a plebiscite confirmed his new position, effectively eliminating all institutional checks on his power.

As Hitler strengthened his political base, he also increased Germany's military might. In October 1934, he directed the army to create a tank fleet; a few months later, he ordered the buildup of the Luftwaffe (air force). He also reintroduced conscription. "At a stroke," historian John Keegan has written, "a German army artificially restricted to inferior status vis-à-vis its neighbors [by the terms of the Versailles Treaty that ended World War I] began to expand, first to match and then to exceed their strengths."

At the same time, Nazi leaders initiated a second phase of persecution against Jews—the Nuremberg Laws. These edicts prohibited Jews from marrying or having sexual relations with individuals of "German or related blood" and excluded Jews from Reich citizenship. The laws also defined a Jew not as someone who espoused a certain set of beliefs or engaged in particular religious practices, but rather as one who had descended from three or four Jewish grandparents. Together with the 1933 civil service law (with its Aryan Paragraph), the Nuremberg Laws laid the legal basis for the Reich's intensifying attacks against Jews, who were now treated as a lower class of nationals with few, if any, political rights.

Against this backdrop, Bonhoeffer became frustrated with the Confessing Church's failure to effect any real change. He worried that the church struggle was becoming an end in itself, focused inwardly on the politics of various factions rather than on what was actually happening in Germany. He wanted to combat the injustice perpetrated by the Third Reich and to do so by peaceful means, as he felt his faith required. Once again, his mind turned to Mahatma Gandhi, and he wondered if the time had come for him to take a sabbatical in India.

But as before, the pilgrimage didn't happen. In early 1935, Bonhoeffer was offered a position as director of a newly created seminary dedicated to training Confessing Church pastors, and this option appealed to him. In April, Bonhoeffer and twenty-three candidates for ordination began a bold experiment in theological training in Zingst, a small town in northern Germany along the Baltic coast. In June, the group moved to more permanent quarters in Finkenwalde, a village located forty miles east (just across the present-day Polish border).

In this remote location, Bonhoeffer established a community that he hoped would stand as a bastion against the false teachings of the Nazi-controlled state church. He wanted to create more than a religious enterprise unto itself; he sought to fashion a program of study and way of life that would educate candidates for ordination in the essential teachings of Christianity at a time when these teachings were threatened from almost every side. This meant, Bonhoeffer wrote, "we need a group of pastors who are completely free and ready for sacrifice. They must be prepared . . . to go where their services are needed. . . .The aim is not the seclusion of the monastery, but innermost concentration for service to the outside world."

From the start, Bonhoeffer threw himself into the work of leading the seminary. This began with designing and teaching a course of study that relied heavily on the Sermon on the Mount. By 1935, he had come to believe that Christ's message in the famous sermon, which incorporated the Golden Rule and the principle of turning the other cheek, had powerful resonance, not only theologically, but also as a moral ballast in the storms of evil buffeting Germany. For him, it was essential that the next generation of ministers—the men and many fewer women now in Confessing Church seminaries—understand the Sermon on the Mount and live their lives according to it. In early 1935, writing to his brother Karl Friedrich, he outlined the sermon's critical importance:

> When I first started in theology, my idea of [the Sermon on the Mount] was quite different—rather more academic, probably. Now it has turned into something else altogether. . . . I think I am right in saying that I would only achieve true inner clarity and honesty by really starting to take the Sermon on the Mount seriously. Here alone lies the force that can blow all this hocus-pocus sky-high—like fireworks, leaving only a few burnt-out shells behind.

With the Sermon on the Mount as his foundation, Bonhoeffer structured the students' daily routine around lectures, worship services, Bible reading, shared song, and meditation (which virtually all the students initially found difficult, and some never felt comfortable with). He also made sure the students had plenty of time for physical activity, including long walks, swimming in the Baltic Sea's bracing waters, table tennis (in which Bonhoeffer excelled), and other organized games.

Teacher and students shared meals and daily chores. In the evenings, they gathered together to play music. On occasion, they performed skits and musical numbers with the minister at the piano. At other times, the group listened to the gramophone records that Bonhoeffer had brought home with him from New York. Eberhard Bethge, who first met Bonhoeffer as a student at Finkenwalde, remembered that the "rooms often rang with then little-known Negro spirituals, such as 'Swing Low, Sweet Chariot.'"

The setting, a dilapidated estate, was simple; some of the students found it primitive. The food was plain, and "in the long run monotonous," one remembered. Most of the furniture had been donated by nearby residents. In these sparse accommodations, Bonhoeffer worked to foster collaboration and commitment. Toward this end, he insisted on several rules, what today we would call behavioral norms. As Otto Dudzus, who lived at Finkenwalde, recalled:

> First, one was not to speak about someone else in the latter's absence nor offer any judgments concerning that person, not even judgments cloaked in the guise of well-meaning criticism. Anything one person wanted to say to another should be said to that person directly. . . . Second, during the [six-month] session every member of the community was to take at least one long walk with every other member. Whenever time permitted, Bonhoeffer himself was particularly fond of taking advantage of this wonderful opportunity. Third, Sundays were to be spent together, in the morning naturally in the worship service, then in the afternoon with communal walks or social games in the garden and house.

But these rules weren't alone in reinforcing the ordinands' commitment to their mission and one another. Dudzus continued:

> What was the secret of this Finkenwalde community that developed so effortlessly and, as it were, on its own initiative? Certainly one

factor was Bonhoeffer's own fascinating personality, his openness to every individual and his sense of play and [talent] for good jokes.

Another key element in the group's sense of shared purpose was Bonhoeffer's kindliness, including his small acts of service and generosity. The seminary leader practiced what one ordinand, Wilhelm Rott, remembered as "matter-of-course brotherly love." When a student was ill, for example, Bonhoeffer was known to disappear into the kitchen, returning with an "opulent breakfast in best English style." "No rule without exception," he said, contrasting the refreshment with the seminary's usual simple fare. "The meal which they shared," Rott recalled, "made the invalid forget his sickness." In later years, when the Nazis arrested Confessing Church ministers, including many of Bonhoeffer's former students, he often visited them in prison. Rott remembered how in 1937, after he himself was released from arrest, "there was Dietrich again. He had tickets for *Don Giovanni*, and with Eberhard Bethge we celebrated my newly won freedom in the opera house."

At Finkenwalde, the focus was on creating and maintaining a strong, vibrant community, one imbued with ethical purpose and committed to fortifying each individual as well as the group. In *Life Together*, a book Bonhoeffer wrote about the Finkenwalde experiment, he explained the importance of the community—including its routines and discipline:

Who can really be faithful in great things, if they have not learned to be faithful in the things of daily life?

Every day brings the Christian many hours of being alone in an unchristian environment. These are times of *testing*. This is the proving ground of a genuine time of meditation and genuine Christian community. Has the community served to make individuals free, strong, and mature, or has it made them insecure and dependent? Has it taken them by the hand for a while so they would learn again to walk by themselves, or has it made them anxious and unsure? This is one of the toughest and most serious questions that can be put to any form of everyday Christian life in community.

From Bonhoeffer's perspective, not only did a healthy community help an individual discover his own deep-seated confidence, it also helped him forge a worthy mission. In 1935, such a community was the church as he believed it ought to exist: anchored in Christ's essential teachings and serving as a resource that impelled its members to "active love, to obedience, to good works." He believed these good works extended beyond one's private sphere and included active opposition to institutions at odds with Christ's Word. Such opposition, biographer Charles Marsh has written, "required spiritual nourishment: prayer, Bible study, and meditation on the essential matters to expand the moral imagination."

The ability to develop and sustain an effective community is a critical skill for today's leaders. Scores of managerial studies demonstrate the key role that engaged, collaborative teams play in innovation, organizational transformation, and other goals. But what Bonhoeffer (and Shackleton) understood as community was distinct from what the word *teamwork* has come to mean today. For both these leaders, community meant more than sharing a mission and acting together toward that end. It meant being bound together not only by obligation, but by mutual caring and affection.

As these two individuals understood, this caring and affection begins with the leader himself. The higher the stakes, the more essential it is for the leader to demonstrate ongoing love, respect, and attention to the details—however small—of his followers' lives. Shackleton knew he needed his men to believe in themselves and their collective power to get home safely, and that a precondition for both was a sense of unity and mutual devotion. Bonhoeffer couldn't have navigated through the crisis of confidence that he faced in New York in mid-1939 without the anchoring comradeship he'd experienced among his brethren in Germany. Small wonder that community was an ongoing concern for each of these leaders.

In 1935, the Reich Ministry of Church Affairs declared the Confessing Church illegal. This meant that Bonhoeffer and other pastors in this church were teaching in full knowledge that at any moment they might be arrested. Their students likewise understood the risks they were taking.

Nonetheless, in the two years that the seminary operated, five groups of roughly twenty-five ordinands each completed the course. Some of these individuals would go on to clash directly with the Nazi government. In 1936, for example, a small group of Confessing Church clerics composed a secret memorandum to Hitler criticizing the Nazi government's legal encroachments, including the Reich's anti-Semitism, concentration camps, and spying. Bonhoeffer was not directly involved in drafting this memo, but he'd followed its writing closely, conferring with one of its authors, Franz Hildebrandt, on its form and content.

Hitler didn't acknowledge the memorandum. But six weeks later, it was leaked and published verbatim in a Swiss newspaper. Shortly after, the Gestapo arrested three of Bonhoeffer's former students in connection with the document: Ernst Tillich, Werner Koch, and Friedrich Weissler; in February 1937, the men were sent to Sachsenhausen concentration camp. Tillich and Koch were eventually released. Weissler, who was Jewish, was not; he died six days after arriving at the camp, likely from repeated beatings.

After the memorandum's publication, life grew more difficult for many Confessing Church ministers, including Bonhoeffer. The Reich Ministry of Education permanently rescinded his right to teach at the University of Berlin, and his post there was terminated. Many of his former students from Finkenwalde also found themselves under increasing attack; Bonhoeffer tried to maintain an informal community of support for them. To this end, he produced a regular newsletter. (Because the Nazis banned such communication, the newsletters were mailed in hand-addressed envelopes and dropped into different mailboxes to deflect suspicion.) Bonhoeffer also invited his former ordinands to connect at organized retreats, and many attended. "The small group [of Finkenwalde students] that survived [World War II and Nazi imprisonment]," biographer Ferdinand Schlingensiepen has written, "had a sense of belonging together which lasted all their lives and was evident to everyone who came into contact with them."

As a leader in the Confessing Church, Bonhoeffer fought a powerful, rising tide of Nazi oppression that, by the late 1930s, effectively limited much of the practical effect he and his students might have in retarding Hitler's depredations. But this fact—one Bonhoeffer was well aware of—doesn't negate the importance of his leadership. Like Frederick Douglass, he understood that part of a leader's responsibility rests in his or her role as a spokesperson for goodness and right action in the face of widespread evil. Bonhoeffer knew that owning and discharging this responsibility was critical to the creation of all forms of resistance—those that were successful and those that weren't—and thus he and his students pushed forward without the tangible confirmation of big wins.

Bonhoeffer and other Confessing Church leaders needed all the strength they could summon as the Reich's persecution intensified. Many ministers were arrested; a few were physically assaulted. In June 1937, for example, the Gestapo burst into a meeting of church leadership in Berlin and arrested eight members. A week later, Martin Niemöller, one of the founders of the Confessing Church, was arrested in his home in the Berlin suburb of Dahlem. After taking their prisoner away, officers conducted an eight-hour search of his study. Niemöller spent the next seven years in Sachsenhausen and Dachau concentration camps.

In September 1937, the Gestapo closed Finkenwalde on the grounds that it was an insurgent institution. "Now, even the place where we could gather for quiet work and brotherly help and reinforcement has been taken from us," Bonhoeffer wrote in his newsletter. "This is a time of testing for us all." And it was only the beginning. By Christmas, nearly thirty of his former students had been incarcerated. "Some are still detained at present," he noted at the time, "and have spent the entire Advent in prison. Among the others there won't be a single person who has not experienced the impact, in his work and his personal life, of the increasingly impatient attacks of the anti-Christian forces."

Even though Finkenwalde didn't survive, the experience of creating and leading the seminary was important for Bonhoeffer. For one thing, he'd thrown his whole self into the enterprise and loved doing it. "The summer of 1935," he wrote the first group of seminary students, "was, I believe, the most fulfilling period in my entire life thus far both professionally and personally. . . . By living together with all of you, I learned more than ever in both respects."

For another, Bonhoeffer had devoted time and attention while he was at Finkenwalde to the concept of discipleship. He'd long been interested in the topic and in 1937 published *The Cost of Discipleship*. The book examined Christ's call to follow him and the relevance of his call in the modern world, not only for the spiritual elite, but also for "the worker, the businessman, the squire and the soldier." Where will such a call lead men and women in their respective lives? What decisions, actions, and states of mind will it demand? Drawing on the Sermon on the Mount, Bonhoeffer tackled these and other questions in a work that has become a classic in Christian thought.

Equally important, Bonhoeffer's students recognized him as a leader of integrity. In this respect, they were like many other people who encountered the serious, compassionate minister. Why did people follow Dietrich Bonhoeffer? Some of what made him credible as a leader was his ability to listen well and take others seriously on their own terms. Some of his power came from his ability to see and articulate the big picture—often before others did. Another aspect of Bonhoeffer's authority came from his ability to move seamlessly between righteous ideals and the concrete actions needed to achieve those ideals.

Finally, Bonhoeffer's effectiveness as a leader owed a great deal to his humanity: his everyday kindness, humor, humility, and accessibility. Like many individuals who motivate others to do harder, better things than they can do on their own, he was perceived to be both removed from the people he led and simultaneously available to them in important respects. There is no evidence that Bonhoeffer dissected his leadership in this kind of detail. But it seems likely that he sensed the impact he had on his students; he certainly understood their abiding commitment and affection. And all of this fed his confidence as a leader going forward.

CHAPTER THIRTY-SEVEN

The Tightening Noose

When 1938 opened, Bonhoeffer was serving as a minister for the Confessing Church in northern Germany and illegally training ordinands. About the same time, the Nazi government banned him from traveling to Berlin on the grounds that he was an enemy of the state. Bonhoeffer and his former students weren't the only members of the Confessing Church who were subject to Nazi persecution. Many people who were deemed enemies of the government felt the state's strong arm against them. Different individuals and groups responded in different ways. Some grew stronger in their opposition to the Reich; others shrank from its threat.

In April 1938, for example, the administrative clerics in the Nazi-controlled Reichskirche ordered that all active pastors in Germany take a loyalty oath to Adolf Hitler on pain of dismissal. The oath of allegiance, church officials stated, was a "personal commitment to the Führer under the summons of God." This oath caused great controversy among Confessing Church leaders, since they did not recognize the ecclesiastical authority of the Reichskirche. After lengthy discussion, these clerics decided they would put the oath before their ministry, allowing individual pastors to choose for themselves whether to take it. Eventually, the majority of Confessing Church ministers elected to do so. In the conservative regions of the country, such as the Rhineland, Brandenburg, and Pomerania (northern Germany), as many as 80 percent of pastors pledged their allegiance to Hitler.

Bonhoeffer found it impossible to follow the clerical directive. (He was not required to take the oath, however, because he was preaching illegally and therefore not on the roster of active ministers.) He protested vehemently against the oath's enforcement, but the majority of Confessing Church leaders ignored him. In the aftermath of this controversy, Bonhoeffer was deeply ashamed of his church and alienated from much of its leadership. He'd devoted enormous amounts of time and energy to help found an institution that would oppose Nazi ideology and ecclesiastical control. Now, he watched as this same institution appeared to be caving in to the very regime it was created to resist.

Isolated from his church and without steady employment, Bonhoeffer lived a nomadic existence from 1938 until he was imprisoned five years later. He was prohibited from traveling to Berlin for anything but family visits and was under the growing scrutiny of Nazi police. In 1940, he would be banned from all public speaking because of what the Third Reich labeled "subversive activity."

All these constraints forced him into frequent travel and extended stays with sympathetic friends. His pastoral work was conducted underground in villages and small towns. In these often remote places, he ministered, as biographers Elisabeth Sifton and Fritz Stern have written, "to the families of dozens of his students whom the Gestapo was persecuting with house searches, interrogations, and arrests." In defiance of the Reich's order, he continued to train ordinands in Confessing Church parishes around the country. As he moved from place to place, he also wrote when he could—sermons, letters, and the beginning of a book on ethics. It cannot have been easy to live like this. But, as Eberhard Bethge has written, Bonhoeffer got on with it:

[He] taught, reflected, and wrote after 1937 with no settled place to work and without his book collection. . . . Only for the work on ethics during the war did he try once more in Berlin to collect any considerable number of relevant books. . . . He could rely on his memory, which generally provided what he needed. Increasingly, however—more than he actually admitted—he longed for settled work, and sometimes he would heave a deep sigh over his gypsy-like

existence. Although he never acknowledged it, the flight in 1939 to
the United States was partly a result of this yearning to settle down.

While Bonhoeffer continued his theological work underground,
larger storm clouds gathered, and the threat of war intensified. In
March 1938, Germany annexed Austria in an event called the Anschluss, or political union. Less than six months later, Hitler threatened
to take the western borderland of Czechoslovakia, an area heavily
populated by Germans and known as the Sudetenland. France and
Britain responded by signing the Munich Agreement, a treaty with
Germany and Italy that allowed German annexation of the Sudetenland in exchange for Hitler's assurance that he would pursue no
future military action without additional discussion.

As the Reich prepared for war, it also increased its assaults on the
Jews. In mid-1938, Bonhoeffer's brother-in-law Hans von Dohnanyi,
who had inside information, warned his wife's family that the Nazis
were planning a widespread campaign against the Jews in the recently
annexed Sudetenland. Dohnanyi also told the Bonhoeffers about
the coming decree, promulgated in August 1938, that required Jews
to publicly identify themselves. Those with first names that were of
"non-Jewish origin" would henceforth have to add *Israel* or *Sara* to
their given names. All Jews would be ordered to carry identity cards
that included their heritage, and Jewish passports would be stamped
with the letter *J*. Dohnanyi was certain that this was a prelude to
more terrible action. The SS newspaper, *Das Schwarze Korps*, wrote
that if war broke out, the outcome for the Jews would be "total
annihilation."

The Bonhoeffers worried for the safety of Sabine, Dietrich's twin
sister, and her husband, Gerhard Leibholz, who was classified a
non-Aryan by government authorities. Even with their well-placed
connections in Berlin, family members were certain they could not
protect Leibholz. Writing to Dietrich in August, Sabine revealed the
couple's rising fear:

> In recent weeks [Gerhard has] no longer been able to maintain his
> old equanimity. Ultimately the resilience of the nerves simply gives

in. At the moment it's hard to think all the way through all the decisions that need to be made, and that makes one so nervous. Unfortunately, he's simply sleeping so badly. So I must hold down the fort for two, and sometimes it's not very easy to keep in mind matters as divergent as existential questions and pressing worries alongside the large and small concerns and wishes of the children.

In early September, the couple and their two daughters safely emigrated to England.

It was a well-timed exit. On November 9, 1938, the Nazis unleashed a wave of violent pogroms against Jews in Germany, Austria, and parts of the Sudetenland. State police and other authorities destroyed synagogues, looted Jewish businesses, and set fire to homes and other buildings. They desecrated Jewish cemeteries and arrested as many Jews as local jails could hold, incarcerating close to thirty thousand. The night and following day of terror were called Kristallnacht (Night of Broken Glass) for all the windows that were smashed. The pogroms claimed at least ninety-one Jewish lives. "Kristallnacht was a brutal signal," historian Victoria Barnett has written, "not just of Nazi intentions but of the extent to which ordinary compassion in German society had become numbed."

In the aftermath of Kristallnacht, the Third Reich pressed aggressively forward with its plans to deprive Jews of their property, occupations, and practical means of daily living. Jewish children were expelled from schools. Jews were no longer permitted to own cars or have driver's licenses. They were forbidden admission to theaters and concert halls. Emboldened by the overall passivity with which most Aryan Germans reacted to Kristallnacht, the Nazi government grew more audacious in its actions, paving the way for future policies that included forced emigration and mass extermination.

During this period, the German churches remained largely silent. Several years earlier, Bonhoeffer had maintained, "Only he who cries for the Jews may sing Gregorian chants." But in the aftermath of Kristallnacht, he said nothing publicly. In his personal Bible, he underlined Psalm 74:8, which reads, "They have burned up all the synagogues of God in the land." He also wrote Kristallnacht's date in the margin: "9.11.38." When some of Bonhoeffer's former students suggested that Kristallnacht was a curse on the Jews, he replied, "When today the synagogues are set afire, tomorrow the churches will burn." Bonhoeffer was privately outraged by the Nazi pogrom. But at the end of 1938, he stood relatively alone and without the widespread influence he'd once known. Frustrated by the Confessing Church's growing unwillingness to take a stand against the Third Reich, on the move to avoid arrest by the Gestapo, and uncertain what he should do to effectively resist a regime he deemed immoral and antithetical to Christ's teachings, he watched and waited for an opportunity to make a real difference.

In March 1939, in clear violation of the Munich Agreement, the German army marched into Prague and occupied Czechoslovakia. Recognizing that Hitler was likely to invade Poland next, British and French leaders extended a diplomatic guarantee to that country, committing their countries to military action if the Poles were attacked. The runway to war had become short and steep.

As international conflict appeared more likely, Bonhoeffer grew less certain of his own path. He could not serve in Hitler's military. He was deeply disillusioned with the Confessing Church and largely without a public voice. What to do? Where to turn? In late May 1939, he decided to leave Germany for the Union Theological Seminary in New York.

Since the mid-1930s, many had seen clearly that Hitler intended to make war. The vast majority of Nazi officials supported these plans, but a number of officers and others at high levels of the Reich were outraged by the Führer's growing ambition and unprovoked military aggression. After the Anschluss in early 1938, this opposition intensified. In some parts of the government, this outrage became covert resistance.

From his post in the Reich Ministry of Justice, Hans von Dohnanyi had long opposed Hitler and his government. Now, as Germany moved closer to war, he and his wife, Christine, resolved to join the resistance against the Führer. Dohnanyi's superior, Minister of Justice Franz Gürtner, also objected to much of what Hitler was doing. In 1938, Gürtner appointed Dohnanyi to a judgeship in Leipzig to help him evade the Gestapo's close surveillance in Berlin. But Dohnanyi remained in contact with high-ranking members of the resistance in the capital. These men included Chief of the General Staff General Ludwig Beck, Admiral Wilhelm Canaris, who was head of the Reich's Department of Military Intelligence (known in German as the Abwehr), and his deputy Hans Oster. In different ways, Dohnanyi supported their activities, which by 1939 came to include the possibility of killing Hitler and toppling the Third Reich. Dohnanyi also kept a secret, meticulous log of Nazi atrocities that he called "the chronicle of shame"; in the event of the Führer's overthrow, Dohnanyi intended to use the record as justification for the coup d'état.

Dohnanyi shared this chronicle and the group's assassination plans with Bonhoeffer, discussing what might follow the end of the Nazi regime. The two men also considered the ethical implications of murdering Hitler. During one evening conversation, for example, Dohnanyi broached the question raised by the passage in Matthew's gospel that reads, "All they that take the sword shall perish with the sword" (Matthew 26:52). Would such a judgment apply to the conspirators? he wondered. Bonhoeffer told Dohnanyi that, yes, it would, and that it was important for the conspirators to take full moral responsibility for their actions.

In 1939, as Bonhoeffer considered where his duty lay, he wrestled with this responsibility. For several years, he had watched what his brother-in-law and other resisters were doing, occasionally advising Dohnanyi on the morality of these actions. Now, Bonhoeffer considered greater involvement in the conspiracy to kill Hitler, overthrow the Third Reich, and stop the train of Nazi evil. Moving from observer to active participant, however, raised thorny questions for the thirty-three-year-old pastor. How could he, a devoted follower of Christ, justify joining a group of would-be assassins? Was he willing to risk his life in such an attempt? These questions pressed in on him—most heavily during his brief time in New York City in mid-1939. But once he'd navigated through this emotional turbulence and returned to Germany, he was ready to assume both the responsibility and the risk.

In July 1939, Wilhelm Canaris, head of the Abwehr, appointed Dohnanyi as an assistant to Canaris's deputy Hans Oster. After the appointment, Dohnanyi and his family moved back to Berlin from Leipzig. The new position increased his access to valuable information and expanded his role in the conspiracy. It also kept him out of military service, since his work was classified as indispensable to the Reich. But the appointment also raised the odds that Dohnanyi would be discovered and arrested. He would certainly be under greater surveillance by Nazi police, because many in the Gestapo and SS viewed the Abwehr as a rival organization and were keen to find fault with anyone or anything in that office.

As the conspirators in the Abwehr formulated their plans, they kept close tabs on the larger situation in Europe. In August 1939, Germany and the Soviet Union signed a nonaggression treaty, with each country promising not to attack the other in the event of war and agreeing to divide the spoils of victory: a conquered Poland and a defeated Eastern Europe. For Hitler, the pact was critical because it allowed him to invade Poland without the possibility of Soviet intervention. And on September 1, 1939, the German army did just that. Two days later, Britain and France declared war on Germany. Despite their joint promise to protect the besieged country, neither nation sent armies to help defend it. On September 17, the Soviet Union, acting as Germany's ally, invaded Poland from the east. World War II had begun.

CHAPTER THIRTY-EIGHT

Double Agent

During the opening months of the conflict, Germany and the Soviet Union scored huge victories. Troops from both nations conquered Poland in weeks, and the country surrendered on September 27, 1939. Few outside Poland were aware of the full brutality of the Nazi campaign. This was defined, as Sifton and Stern have written, "by savage plundering and rape, by arbitrary shootings, burning of synagogues, and excesses of cruelty unleashed not only by the Wehrmacht [the German army] but especially by the SS and police battalions." Most of these police personnel, who followed in the wake of advancing armies, were organized as Einsatzgruppen, or mobile killing squads. Their duties included the annihilation of those perceived to be political or racial enemies; during the four months after Germany invaded Poland, these killing squads shot and murdered as many as sixty-five thousand people, many of them Jewish men, women, and children.

Canaris, Oster, Dohnanyi, and other conspirators inside the Abwehr knew of some of these atrocities and were outraged. They began to make new plans to overthrow the Nazis, reaching out to other countries about the possibility of a coup d'état and requesting support for the new government if and when Hitler was assassinated. The resisters understood that the outcomes of their actions against the Führer were heavily dependent on German military fortunes. Defeats for the Third Reich would make the regime more vulnerable and thus increase the likelihood of overturning it; victories on the battlefield would make a coup attempt much more difficult.

In April 1940, German troops invaded Denmark and Norway. The next month, Nazi armies moved into France, Belgium, Luxembourg, and Holland; the last three countries quickly surrendered, and the fall of France seemed likely. Hitler's goal of world domination suddenly appeared much more achievable than it had even eight months earlier. On June 17, 1940, France capitulated to the Third Reich. Eberhard Bethge was with Bonhoeffer in an open-air café in Germany when the news came:

> While we were enjoying the sun, suddenly the fanfare boomed out of the café's loudspeaker, signaling a special announcement: the message that France had surrendered. The people around the tables could hardly contain themselves; they jumped up, and some even climbed on the chairs. With outstretched arms they sang "*Deutschland, Deutschland über alles.*" . . . We had stood up, too. Bonhoeffer raised his arm in the regulation Hitler salute, while I stood there dazed. "Raise your arm! . . ." he whispered to me, and later: "We shall have to run risks for very different things now, but not for that salute!"

That fall, Bonhoeffer's double life began. Dohnanyi arranged for him to join the civilian staff of the Abwehr; the justification was that Bonhoeffer's relationships with European church leaders would be a valuable source of information for the Nazi war effort. Dohnanyi made sure that his brother-in-law was designated an indispensable member of the department and thus not subject to conscription.

For the next two years, the pastor traveled between eastern Pomerania, Berlin, Bavaria, Switzerland, Norway, and Sweden. His work operated on two levels. On the first level, he served as a conduit for the Abwehr, collecting and reporting data during his travels that might be useful to the Reich. On the second and more important level, he was a member of a conspiracy planning a coup d'état; thus, as he traveled, he assembled a different kind of information for use by his fellow resisters. This work also included trying to mobilize support from different countries for a post-Nazi regime. As he moved between these roles, Bonhoeffer also served as a spiritual and ethical backboard for some of the conspirators, particularly Dohnanyi.

This was hard work. For all practical purposes, Bonhoeffer had two separate identities, and this demanded keen attention to exactly what he said, to whom, and in what circumstances. It also required ongoing vigilance since the conspirators knew they were subject to frequent surveillance by the Gestapo and Reich Security Office. Bonhoeffer and his fellow resisters had to keep their stories meticulously straight; they also had to make plans about what they would say and do if they were captured.

Toward this end, the Bonhoeffer family devised codes to use on the phone and in correspondence. If one or more of them were arrested, they agreed they would communicate by using books delivered to the prisons. Each book that carried a message would have a small pencil indication on the title page. Subsequent pages would have tiny dots placed under individual letters: one letter per page, or one letter every few pages. The recipient would then string together the dots throughout the volume to form words and sentences that comprised news, instructions, and details about the interrogations of other imprisoned conspirators. Family members also planned to communicate by notes written in microscopic hand that could be stashed in a box of food or tucked into the lining of a piece of clothing. "Among people who to the core of their being valued honesty and truth," Sifton and Stern have written, "these techniques, which only the most urgent crisis permitted, aroused a sometimes comic spirit and at other times moral repugnance."

Bonhoeffer and the other conspirators also took precautions with their personal papers. The minister excised important pages of his diaries, particularly specific phone numbers and addresses, so that if he was arrested, the Gestapo could not question him about these. He hid some of his manuscripts and he backdated letters to minimize the chance that Nazi authorities would find incriminating evidence. He also learned to lie to authorities and to keep former friends and colleagues at a distance.

From 1940, he led a life of duplicity and instrumental falsehood.

He continued his pastoral work, ministering illegally to his former students and colleagues in the Confessing Church. He also began work on a book he called *Ethics*. But he was a double agent for a group of men working to assassinate Hitler. Bonhoeffer had spent much of his adult life speaking out publicly against what he took to be wrong actions and deceptive ideologies; he had tried to create a community based on discipleship and the peaceful dictates of the Sermon on the Mount. This new existence required a big internal shift.

As he made this shift, he remained acutely aware of what he was doing morally, spiritually, and practically. He understood that the barbarism of the Third Reich and the global conflict it had brought had effectively turned the world upside down. In a late-1942 letter to his family and fellow conspirators, Bonhoeffer articulated what this new moment meant—its costs and its imperatives:

> We have been silent witnesses of evil deeds; we have been drenched by many storms; we have learnt the arts of equivocation and pretence [sic]; experience has made us suspicious of others and kept us from being truthful and open; intolerable conflicts have worn us down and even made us cynical. Are we still of any use? What we shall need is not geniuses, or cynics, or misanthropes, or clever tacticians, but plain, honest, straightforward men. Will our inward power of resistance be strong enough, and our honesty with ourselves remorseless enough, for us to find our way back to simplicity and straightforwardness?

Bonhoeffer never shrank from the moral challenges of killing Hitler. But he believed that the German leader and all he had unleashed had to be stopped. From the time Bonhoeffer joined the conspiracy, he worked to articulate both sets of ethical issues: the inescapable sin of tyrannicide and the urgency of ending the Third Reich.

He also thought long and hard about Christianity and the pursuit of goodness in a world that was living through the atrocities of Nazi rule. Much of this thinking became part of his book on ethics. In it, he shared the insights he'd gleaned from moving back and forth between his resistance and theological work. These were lessons about the choices each individual makes every day about *how* to live his or her life, and about what it means—day in and day out—to do so fully and thoughtfully. For Bonhoeffer, this meant answering Christ's call to help those who suffer. This call was even more relevant, Bonhoeffer wrote in a 1942 letter to friends and family, amid the horror of the Third Reich:

> We are not Christ, but if we want to be Christians, we must have some share in Christ's large-heartedness by acting with responsibility and in freedom when the hour of danger comes, and by showing a real sympathy that springs, not from fear, but from the liberating and redeeming love of Christ for all who suffer. Mere waiting and looking on is not Christian behaviour [*sic*]. The Christian is called to sympathy and action, not in the first place by his own sufferings, but by the sufferings of his brethren, for whose sake Christ suffered.

With this as a foundation, Bonhoeffer surveyed what he did, the reasons behind the choices he made, and how all this action stacked up against goodness, which for him was made manifest in the teachings of Christ. Indeed, his unfinished *Ethics*, which many theologians regard as his magnum opus, grew partly out of his efforts to get right with himself about what he was doing as a conspirator. Here is how Bethge described Bonhoeffer's thinking:

> Now a period began when it was of the utmost importance that people of character remained at the controls at all costs, and did not let themselves be pushed out. . . . Even if it meant giving up a "clean slate," they had to try to get into key positions. The use of camouflage became a moral duty. . . . If there was to be a conspiracy, then they had to enter the lion's den and gain a foothold there. . . . Bonhoeffer never tried to dissuade Dohnanyi [and the other resisters] from [their] course of action. The situation had been clear to him since the spring of 1938: someone had to take on this disreputable task.

Leaders today, operating in a different kind of turbulence, can learn from Bonhoeffer's willingness to own the moral challenge. Around the world today, people are searching for leaders of character—men and women willing to speak out for goodness and bring it to bear—despite the difficulties of doing this. As the stories in this book demonstrate, leading on the higher road is not easy. It was extremely difficult, for example, for Shackleton to bring his men home safely, for Lincoln to lead the nation through civil war, and for Frederick Douglass to keep the abolitionist flame burning through the 1850s. None of the individuals here were born extraordinary. Step by step, they *made* themselves into people of character and strength capable of doing extraordinary things. In the early twenty-first century, with public trust in politicians and business executives at an all-time low, the world cries out for ordinary people to make the same commitment that those in this book did: to fashion themselves into leaders who will stand fast for a worthy cause and help others to do the same.

In mid-1941, Germany's aggression increased. In late June, Hitler launched Operation Barbarossa, a massive invasion of the Soviet Union and a flagrant violation of the treaty that the two countries had signed in 1939. The invasion took the Soviet Union by surprise, and Nazi forces initially won decisive victories as they moved east through what is now Ukraine and Belarus. At the end of the year, however, German armies stalled outside Moscow just as the Russian winter was setting in, and Soviet military leaders launched a successful counterattack. It was the first major defeat for Nazi armies.

The war in the Soviet Union took a huge human toll. Germany suffered more than 750,000 casualties. More than 800,000 Soviet soldiers were killed, and as many as 6 million were wounded or captured. The war expanded; on December 7, 1941, Japanese planes bombed Pearl Harbor, and the United States entered the conflict.

Watching these events, Bonhoeffer and his fellow conspirators hoped that Germany's long string of military victories had now ended, and that this would increase support for their plans to oust Hitler. The resisters knew that the Nazi government was using its military movements on the Eastern Front to escalate its efforts against Jews and other enemies of the regime. The Final Solution to the Jewish question was gathering momentum (the Final Solution was the Nazi code name for the organized annihilation of European Jewry).

Within the next four months, the SS and other Nazi security forces began the systematic deportation of Jews from all parts of Nazi-controlled Europe to extermination camps located in German-occupied Poland. Among the largest of these camps were Treblinka and Auschwitz-Birkenau. Hitler and his army now forbade Jews from leaving Germany and other occupied countries, effectively trapping millions of men, women, and children in an empire committed to their extermination.

Bonhoeffer and Friedrich Justus Perels, a colleague from the Confessing Church and fellow resister, wrote two reports on the deportations and gave these to Dohnanyi, who then passed them to his superiors, Ludwig Beck and Hans Oster. Knowledge of the deportations added additional urgency to the conspirators' work. As in 1939, when the men had learned about the Einsatzgruppen moving in the wake of German armies and murdering tens of thousands of Jews, Gypsies, and other civilians, the conspirators realized that each day Hitler remained in power, thousands more innocent people were slaughtered. (When World War II ended, a total of 6 million Jews had been killed in the Holocaust. The Einsatzgruppen murdered about 1 million of these people. An additional 3 million were killed in Nazi extermination camps. The remaining 2 million perished in concentration (or labor) camps, euthanasia programs, and other settings.)

In 1942, Bonhoeffer became involved in a plan devised by Dohnanyi to save seven Jews by smuggling them out of Germany to Switzerland. (Though the final number grew to fourteen, the plan was known as Operation 7.) This was a risky undertaking. The plot called for high-ranking members of the Abwehr to hire the fourteen men and women as confidential agents and then send them abroad, ostensibly as spies for the Reich. Through Bonhoeffer's ecumenical connections in Switzerland, visas were obtained for all fourteen. Gestapo officials were suspicious, but the mission succeeded. By late fall 1942, all fourteen people were safe outside Germany. One of the émigrés, Charlotte Friedenthal, was a colleague of Bonhoeffer's from the Confessing Church. Her parents, whom she left behind, died in concentration camps.

Bonhoeffer continued to travel, returning often to northeastern

Germany, where he visited his friend and longtime supporter Ruth von Kleist-Retzow, at her home in Pomerania. During his visit in June 1942, he became reacquainted with von Kleist-Retzow's granddaughter, eighteen-year-old Maria von Wedemeyer. Dietrich had not seen Maria since she was a precocious eleven-year-old who had been his confirmation student. Now a well-read, sprightly young woman with striking blue eyes, Maria captured Bonhoeffer's attention. After the visit ended, he debated what to do about his attraction to her, exploring this in a letter to his friend Eberhard Bethge: "I have not written to Maria. It is truly not time for that yet. If no further meetings are possible, the pleasant thought of a few highly charged minutes will surely eventually dissolve into the realm of unfulfilled fantasies, a realm that in any case is already well populated." In October 1942, after learning that Maria's brother had been killed on the Eastern Front, he sent his condolences to her. Not long after, he visited her family at their estate in northeastern Germany; by the end of the visit, Dietrich and Maria had established a deep personal connection.

Bonhoeffer was thirty-six and had had little, if any, romantic experience. (He may have been involved with another theology student, Elisabeth Zinn, in the mid-1930s, but the two moved apart, and Zinn married another theologian.) Why, in 1942, did he become so swiftly and strongly attracted to Maria von Wedemeyer? Biographer Charles Marsh has suggested that the couple's affection for each other was rooted in an "all-too-common desire for intimacy in those days of mounting personal losses for everyone." Just months before her brother died, Maria's father had been killed in combat in Ukraine; two of her close cousins would die before the year was out. Given the war's growing casualties, it is understandable that Dietrich's pastoral instincts would have drawn him closer to Maria, and that she would have responded positively to these overtures.

Dietrich may also have been interested in a romantic relationship because Eberhard Bethge had embarked on one of his own with Dietrich's niece, seventeen-year-old Renate Schleicher. Renate was the daughter of Dietrich's older sister Ursula and her husband, Rüdiger Schleicher, who was also involved in the conspiracy to overthrow Hitler. At the time of Dietrich's visit to Maria's family, Eberhard and

Renate's relationship had become serious, and in November 1942 the couple became engaged.

During the seven years since they'd met at Finkenwalde, Dietrich and Eberhard had grown close. Now, like Lincoln in 1842 anticipating the marriage of Joshua Speed, Dietrich may have feared that Bethge's upcoming nuptials would drive a wedge between the two longtime confidants. Certainly, Dietrich took this in as he considered whether to pursue a relationship with Maria von Wedemeyer. Maybe he was anxious about losing the person to whom he had been closest. It may also be that, like Lincoln one hundred years earlier, Bonhoeffer was encouraged by the happiness that his good friend had found with his fiancée.

Bonhoeffer was likely deeply smitten with the intelligent, attractive, and spontaneous young woman whose family he greatly respected. For her part, Maria admired the handsome, athletic pastor and scholar who'd long been a favorite of her grandmother's. Within three months, the two were engaged. With both the joy and anxiety of young love, Maria wrote her fiancé:

> I find it hard to have to tell you in writing what can scarcely be uttered in person. I would rather disown every word that demands to be said on the subject, because it makes things that were better conveyed quietly sound so crude and clumsy. But, knowing from experience how well you understand me, I'm now emboldened to write to you even though I've really no right whatever to answer a question which you have never asked me. With all my happy heart, I can now say yes.

With this new relationship as backdrop, Bonhoeffer entered the New Year with considerable momentum. He had found the woman he wanted to marry, and his book on ethics, the work he believed would be his most important to date, was well under way.

CHAPTER THIRTY-NINE

Tegel Prison

B onhoeffer and other members of the conspiracy now had reason to hope that the tide of war had begun to turn against the Third Reich. The Wehrmacht's eastern offensive against the Soviet Union remained stalled; in some places, German troops had been repelled. British forces fighting in North Africa had defeated Nazi troops in late 1942; a few months later, the Reich army in Stalingrad surrendered to Soviet soldiers.

By late February 1943, the conspirators were ready to act. They planned to assassinate Hitler and then quickly seize power in key German cities. The plot called for an army officer to smuggle a bomb onto a plane, which Hitler was scheduled to take from German-occupied Smolensk in the Soviet Union to his East Prussian head-quarters. The bomb, disguised as two bottles of Cointreau, made it onto the plane and was timed to detonate roughly half an hour after the flight departed. Dohnanyi, Bonhoeffer, and even Eberhard Bethge were involved. Dohnanyi carried the explosives on the first leg of their journey east, with Bethge driving him to the train station.

On March 13, the Führer boarded the plane as scheduled, and the flight took off. But the detonation mechanism malfunctioned, and the bomb failed to explode. Unharmed and ignorant of the attempt on his life, Hitler disembarked at his headquarters. (One of the plotters subsequently secretly removed the bomb from the plane.)

Undeterred, the conspirators tried again. On March 21, 1943, a military intelligence officer, Rudolf Christoph von Gersdorff, filled his coat pockets with explosives as he prepared to accompany Hitler on a tour of a Berlin arsenal. The plan was for Gersdorff to detonate the bombs when he was close to the Führer, killing the leader and himself. At the last minute, however, Hitler changed his itinerary, preventing the officer from getting within striking distance, so this plot, too, came to nothing. Fortunately for the conspirators, neither the Gestapo nor the SS learned about the scheme.

At the end of March, the Bonhoeffers gathered with friends at the family's Berlin home to celebrate Karl Bonhoeffer's seventy-fifth birthday. Eberhard Bethge was there, as was Friedrich Justus Perels, Dietrich's clerical colleague and fellow resister. There was fine food, music, laughter, and the warm energy of several generations enjoying one another's company. In a photograph taken on the sunny day, Dietrich appears in buoyant spirits as he stands alongside his brother Klaus and brothers-in-law Rüdiger Schleicher and Hans von Dohnanyi.

Five days later, on April 5, 1943, Manfred Roeder, a prosecutor and judge advocate for the Reich War Court, accompanied by a Gestapo official, arrested Hans von Dohnanyi at the Abwehr offices in Berlin. They took him to a prison in the center of the city. The men also arrested his wife, Christine. (She was detained for approximately four weeks at a women's prison in another part of Berlin before being released.) Hours later, the same Nazi officials came for Dietrich at his parents' home. Bonhoeffer was upstairs, seated at his desk. His fabricated diary lay nearby. Much of his other work was hidden in the room's rafters. Roeder and the Gestapo agent did not explain why they were apprehending Bonhoeffer, and they did not have a warrant for his arrest. He surrendered quietly as he was handcuffed and marched to the waiting Mercedes on the street. He was taken to Tegel military prison in northwest Berlin.

Once inside Tegel, Bonhoeffer was stripped of all his personal possessions, including his Bible. Prison officials offered no information about his arrest or how long he might be detained. He was locked in a cell that had a wooden bed covered by foul-smelling blankets. The next morning, a piece of bread was thrown onto the floor of his cell, and he was handed a cup of coffee. The pastor remembered hearing "the sound of the prison staff's vile abuse" of other inmates. He heard these sounds every day, morning to night.

The day after Bonhoeffer arrived, guards took him to the solitary-isolation ward. His cell there was even smaller, and he was denied the thirty minutes outdoors in the prison yard that other inmates were allowed each day. His only human contact was with the guards who opened the cell door to retrieve his latrine bucket. He remained in solitary confinement for almost two weeks.

When officials learned that Bonhoeffer was the son of the famed psychiatrist Dr. Karl Bonhoeffer, and the nephew of the former city commandant of Berlin, General Paul von Hase, the prisoner's living conditions improved markedly. Dietrich was moved to a large cell on the top floor of the building overlooking the prison yard. He was given back his Bible, granted books from the prison library, and allocated some writing paper. His parents were allowed to leave parcels for him, and he was permitted to correspond with family members and a few other individuals approved by prison officials (all letters were subject to censorship). Prison staff gave him better coffee, and even cigarettes. They also offered him larger food portions; he refused these, saying that the bigger allotments "would have been at the expense of the other prisoners." By late April, officials allowed Bonhoeffer to spend thirty minutes outside each day; at times, Tegel commandant Captain Walter Maetz accompanied him on walks around the prison yard.

Bonhoeffer benefited enormously from corresponding with his family. Even though he wrote letters in full knowledge that the Nazis might read them, these nonetheless provided him with a vital connection to the people to whom he was closest. This connection helped sustain his spirit during the agonizing uncertainty of his imprisonment. Writing and receiving letters also helped Bonhoeffer make sense of what he was experiencing inside his prison cell as he *waited*: waited for Nazi prosecutors to present a case against him, waited to see if the conspirators still working within the Abwehr and larger military would kill Hitler and topple the regime, waited to see if Berlin would come under attack by Allied bombing raids that were buffeting other areas in Germany, and waited to observe what he himself would become as the days in prison piled on top of each other.

The packages that Bonhoeffer received, mostly from his parents, also buoyed his spirits. Karl and Paula Bonhoeffer regularly left boxes of bread, vegetables, fruits, meats, cookies, writing paper, clean clothes, and toiletries. A welcome respite from prison rations, the food his parents provided helped nourish Bonhoeffer and soften the sharp edges of prison life. The clean clothes and well-polished shoes provided some modicum of control (and normalcy) for a man who'd always been a fastidious dresser. His parents also brought books. Some contained coded information about the progress of the Nazis' case against him and Dohnanyi and other issues pertaining to the resistance. All of the books he received were important to his ability to keep thinking about theological and political subjects.

This reading and reflecting led Bonhoeffer to write: letters, book pages, reports on his experience, poetry, notes to himself, prayers for fellow prisoners, and a last will and testament. Composed within the crucible of his imprisonment, these letters and papers represent his attempt to find some kind of real determining power when almost all of his external agency had been stripped away. With the help of sympathetic guards, many of these papers have survived. Some that relate to work he did on his book *Ethics*, and to religionless Christianity, continue to influence thinkers to this day. Others, such as his letters, poetry, and private musings, leave unmistakable evidence of effective leadership from within, of the impact that one person can have by choosing *how* to live in the midst of a dreadful—and, at times, seemingly unbearable—crisis.

When he could, Bonhoeffer used his special status to advocate for his fellow inmates. For example, he protested the quality of prison food, calling officials' attention to its poor taste and nutritional inadequacy. Criticizing a meal of cabbage soup made with no fat, meat, or potatoes as "beyond contempt," he claimed that the inmates' fare owed its good reputation to trickery. "I know for a fact," he wrote, "that when the doctors or officers inspect the prisoners' food, a nourishing sauce of meat or cream is added to the plates concerned." On at least one occasion, he summoned a warden to watch him weigh

The crew enjoys a midwinter's day feast aboard the *Endurance* in June 1915. (*Courtesy of the Royal Geographical Society*)

The *Endurance* crew in August 1915, standing alongside the ship trapped in ice. (*Courtesy of the Royal Geographical Society*)

The *Endurance* in the grip of the pack ice, in September 1915. (*Courtesy of the Royal Geographical Society*)

The launching of the *James Caird* for Elephant Island on April 24, 1916. Shackleton hoped to sail the lifeboat, fitted with a mast, sail, and canvas deck, eight hundred miles northeast to South Georgia Island. (*Courtesy of the Royal Geographical Society*)

Rescue! August 30, 1916. Shackleton's crew leaves Elephant Island for the *Yelcho*, bound for Chile. (*Courtesy of the Royal Geographical Society*)

A portrait of Mary Todd Lincoln by Mathew Brady, c. 1850s. (*Courtesy of Getty Images*)

A photograph of a young Lincoln, taken in Chicago in February 1857, immediately before his campaign for the US Senate. (*Courtesy of the Library of Congress*)

Lincoln with General George McClellan and a group of officers after the hard-fought Battle of Antietam in October 1862. (*Courtesy of the Library of Congress*)

Lincoln stepping down from a platform after delivering the Gettysburg Address on November 19, 1863. The speech was so short that the photographer did not have time to set up his camera while the president was speaking. So the surviving images of the moment capture Lincoln after his address. (*Courtesy of the Library of Congress*)

Lincoln reading to his youngest son, Tad, in the White House in February 1864. (*Courtesy of the Library of Congress*)

Dead Confederate soldiers collected for burial after the Battle of Spotsylvania Court House, May 20, 1864. (*Courtesy of the Library of Congress*)

Frederick Douglass in 1847.
(*Courtesy of the National Portrait Gallery, Smithsonian Institution*)

A slave wedding at a plantation in Mississippi. (*Courtesy of J. Mack Moore Collection, Old Court House Museum, Vicksburg, Mississippi*)

This painting, *Slave Auction, Virginia* (1862) by LeFevre J. Cranstone, shows an idealized image of the harsh realities of the slave auction. (*Courtesy of the Virginia Historical Society*)

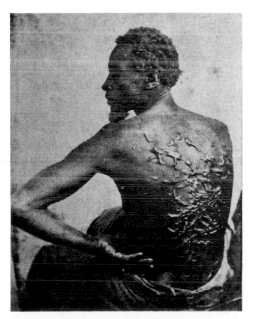

A photograph of "Peter" Gordon, a former slave who escaped from a Louisiana plantation in 1863. The horrific scarring on his back is a result of vicious whippings, and this image quickly became a sensation. (*Courtesy of the National Portrait Gallery, Smithsonian Institution*)

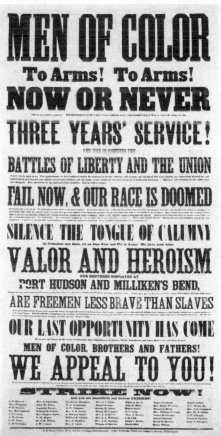

A recruiting broadside for the Union army, printed in 1863 and endorsed by Douglass. (*Courtesy of the Library Company of Philadelphia, Philadelphia, Pennsylvania*)

Paula Bonhoeffer with her eight children in the 1910s. Dietrich Bonhoeffer is in the first row, second from left. (*Courtesy of bpk-Bildagentur/Art Resource, New York*)

Adolf Hitler greets the Catholic abbot Albanus Schachleiter, saluting, and Reich bishop Ludwig Müller, head of the newly created Reich Church, during the 1934 Nuremberg Rally. (*Courtesy of Süddeutsche Zeitung Photo/Alamy Stock Photo*)

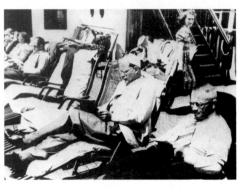

Bonhoeffer on the deck of a ship bound for America, summer 1939. (*Courtesy of bpk-Bildagentur/Art Resource, New York*)

Bonhoeffer in the courtyard of the military prison at Tegel, July 1944. (*Courtesy of bpk-Bildagentur/Art Resource, New York*)

This is the house that Karl **and Paula** Bonhoeffer built as a retirement home in 1935, and it was here in April 1943 that the Gestapo arrested Dietrich. (*Courtesy of photographer Martin Dubberke of the Bonhoeffer-Haus*)

Rachel Carson with Grace Croff, assistant professor of English, Pennsylvania College for Women, in 1926. (*Courtesy of NCTC Archives/Museum*)

Carson at her microscope, 1951. (*Courtesy of Getty Images*)

A detail of a 1947 Pennsalt Chemicals advertisement that ran in a number of magazines, including *Time*. (*Courtesy of Crossell Library, Bennington College*)

A DDT truck spraying New York's Jones Beach—and the children playing in the sand—in 1947. (*Courtesy of Getty Images*)

Carson photographed in the woods near her home, September 1962. (*Courtesy of Getty Images*)

Carson being interviewed by Eric Sevareid for *CBS Reports* in late November 1962. The show aired on April 3, 1963, and was watched by between 10 and 15 million Americans. (*Courtesy of Getty Images*)

a piece of sausage that totaled fifteen grams rather than the legally mandated twenty-five.

Few of these efforts had any marked effect, but Bonhoeffer continued to voice his objections. He also remained conscientious about which privileges he utilized and which he refused. During a hot spell in August 1943, for example, his mother urged him to request a cell on a lower, cooler floor. Bonhoeffer declined, explaining, "I don't want to ask to be moved to another floor, as that would not be fair to the other prisoner who would have to come into my cell, probably without such things as tomatoes," referring to a parcel his parents had recently delivered containing vegetables, fruit, and cooling salts. "Please don't worry; I've often had to put up with worse heat in Italy, Africa, Spain, Mexico, and, almost the worst of all, in New York in July 1939."

From mid-April when he was first allowed to write his parents, Bonhoeffer took pains to reassure them that he was all right. "Strangely enough," he wrote early on, "the discomforts that one generally associates with prison life, the physical hardships, hardly bother me at all. One can even have enough to eat in the mornings with dry bread (I get a variety of extras too). The hard prison bed does not worry me a bit, and one can get plenty of sleep between 8 p.m. and 6 a.m." He continued:

> I think that in all this the psychic factor has played the larger part. A violent mental upheaval such as is produced by a sudden arrest brings with it the need to take one's mental bearings and come to terms with an entirely new situation—all this means that physical things take a back seat and lose their importance, and it is something that I find to be a real enrichment of my experience. I am not so unused to being alone as other people are, and it is certainly a good spiritual Turkish bath. The only thing that bothers me or would bother me is the thought that you are being tormented by anxiety about me, and are not sleeping or eating properly. Forgive me for causing you so much worry, but I think a hostile fate is more to blame than I am.

Behind this genuine concern for his family and the brave front he put up, Bonhoeffer struggled to deal with life in an eight-by-ten-foot prison cell. In this existence virtually all of his external power was gone; his future—indeed, his immediate present—was uncertain; and the communities from which he'd always drawn strength—his family, friends, colleagues, and more recently his fiancée—were largely out of reach. In this existence the clock had also become his enemy. Time now dragged on, Bethge has written, "with no fixed points to look forward to." As Bonhoeffer paced round the cell in which he was confined for twenty-three and a half hours each day, he noticed that one of his predecessors had relieved some of the same suffering by scratching a sentence on the wall: "In a hundred years it'll all be over."

Like Shackleton stranded on the ice in 1915 without a ship or any other way of getting his team home, time presented a formidable challenge: What was one to do in its vast, unexpected emptiness? How was one to endure when there appeared to be so little to hope for? Bonhoeffer did not keep a diary or journal while he was in prison. But on a slip of paper dated May 8, 1943, and in a series of reflections probably composed at the same time, he revealed something of his emotional state:

Separation from people
     from work
     from the past
     from the future
     from marriage
     from God . . .

Overcoming memories
     self-pity . . .

Dissatisfaction
Tension
Impatience
Longing
Boredom
Sick—profoundly alone
Indifference

Urge to do something, change, novelty
Being blunted, tiredness, sleep . . .
Order
Fantasy, distortion of past and future
Suicide, not because of consciousness of guilt but because basically
   I am already dead, draw a line,
Summing up the balance . . .

Overcoming in prayer

Like Lincoln during the darkest moments of his presidency, Bonhoeffer thought seriously about taking his life in the weeks after he
was arrested. Bethge, who knew him well, has speculated that his
friend may have considered suicide not only as a response to the
isolation and uncertainty of being locked up, but also because he
was worried that he might betray his fellow conspirators if he was
physically tortured and broke under the strain of Nazi interrogation.

In the spring of 1943, how did Bonhoeffer navigate the thick,
dank fog of emotions that kept him company? How did he make
the choice to fight for his life rather than end it? He left only small
bits of evidence about his thoughts and feelings during this criti
cal period. In November 1943, for example, he wrote Bethge that
immediately after his imprisonment, he had resolved not to give
way to the *tristitia* or melancholy he'd occasionally known: "I told
myself from the beginning that I was not going to oblige either man
or devil in any such way—they can do what they like about it for
themselves; and I hope I shall always be able to stand firm on this."
This resolution was accompanied, he added, by the certainty "that
the duty had been laid on me to hold out in this boundary situation
with all its problems; I became quite content to do this, and have
remained so ever since."

These were brave words. They represented an obligation Bonhoeffer felt to his fellow conspirators and his country's future. But mission
alone was not enough to sustain him or the other four leaders in this
book during their worst moments. At these important junctures, the
five people here also made a kind of emotional pact with themselves.

Each explicitly refused to spend a lot of time or energy mentally playing out worst-case scenarios. Bonhoeffer, for example, resolved not to oblige the "man or devil" that put these possibilities before him. Shackleton determined he would not entertain the prospect of failure. Douglass purposefully closed his eyes to the nightmare of being captured as he tried to escape. In the midst of her worsening medical situation, Carson turned away from her deteriorating health and focused on the book she was trying to finish.

This was not a willful blindness to the realities each leader faced. Nor was it some kind of forced optimism. These five individuals knew exactly what they were up against. Because they did, they used their emotional awareness and discipline to concentrate directly, almost exclusively, on how to move forward, how to take the next step, however small. Each leader realized that to do this, he or she had to consciously turn away from his or her worst fears and biggest doubts. For Bonhoeffer, in the spring of 1943, this meant walking away from— refusing to give in to—thoughts of suicide. Instead, he chose life.

The ability to manage one's emotions during times of turbulence is a vital lesson for leaders today. We live in an era largely defined by widespread fear. A great deal of this collective anxiety is held in place by hyperconnectivity. We learn of the latest natural disaster across the globe before local emergency workers have even reached the scene. Our financial markets react in seconds to lower forecasts in a particular country's budget. Politicians and journalists fill the airwaves and social media with dire predictions about everything from geopolitics to planetary weather. Facebook encourages us to keep precise track of the people, experiences, and things that each of us lacks relative to our friends. It is hardly surprising that most people spend a significant part of each day reacting, consciously or not, to some kind of worry. In this context, it is important that leaders learn how to acknowledge and then deal effectively with their own fears. This capability begins with individuals summoning the emotional discipline to turn away from their worst fantasies, turn their attention to the road ahead, and then take the next step forward.

One of the first things that Bonhoeffer did, as the initial mental upheaval of his imprisonment subsided, was to establish a daily schedule. He rose at six o'clock each morning and went to bed at eight o'clock in the evening. He divided his waking hours among meditation, Bible reading, and reading more generally, writing, work on the Nazis' case against him, and his allotted thirty minutes out of doors. He also made sure to get physical exercise within his cell. He paced for hours around the small space, purposefully logging several kilometers each day.

He also kept the church calendar, living by this and the seasons more than by the months and days. (Indeed, his fiancée, Maria, remembered that his letters to her from Tegel were sometimes misdated because Bonhoeffer kept a different account of time.) She recalled his description of Advent 1943, traditionally a season of waiting and preparation for the Nativity. "A prison cell like this," he wrote, "in which one watches and hopes and performs this or that ultimately insignificant task, and in which one is wholly dependent on the door's being opened from the outside, is a far from inappropriate metaphor for Advent."

Like Shackleton, who created a new duty roster for his men every week, Bonhoeffer instinctively knew that a structured day would provide stability and a sense of control in the midst of a crisis. He needed such stability; to survive, he needed to believe he could exercise some influence on the course of his life—not only life in prison, but also whatever was to come in the Nazi government's case against him and other members of the resistance. (In early April, Josef Müller, a fellow conspirator, and his wife were arrested. At roughly the same time, Hans Oster, Dohnanyi's direct superior in the Abwehr, was dismissed from his post.)

During the four months following Dohnanyi's and Bonhoeffer's arrests, Manfred Roeder, the prosecuting attorney for the Nazi War Court, repeatedly interrogated each prisoner. Both men feared the specter of physical torture, but Roeder did not use such methods. He was, however, harsh and relentless in his questioning, particularly with Dohnanyi, who, from the time he was imprisoned, Roeder believed more culpable than Bonhoeffer. Pushing, probing, abruptly changing his line of attack, the Reich official conducted long, separate sessions with each man.

Both had been arrested without being told the charges against them, and for several months they lived in legal limbo. But then a pattern emerged in Roeder's interrogations. With Bonhoeffer, the prosecutor was interested in the circumstances surrounding his exemption from war service, the details of Operation 7, and the international trips he made on behalf of the Abwehr. The legal official pushed hard on each of these areas, particularly the military exemption, arguing that the minister had used this as a means of continuing his illegal activities with the Confessing Church while avoiding Gestapo surveillance.

Both Bonhoeffer and Dohnanyi had prepared for such questions. With scrupulous care not only to what he said, but also to the tone he used and the body language he assumed, Bonhoeffer met his adversary time and again during the summer of 1943. During face-to-face interrogations and in letters he wrote the prosecutor from his prison cell, the pastor successfully countered many of Roeder's attacks. Some of this success was a result of the information he and Dohnanyi obtained about what was happening during the other person's interrogations; this was conveyed in coded messages that came in books and gifts from Bonhoeffer's family. Both prisoners used this knowledge to maintain consistent stories and, in some cases, to lead Roeder down dead-end roads of irrelevant detail.

Bonhoeffer worked diligently during the interrogations to present himself as a minister focused on ecclesiastical matters and largely ignorant of military and bureaucratic operations. He stressed his family's long history of service to Germany. He explained his interest in working for the Abwehr as a way to rehabilitate his reputation in the eyes of state authorities who'd been suspicious about his affiliation with the Confessing Church. He used his engagement to Maria to demonstrate his patriotism. All of these actions, Bonhoeffer argued, were evidence of deep commitment to his country. Professing to be incredulous that Nazi authorities were considering charges of disloyalty, much less treason, he wrote Roeder:

[If I were actually disloyal] would I have found my fiancée in an old officer's family, all of whose fathers and sons have served as officers since the beginning of the war, some with the highest distinction, and have made the greatest sacrifices? My fiancée has lost both her father and her brother at the front. If [I were actually disloyal], would I have cancelled all the engagements that I had made in America and have returned immediately upon the outbreak of war to Germany, where I had to expect to be called up straight away? . . . If anyone wants to learn something of my conception of the duty of Christian obedience towards the authorities, he should read my exposition of Romans 13 in my book *The Cost of Discipleship*. The appeal to subjection to the will and the demands of authority for the sake of Christian conscience has probably seldom been expressed more strongly than there. That is my personal attitude to these questions. I cannot judge how far such personal arguments have any legal significance, but I cannot imagine that one can simply pass over them.

It was not easy for Bonhoeffer to write such letters. It was harder, still, to remain vigilant, focused, credibly deferential, and composed during the ongoing questioning. He prepared physically for these sessions by exercising every day, eating all the nourishing food his family brought, and sleeping as much and as well as he could. He readied himself mentally by rehearsing the explanations of events that he, his brother-in-law, and their fellow resisters had prepared. He went over what he knew about the lines of investigation that Roeder was pursuing with Dohnanyi. He also played out a series of possibilities in his head as he tried to envision the high-stakes chess game that the Nazi prosecutor would play with him during the next day's interrogation.

Perhaps most important was Bonhoeffer's emotional preparation. He knew he was frightened of being tortured (although this worry receded as the investigation stretched on). He was anxious about whether he would accidentally implicate another person; both he and Dohnanyi lived in dread of the harm they could bring to their families as well as fellow conspirators. Bonhoeffer was also worried about maintaining his composure under Roeder's onslaught, relying on several tools to help manage his fear. He walked a great deal around his cell. He wrote as an outlet for the energy behind his fright. As important, he harnessed his reserves of emotional discipline to present a calm, confident appearance during prosecutorial sessions. Like Shackleton, who understood that his mission would fail if his men saw him sweat, Bonhoeffer realized how critical it was for him to show up in a very specific way before the Nazi lawyer and his associates in the War Court.

This was serious, scary business. But somehow, Bonhoeffer and Dohnanyi found the reserves of strength and courage required to remain steadfast during the four months of Roeder's questioning. They didn't break, and they didn't name names. By the end of the summer, when the state finally issued its indictments, the case against each man was not as strong as either defendant had feared. Dohnanyi was charged with currency violations, procedural errors, and improper military exemptions for pastors. Bonhoeffer was charged with antimilitary acts for obtaining exemptions from military service for himself and for a colleague in the Confessing Church. Neither prisoner was indicted for high treason; but the charges were still formidable. Each of the indictments was made under a broad Reich statute against subversion of military power, a crime punishable by death.

In late June 1943, in the midst of the interrogation sessions with Roeder, Bonhoeffer received an unexpected visit from his fiancée. "I've just come back and have seen Maria," he wrote his parents. "An indescribable surprise and joy. I knew about it only a minute beforehand. It's still like a dream—really an almost unimaginable situation—what will we think of it one day? . . . It was so brave of her to come; I wouldn't have dared suggest it to her. It's so much more difficult for her than for me. I know where I am, but for her it is all unimaginable, mysterious, terrifying. Think how things will be when this nightmare is over!"

From July 1943 until he was moved from Tegel late the next year, Maria was permitted to visit Bonhoeffer about once a month. He, in turn, was allowed to write a one-page letter to her or his family every four days. The communication with his fiancée became an important source of energy and possibility for the prisoner, and Bonhoeffer began to hang his hope for the future on his vision of the couple's life together. "When I also think about the situation of the world," he wrote Maria,

> the complete darkness over our personal fate and my present imprisonment, then I believe that our union can only be a sign of God's grace and kindness, which calls us to faith. We would be blind if we did not see it. Jeremiah says at the moment of his people's great need "still one shall buy houses and acres in this land" as a sign of trust in the future. This is where faith belongs. May God give it to us daily. And I do not mean the faith which flees the world, but the one that endures the world and which loves and remains true to the world in spite of all the suffering which it contains for us. Our marriage shall be a yes to God's earth; it shall strengthen our courage to act and accomplish something on the earth.

The couple's letters to each other are also filled with details about their wedding plans, setting up a household, places to which they might travel, and individual pursuits they hoped to share with each other. Dietrich wanted Maria to teach him to dance and ride horses. She wanted to understand more of her fiancé's religious work. The letters are also rich with the intensity of romantic love that had only recently been avowed. "My dearest Maria," Bonhoeffer wrote in August 1943, "how can I convey what your visits mean to me? They dispel every shadow and every heartache and remain a days-long source of great, serene happiness—and if you knew how much that means to a prisoner you would also know that nothing could be more important." He went on:

> When I return to my cell after being with you, my prevailing emotion is not, as you may possibly suppose, one of despair at my captivity; no, I'm overwhelmed by the thought that you accepted me. There were so many understandable reasons why you could have said no, but you said yes in spite of them all, and I seem to sense that you say it with ever greater freedom and assurance. In view of that, all the bars over my window melt away and you are with me. Why should I care about the locked door?

For all the happiness he expressed to his fiancée, Bonhoeffer was never far away from the uncertainty of his larger fate. Once they'd received their respective indictments in the early fall of 1943, both he and Dohnanyi were hopeful they'd soon be exonerated. But then, nothing happened. Allied air raids interrupted War Court business, thwarting Bonhoeffer's expectations of a speedy trial; a new date was set for December 17, 1943. But in November, Hans von Dohnanyi suffered a brain embolism when an incendiary bomb from an air raid hit his cell. He had to be moved from prison to a Berlin hospital, putting off any judicial proceedings until he was sufficiently recovered.

The indefinite postponement of his and Dohnanyi's trials was deeply disappointing for Bonhoeffer. He wanted to know his future. He wanted to move on with his life. He wanted to rejoin the people he loved and pined for. Perhaps most of all, he wanted the waiting—what Sifton and Stern have called "the up-and-down uncertainty" of his imprisonment—to end.

But it did not. In October, Allied air raids had begun to pummel Berlin, including Tegel and a nearby munitions factory. With this as backdrop, Bonhoeffer revealed his deepest doubts and fears in a series of uncensored letters to his good friend Eberhard Bethge—letters that a sympathetic guard smuggled out. "Now there's something I must tell you personally," Bonhoeffer wrote in late November. "The heavy air raids, especially [that three days earlier], when the windows of the sick-bay were blown out by the land mine, and bottles and medical supplies fell down from the cupboards and shelves, and I lay on the floor in the darkness with little hope of coming through the attack safely, led me back quite simply to prayer and the Bible." During the raids, Bonhoeffer also tended to his fellow inmates. The prisoners came to rely on his steadiness and calm. Still, the sense of peril never left him. As the bombings increased, Bonhoeffer sent Bethge his last will and testament. The prisoner left most of his possessions to his friend, asking him to "please be very good to Maria, and if possible, write to her in my stead from time to time, just a few kind words, as you can do so well, and tell her gently that I asked you to."

In mid-December, faced with seemingly endless air strikes and the prospect of spending Christmas in prison, Bonhoeffer laid bare some of his despondency. "In spite of everything that I've written so far, things here are revolting," he wrote to Bethge. "My grim experiences often pursue me into the night and . . . I can shake them off only by reciting one hymn after another." He continued:

It's possible to get used to physical hardships, and to live for months out of the body, so to speak—almost too much so—but one doesn't get used to the psychological strain; on the contrary, I have the feeling that everything I see and hear is putting years on me, and I'm often finding the world nauseating and burdensome. You're probably surprised now at my talking like this after all my letters; you wrote very kindly that I was making "something of an effort" to reassure you about my situation. I often wonder who I really am—the man who goes on squirming under these ghastly experiences in wretchedness that cries to heaven, or the man who scourges himself and pretends to others (and even to himself) that he is placid, cheerful, composed, and in control of himself, and allows people to admire him for it.

As he struggled to navigate through self-doubt and despair, Bonhoeffer, like the other leaders in this book, tried to make sense of his emotions. Caught in the grip of what mystics have termed "the dark night of the soul," all of the five people here made a conscious effort to understand their feelings not only in terms of their own distress, but also in terms of the larger moment in which they found themselves. This moment included the mission they were pursuing and the losses and suffering of others. As he lay sleepless in his tent on the ice, Shackleton understood his anxiety was connected to the responsibility he felt for his men's well-being. In 1862 and 1864, Lincoln slogged through the trenches of his depression partly by visiting battlefields and army hospitals. For both leaders, as for Bonhoeffer, personal anguish was not only a solitary experience; they gave it proportion by relating it to that of other people to whom they felt obligated.

In late 1943, the pastor reflected on the countless other victims of Nazi aggression: his former students killed at the front, Jews and others who'd been murdered by the regime, and his fellow prisoners. He also thought about how he'd tried to stop some of this terrible suffering.

Even in his desolation, Bonhoeffer reassured Bethge that he hadn't "for a moment regretted coming back [to Germany] in 1939—nor any of the consequences, either. I knew quite well what I was doing, and I acted with a clear conscience." He believed that he'd done the right thing; failing to do this would have been a grave mistake. "Faithless vacillation, endless deliberation without action, refusal to take any risks—that's a real danger," Bonhoeffer explained. "We must learn to act differently from those who always hesitate, whose failure we know in a wider context. We must be clear about what we want, we must ask whether we're up to it, and then we must do it with unshakable confidence. Then and only then can we also bear the consequences."

This isn't to say that Bonhoeffer easily bore the repercussions of his choices. He oscillated between anguish and hopefulness— between the powerful, insidious doubt that he would ever be free, and the possibility of his path ahead as a minister, writer, husband, and father. He made these shifts with the knowledge that sustaining oneself through extreme circumstances required thoughtful, concerted effort. "There are two ways of dealing psychically with adversities," he wrote Bethge. "One way, the easier, is to try to ignore them; that is about as far as I have got. The other and more difficult way is to face them deliberately and overcome them; I'm not equal to that yet, but one must learn to do it, for the first way is a slight, though, I believe, a permissible, piece of self-deception."

During this time, and throughout the eighteen months he spent in Tegel Prison, Bonhoeffer never stopped trying to reassure the people who cared for him that his spirits were strong and his outlook positive. In his letters and during visits from select family members, he projected a calm, uncomplaining presence. When he expressed strong emotion, it was generally appreciation and joy. One evening, for example, he wrote his parents about the tolling of nearby chimes. "It's remarkable what power church bells have over human beings, and how deeply they can affect us. So many of our life's experiences gather round them. All discontent, ingratitude, and selfishness melt away, and in a moment we are left with only our pleasant memories hovering round us like gracious spirits."

CHAPTER FORTY

In Service to Others

As 1944 dawned, Bonhoeffer and Dohnanyi, whose health slowly improved, still did not have a court date. Winter gave way to spring, and the two continued to wait. This was frustrating for Bonhoeffer, but after a year in prison, he'd developed tools for reestablishing his equanimity. Since his first weeks in Tegel, he'd read widely in theology, literature, and history. He also spent a great deal of time immersed in the Bible. His time with such books served several purposes. It took his mind away from his own circumstances. It fed his curiosity about art and other fields within the humanities. Studying the sweep of history also offered perspective on the war, showing him how other people in other times had dealt with adversity. Some of what he read, such as the Psalms, provided emotional support and clarity.

Bonhoeffer absorbed it all, falling back on his deep knowledge of Christian theology and returning to some of the issues he'd wrestled with at the University of Berlin. But now, he was also working from his experience in the Confessing Church, his involvement in the conspiracy, *and* the exigency of being imprisoned and at risk for his life. In surveying his former existence, which was now completely out of reach, he saw continuity. His journey, he wrote Bethge, "has been an uninterrupted enrichment of experience, for which I can only be thankful. If I were to end my life here in these conditions, that would have a meaning that I think I could understand; on the other hand, everything might be a thorough preparation for a new start and a new task when peace comes."

He continued writing Bethge. In these letters, composed between April and September 1944 and again smuggled out by a friendly guard, Bonhoeffer considered the future of Christianity in the twentieth century. "What is bothering me incessantly is the question [of] what Christianity really is, or indeed who Christ really is, for us today." We live, he asserted, in a "world come of age," an increasingly secular world that no longer needed God to explain reality or answer human needs. "Man has learnt," Bonhoeffer said, "to deal with himself in all questions of importance without recourse to the 'working hypothesis' called 'God.'" It is becoming evident, he added, "that everything gets along without 'God'—and, in fact, just as well as before." In science, ethics, religion, and other realms, "'God' is being pushed more and more out of life, losing more and more ground."

Against the onslaught of secularism and man's self-absorption, Bonhoeffer argued, the church had tried to defend Christianity by resorting to "the so-called 'ultimate questions'—death, guilt—to which only 'God' can give an answer." But this reasoning was deeply flawed. By restricting God to the so-called ultimate questions, Bonhoeffer asserted, modern religion had made Him into "the answer to life's problems, and the solution of its needs and conflicts." This conception effectively restricted God to a utilitarian role, located largely on the periphery of human activity. But soon, Bonhoeffer added, even this role would be eclipsed. As man's confidence grew, the ultimate questions would be answerable without the Almighty, and He would become superfluous even as the solution to previously insolvable problems.

In sharp contrast, Bonhoeffer sought a God at the center of everyone's life, a divine power who spoke to men and women in their strength rather than in their weakness, who dealt in life and goodness rather than death and guilt. As theologian John W. de Gruchy has written, Bonhoeffer's study of the Old Testament strengthened his conviction that biblical faith is focused not on man's salvation after death, but rather on man's life on earth—"not on withdrawal from the world but on engagement with its life, not on asceticism but on a genuine appreciation of the body and sexuality, not on private piety but on [direct] engagement with the world." The more time in prison that Bonhoeffer devoted to studying the Scriptures, the more convinced he became that the God of the Bible was not God as He was conceived of by most established religions. This realization, de Gruchy has pointed out, demanded a "'nonreligious' interpretation of Christian faith."

Bonhoeffer intended to write a book about this subject, and he was most likely working on this throughout 1944. But no manuscript has survived. What he envisioned in his letters to Bethge that spring and summer was a profound transformation of Christian faith—one in which the church and its members identify with Jesus in his earthly sufferings. In Bonhoeffer's vision, this identification was not intended as a means to redemption or access to an afterlife. Instead, it was a way of liberating man from his overriding worry about his own sinfulness and what this meant for his fate. Even more important, it was also a means of propelling man into a new life on earth—one rooted in "being there for others," as Christ had been. It presented man with the challenge and the *grace* of living in solidarity with and in service to others—particularly those who are powerless, oppressed, and reviled—in short, those who suffer.

In Bonhoeffer's eyes, a church that existed for others, that sought to embody Christ's concern with those who suffered, was not primarily concerned with its own survival or aggrandizement. Nor was it a community of ascetics or saints living in monastic seclusion—quite the opposite. The Christian life, he argued, was rooted in being truly human, in anchoring oneself in what he termed "this-worldliness." Only by "living unreservedly in life's duties, problems, successes and failures, experiences and perplexities," Bonhoeffer wrote, can "we throw ourselves completely into the arms of God, taking seriously, not our own sufferings, but those of God in the world—watching with Christ in Gethsemane [the garden where Jesus waited for Roman soldiers to take him and then crucify him]. That, I think, is faith . . . and that is how one becomes a man and a Christian."

Composed in the thick of great uncertainty—about his own fate and that of his loved ones, and the outcome of the conspiracy's plans to assassinate Hitler—Bonhoeffer's letters to Bethge were a tour de force. In mid-1944, neither man could see the widespread impact these writings would come to have on Christian theology and on the faith and actions of countless men and women in the ensuing seventy years. For example, during the late 1980s and early 1990s, Bonhoeffer's ideas on religionless Christianity played an important role in the opposition to South African apartheid. A few years later, these same ideas were influential in the reconstruction of German church life that occurred in the wake of Germany's reunification. This, of course, was unknowable as Bonhoeffer scribbled his letters to Bethge from his prison cell in 1944. What the two ministers could see then was that one of them had laid down a compelling vision for Christianity, and that the letters should be preserved. Bethge took this charge seriously, safeguarding them, typing some of them up, and then carefully hiding all of them. In 1951, he published the letters.

During the first half of 1944, the Reich War Court made no noticeable advance in its cases against Bonhoeffer and Dohnanyi. But both men suspected that Gestapo officers were still looking for incriminating evidence involving anyone connected to the Abwehr. As Germany's military fortunes continued to decline, and Allied air strikes intensified, Bonhoeffer and his fellow conspirators hoped they could outlast the Nazis. If the prisoners were lucky, British or US forces would liberate Berlin before they could be tried or executed. After the Allied invasion of France on June 6, 1944, this possibility would seem more and more likely.

In the spring of 1944, Dohnanyi tried to delay the legal proceedings against him—and since the two men were to be tried together, those against Bonhoeffer as well—by arranging for his wife, Christine, to bring him food infected with diphtheria. She delivered the infected foodstuffs to her husband, and he swiftly developed paralysis and was transferred to a military hospital in nearby Potsdam, where he was quarantined.

At about the same time, both men were keenly awaiting the outcome of another attempt to kill Hitler, which was scheduled for mid-July. Although neither prisoner had played an active role in its planning, Dohnanyi had helped set the plot in motion. While they were in prison, he and Bonhoeffer were kept informed of what was going on by coded messages. The brothers-in-law were optimistic they would each be freed after Hitler was dead and a new regime came to power.

The assassination plan, code-named Operation Valkyrie, called for staff officer Claus Schenk Graf von Stauffenberg to carry a bomb, hidden inside his briefcase, into a meeting of Hitler and his generals. The meeting was to be held on July 20 in Hitler's East Prussian headquarters in Rastenburg (today, a part of Poland). On the appointed day, von Stauffenberg took the briefcase into the conference room and placed it under the wooden table near the Führer. The staff officer then excused himself to take a planned telephone call. While trying to get a closer look at the maps spread across the conference table, another military officer moved the briefcase farther away from Hitler, pushing it behind one of the table's thick legs. Within minutes, the bomb went off, killing several people. But aside from a perforated eardrum, Hitler was uninjured. Von Stauffenberg, escaping from the headquarters, heard the explosion and assumed the leader was dead; he then flew to Berlin. Although a number of conspirators quickly tried to take control of the government, these efforts collapsed as soon as news of Hitler's survival spread.

Nazi reprisals were swift and brutal. General Beck, Colonel von Stauffenberg, and others were shot in a Berlin courtyard in the first minutes of July 21. Dohnanyi's direct superior at the Abwehr, Hans Oster, was arrested the same day; Admiral Wilhelm Canaris, former chief of the Abwehr, was imprisoned the next. The SS launched a massive investigation. During the succeeding weeks, police and Gestapo officers arrested more than six thousand people, executing more than three-quarters of them.

When Bonhoeffer, Dohnanyi, and their families learned that the recent plot had failed, they knew that the ensuing manhunt might well seal the prisoners' fates. But for two months the prisoners heard nothing to indicate a change in their status. Family members hoped that Hans's and Dietrich's arrests in 1943 would prevent accusations that they were involved in Operation Valkyrie.

But on September 20, 1944, a Gestapo officer discovered some files at an Abwehr outpost in the Berlin suburb of Zossen that directly connected Dohnanyi to many of the people implicated in the July 20 assassination attempt. The files also linked him to virtually every effort to topple the Third Reich since 1938. Among the papers found was correspondence concerning Bonhoeffer's travels, ostensibly on Abwehr business. Although none of the files indicated that the minister had been involved in the recent attempt on Hitler's life, the letters connected him to the Abwehr-based resistance. The discovery of the Zossen files put Bonhoeffer and Dohnanyi in grave danger.

Once Bonhoeffer knew that the Gestapo had these papers, he considered trying to escape from Tegel. Some of his guards liked and respected him, and the most loyal among them, Ernest Knobloch, agreed to help. With the Bonhoeffer family's assistance, Knobloch planned to escort Dietrich, dressed as a mechanic, out of the Tegel gate and then disappear with him. The escape was planned for early October. But on the first day of that month, Klaus Bonhoeffer, Dietrich's older brother, was arrested as a part of the Abwehr conspiracy. Two days later, Rüdiger Schleicher, Bonhoeffer's brother-in-law, was imprisoned on the same charges (Eberhard Bethge was also arrested, but was later released). When Dietrich became aware of his brother's and brother-in-law's incarcerations, he decided against trying to escape. He feared his flight would make things more difficult for his family members, including his parents and fiancée.

A few days later, Bonhoeffer was moved from Tegel to the Gestapo prison in the basement of its Berlin headquarters. This was a terrible place in which, as Sifton and Stern have pointed out, thousands of Socialists and Communists had been imprisoned and tortured in the 1930s. Bonhoeffer's transfer there indicated that the government's case against him had become far more serious. During the four months that he spent in the Gestapo prison, he met colleagues and old friends who were also held there, including Oster, Canaris, and, briefly, Dohnanyi. The prisoners were kept in separate cells, but they could snatch conversation together during the chaos of the frequent air raids or in the communal lavatory at the end of the corridor.

There is little historical record of how Bonhoeffer spent his days in the prison. It seems likely that he continued work on his theological writing, but these papers were either destroyed or lost. We know that the Gestapo interrogated him, and that he found these sessions repulsive. (There is no evidence that he was physically tortured.) He was allowed no visitors and little communication with his family. His correspondence with his parents was limited to two letters, and with Maria, to one. Bonhoeffer was, however, allowed to enjoy at least some of the food parcels that his parents or fiancée brought him each week.

In late December, he wrote a Christmas message to Maria. Composed in his five-by-eight cell, this brave, loving letter was written in a moment of self-knowledge and with an eye to preventing his fiancée from worrying. After thanking Maria for her support and asking her to convey similar sentiments to his parents, Bonhoeffer reflected on his love for the people he cared about:

> Our homes will be very quiet at this time. But I have often found that the quieter my surroundings, the more vividly I sense my connection with you all. It's as if, in solitude, the soul develops organs of which we're hardly aware in everyday life. So I haven't for an instant felt lonely and forlorn. You yourself, my parents—all of you including my friends and students on active service—are my constant companions. Your prayers and kind thoughts, passages from the Bible, long-forgotten conversations, pieces of music, books—all are invested with life and reality as never before. I live in a great, unseen realm of whose real existence I'm in no doubt. . . . So you mustn't think I'm unhappy. Anyway, what do happiness and unhappiness mean? They depend so little on circumstances and so much more on what goes on inside us. I'm thankful every day to have you—you and all of you—and that makes me happy and cheerful. . . . We've now been waiting for each other for almost two years, dearest Maria. Don't lose heart! I'm glad you're with my parents. Give my fondest love to your mother and the whole family.

Bonhoeffer also enclosed a poem he had written as a Christmas greeting to her and his family. Here is the last stanza:

> By kindly powers so wondrously protected
> We wait with confidence, befall what may.

We are with God at night and in the morning,
And, just as certainly, on each new day.

In early February 1945, Bonhoeffer was moved to Buchenwald concentration camp, located about 180 miles southwest of Berlin. He remained there until April 3, when he began a five-day journey to Flossenbürg concentration camp near the Czechoslovakian border. From the time he left the Gestapo prison in Berlin, his family had no idea of his whereabouts.

On April 4, Nazi officials discovered the diaries of former Abwehr chief Wilhelm Canaris. In these papers, Canaris, who had headed the resistance effort within the Abwehr, detailed his life as a double agent. These diaries were shown to Hitler, who was enraged and ordered the summary execution of all suspected Abwehr-based conspirators, including Dohnanyi and Bonhoeffer. On the evening of April 8, Bonhoeffer arrived at Flossenbürg concentration camp, where he was quickly arraigned, convicted, and condemned to death.

Early the next morning, April 9, 1945, Bonhoeffer and five other prisoners, including Canaris and Hans Oster, were hanged in a small courtyard at Flossenbürg. (Two weeks later, US armed forces liberated the camp.) On the same day that Bonhoeffer and his colleagues died, Hans von Dohnanyi was hanged at Sachsenhausen concentration camp, thirty miles north of Berlin. On April 22, Klaus Bonhoeffer and Rüdiger Schleicher were shot in the street outside the Berlin prison in which they had been incarcerated.

During the next several months, the Bonhoeffer family learned the fate of the four men. Their surviving parents, siblings, wives, and children tried to carry on with fortitude and grace. "I believe it is better," Christine Dohnanyi wrote a friend in 1945, "to know for what one dies than not to know what exactly one is living for." She said to her mother, Paula Bonhoeffer, that she could not believe she would ever be happy again, "and yet that is precisely what we owe the dead." In the fall 1945, Karl Bonhoeffer wrote a colleague in Boston about having two sons and two sons-in-law murdered by the Nazis:

I understand that you have heard that we have had a bad time and lost two sons (Dietrich the theologian and Klaus the head of Lufthansa) and two sons-in-law (Professors Schleicher and Dohnanyi) at the hands of the Gestapo. You can imagine that that has not been without its effects on us old folk. For years we had the tension caused by anxiety for those arrested and for those not yet arrested but in danger. But since we were all agreed on the need to act, and my sons were also fully aware of what they had to expect if the plot miscarried and had resolved if necessary to lay down their lives, we are sad but also proud of their attitude, which has been consistent.

CHAPTER FORTY-ONE

The World after Dietrich Bonhoeffer

U nlike the other leaders in this book, Dietrich Bonhoeffer didn't live to see his mission accomplished. He died three weeks before Adolf Hitler killed himself and Nazi rule was destroyed. The theologian's writings from prison remained hidden into the early 1950s, when they were first published. It would take more time before Bonhoeffer's late work on religionless Christianity and living a right life in community with others would become famous. His leadership in the Confessing Church and the European ecumenical movement during the 1930s would not be well documented until 1967, when his friend and colleague Eberhard Bethge published the definitive biography of Bonhoeffer (in German). Even then, few outside his native country and theological circles knew much about the committed minister and concerned citizen who, along with family members Hans von Dohnanyi, Klaus Bonhoeffer, and Rüdiger Schleicher, risked his life to try to stop the barbarity of the Third Reich.

In 1970, the English translation of Bethge's biography appeared, and general interest in Bonhoeffer expanded. As his name became better known, especially in Europe, Africa, and other parts of the world, some critics charged that Bonhoeffer had failed in most of what he tried to do. He'd failed to make the Confessing Church a viable source of opposition to the Nazi regime, and he didn't succeed in uniting European churches against Hitler. Other detractors pointed out that Bonhoeffer, Dohnanyi, and other family members directly saved only fourteen victims of Nazi atrocities. And, of course, the conspiracy's various attempts to kill Hitler all miscarried.

On the surface, this assessment has a certain logic. But it ignores much more than it captures about the impact of Bonhoeffer's life. It takes no account, for example, of the enormous theological influence his work, including that on religionless Christianity, has had in the more than seven decades since his death. Bonhoeffer's writing has helped shape church movements in various parts of the world. The same work has affected how ordinary people think about the role of Jesus Christ and what the commitment to goodness in the world means today. Some of this work has reached into social and political activism, inspiring civil rights and other leaders. On a broader level, thousands of Christians, and other spiritually minded people who do not identify themselves as Christian, have been motivated by Bonhoeffer's thoughtful invocation of "this worldliness" and finding one's true self in service to others.

All of this impact has been important. But Bonhoeffer's significance as a leader reaches beyond his work. Of the five people in this book, no one else so clearly exemplifies the power of Mahatma Gandhi's riveting claim "My life is my message." Bonhoeffer's leadership—of those who knew him during his life and the millions of people who have encountered that life after it ended—has consisted of much more than his external achievements. It has been felt in *how he made his way through the world*: the mission he undertook, the choices he made, the courage he summoned, and the respect that he accorded himself, others, and goodness in the midst of moral ambivalence and inversion.

Today, in a world that struggles with racism, oppression, global violence, and widespread disillusionment about leadership at high levels, each of us can find motivation in Bonhoeffer's efforts to discern, and then live by, right action. We can take inspiration from his and his family's opposition to Hitler, and we can learn from his commitment to love and serve others as a path to self-fulfillment. Perhaps most important, Bonhoeffer teaches us that the lives we make, including the purposes we embrace, the roads we travel, and the integrity we bring to the small and large aspects of our respective journeys, have the potential to exert great influence on external circumstances and other people. Living thoughtfully, living rightly, are powerful acts of leadership unto themselves. This lesson has never been more important than here and now in the early twenty-first century.

PART FIVE

Protect the Earth and Its Creatures

RACHEL CARSON'S CHALLENGE

CHAPTER FORTY-TWO

Stay the Course

In April 1960, Rachel Carson entered a hospital in Washington, DC, for surgery to remove two small growths in her left breast. It would be the third such procedure in twelve years for the well-known scientist and author, and she hoped it would prove as uncomplicated as the others. During recent months, illness had plagued the fifty-two-year-old, robbing her of energy she needed to work on her latest book—a wide-ranging investigation of the dangers of synthetic pesticides.

Carson's surgery was anything but simple; her doctors found one of the tumors sufficiently "suspicious" to justify a radical mastectomy. They also removed all of the lymph nodes on her left side. When Carson asked her surgeon about the pathology report, he said that she had "a condition bordering on malignancy," and advised no further treatment. She knew a long, painful recovery lay ahead, but she was greatly relieved. The author was eager to get back to her work.

She recovered sufficiently to work steadily during the summer and fall. But as 1960 wound down, the manuscript that would become *Silent Spring* remained far from finished. Several chapters needed revision; others were still only outlined. Thousands of notes that still had to be incorporated into the manuscript sat in boxes in her study, alongside newspaper clippings and correspondence. At times, she considered all the work ahead of her and wondered how she could complete it.

In November, Carson found what she described as a "curious, hard swelling" on her left side, and she went back to the doctors who'd treated her in the spring. X-rays revealed a hard mass between her ribs and skin. Claiming to be confounded, her physicians recommended radiation treatments. Carson consented, but she decided to seek a second opinion.

She reached out to the well-known oncologist Dr. George Crile Jr. of the Cleveland Clinic. He agreed to help, inviting her to come to Ohio. She warned the cancer specialist she was willing to undergo only so much treatment. "I want to do what must be done, but no more," she told him. "After all, I still have several books to write, and can't spend the rest of my life in hospitals."

When she arrived at the Cleveland Clinic, Crile examined Carson and reviewed her medical records. He said her doctors in Washington, DC, hadn't given her the correct diagnosis. Contrary to what they'd said in April, she *did* have metastasizing breast cancer, and the disease had spread to her lymph nodes. Crile recommended that she begin targeted radiation treatments at once, referring her to cancer specialists based near her home in Silver Spring, Maryland. Carson agreed, and after she returned home, she wrote Crile to thank him: "I appreciate . . . your having enough respect for my mentality and emotional stability to discuss all this frankly with me. I have a great deal more peace of mind when I feel I know the facts, even though I might wish they were different."

The diagnosis was shattering. She was still a young woman; she was also the sole support and legal guardian for her nine-year-old grandnephew, Roger, whom she'd adopted in 1957, when her niece had died. Carson had no idea how the boy would be cared for should she die as well. Then there was her work. She was trying to complete what she believed was the most important project of her life. In the wake of Crile's diagnosis, she explained to a friend, "I knew then that if my time were to be limited, the thing I wanted above all else was to finish this book."

Through the winter of 1961, Carson wrote and rewrote chapters as she underwent radiation treatments. These left her nauseated and drained her energy, but she worked as well as she could in between the X-ray sessions. She also contracted a bladder infection; then the duodenal ulcer that had plagued her for more than a year flared up again. Next, she came down with a staph infection that caused her legs to swell and ache, a condition that intensified until she could no longer walk. For weeks, she was confined to a wheelchair.

Carson gradually recovered. But she lived in constant pain. When doctors diagnosed rheumatoid arthritis—one more in a seemingly endless catalog of illnesses—she could hardly bear it. At points, she wondered if she could go on. Writing to a good friend, she described waking from a deep sleep feeling "so indescribably weak and ill that I was frightened. I just had the feeling that at that moment life had burned down to a very tiny flame, that might so easily flicker out."

She grew more frustrated with the toll her poor health was taking on her writing. In a letter to a friend, she lamented the "loss of any creative feeling or desire" and "the complete and devastating wreckage" of her work schedule. But she kept her darkest thoughts to herself. "I moan inside," she scribbled in a notebook's margin. "And I wake in the night and cry out silently for Maine [where she had a summer cottage]. I prayed very graciously to God that he would make it a nice day."

Still, Carson carried on. As her energy returned, she reverted to her lifelong habit of writing at night when the house was quiet, leaving handwritten pages for her research assistant to type when she arrived in the morning. By March 1961, Carson's momentum had returned. She believed she'd turned a corner in her work and could almost see the finish line.

The author and her nephew Roger spent the summer of 1961 in Southport, Maine. Always happiest at her small house there, Rachel remained strong enough to maintain a steady writing schedule. "I feel really over the hump now," she told a friend in mid-August. "There remain only two new chapters [of seventeen] to do. . . . There has been good solid progress this summer and at last it moves with its own [energy]." During these months, Carson tackled some of her most formidable compositional challenges. "How to reveal enough to give understanding of the most serious effects of [pesticides] without being technical, how to simplify without error—these have been problems of rather monumental proportions," she explained to another confidant. By late summer, she believed she'd overcome the worst of these. "Now I understand myself and my way of working well enough," she said in the same letter, to know that "it is all fitting together about as it should."

But then in November 1961, Carson's health took another sharp turn for the worse, and everything came to a halt. She began to suffer from angina, a condition caused by inadequate blood supply to the heart. Arthritis continued to plague her, and she discovered a small melanoma on her nose. Physicians again prescribed radiation, and she was again nauseated by the therapy. At the end of the year, Carson also fell victim to iritis, a painful inflammation of the eye that left her virtually sightless. For weeks, she couldn't read, and her work slowed dramatically. Her assistant read draft chapters aloud, so the author could edit them. But the work-around was exasperating. Writing to a good friend in January 1962, Carson tried to make sense of her "catalogue of illnesses":

> If one were superstitious it would be easy to believe in some ma-levolent influence at work, determined by some means to keep the book from being finished. . . . I just creep along, a few hours a day. . . . [Finishing the book] not swiftly and easily, but draggingly with the impediments of the arthritis and now the iritis, has been rather like those dreams where one tries to run and can't, or to drive a car and it won't go.

At times, Rachel became hopeless. But she didn't give in completely to this feeling. Resolved to outrun her illnesses, she kept working even as new complications arose and her writing slowed to a virtual standstill. As her health deteriorated, where did she find the fortitude and will to keep taking the next step? She left few clues about the determination that lived within her. Maybe at some deep level, the gravity of her medical situation emboldened and motivated her. She knew the stakes for her could not be higher, and acting from this sobering realization, she summoned all her strength to keep going.

Carson's moment of forging—her crucible—stretched out for more than two years. This long, slow burn demanded, again and again, that she find her way back from the precipice of despair and then recommit to her mission. Her ability to stay the course, finish her book, and exert enormous impact was fueled by her unrelenting dedication to a mighty cause. A quiet, reserved woman, Rachel Carson became one of the most important leaders of the twentieth century. The story of how she did this offers valuable insights for all who would make the world better—on their own terms.

CHAPTER FORTY-THREE

The Young Writer

Rachel Carson was born on May 27, 1907, in Springdale, Pennsylvania, a rural town sixteen miles northeast of Pittsburgh. She was the youngest of three children of Robert Warden Carson and Maria McLean Carson. Robert had no formal education and worked as a traveling insurance salesman and electrician. Maria Carson had been educated at the Washington Female Seminary nearby; she worked as a schoolteacher until she married, when by law she was forbidden from teaching school. To add to her husband's income, she offered piano lessons to neighboring children.

The Carsons lived on a small farm. Their four-room house was Spartan, without indoor plumbing or central heat. But it sat on sixty-five acres of pristine land; apple and pear orchards, fields, and woods beckoned Rachel and her older brother and sister outside. The family kept chickens, goats, and, for a time, a horse. They also had dogs and cats.

For Rachel, the woods and fields surrounding her home became her classroom, her mother her guide. An amateur ornithologist and botanist, Maria spent hours exploring nature with her children, teaching them what she knew. She was particularly interested in nurturing the young people's admiration for the natural world and their sense of responsibility toward it. When the Carson children brought creatures home from the forest, for example, Maria insisted they return them to their habitat. Rachel drank this all in. "I can remember no time when I wasn't interested in the out-of-doors and the whole world of nature," she recalled years later. "Those interests, I know, I inherited from my mother and have always shared with her."

Maria was also a student of literature. She read aloud to her children, encouraging them to discover great authors on their own, including Herman Melville, Robert Louis Stevenson, and Joseph Conrad. She subscribed to a popular children's literary magazine, *St. Nicholas*, which featured essays, stories, and illustrations by well-known writers such as Louisa May Alcott and Mark Twain as well as work by young authors. Rachel, her brother, and her sister became avid readers.

From her earliest days, Rachel enjoyed reading, writing, and drawing, and eventually the assumption set in that she would become an author. "I have no idea why [I thought this]," she remembered. "There were no writers in the family. I read a great deal almost from infancy, and I suppose I must have realized someone wrote the books, and thought it would be fun to make up stories, too." As a child, she created and illustrated her own small books—some held together with flour-and-water paste—that told stories of her woodland friends: mice, bunnies, frogs, and owls. Maria encouraged her youngest child in all her literary pursuits.

At age eleven, Rachel published her first story. By the time she was fourteen, she'd seen several more in print, all in *St. Nicholas*. In 1922, she published another story in the magazine, titled "My Favorite Recreation," about exploring her family's land with her dog, Pal. "The call of the trail on that dewy May morning was too strong to withstand," she wrote. "The sun was barely an hour high when Pal and I set off on a day of our favorite sport with a lunch-box, a canteen, a note-book, and a camera." After a day of exploring, "the cool of approaching night settled," she wrote. "The wood-thrushes trilled their golden melody. The setting sun transformed the sky into a sea of blue and gold. A vesper-sparrow sang his evening lullaby. We turned slowly homeward, gloriously tired, gloriously happy!"

Until she was sixteen, she went to school in Springdale. The town offered no instruction beyond tenth grade, so beginning in 1923 she attended high school in nearby Parnassus. A diligent student, she earned top marks in all her classes. She also joined the field hockey and basketball teams and, despite her small frame, became skilled in both sports. In 1925, she graduated first in her class at Parnassus High School.

Neither Robert Jr. nor Rachel's older sister, Marian, had attended school beyond tenth grade. But Rachel and her mother, Maria, had long planned that the youngest sibling would enroll at a four-year college. Intent on making her way as a writer, she planned to major in English, so she set her sights on the Pennsylvania College for Women (PCW, later renamed Chatham College) in Pittsburgh. The prestigious private school was located just a sixteen-mile train ride from Springdale. This was important because neither Rachel nor her mother wanted to be too far from the other. In the spring of 1925, the school admitted Rachel for the upcoming fall.

The Carsons immediately faced the formidable hurdle of paying college tuition, room, and board. PCW and the State of Pennsylvania each granted Rachel a small scholarship, but this money didn't come close to covering the total cost. Rachel's father, Robert Carson Sr., sold off some of the family's acreage, while Maria took on more piano students. She also sold the family china, as well as apples and chickens from the backyard. By early fall, the Carsons had scraped together the fees for Rachel's first semester. In September, Robert Sr. borrowed a Ford Model T, and he and Maria delivered their daughter to campus.

Rachel enjoyed her courses at PCW, including history, sociology, French, and physical education. But she devoted the majority of her time to her English and composition classes. One was taught by a dynamic, Radcliffe-educated woman named Grace Croff. The professor was impressed with Rachel's talent, awarding her high marks for her essays and stories. Croff also encouraged her to submit some of these to the school's literary magazine, which she did, publishing her first story in the spring of 1926.

Outside the classroom, Rachel had a limited social life. This may have been rooted in her innate shyness or intellectual seriousness. Perhaps she felt insecure about her plain, homemade clothes or her persistent acne. As in high school, she joined the field hockey and basketball teams. But she avoided the frequent tea parties and social mixers with boys from nearby schools. She also refused to go to most of the dances that PCW girls were invited to attend.

Her mother's frequent presence at the college also limited Rachel's interactions with other students. Most Saturdays, for example, Maria arrived on the train from Springdale carrying homemade sweets and treatments for Rachel's acne. The two women strolled around campus and read together in the library, with Maria often typing up assignments that Rachel had written in longhand. The women also spent hours chatting in Rachel's dorm room. Years later, her freshman roommate, Dorothy Appleby, recalled coming upon the pair perched on Rachel's bed over a plate of homemade cookies, and neither offering to share.

In the fall of 1926, Rachel began her sophomore year. She took two English classes, an additional year of French, an elective in psychology, and, to fulfill a requirement, an introductory course in biology. From the start, she loved the science class. Nature had always compelled her. Now she discovered a logic, system, and level of detail to the natural world. She was hooked.

Mary Scott Skinker, who taught the biology course, encouraged Rachel's innate curiosity. Skinker had no formal training in what we would today call ecology, but she had a strong interest in the preservation of the environment. She often shared with her students her concerns about growing industrialization and the attendant pressures on open space, clean air, and water. Listening to Skinker, Rachel remembered the foul smell from Springdale's glue factory, the smoke billowing from Pittsburgh's steel factories, and the gray ash that settled on the trees and fields near her home. These conditions had bothered her as a child; now her interest in them deepened.

During her sophomore year, Rachel found herself torn between her love of writing and her growing commitment to science. She earned A's in both pursuits. But she knew that she'd soon have to choose either English or biology as her major. Abandoning English would mean disappointing two important supporters, her mother and Grace Croff, women to whom she was deeply devoted. There were also practical issues to consider. As difficult as it would be for the young woman to earn a living as a writer, making her way as a scientist would be harder still. In the 1920s, few women worked as professional research scientists. Most were discouraged from even applying to graduate school on the grounds that they possessed neither the intellectual ability nor the physical stamina to keep pace with men. PCW president Cora Coolidge was a vocal proponent of women's advancement; she was also Rachel's strong backer. But even she warned her student that completing a PhD program and building a career in biology would be all but impossible.

Despite the potential obstacles, Rachel decided to major in biology. During her senior year, she took courses in histology, embryology, and genetics, organic chemistry, physics, and qualitative analysis, all in preparation for graduate-level work. In late 1928, she applied to the PhD program in zoology at Johns Hopkins University and was admitted for the following autumn. Based on her strong academic performance, the university granted her a full-tuition scholarship.

Paths Converge

Before she graduated from college, Carson won a six-week summer fellowship at the renowned Marine Biological Laboratory (MBL) in Woods Hole, located on Cape Cod in Massachusetts. The MBL drew scientists and scholars of all ranks—from graduate students to Nobel laureates. At Woods Hole, named for the maritime passage between Vineyard Sound and Buzzards Bay, Rachel carried out research into the cranial nerves of reptiles, a project she'd begun at PCW and hoped to continue at Johns Hopkins.

Rachel's arrival at the MBL marked the first time she'd seen the ocean, and this introduction proved critical to her development as a scientist and a writer. Years later, she recalled the variety and wonder of marine life that she encountered aboard the MBL trawler:

> After a time, with much violent rocking of the little boat, the dredge would be pulled up and its load of sea animals, rocks, shells, and seaweeds spilled out on the deck. Most of these animals I had never seen before; some I had never heard of. But there they were before me, dripping with sea water and perhaps clinging to a piece of rock or shell or weed that they had brought up from their home down there on the bottom of the sound. Probably that was when I first began to let my imagination go down through the water and piece together bits of scientific fact until I could see the whole life of those creatures as they lived them in that strange sea world.

Rachel also came to know life onshore. Day and night, she walked the beaches along Buzzards Bay, observing the winds, undulating waves, swooping birds, and teeming life in the tide pools. She tried to make sense of the marine life she saw, taking careful notes and then going back to books and scientific journals to learn more.

In the autumn, Rachel moved to Baltimore to begin graduate work. The twenty-two-year-old was energized about her path ahead. But within weeks, she ran into practical and emotional difficulties. She struggled in some of her courses, including organic chemistry, and lab work frustrated her because the equipment was more technologically advanced than any she'd used before. Uncertain how to make friends and lonely without her mother, she did what came naturally: she logged long hours alone in libraries and labs. Maria would have liked to visit her daughter, but the Carsons couldn't afford the travel costs. Even phone calls were beyond the household's tight budget.

Rachel didn't just *miss* her family; she worried about them. Her father had begun to suffer from a worsening heart condition, and as always, finances were precarious. Her parents were particularly concerned about a series of loans coming due, while Rachel's siblings had money troubles of their own. Rachel's sister, thirty-two-year-old Marian, was twice divorced with two young daughters and had moved back in with her parents, and Rachel's older brother, Robert Jr., was also living at home. At age thirty, he'd tried and failed to run his own radio-repair business and was working part-time at a power plant.

In late 1929, Rachel proposed a solution to her loneliness and her family's woes: she would bring her parents, siblings, and nieces to Baltimore to live with her. This would give her father a chance to recuperate without the responsibilities of overseeing the family home and land in Pennsylvania. Rachel also hoped her brother and sister would find decent work in the city. She calculated that between her graduate student stipend and what the two might earn, she and her family could get by.

Rachel realized she and her family would need a large house. They were seven now, including Marian's daughters, Virginia and Marjorie. Outside Baltimore, Rachel found an affordable dwelling to rent. The house had no central heat, but it did have indoor plumbing and sufficient space. By June, her parents, Marian, and her two nieces had all moved in; Robert Jr. relocated some months later.

In 1930, Baltimore's economy was better than Pittsburgh's, but nonetheless, her brother and sister struggled to find good jobs. At the beginning of the Great Depression, the national unemployment rate was rising quickly and work was hard to come by. Marian worked intermittently as a clerk, and Robert Jr. earned a small income as a radio repairman. But neither could contribute much to the family's finances. Nor could their parents; Robert Sr. was too ill to look for employment, and Maria had her hands full, taking care of him and keeping house for five adults and two young girls.

This left Rachel as the primary breadwinner, which posed a big challenge. Month after month, Rachel struggled to meet household expenses, agonizing over incomings and outgoings. She soon realized she could no longer afford to be a full-time student and earn enough money to support her family. During her second year of graduate work, she cut her course load in half and took a job as a lab assistant at Johns Hopkins Medical School. In between attending classes, working in the lab, and helping her mother take care of the household, Rachel began researching her master's thesis. But she struggled to get much done. "I pretend to be carrying on [my] research . . . [but] it's a pretty uphill business to do even the work for the courses," she wrote a college friend. "It's worse this year than ever before. . . . It's just that this business of doing two things at once doesn't work."

During the next twenty-four months, she continued with her research, courses, and part-time work. In June 1932, at age twenty-five, she was awarded her master's degree in zoology. This was a big achievement, but Carson allowed herself no time to enjoy it. Instead, she resolved to push herself even harder: to continue to support her family—financially, emotionally, and practically—*and* get her doctorate.

Rachel had to fit into her crowded days both researching her dissertation and earning an income. In the next academic year, 1932–33, she taught undergraduate biology at the University of Maryland in College Park and worked as a teaching assistant at Johns Hopkins during the summer. In between the cracks and crevices of her work and domestic obligations, she eked out what research she could.

Despite this extremely heavy workload, she managed somehow to fulfill her commitments into the summer of 1933.

At the end of that year, however, the situation at home deteriorated. Marian was diagnosed with diabetes. She could care for her daughters, but she was often too ill to leave the house. Robert Jr. decided to move out, taking what income he earned with him. Maria Carson was willing to try to find paid work, but at sixty-four years old, she was hardly a strong job candidate. By early 1934, the family had cut all of the corners they could, but money was still tight. A neighbor recalled dropping in on the Carsons around this time and finding the family seated at the dinner table with only a bowl of apples in front of them.

In January, Rachel officially withdrew from the graduate program at Johns Hopkins and tried to find a full-time teaching position. The historical record is silent on how the twenty-six-year-old came to terms with this decision. But for a young woman who harbored great ambition, it must have been a wrenching choice. Like Lincoln after his political defeats, Rachel was greatly disappointed, but she didn't give up or allow herself to become bitter. Yes, she was dejected at certain points. Yes, she experienced frustration, and yes, undoubtedly, she considered packing it all in and settling for much less. But time after time, she refused to give these emotions final say in determining her next move—and thus her future.

This is a critical lesson for leaders in our time. We live an era when, because we are connected every hour of every day, we constantly compare ourselves to others. We learn of a young software entrepreneur who sold her company for $100 million, and we worry that we have somehow failed. We meet an old friend at a college reunion who has written a bestselling book, and we wonder how, in all the time that has passed, we've accomplished so little. Amid this anxiety and self-flagellation, we forget that doing really good work—work that endures, work that makes the world better, and work that offers abiding satisfaction—takes time and the mileage of experience. It also requires navigating through disappointment, exhaustion, and failure without abandoning one's mission.

By late 1934, Rachel had nothing to show for her job search, so she contacted Mary Skinker, her former mentor from PCW. Skinker told her that academic teaching positions were in short supply and urged her to look for a position as a full-time scientist for the federal government. Taking the older woman's advice, Carson sat for the civil service examinations in early 1935. She scored well on all of the tests, but no suitable jobs were open at the time, so she continued teaching and looking for other employment. She also pulled out some of her college writing and began to revise and submit it to well-paying national magazines such as the *Saturday Evening Post*, *Collier's*, *Poetry*, and *Reader's Digest*. In 1935, all of Carson's articles were rejected, but she wasn't deterred. Going back to her literary work had reawakened her desire to write for a larger audience.

Then, tragedy struck. On July 6, 1935, Robert Carson Sr. suffered a heart attack in the family's backyard. Minutes later, he died in his wife's arms. With no money for a funeral, Rachel and Maria shipped his body back by train to Pennsylvania, where Robert's three surviving sisters saw to his interment. Rachel said little about her father's passing. But this event undoubtedly brought her financial and other responsibilities into stark relief. Now there was no one else to feed, clothe, and house three women and two children. Her sister Marian's fragile health also added to Rachel's worries.

She continued to search for full-time work. In October, she got a break when Skinker recommended that she meet with Elmer Higgins, a division chief at the US Bureau of Fisheries. The government official was looking for a writer for an educational radio program called *Romance Under the Waters*. The program's objective was to introduce a general audience to marine life in the Chesapeake Bay. Several of Higgins's staff had tried to write the content themselves. But none of their efforts was sufficiently accessible or engaging. Higgins had then hired a professional writer, but his script failed because he didn't know anything about science. When Carson interviewed for the job, Higgins told her he was out of options and was considering writing the segments himself. "I've never seen a written word of yours," he told her, "but I'm going to take a sporting chance [on you]."

For the next eight months, Carson spent two days a week writing scripts for the program, receiving $6.50 per day for her work. When they aired, the radio broadcasts were well received, and Higgins and his superiors were pleased. Carson had achieved what other writers couldn't; she'd translated scientific material for a lay audience, making it both comprehensible and interesting.

This success prompted her to try to do the same thing for general readers. In February 1936, she shelved the older writing she'd been revising, and in its place she wrote what she hoped would become a feature article on shad fishing in the Chesapeake Bay. Titling the piece "It'll Be Shad Time Soon," she submitted it to the *Baltimore Sun*. Mark Watson, an editor at the newspaper, quickly offered her $20, and the article ran on March 1, 1936. Excited about Carson's content and voice, Watson encouraged her to submit other work.

At about this same time, Elmer Higgins asked Rachel to write an essay about the ocean that would serve as an introduction to a new Bureau of Fisheries publication. Given no guidelines or restrictions, she wrote a ruminative, lyrical piece titled "World of Waters." Here, she invited readers to consider the sea as the element that connects all life on earth:

> Every living thing of the ocean, plant and animal alike, returns to the water at the end of its own life. . . . Thus, there descends into the depths a gentle, never-ending rain of the disintegrating particles of what once were living creatures of the sunlit waters, or of those twilight regions beneath. . . . Thus, individual elements are lost to view, only to reappear again and again in different incarnations in a kind of material immortality.

Higgins was impressed. But he thought the essay too literary for a government publication. "Better try again," he told the young scientist. "But send this one to the *Atlantic*."

A light bulb turned on. Perhaps, Carson reasoned, she shouldn't give up on her larger ambition to become a famous author. Perhaps the answer was to combine her gifts as a writer and her passion for science. Perhaps, she speculated, she could write about what she already knew about the natural world in a graceful, compelling way that would get the scientific story right *and* make it accessible to a wide audience. This powerful realization was much more than a smart bet on her next professional move. It was a vision of how she could marry what had once seemed radically divergent interests—serious writing and scientific research—to create a path forward that used her most important gifts. (Many years later, Apple cofounder Steve Jobs would describe a similar realization about integrating art and technology during a 2005 commencement speech at Stanford University. He would call this integration "connecting the dots" and attribute much of his impact as a leader to it.)

In June 1936, the Bureau of Fisheries advertised for a full-time junior aquatic biologist, and Rachel successfully applied for the position. She was the second woman to be hired by the bureau as a full-time scientist, and she was paid $33.48 weekly. In her job she collected data from scientists in regional field stations, analyzed the information, and wrote reports. Rachel thrived in her new surroundings, and she took copious notes on whatever she was doing—notes she used for both her bureau work and as story possibilities.

We can picture this woman, standing five feet four inches tall, slight of build, with delicate features and curly auburn hair done in a fashionable style. We can see her carefully dressed, wearing high heels and straight-seamed stockings as she walked down the hallways of government office buildings. We can imagine her in her office: thinking, jotting down ideas, and interacting with colleagues. We can also picture her in more relaxed dress, wearing a sun hat and carrying a pen and notebook as she interviews researchers and fishermen working in field stations along the Chesapeake Bay. At age twenty-nine, she was beginning to lay down the wide, solid floorboards of a professional career.

After she left the office and on weekends she wrote articles for the *Baltimore Sun*. By the late 1930s, she was publishing an average of one every month. She was happy for the extra income and the opportunity to write for general readers. It was a satisfying combination of professional activity that she was creating for herself, a kind of virtuous cycle of observation, analysis, ongoing learning, and communication with different readers.

In early 1937, as Rachel was settling into a steady rhythm in her government work and freelance writing, her sister, Marian, died of pneumonia. This was tragic—for Rachel, her mother, and Marian's two daughters. Marian's passing left the two adults to care for the children and keep house, and this meant more domestic responsibility for Rachel, which left her less time and energy for her writing. Now she was often too tired after a day at the bureau, cleaning up from dinner, and putting her nieces to bed, to sit down at her desk and get much done. Her mother, Maria, also had more to do at home and could do less to help Rachel with her writing. At times, the reality of Carson's daily life—which included financial responsibilities, a government job, never-ending demands at home, and the frustration of not having enough time for freelance writing—weighed heavily on her.

Carson's burden was a particularly female one. In each of the other stories in this book, the protagonists—Shackleton, Lincoln, Douglass, and Bonhoeffer—experienced critical years of what I call gathering. These were times of self-conscious learning; in some cases, trying careers on; and looking for one's purpose. Consider Lincoln's experience practicing law in the early 1850s as the issue of slavery grew more prominent, or Bonhoeffer's time in London in the mid-1930s as the Nazis tightened their grip on Germany. For each man, these were crucial, formative years. Each moved through this time without shouldering hefty domestic burdens. Each had more room, freedom, and energy, by some measure, than Carson.

In our time, women (and fewer men) face challenges that resemble those Carson confronted. Her commitment to her work, her own gifts, and the people she loved offers an alternative way to think about what is referred to today as work-life balance. As Carson understood, the challenge and satisfaction of dealing with our obligations to others as we follow our professional drive is not about living a double life. Instead, it's about living *one* life of which work is often a vital part, and in which the competing demands of personal responsibility and career advancement can rarely be negotiated smoothly. For Carson, as for many people today, periods of great productivity were sandwiched between those when her calling—writing—had to be put aside in the interest of family commitments, including health issues. These moments weren't easy for Carson. And they aren't easy for us.

CHAPTER FORTY-FIVE

The Sea Around Us

In the wake of her sister's death, Rachel tried to continue her freelance writing. She published several articles in the *Baltimore Sun*. Then, she started revising her essay "World of Waters," which she'd first written for Elmer Higgins; as he'd suggested, she submitted it to the *Atlantic Monthly*. "We have everyone of us been impressed by your uncommonly eloquent little essay," the magazine's acting editor Edward Weeks wrote Carson. "The findings of science you have illuminated in such a way as to fire the imagination of the layman." Weeks suggested a few edits, including changing the title to "Undersea." Carson agreed, and the piece ran in the magazine's September 1937 issue. It opened with grace and confidence:

> Who has known the ocean? Neither you nor I, with our earthbound senses, know the foam and surge of the tide that beats over the crab hiding under the seaweed of his tide-pool home; or the lilt of the long, slow swells of mid-ocean, where shoals of wandering fish prey and are preyed upon, and the dolphin breaks the waves to breathe the upper atmosphere. Nor can we know the vicissitudes of life on the ocean floor, where the sunlight, filtering through a hundred feet of water, makes but a fleeting, bluish twilight, in which dwell sponge and mollusk and starfish and coral, where swarms of diminutive fish twinkle through the dusk like a silver rain of meteors, and eels lie in wait among the rocks. Even less is

it given to man to descend those six incomprehensible miles into
the recesses of the abyss, where reign utter silence and unvarying
cold and eternal night.

When it was published, the article attracted great interest, including enthusiastic letters from Quincy Howe, the senior editor at
the publishing house Simon & Schuster, who urged her to consider
writing a book based on "Undersea." Within a month, she proposed
a structure for the work, organizing it around stories told from the
perspective of sea creatures living in different ocean environments.
Howe liked the proposal and promised to publish the book.

Carson was excited to get started. But making progress proved difficult. At home, domestic responsibilities took up enormous amounts
of energy. Her government job also expanded, increasing her professional obligations. (In the late 1930s, the Bureau of Fisheries had
merged with the US Biological Survey to form the new, larger US
Fish and Wildlife Service (FWS), which became her employer.) Rachel
continued to compose essays for the *Baltimore Sun*, *Atlantic Monthly*,
and other publications. With what time was left, she chipped away
at her book manuscript. She worked late at night, with only her
cats Buzzie and Kito for company. (In her notebooks from the time
are sketches of Buzzie sleeping on her writing table, curled on top
of manuscript pages.) She wrote slowly, in longhand, revising each
paragraph before moving on to the next. While she was at work
during the day, Maria typed up these pages; in the evenings, Rachel
returned home to find them stacked on her desk. Then, she often
revised them again.

As the months piled on, so, too, did the pages. It took Carson
three years to deliver the roughly 160-page manuscript to Simon &
Schuster, which published the work on November 1, 1941, as *Under
the Sea-Wind*. Scientific experts and literary critics were quick to
praise it. The book, wrote a *New York Times* reviewer, is "so skillfully
written as to read like fiction, but [is] in fact a scientifically accurate
account of life in the ocean and along the ocean shores." "There is
poetry here, but no false sentimentality," asserted the *Scientific Book
Club Review*. "Miss Carson's science cannot be questioned," wrote the

naturalist and deep-sea diver William Beebe in the *Saturday Review of Literature*. "I have been unable to detect a single error."

On December 7, 1941, just weeks after the book's publication, Japanese fighter planes bombed Pearl Harbor, and the United States entered World War II. Overnight, the nation's attention turned to war. Sales of most books slowed dramatically, and *Under the Sea-Wind* was no exception. During its first year, the book sold only 1,348 copies. Carson was terribly disappointed. She'd poured the best of herself into the work, and yet, she remembered, "the world received the event with superb indifference." By the time the book went out of print six years later, it had sold fewer than 1,600 copies; the author's royalties totaled $689.17.

Frustrated and disheartened, Carson focused on publishing in magazines. During World War II, she successfully submitted articles to *Collier's*, *Reader's Digest*, and other serials. In 1944, for example, she sold a piece about the sonar detection system of bats and how this related to modern radar. (After *Reader's Digest* reprinted it, the US navy made the article required reading for any officers or enlisted men involved with the technology.) In 1945, Carson tried to interest editors at *Reader's Digest* in an article about the potential hazards of a new pesticide called DDT, which had been used to fight insect-borne diseases during the war and was now slated for industrial and consumer uses. Citing the controversial nature of the material, the magazine declined the piece.

At forty years old, Carson was trapped in the classic writer's dilemma: she needed a steady income to support herself and family while she tried to build an independent literary career. But her day job took time away from the writing she needed to do to create that track record. Carson briefly tried to find a job that didn't have the bureaucratic responsibilities of her government position, but would still use her writing skills and scientific knowledge. She looked for jobs at *Reader's Digest*, the New York Zoological Society, and the National Audubon Society, but came up cold.

During the late 1940s, she returned to the possibility of writing another book. As before, she conducted her research while doing her work for FWS. A colleague, Shirley Briggs, joked that Carson was "concocting a fine scheme whereby she writes a [bestseller] . . . and is so wealthy and can retire and write natural history." For her next project, Carson envisioned what she termed a naturalist's profile of the ocean. As she had in *Under the Sea-Wind*, she wanted to give readers a holistic account of life in the earth's oceans. She also wanted to challenge them to consider the sea as something to which human beings are inexorably connected. "I am much impressed by man's dependence upon the ocean, directly, and in thousands of ways unsuspected by most people," Carson explained to naturalist William Beebe. "These relationships, and my belief that we will become even more dependent upon the ocean as we destroy the land, are really the theme of the book and have suggested its tentative title, 'Return to the Sea.'"

Unhappy with the poor performance of *Under the Sea-Wind*, Carson wanted to find a different publisher for her second book. Rather than look on her own, in 1948 she hired a literary agent named Marie Rodell. A successful editor and mystery writer in her own right, Rodell was fast becoming a force in the industry. She was also fiercely intelligent and relentlessly hardworking. The two women immediately liked each other and began planning Carson's short-term future. They agreed Rachel would finalize an outline for her new work, and Marie would sell it to a publishing house that she and Carson trusted to aggressively market the book. Rodell also planned to pitch individual chapters to popular magazines to generate interest in advance of the book's release. The pair went to work. By June 1949, Carson had finished four chapters. Rodell then sold the book to Oxford University Press for an agreed-upon advance of $1,000.

Writing the book wasn't easy, but Carson continued to turn out chapter after chapter. In June 1950, she submitted the final manuscript, now titled *The Sea Around Us*, to Oxford. Rodell had also been busy, selling chapters to the *Yale Review*, *Naturalist*, *Atlantic Monthly*, *Vogue*, and *Nature*. She'd also negotiated a lucrative deal with William Shawn, an editor at the *New Yorker*, to excerpt parts of the book in three separate issues of the magazine. These would hit newsstands roughly a month before the book's publication. The *New Yorker* promised to pay Carson $7,200 for the serialized chapters.

This was a huge sum for the forty-three-year-old author, more than she'd ever made from writing and more than her $6,700 annual salary at FWS.

When *The Sea Around Us* was published on July 2, 1951, it received immediate, widespread acclaim. Reviewers praised both Carson's scientific contributions and her singular writing style. "The sea is alive with rhythm and cycles, some of them centuries long," wrote the *New York Times*. "This branch of science is formidable, but Miss Carson explains it in language that is soft and disarming. . . . Her book adds up to enjoyment that should not be passed by. Every person who reads it will look on the sea with new pleasure." *Atlantic Monthly* called the work a "first-rate scientific tract with the charm of an elegant novelist and the lyric persuasiveness of a poet." Baltimore's *Evening Sun* described the book as "not only a superb example of scientific reporting but also a work of art." Scientists also praised the book. "The amount of material you have assembled amazes me," wrote Henry Bigelow, an oceanographer and director of Harvard's Museum of Comparative Zoology. "Although I have been concerned with the sea for fifty years, you have found a good many facts I hadn't."

All this approval quickly translated into book sales. Within a month *The Sea Around Us* appeared on the *New York Times* bestseller list, and by early September, it had risen to the number one spot, remaining there for thirty-two of its record eighty-six consecutive weeks on the list. By the end of 1952, the book had sold 250,000 copies. This put *The Sea Around Us* on par with two other bestsellers that year: J. D. Salinger's *Catcher in the Rye* and Thor Heyerdahl's *Kon-Tiki*. International publishers translated Carson's work into twenty-eight languages. RKO Pictures optioned the film rights. Oxford University Press also paid Carson $20,000 for the reprint rights to her first book, *Under the Sea-Wind*. That book sold nearly forty thousand advance copies, and shortly after it was published in April 1952, it joined *The Sea Around Us* on the *New York Times* bestseller list.

Why did so many different people respond so strongly to *The Sea Around Us*? Certainly, as biographer Linda Lear has pointed out, Carson's love for the ocean was contagious. Certainly, the prose was clear, clean, and graceful. No doubt the *New Yorker* serialization generated important advance publicity. But these factors don't fully explain the public's enthusiasm. Carson had foreseen that after World War II, people would be especially interested in the oceans. The seas had been key battlegrounds during the conflict and had helped protect the country. As significant, in the early 1950s, was the growing awareness of the ocean as a repository of physical resources—not just oil reserves, a focus today, but mineral deposits and fishing stocks.

Perhaps something else was going on as well. Perhaps at a moment when scientific progress—in the form of innovations such as the mainframe computer, jet air travel, and nuclear weapons—was at the forefront of American culture and prosperity, people longed for greater connection with nature. They sought access to its timelessness, majesty, and power. Reading her fan mail, Carson discerned "an immense and unsatisfied thirst for understanding of the world about us, and every drop of information, every bit of fact that serves to free the reader's mind to roam the great spaces of the universe, is seized upon with . . . eagerness."

This curiosity was a good thing, she asserted, and it meant that science shouldn't be confined to a small cadre of experts. Understanding the natural world was the obligation of all citizens, Carson believed. This was her animating imperative, as she explained in a 1952 speech:

> We live in a scientific age; yet we assume that knowledge of science is the prerogative of only a small number of human beings, isolated and priestlike in their laboratories. This is not true. The materials of science are the materials of life itself. Science is part of the reality of living; it is the what, the how, and the why of everything in our experience. It is impossible to understand man without understanding his environment and the forces that have molded him physically and mentally.
>
> The aim of science is to discover and illuminate truth. And that, I take it, is the aim of literature, whether biography or history or fiction. It seems to me, then, that there can be no separate literature of science. . . .

The winds, the sea, and the moving tides are what they are. If there is wonder and beauty and majesty in them, science will discover these qualities. If they are not there, science cannot create them. If there is poetry in my book about the sea, it is not because I deliberately put it there, but because no one could write truthfully about the sea and leave out the poetry.

The Sea Around Us won numerous awards, including the National Book Award for Nonfiction and the John Burroughs Medal for distinguished writing in natural history. Accolades poured in for the author as well. She was elected to the National Institute of Arts and Letters and to the Royal Society of Literature in Britain. The New York Zoological Society awarded her its Gold Medal for service in interpreting the sea, and the Geological Society of Philadelphia conferred the Henry Grier Bryant Gold Medal on her; she was the first woman to receive this honor.

This was heady stuff. But Carson quickly realized that fame had a steep price. An introvert by nature, she found national recognition surprising and discomfiting. Overnight celebrity also brought a range of misperceptions about Carson's gender and appearance. Some readers assumed that the author must be a man. For example, one wrote that he "had always been convinced that the males possess the supreme intellectual powers of the world." Others, who knew *The Sea Around Us* had been written by a woman, were nonetheless startled when they laid eyes on Carson. "You are such a surprise to me," commented an Oxford University Press editor. "I thought you would be a very large and forbidding woman." A *Boston Globe* reporter tackled this preconception head-on, writing, "Would you imagine a woman who has written about the seven seas and their wonders to be a hearty physical type? Not Miss Carson. She is small and slender, with chestnut hair and eyes whose color has something of both the green and blue of sea water. She is trim and feminine, wears a soft pink nail polish and uses lipstick and powder expertly, but sparingly." Speaking shortly after *The Sea Around Us* was published, Carson described her experience as an accomplished female author in a man's world:

People often seem to be surprised that a woman should have written a book about the sea. This is especially true, I find, of men. Perhaps they have been accustomed to thinking of the more exciting fields of scientific knowledge as exclusively masculine domains. In fact, one of my correspondents not long ago addressed me as "Dear Sir"—explaining that although he knew perfectly well that I was a woman, he simply could not bring himself to acknowledge the fact.

Behind the scenes, Carson's domestic life was troubled. In late 1951, she learned that her twenty-six-year-old niece, Marjorie, had had an affair with a married man and was several months pregnant. Carson took pains to keep the scandal hidden, arranging for a physician to quietly care for Marjorie until she delivered her son, Roger Christie, in February 1952. This moment was particularly hard for the now-famous author. "All that followed the publication of *The Sea* [*Around Us*]," Carson remembered, "the acclaim, the excitement on the part of critics and the public at discovering a 'promising' new writer—was simply blotted out for me by the private tragedy that engulfed me at precisely that time. I know it will never happen again, and if ever I am bitter, it is about that."

Carson was also dealing with a number of health issues. Between 1945 and 1947, she was hospitalized for an appendectomy, had a cyst removed from her left breast, and underwent hemorrhoid surgery. In 1948, she suffered a debilitating case of shingles. She tended to minimize—and at times ignore—problems with her health. In the summer of 1950, when Carson was forty-three, doctors discovered a second tumor in her left breast and planned to remove it. When she mentioned the upcoming surgery to Marie Rodell, it was almost as an afterthought at the end of a long letter. When the literary agent sent a note expressing concern, her client rebuffed it. There was no need to worry, Carson responded. "The operation will probably turn out to be so trivial that any dope could do it." Following the surgery in September, doctors told Carson a biopsy indicated no signs of malignancy.

In hindsight, we can see how hard Rachel drove herself, how little she slept, and how heavy an emotional load she carried. During all of her twenties, thirties, and forties, she worked extremely hard—on virtually every front. Some of this labor was for professional advancement; some was to keep food on the table and to care for her family; and some was internal as she fought through worry, sadness, and, at times, great loneliness. All of this took a toll on her physical well-being. Today, medical science is just beginning to identify the physiological effects of depression, grief, stress, and persistent fear.

In the early 1950s, Carson and other scientists knew much less about possible linkages between lifestyle and the onset of illness. But even if Carson had understood such connections, it isn't clear that she would have taken better care of herself. For example, in the 1950s, as her medical problems intensified, she was often dismissive about them. At certain moments, she was also surprisingly passive with her physicians.

How are we to explain this attitude? How could a scientist who was so careful to get the facts and the larger story right not bring the same diligence to her own health? There is little in the historical record to help answer these questions. My own reading is that Carson conceived of her life chiefly in terms of its value for others (today, we might call her a servant leader). Since she'd graduated from college, she'd felt a deep obligation to take care of her birth family. As her professional career expanded, particularly as a writer, she felt a larger and more solemn responsibility to bring the wonders of the natural world to the public. By the time she entered her late forties, this commitment would become an urgent calling to help protect the environment and the life it sustains.

Time and time again, Carson's mission remained paramount. It simply trumped many personal concerns, including her physical well-being. She always believed she had important work. She also believed that she was uniquely suited—even destined—to do this work. Given this, perhaps she felt she couldn't afford to devote time or attention to her own care. Her job, as she seems to have conceived it, was to get on and accomplish her purpose.

In this respect, today's leaders can learn from Rachel Carson. It's a privilege to find one's calling in service to others as she did, and certainly, the world needs effective leaders to move goodness forward.

But being able to do this in the midst of great turbulence requires that individuals take good care of themselves. It is much harder to motivate others to do difficult things if one is not healthy and strong in both mind and body. This means that some of a leader's most important work is being a good steward of him- or herself—physically, emotionally, intellectually, and spiritually. Executives need to make time to get their annual physicals, working mothers must get enough sleep, and politicians have to create plenty of time for reflection and moral questioning. Leaders face pounding pressures and never-ending demands. In this environment, individuals who aspire to make a real difference *have* to feed and water themselves.

CHAPTER FORTY-SIX

New Beginnings

By mid-1952, Carson had made enough money from the royalties on *The Sea Around Us* to leave her job at the Fish and Wildlife Service; now she would earn her living solely by writing. She was already at work on another book about the sea. Rodell had negotiated a publishing contract with Houghton Mifflin, and Carson had agreed to deliver the manuscript by early 1953.

The author was busy, dealing with publicity surrounding her bestseller, conducting field research for the new project, and, as always, supporting her family, which included her aging mother, her niece Marjorie, and her grandnephew, Roger. Nonetheless, she found the time and energy to give herself one great gift. With some of the royalties from *The Sea Around Us*, she bought land on Southport Island in southern Maine with an eye to building a house there. She'd visited the area on two past occasions and been enthralled by its beauty. Now, in 1952, she was going to realize her dream of having a second home there. In a letter to Marie Rodell, she could hardly contain her excitement:

> By next June I am to have a sweet little place of my own built and ready to occupy! The place overlooks the estuary of the Sheepscot River, which is very deep, so that sometimes—you'll never guess—*whales* come up past the place, blowing and rolling in all their majesty! And lots of seals, and there is a long pool left in

the rocks at low tide, where sculpins and other fish sometimes get
stranded. . . . Are you excited?

The cottage was ready in the summer of 1953, and Rachel and
her family headed to Maine. She was delighted to be there. "I can't
think of any more exciting place to be than down in the low-tide
world," Carson told an audience at an Audubon Society lecture,
"when the ebb tide falls very early in the morning, and the world is
full of salt smell, and the sound of water, and the softness of fog."
This summer was a watershed moment for Carson in another way.
Six months earlier, she'd received a letter from Dorothy Freeman,
who'd loved *The Sea Around Us*. Freeman and her husband, Stan,
spent summers in Southport, Maine, and were keen to welcome the
famous author to the area. In July 1953, the Freemans joined Rachel
and Maria for dinner.

At fifty-five, Dorothy was nine years older than Rachel; she was
well educated and an accomplished naturalist with a special interest
in birds and marine life. From the get-go, she and Rachel struck up a
strong friendship, talking about nature, literature, and other shared
interests. By their second meeting that summer, the two women were
wading in the tide pools along the shore and collecting anemones
and other specimens, which they examined together under Rachel's
microscope in her study.

By their calculations, the pair spent only six and a half hours
together during the summer of 1953. But the correspondence they
began that autumn created strong bonds of affection, respect, and
humor. "It seems as though I had known you for years instead of
weeks," Rachel wrote Dorothy in September, "for time doesn't matter when two people think and feel in the same way about so many
things. I, too, am looking forward to lazy hours when we can sit on
our beach next summer and just talk!"

Rachel, as she struggled to make progress on her new book, rel-
ished the letters and support she received from Dorothy. The work
was to be titled The Edge of the Sea and was intended as a companion
to her second book. The work in progress explored three distinct
ecosystems found along the eastern coast of the United States: the

rocky shores north of Cape Cod, the sandy beaches of the mid-Atlantic region, and the coral and mangrove coasts of the southern states. Rachel could see the book's structure and substance in her mind, but the writing came more slowly than she'd expected. "I'm still so far from the end," she wrote Dorothy in autumn 1953, "that at times I feel pretty desperate about it in spite of my publisher's understanding indulgence." When Carson submitted the final manuscript in early 1955, she was more than eighteen months late.

Given her previous book's success, Carson worried that the new work would fall short. Her anxiety quickly proved unfounded. Paul Brooks, her editor at Houghton Mifflin, told her that *The Edge of the Sea* contained some of the best writing she'd done, including passages that were superior to anything in *The Sea Around Us*. William Shawn at the *New Yorker* was equally enthusiastic, agreeing to publish two excerpts in advance of the book's October 1955 release.

Critics and the general public embraced *The Edge of the Sea* when it hit the bookstores on October 26, 1955. "Miss Carson's book is beautifully written and technically correct," wrote the *New York Times*. "People who get bored by too much lolling on beaches should read it as a guide book. All around them, even beneath them, are fascinating worlds. A little wading, searching and poking will open their doors." "Miss Carson's pen is as poetic as ever," noted the *Christian Science Monitor*, "and the knowledge she imparts is profound." Writing in the *New Republic*, archaeologist Jacquetta Hawkes observed, "Miss Carson succeeds admirably in conveying a sense of the richness and intricate interrelatedness of the life she describes. No jeweller [sic] could create a work so delicately interlocked and encrusted."

The new work did not enjoy the blockbuster sales of its predecessor. But in November 1955, *The Edge of the Sea* appeared on the *New York Times* bestseller list at number eight and rose as high as number three during the 1955 holiday season, spending five months on the list. The National Council of Women of the United States named *The Edge of the Sea* its "outstanding book of the year," and the American Association of University Women honored Carson with its Achievement Award.

For the next two years, Rachel published relatively little. She penned a script for an educational television program and wrote a popular article for *Woman's Home Companion* titled "Help Your Child to Wonder." Basing the piece on time she spent in Maine with her nephew, Roger, she explained that parents have to nurture a child's innate sense of wonder about nature. This, she wrote, would not only help a child understand and appreciate the larger environment, it would also help develop his or her curiosity and idealism:

> A child's world is fresh and new and beautiful, full of wonder and excitement. It is our misfortune that for most of us that clear-eyed vision, that true instinct for what is beautiful and awe-inspiring, is dimmed and even lost before we reach adulthood. If I had influence with the good fairy who is supposed to preside over the christening of all children I should ask that her gift to each child in the world be a sense of wonder so indestructible that it would last throughout life, as an unfailing antidote against the boredom and disenchantments of later years, the sterile preoccupations with things that are artificial, the alienation from the sources of our strength.

During the mid-1950s, Rachel continued to spend her summers in her Maine cottage. She found her time there energizing and restorative. She devoted long hours to exploring the tide pools nearby and lying on her deck, watching the birds overhead. Writing to Dorothy in August 1956, she described a late-night walk along the shore with her niece Marjorie. "There had been lots of swell and surf and noise all day, so it was most exciting down there toward midnight—all my rocks crowned with foam, and long white crests running from my beach. . . . To get the full wildness, we turned off our flashlights—and then the real excitement began." Describing the fitful phosphorescence on the top of the water, Carson wrote, "The surf was full of diamonds and emeralds, and was throwing them on the wet sand by the dozen."

In the fall of 1956, Carson's family obligations again moved center stage. Her mother, Maria, was eighty-seven now. She was plagued by arthritis and required a great deal of care. Roger was a healthy, rambunctious four-year-old who also needed a lot of attention. His mother and Rachel's niece, Marjorie, had been diagnosed with diabetes and was suffering from a range of associated health problems. As the year wound to a close, yet more illnesses overtook the Carsons. In November, Maria contracted pneumonia. The next month, Rachel and Roger came down with severe flu-like symptoms.

Then, in January 1957, Marjorie was hospitalized with anemia. Late in the month, she was released and returned home to convalesce. Optimistic her niece would recover in the coming months, Rachel hired a nurse to help. But on January 30, Marjorie took a sudden and devastating turn for the worse. Within hours, she was dead at age thirty-one.

Rachel was devastated. Not only had her young niece died suddenly, she'd left a five-year-old child behind. It wouldn't be easy to become Roger's de facto mother, but Rachel had no choice. Other relatives could not or would not take him, and she began adoption proceedings for the boy, whom she described as "lively as 17 crickets."

She feared this new responsibility. She had virtually no experience as the primary caretaker for a child and worried about her ability to love him, educate him, discipline him, and make good choices on his behalf. At times, her anxiety spilled over into despair. "Somehow I feel terribly alone with my problems," she wrote Dorothy, "as I suppose I must inevitably be. And sometimes I even have a panicky feeling that I *can't* go through with it, but then I see again that there is no gate in the wall; there is no alternative. And then I'm haunted by the thought 'what would become of Roger if something happens to me?'—and for that, as yet, I've found no answer and it frightens me." (Late in her life, Carson added a codicil to her will nominating her editor, Paul Brooks, and his wife, Susie, as possible guardians for Roger.)

In early 1957, as she approached her fiftieth birthday, Rachel took stock of her life. As always, she wanted to write and had committed to a few projects. But she'd been unable to generate real momentum behind any. Some of what felt like literary stagnation was a result of not having sufficient time or energy. "I find a little time to work— then interruption!" Rachel wrote Dorothy. "I think 'Tonight perhaps I can work all night.' But when I get the household settled—or even before—I'm in such a state of exhaustion I can't." Some of Carson's inability to move her work forward ran deeper than lack of hours in the day or cumulative tiredness. She simply didn't have the space to do her best thinking and writing. "My freedom of movement is now greatly curtailed," Carson wrote her Houghton Mifflin editor, "and the sad truth is that I have done no new work for very many months." As the year stretched out, she squared her shoulders, tried to meet her complicated family obligations, and hoped to be able to immerse herself in a compelling project.

CHAPTER FORTY-SEVEN

Elixirs of Death

In 1939, Swiss scientist Paul Müller discovered that the chemical compound DDT (dichloro-diphenyl-trichloroethane) killed a range of insects, apparently causing little or no harm to plants or warm-blooded animals. Tests demonstrated DDT's efficacy against crop-destroying pests such as potato beetles and gypsy moths as well as insects responsible for the spread of diseases such as malaria and typhus. During World War II, Allied troops used DDT to kill lice and mosquitoes; the compound was so effective that this was the first conflict in which more soldiers were killed by enemy fire than by insect-borne diseases. American chemical manufacturers rushed to meet the wartime demand, and as the conflict wound to a close in late 1944 and 1945, producers shifted their focus to the potential peacetime uses of DDT.

During the postwar decade, manufacturers brought DDT and similar pesticides to market. Between 1947 and 1960, the annual production of these chemicals increased more than fourfold, rising from roughly 124 million pounds to 637 million. Companies, including Dow Chemical, DuPont, and Monsanto, produced over two hundred herbicides, insecticides, and pesticides, many sold under different brand names. Some of these products were targeted at households and commercial customers; others were intended for government agencies. By the late 1950s, grocery and hardware stores stocked powders, sprays, and even treated wallpaper that promised to rid homes and gardens of all kinds of pests. Hundreds of crop dusters were treating huge rural areas across the country, and thousands of trucks spraying poisons rolled through suburban streets.

In 1957, controversies surrounding synthetic pesticides broke out. One involved the US Department of Agriculture's (USDA) initiative to eradicate the fire ant. Launched with the strong support of chemical makers, the program proposed to spray two new pesticides, dieldrin and heptachlor, over 20 million acres of land in nine southern states. These compounds were more potent than DDT and had proven effective in killing locusts, mosquitoes, and other insects that attacked crops. Many scientists were critical of the initiative, arguing that, although fire ants were a nuisance, they didn't seriously threaten harvests, livestock, or humans. The same critics asserted that the long-term environmental impact of these new chemicals was largely unknown and more research was needed before undertaking mass spraying.

Despite these concerns, the USDA began aerial spraying. Within weeks, reports of widespread destruction poured into government agencies and news outlets. In Texas, for example, residents found thousands of dead birds and mammals, including raccoons, opossums, and armadillos. In Alabama, songbirds perished by the thousands. Farmers expressed outrage as their livestock, poultry, and household pets dropped dead in the wake of spraying. Photographs and film footage captured squirrels, birds, and dogs writhing in death throes. Other animals died as an indirect result of the applications. One farmer reported that he lost nineteen cattle and several calves after they'd consumed sows' contaminated milk.

A group of Long Island residents also now filed suit against the USDA and the State of New York to halt government spraying of their private property with DDT. Among the plaintiffs were Robert Cushman Murphy, curator emeritus of the American Museum of Natural History; Marjorie Spock, younger sister of the famous pediatrician Benjamin Spock; Jane Nichols, daughter of the banker J .P. Morgan Jr.; and Archie Roosevelt, son of former president Theodore Roosevelt.

These and other individuals alleged that government spraying had destroyed plants, insects, and animals and endangered human health.

They also claimed that federal and state governments had "[deprived] them of property and possibly lives without . . . just compensation," thereby violating their constitutional right to due process. In early 1958, when the case came to trial, the court heard testimony from scientists and medical experts that DDT and other similar pesticides accumulated in the environment and were likely to contribute to the development of leukemia, lymphoma, and other diseases in humans.

Carson closely followed the controversy surrounding synthetic pesticides. In late January 1958, for example, she received a letter from Olga Huckins, a former literary editor of the *Boston Globe*. She wanted to make Carson aware of a recent government spraying program in her home town of Duxbury, Massachusetts. Huckins was incensed about what she described as the "aerial intrusion" into her home and garden. The DDT application

> killed seven of our lovely songbirds outright. We picked up three dead bodies the next morning right by the door. They were birds that had lived close to us, trusted us, and built their nests in our trees year after year. The next day three were scattered around the bird bath. (I had emptied it and scrubbed it after the spraying but YOU CAN NEVER KILL DDT.) On the following day one robin dropped suddenly from a branch in our woods. We were too heartsick to hunt for other corpses. All of these birds died horribly, and in the same way. Their bills were gaping open, and their splayed claws were drawn up to their breasts in agony.

Carson had long been concerned about the growing use of DDT and similar compounds; now she decided to learn all she could about aerial spraying programs. She began contacting scientists, government officials, and concerned citizens, most of whom she'd known during her years at FWS. Within a month of receiving Huckins's letter, Carson had spoken with several people, including an official from the Department of Health, Education, and Welfare (HEW), who was examining groundwater pollution, and a Food and Drug Administration (FDA) staffer, who agreed to send her information regarding possible pesticide contamination of baby food. She soon secured testimony from the Long Island court case and from hearings of the former House Select Committee to Investigate the Use of Chemicals in Foods and Cosmetics. "The more I learned about the use of pesticides," Carson recalled, "the more appalled I became."

Initially, she wanted to write a feature article on the subject; Marie Rodell pitched the idea to major magazines such as *Ladies' Home Journal* and *Good Housekeeping*, but none was interested. Carson next tried to sell the story to *Reader's Digest*, but the magazine declined because it was already publishing a piece supportive of aerial spraying programs. She then reached out to E. B. White, a staff writer at the *New Yorker* and an environmentalist, asking him to consider writing an article about the dangers of DDT. White had been openly critical of widespread pesticide use. However, he said no to Carson, urging her to consider writing such a piece herself.

Carson was disappointed by White's decision, but she wasn't surprised. Criticizing pesticides meant taking on the major chemical companies that produced the compounds and government officials who'd authorized their large-scale use. Like anyone who intended to publicize the growing evidence of pesticides' hazards, she had to be prepared for an uphill battle. Carson also realized that such an exposé would be a big departure from the work that had made her famous. The world knew her for books that extolled nature's beauty, power, and grace and invited readers of all ages to explore these wonders. Now she proposed to examine the destructive—and possibly deadly—effects of synthetic insecticides. This endeavor was likely to produce a dark, depressing, and controversial story.

Despite such concerns, Carson decided in early 1958 to take the next step. She contacted Paul Brooks, her editor at Houghton Mifflin, about the possibility of a short book on pesticides, and he quickly agreed to the idea. She also sent a proposal to William Shawn at the *New Yorker*, beginning her letter to him with a recent statement from Albert Schweitzer. "Modern man no longer knows how to foresee or to forestall," the French theologian had written. "He will end by destroying the earth from which he and other living creatures draw their food." Shawn was immediately interested and asked for a multipart essay on pesticides.

Carson was excited about publishing her research in the *New Yorker* and the potential impact it might have. The author now had tangible momentum behind her project and became increasingly invested in it. "Knowing what I do," she wrote Dorothy, "there would be no future peace for me if I kept silent. . . . I wish you could feel, as I do, that it is, in the deepest sense, a privilege as well as a duty to have the opportunity to speak out—to many thousands of people—on something so important."

By summer 1958, Carson recognized that a moment had arrived that demanded her leadership, and she went to work in earnest. For the next several months, she made good progress. But then circumstances at home took a grave turn. In late November, Rachel's mother suffered a massive stroke. Pneumonia set in, and on December 2, Maria Carson died at home. She was eighty-nine. "During that last agonizing night," Rachel wrote Dorothy, "I sat most of the time by the bed with my hand slipped under the border of the oxygen tent, holding Mama's [hand]. . . . Occasionally I slipped away into the dark living room, to look out of the picture window at the trees and the sky. Sometime between 5:30 and 6:00 [in the morning] I did so. . . . Then I went back into the room and at 6:05 she slipped away, her hand in mine."

In a second note dated that same day, the author described her mother's influence: "Her love of life and of all living things was her outstanding quality." Remembering Maria's spirit, Rachel continued, was itself a form of inspiration for her new project: "Knowing how she felt about [the danger of pesticides] will help me to return to it soon, and to carry it through to completion."

An intensely private person, Carson said little to others about her mother's passing. But undoubtedly this was an extraordinary loss. Maria Carson had always believed in Rachel's talent as a writer and a scientist. The older woman had done all she could—practically, intellectually, and emotionally—to nurture her daughter's gifts and to move her career forward. Maria had also seen Rachel through the loneliness and doubt that every serious writer lives with, supporting and encouraging her when she agonized about her work.

As 1958 drew to a close, Maria was gone, and Rachel was left to care for her six-year-old grandnephew, Roger. But she sensed that she had stumbled into the most important work of her life. She knew the project on pesticides would demand all the talent, experience, and emotional strength she could muster. It might also make a huge impact. She had no choice but to see it through. She'd never been more alone.

CHAPTER FORTY-EIGHT

Throwing Down the Gauntlet

B y February 1959, Carson had returned to steady work. She was excited about the connections she was seeing between different aspects of her research. "I have a comforting feeling," she wrote Brooks, "that what I shall now be able to achieve is a synthesis of widely scattered facts, that have not heretofore been considered in relation to each other." She added, "It is now possible to build up, step by step, a really damning case against the use of these chemicals as they are now inflicted upon us."

Carson had always been a diligent investigator. Now she applied her detective skills to understanding how synthetic pesticides worked, how insects responded to (or resisted) the chemicals, what their effects on human health were, and what the proliferation of these substances meant for wildlife, birds, and the larger environment. She worked inductively, assembling all the relevant facts she could find, formulating hypotheses, considering and testing her theories, and then revising her ideas. To help gather data, she hired a research assistant, Bette Haney, and the two women logged weeks in the libraries of Washington, DC.

Carson also reached out to a growing network of scientists, physicians, librarians, conservationists, farmers, and government officials. Harvard entomologist Edward Wilson, for example, offered her some of his research on the effects of pest control on fire ants. Wilhelm Hueper, at the National Cancer Institute, shared some of

his findings with Carson, and a Connecticut physician, Morton Bis-
kind, also helped her think through the effects of pesticides on the
body's cells. George J. Wallace, an ornithologist at Michigan State
University, had become interested in pesticides' effects on birds after
witnessing the collapse of the robin population on campus, and he
offered his perspective. So did Harold Peters, field biologist for the
National Audubon Society. Carson found scientists in the Netherlands
who sent her on to counterparts in the United States working on
groundwater studies and chemical toxicology. Edward F. Knipling,
chief of the USDA's Entomology Research Branch, wrote the author
about experiments on sterilizing male insects as a means of effective, nontoxic pest control. Clarence Cottam, a biologist and former
FWS colleague, provided data on the repercussions of pesticides on
wildlife populations. He and Carson corresponded throughout her
research and writing.

Some of these people knew the writer from her years in government. Others knew her by literary reputation, or by her scientific
contributions. Still others responded because a trusted colleague had
referred her to them. Virtually all of these people moved Carson's work
forward, communicating with her by phone or post, sending relevant
information, or suggesting another lead to follow. More than a few of
these people, as Linda Lear has written, aided the author by sharing
confidential information—often at risk to their jobs and reputations.

Carson was particularly interested in possible connections between
human exposure to pesticides and cancer incidence. At the start of
the project, she wrote Brooks in late 1959, "I felt the link between
pesticides and cancer was tenuous and at best circumstantial; now I
feel it is very strong indeed. This is partly because I feel I shall be able
to suggest the actual mechanism by which these things transform a
normal cell into a cancer cell." She went on to outline her research
methods: "This has taken very deep digging into the realms of phys-
iology and biochemistry and genetics, to say nothing of chemistry.
But now I feel that a lot of isolated pieces of the jig-saw puzzle have
suddenly fallen into place." (Carson would devote three chapters of
Silent Spring to the link between pesticides and cancer, concluding
that the subject "warrants the most serious concern.")

The puzzle expanded. As it did, she checked and rechecked her theories with experts, calling, sending letters, and—as she began to write the manuscript—mailing off chapters to solicit feedback. Bette Haney described her boss's rhythms in this slow, painstaking process: "Working with Rachel was like seeing the fable of the hare and the tortoise come alive. I honestly thought she would never finish that book. It was not because of all the obvious difficulties; her illness, her mother's death, care of Roger, but more with her pace of work. . . . It seemed so slow. As a child of my culture, I had not yet learned to associate progress with that pace . . . and I did not know then the extent of her determination and what a powerful force that kind of determination can be. It was a valuable lesson."

By late 1959, Carson knew that the book would take longer than she'd originally planned. But she remained committed, she wrote Brooks, to building her work "on an unshakable foundation." This was crucial because "too many people—with the best possible motives—have rushed out statements without adequate support, furnishing the best possible targets for the opposition. That we shall not have to worry about."

Carson's experience researching her book reminds us of the importance of doing one's homework. This means looking carefully for credible sources of information, absorbing and analyzing that information, confirming what we're learning, and revising our work accordingly. Her process also illuminates the need for leaders to move beyond data and facts. These matter, as Carson clearly understood, but they're not enough. Leaders are obligated—whether they work on paper, in a conference room, or in front of a camera—to translate information into knowledge, to use this knowledge to develop understanding, and, if possible, to turn that understanding into wisdom.

As 1960 opened, Rachel was optimistic about her book. She'd hired a second assistant, Jeanne Davis, who was well versed in scientific and technical literature, and Rachel completed chapters about pesticides' effects on birds, wildlife, soil, and groundwater. She drafted another on insect resistance and was well along on two chapters dealing with pesticides and cancer. Also encouraging was her progress on one of the book's most difficult subjects: the connection between pesticides and genetic mutation. This work had taken her deep into the study of cell biology; she was fascinated and frightened by what she was learning.

Then, illness overtook her. Beginning in the spring of 1960, Carson wrestled with a number of serious medical conditions. The most dangerous was metastasizing cancer. In the midst of her radiation treatments in early 1961, another spate of difficult, painful, and energy-sapping infirmities set in, including rheumatoid arthritis and temporary blindness. She fought these medical battles privately, telling only a few close friends. Carson dreaded the possibility of her cancer becoming public knowledge. She feared that if her critics learned of her disease, they'd question her objectivity and thus the validity of her findings. The author knew the book was going to be controversial enough on its own merits; she didn't want to give her opponents any additional ammunition. "Somehow I have no wish to read of my ailments in literary gossip columns," she wrote a friend. "Too much comfort to the chemical companies."

As the weeks of medical appointments and countless accommodations to illness turned into months, she labored without a great deal of emotional support. She had people around her to help with Roger and her house, as well as her research and writing. She was in frequent contact with Dorothy Freeman, Paul Brooks, and Marie Rodell. Nonetheless, in the last two years that Carson worked on *Silent Spring*, she had many moments of galling isolation. As a writer, she'd known the sense of aloneness that often accompanies the creative process. But this isolation was different. It was bitter and steely edged. At times, it was frightening. She felt utterly cut off from other people by virtue of battling a life-threatening disease. She knew that for all her hard work, accomplishments, loyalty to those she loved, and commitment to goodness, her time might soon be up. This was the isolation of living with the specter of dying.

Late at night when she couldn't sleep, what did Carson make of her situation? She left only a few traces of her feelings. In early 1961, for example, she wrote Dorothy about wanting to take Roger with her on a speaking trip to California. "You know that I can see many reasons for a hopeful attitude," Rachel explained, "but you also know that I have faced all the possibilities. Out of that has come, I think, a deepened awareness of the preciousness of whatever time is left, be it long or short, and a desire to live more affirmatively, making the most of opportunities when they are offered, not putting them off for another day."

As best she could, Carson took pleasure in the poetry of everyday life. She found small joys when she could take a walk outside or call Roger to the picture window to watch a flock of geese overhead. She doted on her two cats, Jeffie and Moppet. She enjoyed the company of her assistant Jeanne Davis and the companionable silence the two women knew working together in Carson's study. The author was happy when close friends called or visited. But mainly—when she was able—she worked on *Silent Spring*. Looking back on this time, Davis remembered that in the five years she knew Carson, her boss never once went out to a concert or a movie.

Linda Lear has pointed out that Carson's work on *Silent Spring* likely benefited from her long battle with cancer. The periods when she had to stop writing made her rethink different aspects of the book. These fallow moments also forced her to confront the gravity of her medical situation. This combination gave her a fresh perspective and clarity on the material; it also made her braver and more determined to get this important story right.

Some of the story concerned the impact of synthetic pesticides on human health. After extensive research, Carson knew that acute contact with DDT and other similar compounds caused potentially fatal damage to major organs. But she was also learning about the impact of lower-level, longer-term exposure to pesticides. As her investigation proceeded, evidence mounted that these chemicals could change genetic material, and she hypothesized that this was related to the incidence of cancer.

In the early twenty-first century, we take for granted that a strong link exists between genetically altering substances and disease. But in Carson's time, these connections were new and largely untested. What she and other scientists *did* know in the late 1950s was that strontium 90, the radioactive by-product of nuclear fission, was a proven carcinogen. This finding afforded Carson a framework in which to present the parallel threat of synthetic pesticides. In the opening pages of *Silent Spring*, she wrote:

> Along with the possibility of the extinction of mankind by nuclear war, the central problem of our age has therefore become the contamination of man's total environment with such substances of incredible potential for harm—substances that accumulate in the tissues of plants and animals and even penetrate the germ cells to shatter or alter the very material of heredity upon which the shape of the future depends. . . . It is ironic to think that man might determine his own future by something so seemingly trivial as the choice of an insect spray.

Carson recognized that it would take years to precisely delineate the relationship between pesticides and disease. But, by that time, she warned, it might be too late. Even if man could somehow adjust to existing chemicals, she argued, this "would be futile, for the new chemicals come from our laboratories in an endless stream; almost five hundred annually find their way into actual use in the United States alone." These were brand-new substances, "totally outside the limits of biologic experience," to which the bodies of humans and animals must somehow adapt every year. It was simply not sustainable, she asserted, for man to continue laying down "such a barrage of poisons on the surface of the earth."

Compounding the problem was that as insects adapted to current poisons, more toxic substances—in greater quantities—were needed to simply achieve the initial targets in their reduction. "This has happened," Carson explained, "because insects, in a triumphant vindication of Darwin's principle of the survival of the fittest, have evolved super races immune to the particular insecticide used." Thus, she continued, "the chemical war is never won, and all life is caught in its violent crossfire."

Still, Carson didn't call for a complete moratorium on synthetic pesticides. She pointed out that in the United States, three thousand species of insects caused an estimated $14 billion in damages each year, and she came down firmly on the side of insect control. But that control, she wrote, "must be geared to realities, not to mythical situations, and . . . the methods employed must be such that they do not destroy us along with the insects."

In place of the large-scale, indiscriminate application of synthetic pesticides, Carson called for the "wider use of alternative methods that are now known," and the development of other safe, effective means of pest control. In one of *Silent Spring*'s final chapters, she explored the effectiveness of biological solutions, including less toxic substances, predator insects, microorganisms that preyed on pests, and species sterilization. She pointed, for example, to the successful sterilization of screwworm flies, the larvae of which prey on the living flesh of livestock and humans. By 1959, sterilization programs had virtually eliminated the insect from the southeastern United States. (These programs continued for several decades; in 1982, the United States officially eradicated the screwworm fly using this method.) Carson closed her discussion of alternate pest controls by stepping back and surveying the big picture of what is today called environmental sustainability:

As crude a weapon as the cave man's club, the chemical barrage has been hurled against the fabric of life—a fabric on the one hand delicate and destructible, on the other miraculously tough and resilient, and capable of striking back in unexpected ways. . . .

The "control of nature" is a phrase conceived in arrogance, born of the Neanderthal age of biology and philosophy, when it was supposed that nature exists for the convenience of man. The concepts and practices of applied entomology for the most part date from that Stone Age of science. It is our alarming misfortune that so primitive a science has armed itself with the most modern and terrible weapons, and that in turning them against the insects, it has also turned them against the earth.

Carson believed that mankind had arrived at a critical juncture in its relationship with the earth. "We stand now where two roads diverge," she wrote, purposefully invoking Robert Frost's familiar poem "The Road Not Taken." "The road we have long been traveling is deceptively easy, a smooth superhighway on which we progress with great speed, but at its end lies disaster. The other fork of the road—the one 'less traveled by'—offers our last, our only chance to reach a destination that assures the preservation of our earth."

More than fifty years later, in an age increasingly defined by the effects of global climate change, natural-resource depletion, and rapid-fire species extinction, these words take on new relevance. We can also acknowledge that for all of the research and prescience that animated *Silent Spring*, the book contains elements of an ecological jeremiad. (Even the title—with its intimation of a future in which the birds are killed by pesticide exposure and thus silenced—has overtones of impending doom.) Since 1962 when the book was first published, critics have taken Carson to task, accusing her of an unrealistic nostalgia for preindustrial agriculture, a fanatic defense of the "cult of the balance of nature," and an alarmist sensibility.

We can understand where her opponents found fuel for their fires. But seen through the lens of Rachel Carson's impact as a leader, *Silent Spring* was clearly not a prediction of imminent Armageddon nor was it a lamentation for an older, simpler world. It was, instead, what its author intended: an integrated analysis of pesticides' impact on man and the larger earth that sounded an unmistakable call to public awareness and action. In the interest of effecting powerful, positive change, Carson intended to disturb and disrupt and to do so on "an unshakable foundation."

Silent Spring offered at least three major sources of disruption. The first, as biographers Linda Lear and William Souder have noted, was a forceful questioning of the paradigm of scientific progress that characterized postwar America. Carson wrote at a time when the Cold War was at its height, when science was credited not only with having helped the United States win World War II, but also with keeping the nation militarily secure through atomic weapons and economically prosperous through chemical and technological innovation. At that time, Lear has written, "the public endowed chemists, at work in their starched white coats in remote laboratories, with almost divine wisdom. The results of their labors were gilded with the presumption of beneficence. In postwar America, science was god, and science was male."

Again and again in *Silent Spring*, Carson challenged the assumption that unbridled scientific advance necessarily leads to favorable ends. Too frequently, she argued, science aims to control nature, mistakenly viewing other life-forms—including other sentient beings—as subordinate to man's dominion. This, Carson insisted, is a flawed, ultimately destructive presumption. Man is not in control of nature. Rather, man is one element in the complex, interconnected web of the global ecosystem. This web sustains all life and thus requires delicate balance in using and interacting with it. Change one component in this elegant, interlocking system, she asserted, and the survival of other parts—and perhaps that of the whole itself—is called into question. "Who has decided—who has the *right* to decide," Carson asked, "for the countless legions of people who were not consulted that the supreme value is a world without insects, even though it be also a sterile world ungraced by the curving wing of a bird in flight?"

The second source of disruption in *Silent Spring* was Carson's evocation of the responsibilities of citizenship. Writing before there existed any broad-based environmental movement, she insisted that Americans had an obligation to remain alert, vigilant, and engaged about the environment and to what authorities in industry and government were doing to it. "Have we fallen into a mesmerized state," she asked, "that makes us accept as inevitable that which is inferior or detrimental, as though having lost the will or the vision to demand that which is good?" Individual men and women have the power and the voice, she contended, to create positive change by challenging existing authorities. But to do this, they must have access to reliable information. She explained:

> When the public protests, confronted with some obvious evidence
> of damaging results of pesticide applications, it is fed little tran-
> quillizing pills of half truth. We urgently need an end to these false
> assurances, to the sugar coating of unpalatable facts. It is the public
> that is being asked to assume the risks that the insect controllers
> calculate. The public must decide whether it wishes to continue on

the present road, and it can do so only when in full possession of the facts. In the words of [French biologist] Jean Rostand, "The obligation to endure gives us the right to know."

Carson's call to active citizenship and her animating belief that ordinary men and women can change the world is as relevant today as when she published *Silent Spring*. In an age of PACs, lobbying groups, and growing income inequality, her life and message remind us that individual agency—fueled by resolution, knowledge, and hard work—can make a tremendous difference.

The third disruptive gauntlet that Carson threw down was unabashedly moral. Individual Americans, she insisted, have a right not to be poisoned in their own homes without their permission. "We have subjected enormous numbers of people to contact with these poisons, without their consent and often without their knowledge," she wrote. "If the Bill of Rights contains no guarantee that a citizen shall be secure against lethal poisons distributed either by private individuals or by public officials, it is surely only because our forefathers, despite their considerable wisdom and foresight, could conceive of no such problem."

The moral transgressions involved in widespread pesticide use extended to other sentient beings. In a carefully researched chapter, Carson detailed the effects of DDT and similar compounds on wildlife and domestic animals. Synthetic pesticides, she wrote, poison "all life with which [they come] in contact: the cat beloved of some family, the farmer's cattle, the rabbit in the field, and the horned lark out of the sky. These creatures are innocent of any harm to man. Indeed, by their very existence they and their fellows make his life more pleasant. Yet he rewards them with a death that is not only sudden but horrible." The animals' corpses, she pointed out, testified to their last minutes. Quoting a report on the application of dieldrin, Carson described the death of a ground squirrel: "'The back was bowed, and the forelegs with the toes of the feet tightly clenched were drawn close to the thorax. . . . The head and neck were outstretched and the mouth often contained dirt, suggesting that the dying animal had been biting at the ground.'" She closed this discussion with a question: "By acquiescing in an act that can cause such suffering to a living creature, who among us is not diminished as a human being?"

Another moral violation, Carson asserted, was against future generations. The contamination of groundwater, like the accumulation of toxic substances in the air and alterations in cells' genetic composition, abused the right that our children and grandchildren have to a clean, safe, and sustainable environment. We cannot abdicate our responsibility to those who come after us, she wrote, by allowing "these chemicals to be used with little or no advance investigation of their effect on soil, water, wildlife, and man himself. Future generations are unlikely to condone our lack of prudent concern for the integrity of the natural world that supports all life."

CHAPTER FORTY-NINE

Silent Spring, Noisy Summer

As 1962 opened, Carson had almost finished her book. In late January, she sent most of the manuscript to her publisher and to the *New Yorker*. Both Paul Brooks and William Shawn were enthusiastic. As she made her final revisions, she considered her purpose in writing the book. Her primary motivation hadn't been to take on big chemical companies. "I myself never thought the ugly facts would dominate," she wrote a friend. "And I hope they don't. The beauty of the living world I was trying to save has always been uppermost in my mind." Nonetheless, the scientist in her was angry about what she believed were "the senseless, brutish things that were being done" to the living world.

As her work on *Silent Spring* wound down, Carson went to see Dr. George Crile. He performed a biopsy that revealed that her cancer had spread to the mammary system on her right side, and in March 1962, she began another round of radiation therapy. Once again, the treatment beat her up. "I know that 2-million-volt monster is my only ally in the major battle," Carson wrote Dorothy. But it is "an awesome and terrible ally, for even while it is killing the cancer I know what it is doing to me. That is why it is so hard to subject myself to it each day."

Still, Carson kept working. She finished her manuscript and the excerpts for the *New Yorker*. She also had a wig made, because as long as her health held, she planned to make select publicity appearances and wanted to cover the hair loss she'd suffered as a result of radiation. In late May, she attended the White House Conference on Conservation, led by Secretary of the Interior Stewart Udall. Many of the individuals there, including Sierra Club director David Brower, had received proof copies of *Silent Spring* and expressed their enthusiasm for the book.

On June 16, 1962, the *New Yorker* began publishing three excerpts from *Silent Spring*. These ignited a firestorm of reaction—with supporters rushing to praise the book and critics clamoring to discredit it and its author. Members of both camps realized that Carson had put a big challenge before all Americans: to reconsider the consequences of rapid technological progress. "How could intelligent beings," she asked early in the work, "seek to control a few unwanted species by a method that contaminated the entire environment and brought the threat of disease and death even to their own kind?"

Supporters were quick to recognize the book's potential impact. Supreme Court justice and naturalist author William O. Douglas, for example, declared *Silent Spring* the "most important chronicle of this century for the human race" and "the most revolutionary book since *Uncle Tom's Cabin*." Writing in the *Saturday Review*, anthropologist Loren Eiseley called the book "a devastating, heavily documented, relentless attack upon human carelessness, greed, and irresponsibility." Carson "has courageously chosen, at the height of her powers, to educate us upon a sad, an unpleasant, an unbeautiful topic, and one of our own making." A review in *Christian Century* called the book a frightening and important work. "It ought to be placed," the writer continued, "on the required reading list of every community leader, every lover of nature, and every citizen who cherishes the great natural resources of our nation."

That summer, another chemical controversy, over thalidomide, grabbed the public's attention, and this fed interest in Carson's work. Thalidomide, a drug prescribed for insomnia and morning sickness, was widely used in Europe and recently linked to serious birth defects, including blindness and stunted limbs. For eighteen months beginning in the fall of 1960, the William S. Merrell Company, a US drug manufacturer, had been trying to market thalidomide in America. But

FDA scientist Frances Kelsey, concerned about the drug's dangerous side effects, had held up government approval.

In July 1962, the *Washington Post* broke the story. Americans were outraged. Kelsey was hailed as a hero for blocking thalidomide's manufacture and sale in the United States and thus preventing thousands of family tragedies. (In August, President John F. Kennedy presented her with the President's Award for Distinguished Federal Civilian Service. Congress passed the Kefauver-Harris Drug Amendment, requiring manufacturers to provide substantial, credible evidence of a drug's safety before submitting it for FDA approval.) When a reporter for the *New York Post* asked Carson about the thalidomide controversy, she said, "It is all of a piece. Thalidomide and pesticides—they represent our willingness to rush ahead and use something new without knowing what the results are going to be." Millions of Americans agreed, and letters protesting thalidomide and aerial spraying of pesticides poured into Congress, as well as the FDA, USDA, and the Department of the Interior.

In the midst of the uproar, a reporter asked Kennedy during an August press conference whether he would call on the USDA and the US Public Health Service to take a closer look at pesticides. The president responded, "Yes, and I know they already are. I think particularly, of course, since Miss Carson's book." A day later, the president announced that the government pesticide program would be reviewed by the Federal Council on Science and Technology and by a panel of the President's Science Advisory Committee (PSAC). Issued in May 1963, the PSAC report called for increased federal oversight and regulation of pesticide use, additional research into the effects of these chemicals, and the "orderly reduction of persistent pesticides." It concluded by noting that "until the publication of *Silent Spring* by Rachel Carson, people were generally unaware of the toxicity of pesticides." Committee members recommended that the federal government provide public education on the use and toxic nature of these compounds.

During the summer of 1962, Carson's critics initiated a series of counterattacks, with the chemical industry leading the charge. The president of Montrose Chemical, the leading producer of DDT, said that Carson wrote "not as a scientist, but as a fanatic defender of the cult of the balance of nature." Invoking Cold War language, Louis McLean, general counsel for Velsicol Chemical Company, suggested that the bestselling author was a front for Communist influences that aimed at restricting "the use of agricultural chemicals in this country . . . so that our supply of food will be reduced to [Iron Curtain] parity." "The major claims in . . . *Silent Spring* are gross distortions of the actual facts," stated a scientist from the chemical company American Cyanamid. These arguments are, he went on, "completely unsupported by scientific experimental evidence and general practical experience in the field. . . . If man were to faithfully follow the teachings of Miss Carson, we would return to the Dark Ages, and the insects and diseases and vermin would once again inherit the earth."

Readers and reporters jumped into the fray. Some journalists lined up with the chemical industry. A writer in the *Economist*, for example, termed *Silent Spring* "a shrill tract," composed of "propaganda written in white-hot anger with words tumbling and stumbling all over the page." A reviewer for *Time* accused Carson of "putting literary skill second to the task of frightening and arousing her readers." He continued, "Many scientists sympathize with Miss Carson's love of wildlife, and even with her mystical attachment to the balance of nature. But they fear that her emotional and inaccurate outburst in *Silent Spring* may do harm by alarming the nontechnical public, while doing no good for the things that she loves." Writing to the editor of the *New Yorker*, one reader accused Carson of being a Communist pawn:

> Miss Rachel Carson's reference to the selfishness of insecticide manufacturers probably reflects her communist sympathies, like a lot of our writers these days. We can live without birds and animals, but, as the current market slump shows, we cannot live without business.
>
> As for insects, isn't it just like a woman to be scared to death of a few little bugs! As long as we have the H-bomb everything will be okay.

Some of Carson's opponents attacked her personally. The director of the New Jersey Department of Agriculture, for example, declared that Carson had aligned herself with a "vociferous, misinformed group of nature-balancing, organic-gardening, bird-loving, unreasonable citizenry that has not been convinced of the important place of agricultural chemicals in our economy." Other critics labeled the author a "priestess of nature," a "bird-lover," a "hysterical woman," and a "member of a mystical cult." Worst of all, Paul Brooks remembered, was a slur attributed to former agriculture secretary Ezra Taft Benson. "She's a spinster, isn't she?" Benson had reportedly wondered in a letter to former president Dwight D. Eisenhower. "Why is she so worried about genetics?"

Several chemical companies threatened legal action. Velsicol Chemical Company, maker of chlordane and heptachlor, tried to prevent the *New Yorker* from publishing the third excerpt of *Silent Spring*, promising a lawsuit if the magazine went ahead. Milton Greenstein, the *New Yorker*'s legal counsel, told his counterpart at Velsicol, "Everything in those articles has been checked and it is true. Go ahead and sue." The manufacturer also threatened Carson's publisher, Houghton Mifflin. After an exchange of letters in which the publisher defended Carson's source material and its decision to issue the book, Velsicol backed away from its warnings. No lawsuits against *Silent Spring* were filed before or after its publication.

On September 27, 1962, *Silent Spring* was published, and as soon as it reached stores, it flew off shelves. Within two weeks, it became a *New York Times* bestseller. It went on to hold the number one spot on the list for most of the autumn. The Book-of-the-Month Club selected it for October; by the end of the year, sales had topped one hundred thousand copies. The hardcover edition went on to sell a half million copies before the paperback version came to market. By mid-1964, total sales exceeded 1 million.

As book sales accelerated, journalists, filmmakers, politicians, and others clamored for Rachel Carson. A private, demure woman who preferred walking the Maine shoreline to the corridors of power, she'd become more famous than she ever dreamed. Thousands of letters arrived, and hundreds of phone calls came in (even though Carson had her number changed to an unlisted one). Marie Rodell helped filter the calls and correspondence. Most people wanted to invite Carson to speak, join an organization, or lead some kind of movement.

Carson said no to almost everything. Her health was precarious, and she was determined to keep her illness out of the public eye. She also knew she had to conserve her energy, so the only invitations she accepted were those she thought would have significant impact. In January 1963, for example, she testified before the President's Science Advisory Committee; her research on pesticides proved critical to the deliberations of the government body. She also agreed to be interviewed on television for the program *CBS Reports*. When this episode aired on April 3, 1963, she brought her message directly into living rooms all across America. CBS estimated that between 10 and 15 million people watched the program; in one hour, Carson became the face and voice of a concerned citizenry.

The program juxtaposed an interview between CBS journalist Eric Sevareid and Carson with a second interview between Sevareid and Dr. Robert White-Stevens of American Cyanamid. "Miss Carson maintains that the balance of nature is a major force in the survival of man," White-Stevens asserted, "whereas the modern chemist, the modern biologist, the modern scientist, believes that man is steadily controlling nature." Speaking in a soft, confident voice from an armchair in her living room, Carson took issue with the idea that man should think about his relationship with nature primarily in terms of conquest:

> Man's attitude toward nature is today critically important simply because we have now acquired a fateful power to alter and to destroy nature.
>
> But man is a part of nature, and his war against nature is inevitably a war against himself. . . . Now, I truly believe that we in this generation must come to terms with nature, and I think we're challenged as mankind has never been challenged before to prove our maturity and our mastery, not of nature, but of ourselves.

The television show, Linda Lear has written, "amounted to nothing less than a special printing of *Silent Spring*." In fact, the program gave the book an entirely new, far larger audience than it had previously enjoyed. Citizen calls for action inundated federal agencies. The day after the show aired, Connecticut senator Abraham Ribicoff, a Democrat, called for a congressional review of synthetic pesticides and other potentially hazardous industrial and commercial products. He also announced that he would chair a Senate subcommittee to investigate the issue and call witnesses. "If it weren't for Rachel Carson," Ribicoff recalled, "I never would have had the hearings. I was not aware of the extent [or] the importance of the problems she raised." To the senator, it was clear that the federal government had a duty and an obligation to intervene.

On June 4, 1963, Carson appeared before Ribicoff's subcommittee, presenting some of her research on the effects of DDT and other pesticides. In detail, she described how toxic chemicals lingered in the earth's soil, water, and living creatures and recommended ways of minimizing the dangers of pesticides. Two days later, Carson testified again, this time before the Senate Committee on Commerce. Here, she proposed the establishment of a Pesticide Commission, composed of independent experts from the fields of biology, genetics, and conservation, who would help resolve disputes surrounding use of these chemicals and make decisions in the public interest.

Along with the recently issued PSAC report, these congressional hearings set the wheels of government action in motion. The coming years would see federal and state governments assume a much larger role in regulating the manufacture and use of pesticides and other toxic substances. At the same time, citizen concern about the environment vastly expanded. These were the foundations of the modern environmental movement, and Rachel Carson had done a great deal to put them in place.

In spite of her public fortitude, Carson was very ill. By early 1963, she knew her time was limited. "I still believe in the old Churchillian determination to fight each battle as it comes ('We will fight on the beaches— etc.')," she wrote George Crile in February. "And I think a determination to win may well postpone the final battle. But still a certain amount of realism is indicated, too." Seven months later, she sent Dorothy Freeman a more pointed farewell. Referring to a walk the two had taken along Boothbay Harbor, Carson wrote:

> For me it was one of the loveliest of the summer's hours, and all the details will remain in my memory: that blue September sky, the sounds of wind in the spruces and surf on the rocks, the gulls busy with their foraging, alighting with deliberate grace, the distant views of Griffiths Head and Todd Point, today so clearly etched, though once half seen in swirling fog. But most of all I shall remember the Monarchs, that unhurried westward drift of one small winged form after another, each drawn by some invisible force. We talked a little about their migration, their life history. Did they return? We thought not; for most, at least, this was the closing journey of their lives.
>
> But it occurred to me this afternoon, remembering, that it had been a happy spectacle, that we had felt no sadness when we spoke of the fact that there would be no return. And rightly—for when any living thing has come to the end of its life cycle we accept that end as natural.
>
> For the Monarch, that cycle is measured in a known span of months. For ourselves, the measure is something else, the span of which we cannot know. But the thought is the same: when that intangible cycle has run its course it is a natural and not unhappy thing that a life comes to its end.
>
> That is what those brightly fluttering bits of life taught me this morning. I found a deep happiness in it—so, I hope, may you. Thank you for this morning.

On April 14, 1964, Rachel Carson died at her home in Silver Spring. She was fifty-six.

CHAPTER FIFTY

The World after Rachel Carson

In the immediate aftermath of the publication of *Silent Spring*, citizens and policymakers called for increased regulation of pesticides and other synthetic chemicals. During the following months, forty states passed legislation tightening restrictions on the use and distribution of these compounds.

Beginning in the late 1960s, a series of environmental disasters confirmed Carson's warnings that efforts to control nature threatened man and other species' survival. In early 1969, for example, an estimated eight thousand barrels of crude oil spilled into the waters off Santa Barbara, California. The public was outraged at the devastation to the coastline and the deaths of thousands of seabirds, dolphins, seals, and sea lions. (The spill remains the third-largest in US history after the 2010 *Deepwater Horizon* disaster and the 1989 crash of the *Exxon Valdez*.) Also in 1969, a chemical fire in Cleveland's Cuyahoga River heightened collective anxiety about the environmental consequences of industrial activity. Civic protests against napalm and Agent Orange, both used in the Vietnam War, underscored the importance of Carson's work on the dangers of certain chemicals. The first Earth Day on April 22, 1970, reflected mounting public concern about, and involvement in, these issues.

On January 1, 1970, Congress enacted the National Environmental Policy Act. This legislation established a broad framework for protecting the environment; it also created the President's Council on Environmental Quality. Eleven months later, the Environmental Protection Agency was established. In 1972, Congress passed the Clean Water Act and banned the sale and use of DDT. The Clean Air and Endangered Species Acts followed the next year.

During the past four decades, federal and state governments have used both legislative and regulatory action to address specific environmental crises as well as longer-standing issues. Many of these actions have provoked great controversy among activists, the larger citizenry, and industrial interests—controversy that continues into our own time in the debates surrounding global warming and other important ecological problems. Today, our understanding of collective responsibility—not only to balance public and private interests but also to ensure citizen access to accurate, fairly sourced information about the environment—is deeply rooted in Rachel Carson's work and its call to thoughtful action.

The scientist and author gave voice to the ecological view of the natural world that has underpinned both our thinking about man's relationship with the earth and related research for more than fifty years. Like Henry David Thoreau writing about Walden Pond more than a century and a half ago, Carson called attention to the right that every person has to participate in nature and to the obligations that such a prerogative entails. These two powerful ideas—that all life on earth is interdependent and that its citizens are responsible for the stewardship of sustainable life—have become more relevant as threats to the global environment have multiplied and grown more serious.

Carson's magnum opus continues to inspire some of the most influential environmental leaders. "For me personally, *Silent Spring* had a profound impact," former vice president Al Gore has written. "It was one of the books we read at home at my mother's insistence and then discussed around the dinner table. . . . Indeed, Rachel Carson was one of the reasons I became so conscious of the environment and so involved with environmental issues. . . . Her picture hangs on my office wall among those of the political leaders, the presidents and the prime ministers. It has been there for years—and it belongs there. Carson has had as much or more effect on me than any of them, and perhaps than all of them together." Writing in 2002, on the fortieth anniversary of *Silent Spring*'s publication, biologist E. O. Wilson echoed this sentiment: "No one can deny that Rachel Carson's book exerted, and continues to exert, a major influence. In immediate impact, it accelerated the resistance to chemical pollution that is all but universal today—in word if not always in deed."

The fiftieth anniversary of *Silent Spring* in 2012 saw another outpouring of interest in Carson's work, including debate about the widespread prohibition of DDT use around the world. That the book has continued to stimulate engagement—at popular, scientific, and governmental levels—is testament to the depth and relevance of the issues that its author raised and how she wrote about them. The enduring importance of *Silent Spring* also speaks to the tremendous positive impact that one person, working in service to a worthy mission, can have. This, alongside the contributions that Rachel Carson made to the field of conservation biology, is her legacy.

Unlike the other leaders in this book, Carson led quietly. She worked mostly in private, exercising resilience, forbearance, and commitment to the cause that had called her. She did some of this work in her study, and some walking along the Maine shoreline with her grandnephew, Roger, watching the seabirds overhead and examining the creatures that lived in the tide pools. She also did some of it reaching out to good friends as she tried to navigate the moments of doubt and despair that at times threatened to overwhelm her. In all these contexts, Rachel Carson demonstrated the importance of steady, diligent work and the determination that powers this. She was a classic introvert who exhibited few of the typical qualities we often associate with leadership, such as charisma and aggressiveness. But as people such as Susan Cain, author of *Quiet: The Power of Introverts in a World That Can't Stop Talking*, have pointed out, leadership comes in different forms.

In her time, Carson was a pathbreaker. She worked as a scientist during an era when men dominated the field. For the last ten years of her life, she worked without an institutional affiliation. She consciously decided to speak out on a large issue that challenged formidable vested interests. She did all this in a reserved, soft-spoken manner even as her opponents launched a noisy nationwide campaign to try to discredit her and her research. Today, millions of people recognize Carson's courage, dignity, and lasting influence. Like the primatologist Jane Goodall, she has become a role model for many of today's women and girls.

The year after *Silent Spring* was published, Carson gave a speech to the Kaiser Foundation Hospitals and Permanente Medical Group in San Francisco. It was the first time she publicly identified herself as an ecologist, and she used the occasion to highlight the connections among species, the larger environment, and the dynamic systems that govern the planet. She also pointed to the perils of man's unconditional embrace of technological innovation: "I suppose it is a rather new, and almost a humbling thought, and certainly one born of this atomic age, that man could be working against himself." "In spite of our rather boastful talk," she continued, "about progress, and our pride in the gadgets of civilization, there is, I think, a growing suspicion—indeed, perhaps an uneasy certainty—that we have been sometimes a little too ingenious for our own good." In words that anticipated aspects of today's debate on global warming, she remarked, "We are beginning to wonder whether our power to change the face of nature should not have been tempered with wisdom for our own good, and with a greater sense of responsibility for the welfare of generations to come."

This was the last speech that Carson gave. Here, as in her larger leadership journey, she did more than simply identify critical problems and potential solutions. She also called others to their stronger selves, pointing them to a path of citizen awareness and action paved with humility and wisdom. She did all this with care, courage, dedication, and grace. Her life and work are indisputable proof of the enormous positive difference that one person can make.

CONCLUSION

The Power of
Courageous Leadership

A t first glance, the five leaders whose stories are told here appear quite distinct. They had diverse temperaments, different ways of getting through the world, and varying degrees of intimacy in their lives. With the exception of Abraham Lincoln and Frederick Douglass, they lived in separate times. They came from three countries, grew up in divergent circumstances, and, as leaders, faced many challenges that were specific to their respective journeys. Only Dietrich Bonhoeffer, for example, was imprisoned and stripped of his determining power in the larger world. Rachel Carson was the only one of the five who suffered serious health problems.

Perhaps most significant, each of the five leaders embraced a mission uniquely his or her own. Ernest Shackleton tried to bring his men home safely; Lincoln sought to save the Union; Douglass wanted to free black Americans held in slavery; Bonhoeffer struggled to resist Nazi evil; and Carson spoke out for the critical importance of environmental sustainability. That, by 1865, Lincoln and Douglass found themselves working toward the same end does not alter the fact that the two began their public work as leaders with dissimilar goals.

For all the diversity among these five individuals, the threads that connect them are considerably more important. The most obvious is that these leaders were made, not born. Certainly, each came into the world with a given set of endowments and with differing degrees of family support. All of these leaders, for example, enjoyed large reserves of physical energy, an asset that it seems likely they were born with. From Shackleton to Carson, these people were intelligent, although their discernment and mental acuity took distinct forms. Bonhoeffer grew into adulthood as a wunderkind in a family of intellectuals. Lincoln was a farmer's son whose outlook was shaped as much by the exigencies of the frontier as by the handful of books that he read as a child. For these people—as for all of us—the gifts they inherited at birth and the circumstances in which they entered the world mattered, yet weren't under their control.

But this is not what chiefly determined their actions or impact as legendary leaders. Frederick Douglass was born curious, for example. Carson was innately sensitive. But there was no guarantee in 1834 or 1928 that either person with their respective attributes would come to make such a difference. These two, like Shackleton, Lincoln, and Bonhoeffer, were *made* into effective leaders as they walked their respective paths, tried to understand what was happening around them, and encountered failure and disappointment. Some of their making was a result of the ambition that powered them in the early and middle stages of their respective journeys. For example, Shackleton wanted more than anything else to be the first man to reach the South Pole. (Indeed, it's hard not to see the *Endurance* expedition, as he originally conceived it, as some kind of personal atonement or redemption for his having lost the Pole.) As a free man, Douglass enjoyed being in the public eye and in the 1850s sought recognition as ardently as Lincoln did. Carson hungered to be a bestselling author.

The drive to make their respective marks was important in shaping them. It took each of them some of the way. But then, interestingly, ambition ceased to motivate and influence them as it once had. As they discovered a larger purpose and embraced it, each found his or her impetus, strength, and validation in the mission itself. Once the *Endurance* became stuck in the ice in 1914, for example, Shackleton's rush to be the first to cross Antarctica was subsumed by a larger responsibility to save his men. Lincoln's refusal to accept a brokered peace that recognized slavery's legality in the South didn't arise from some kind of concern with his reputation. He continued to prosecute the war because only surrender by the Confederacy would restore the Union *and* end slavery. Rachel Carson's determination to finish *Silent Spring* was not about earning royalties or winning literary awards. The will to complete the book was a result of what she saw as her obligation to speak out on a vitally important subject. In the case of all five individuals, their leadership was partly shaped by a willingness to subordinate personal drive in a broader end, one inexorably linked with service to others. In the language of philosopher Martin Buber, the "I" became "Thou" for each of these people, and their actions and impact were greatly enhanced by this shift.

All five leaders were willing to work on themselves. Shackleton watched other naval commanders as he was coming up the ranks and put this experience to use in leading his own expeditions. Both Lincoln and Douglass exercised remarkable ingenuity in educating themselves: the former absorbed legal precedents as he delivered mail in New Salem; the latter bribed boys in the street to teach him to read. Bonhoeffer read voraciously, initially on religion and then on a much wider swath of subjects. Born to hardscrabble parents in a house without indoor plumbing, Carson learned to write for the popular market, manage her reputation as a nationally famous author, and, in 1963, lobby at the highest ranks of government for brand-new environmental regulations. This drive to improve themselves was a function of keen—almost entrepreneurial—observation in which each of the five people here looked for opportunities in all kinds of situations, particularly difficult ones, and then tried to make something good of such knowledge.

The protagonists did this kind of work all their lives, and it played a big role in what they achieved as leaders. But the most important work they undertook on themselves was less obvious and came from a deeper place. They committed to cultivating their emotional awareness and using this to access their stronger selves. Long before the term *emotional intelligence* was coined, these five people realized that their greatest source of power came from within—from the insights they gleaned about their feelings and how they could use these insights to make something happen in the larger world. Ernest Shackleton did not use modern psychological language when he wrote in his diary about trying to sustain the courage he needed to get his men home after his ship sank. Lincoln would have been flummoxed by talk of authentic leadership when he told a few constituents in 1862 that he did not have the luxury of publicly expressing his disappointment about Union army defeats.

The parlance was different, but the goal was the same. Like modern-day coaches, therapists, and spiritual guides focused on helping individuals nurture their better selves, the five leaders here picked up this gauntlet. They did not do this as a single endeavor, but rather as a lifelong project in which they each kept working on themselves, learning specific lessons, developing more resilience, and using these resources to lead more effectively.

Some of the insights, such as the importance of solitude and re-flection, they understood from an early age and relied on as they moved forward. Others, such as detachment and the discipline to survey the situation from different perspectives, they stumbled on as they walked their respective paths. Still other lessons, such as the ability to focus on one overarching issue and thus not be distracted by smaller concerns, they absorbed by experience, by the mileage of their lives. Bonhoeffer, for example, learned to concentrate his vision on what the resistance needed to do partly by living for years under Nazi surveillance. In another instance, during more than three de-cades of juggling caretaking and professional responsibilities, Carson became adept at using every minute efficiently when she sat down at her desk in the late evenings to write.

Mileage, happenstance, and early inclinations offered up sub-stantial lessons to these five people, and these insights helped shape them as leaders. But their encounters with failure, doubt, and despair were even more significant. In these moments, particularly when the problems confronting each person had reached crisis proportions, the real forging took place. Remember Shackleton pacing the ice while his men slept or Lincoln with his back up against the wall in June 1862. Think about Douglass hiding in the woods from the slave breaker Edward Covey on a hot summer day in 1834 or Bonhoeffer walking restlessly around New York in mid-1939, almost unhinged by being away from Germany when war was coming. Recall Carson learning in late 1960 that she had aggressive breast cancer.

More than once, all five individuals here found themselves in the middle of calamity. They didn't engineer these moments; with one exception, none saw disaster coming; and none suspected that they'd be brought to their knees by the difficulties they faced. But once each found themselves in what Bonhoeffer called a "boundary situation," they understood they had to navigate through the moment to endure. They didn't do this by grand design, but instead point to point, with each individual taking a single step forward into the turbulence and then taking the next step after that.

This was messy, grueling, exhausting work. And like everyone in the midst of a personal crisis, these five people were at their most vulnerable. Because they were so vulnerable—hemmed in by doubt, fear, and, at times, hopelessness—they were also porous, pried open by the shock and awe of their respective situations. What was each to do in this perilous, fertile space? Somehow, these four men and one woman realized that the emotional penetrability they experienced and that caused them so much suffering was also a door into new insights about themselves and new ways of being in the world.

Each decided to walk through this door, to use the subtle but powerful opportunity for personal growth contained in every crisis. Underneath the angst that Shackleton worked to conceal from his men, the melancholy that Lincoln battled in the darkest moments of his presidency, and the loneliness that surrounded Bonhoeffer in his cell at Tegel was the choice these individuals made not to succumb to the adversity around them or to be defined by it going forward. Instead, all five squared their shoulders and tightened their core muscles, so to speak, and decided to learn what they could in the midst of the storm, including how they might be transformed for the better.

In several ways, this choice proved critical to their development as effective leaders. By resolving to make something good from catastrophe, each took in other valuable lessons. For example, during the long months after his ship sank, Shackleton worked to keep his own confidence level high. This effort helped him manage the morale of his men, which he did by using his own emotional awareness to gauge their individual and collective energy, and then, if necessary, to take what steps he could to improve it. Similarly, Carson's reckoning with a life-threatening illness became a crucible for the writer and scientist, clarifying the importance of what she was trying to do in *Silent Spring* and pushing her to do what she must to tell the bold truth about pesticides.

Bonhoeffer also grappled with the prospect of dying before his time—not from illness but at the hands of the Gestapo. When he was first imprisoned in April 1943, he considered giving up. During at least one other moment while he was incarcerated, he despaired about his future. But these were exceptions. With the hindsight afforded by history, we can observe his emotional and spiritual growth during the two years he spent locked up. We can see that he accessed the fortitude required to keep from breaking under police interrogation, the compassion to comfort his fellow inmates during bombing raids, the caring to try to keep his parents and fiancée from worrying, and, drawing from all of these resources, the focus and integrity to envision a new kind of Christianity anchored in man's life on earth.

The five leaders discovered three additional insights in the crises they faced. One was the need to slow down and forbear reacting in the immediacy of a particular moment. "Make not haste in time of trouble," Ecclesiasticus advised in the King James Bible. Whether they read the Bible or not—and there is no indication that Carson did—these protagonists came to understand that the more adverse the circumstances, the higher the stakes, the more crucial it was for them to take plenty of time before responding to the latest obstacle or disappointment.

At times, *doing nothing at all* was the best action each of these leaders could take. Lincoln, who was born with a phlegmatic disposition—and so perhaps enjoyed a head start in this respect—honed to a fine edge the art of not immediately responding. Time and again as president, he refused to be goaded by the force of his own emotions or of those around him into taking precipitate action that might compromise his larger mission. Even when he was at his most frustrated, he managed somehow to acknowledge his feelings *without* acting on them in a way that was destructive to larger matters.

The classic example of this is the July 1863 letter that he wrote to General George Meade in which the president expressed his disappointment that the Union commander had not pursued Confederate military leader Robert E. Lee and his battered army as they retreated south after the Battle of Gettysburg. After telling Meade of his immense distress, Lincoln thought better of actually *sending* the communication. He stepped back, maybe he took a deep breath, and realized he couldn't afford to alienate the Union officer at that juncture. (In mid-1863, the chief executive had few fighting generals.) Lincoln folded up the letter, put it in an envelope, and wrote on it, "To Gen. Meade, never sent or signed."

Lincoln isn't the only leader in this book who understood forbearance and the value of taking one's time before making a move. Shackleton, Douglass, Bonhoeffer, and Carson also learned how to step back from a specific instant, assess the larger landscape, take the measure of their own emotions, and only then make a decision about what, if anything, they wanted to do.

As with the other insights that these five individuals absorbed in crisis—and then came to rely on—this is valuable for leaders in our time. Much of what leaders experience every day is emotionally difficult. Constant, instantaneous communication, including e-mail and social media, often stirs up even more turbulence within. Politicians, executives, parents, surgeons, teenagers, and others face the challenge of navigating their own and others' emotions with forethought and consideration. As Lincoln realized, the first action that comes to mind isn't always the wisest.

The second thing that each of the five leaders learned as they navigated through great turbulence was the significance of committing to a worthy goal. Shackleton was determined to bring his team home alive. Lincoln vowed to save the Union and then change it. Douglass gave all he had to abolishing slavery. Bonhoeffer risked a great deal to try to stop Hitler and the atrocities of the Third Reich. Carson repeatedly summoned the will to write *Silent Spring* and, while she was alive, increase its impact.

As these leaders took responsibility for a big, worthy mission, they also evidenced great suppleness in how they tried to achieve their goals. Shackleton used every method he could get his hands on—extra rations, duty rosters, walking across the ice, and sailing from Elephant Island to South Georgia in a small lifeboat—to try to save his men. Douglass, once he broke with William Lloyd Garrison in the early 1850s, entertained a number of ways to eradicate slavery, from political reform to civil war. This combination of a steadfast commitment to a larger purpose and flexible methods is increasingly important for leaders in our own tumultuous time.

The third lesson that the five individuals here learned in crisis was the value of resilience. When each person found him- or herself besieged by trouble, each resolved not to falter. In the heat of the moment, they didn't necessarily see a way out, but they vowed to find a way *through* the obstacles they confronted. One way or the other—in some instances, by a hair's breadth—all five people did this. All five endured. They came out on the other side of calamity without falling through the floorboards of doubt, without giving up on their mission and themselves. Because they survived, their missions and the other people who were invested in such effort—not only those who lived in that particular moment, but also all the people going forward who were affected by what these leaders did—also survived. And this, at some fundamental level, was everything.

Beyond calamity and what these people made of it, other skeins run through these five stories. One such thread is the power of writing and writing well. Each leader depended on writing to accomplish his or her goals. Shackleton wrote in his diary as a way of parsing his emotions and clarifying his next steps in leading his men. All his life, Lincoln relied heavily on the written word to accomplish what he sought—win a legal case, advance a political position, command his generals, or explain the meaning of the Civil War. He invested great care in how he used the written word, knowing that this form of communication was a vital leadership tool. (His collected works fill more than ten volumes, hefty evidence of the importance he placed on writing.)

Frederick Douglass took the art, craft, and power of writing no less seriously. His three autobiographies, scores of speeches, and other papers reveal not only an interest in using his experience and perspective as weapons in the fight for human freedom, but also an understanding that forceful, in-depth communication comes from careful exposition rather than hasty scrawls or extemporaneous musings.

Bonhoeffer loved to teach and was a gifted instructor. But he, like the other four leaders in this book, put his most important thoughts and feelings down *on the page* with diligence and discernment. He didn't ask for notebook paper when he arrived at Tegel Prison because he wanted to become a great author and intended to use his time behind bars to this end. He wanted writing paper because he believed that the weightier the issue at hand, the more time and effort one should invest in trying to clarify one's thoughts about the subject, and nothing, he knew, so impelled one to think deeply and incisively about a given question as writing.

Carson was less functionalist in her dependence on writing than Shackleton, Douglass, and Bonhoeffer. From her youth, she found writing compelling. Some of this was from the sheer difficulty of trying to tell a story well; some of the attraction was in the grace and poetry she unearthed within herself to help her relate that story; and some of the appeal of writing was in the impact that she later discovered her work could have on a general audience. By the time she came to write *Silent Spring*, she understood how powerful the pen (or typewriter) could be. She worked from this place, investing enormous time and energy in how and what she said on paper. The result of her efforts was one of the most important books of the twentieth century—a book that helped launch the modern environmental movement and changed the world in big, positive ways. Leaders today need to consider the kind of writing these five people did. Perhaps e-mail, text messages, and Twitter posts aren't enough.

The ability to see the big picture and envision the potential impact is another thread weaving together these five individuals and their stories. Each person worked to observe the larger moment around them, whether it was Shackleton trying to identify his next move once the South Pole had been discovered or Carson contemplating the possible connections between nuclear weapons and synthetic pesticides. They all stepped back, observed carefully, attempted to make sense of some of the seemingly disparate pieces they saw, and then, more often than not, considered what this meant for their work, for their purpose.

At times they grew frustrated when, despite such vision, they couldn't act on it. For example, in the mid-1850s, some time before Lincoln or other politicians and reformers, Douglass could see that slavery was so deeply entrenched that it wouldn't be abolished without armed conflict. Analogously, in the mid-1930s, Bonhoeffer saw the writing on the wall with respect to Nazi ambition. But few of his colleagues shared this view; and his efforts to combat the Reich government by working through the Confessing Church came to little.

Despite such disappointment, none of these people abandoned their perspective on the larger moment or the possibility that they might make a real difference in it. They watched and nourished big thoughts about what they saw. The theater director Tyrone Guthrie once said, "We are looking for ideas large enough to be afraid of again." These leaders cultivated ideas big enough to be afraid of—from saving the Union to inspiring American citizens to take responsibility for the environment. The five individuals here also spent plenty of time waiting for an opening—an issue, an event, or a coincidence of bigger forces—that would allow them to step onto a wider stage and use all that they'd observed and learned to make a worthy impact. When the opening appeared, they knew it was a moment that demanded their leadership, and they moved into it. They embraced the cause and got in the game.

The last essential thread among these people and their stories is that Shackleton, Lincoln, Douglass, Bonhoeffer, and Carson all worked from their humanity. This sounds cliché. But as we step back and consider these stories, we can see nothing hackneyed about the humanness of the protagonists. Like everyone else, these legendary leaders were overwhelmed at times. They grew depressed. They knew great joy. They struggled, at moments, in their intimate relationships, and they also drew vital support from friends, family, and the kindness of strangers.

The five people here experienced the problems and poetry of everyday life. Shackleton was frustrated by the debts he incurred funding his expeditions. As a young man, Lincoln felt awkward around well-dressed women. Douglass enjoyed mingling with fashionable people. Bonhoeffer loved the tomatoes that his parents included in the parcels they left at prison. Carson marveled at the geese outside her Maryland window.

These leaders also used small props, behaviors, and tactics to keep on keeping on. For example, when he couldn't sleep, Lincoln sang raunchy songs or told dirty jokes. Bonhoeffer had an athlete's competitive streak and enjoyed besting his colleagues or siblings at table tennis and other games. Carson was attached to her pets, particularly her cats, Jeffie and Moppet. They were a source of ongoing comfort, especially as she wrote *Silent Spring*. In these and other respects, the individuals chronicled here were ordinary people like the rest of us.

Part of the reason that these five ordinary people could do extraordinary things was that *they led from their humanity*. They used their personal experience, particularly their empathy, to help motivate and sustain others. For instance, as Shackleton sailed on the lifeboat for South Georgia in April and early May of 1916, he offered hot milk to every man on board when he saw one crew member tire. Why pour drinks all round? Because he didn't want to embarrass the weaker man by handing only him a steaming cup. In late 1862, Lincoln wrote a short letter of condolence to the daughter of an Illinois friend who'd recently been killed in battle. "It is with deep grief," the president wrote to eleven-year-old Fanny McCullough, "that I learn of the death of your kind and brave Father, and especially that it is affecting your young heart beyond what is common in such cases. . . . I am anxious to afford some alleviation of your present distress." Two and a half years later, Lincoln brought this same compassion to bear on all Americans who'd suffered in the Civil War: "With malice toward none, with charity for all; with firmness in the right, as God gives us to see the right, let us strive on to finish the work we are in; to bind up the nation's wounds; to care for him who shall have borne the battle, and for his widow, and his orphan."

This compassion, the attention these leaders paid to small details, and the humility that came with having endured and learned from crisis were as important to the influence they exercised as their larger respective visions and political canniness. We can thus only fully comprehend their leadership by considering how each built such capability and power. Their separate endeavors weren't neat or clean. Long stretches were two steps forward and one back, especially when slogging through great difficulty. But these individuals didn't give up. They tried to walk with integrity, thoughtfulness, and a sense of purpose. In this sense, the very way that each lived was an act of leadership unto itself, whose impact resonates—and calls to us—in the early twenty-first century.

Acknowledgments

This book has been more than ten years in the making. Any creation that involves so much time entails many debts. And this work is no exception. It's a great pleasure to thank all those who've helped my literary child and me along the way to publication.

To tell the stories of the five individuals here, I've relied on a large number of dedicated scholars, biographers, and institutions. I want to offer special thanks to Roland Huntford, Alfred Lansing, Caroline Alexander, Frank Worsley, and Margery Fisher and James Fisher. Their careful research on Shackleton was indispensable to my work on the explorer. I also want to thank the Royal Geographical Society for permission to use some of the extraordinary photographs from the *Endurance* expedition.

My interest in Lincoln began with his writings, and for this I'm indebted to *The Collected Works of Abraham Lincoln*, edited by Roy Basler and his team. I'm also grateful to the Library of Congress, which maintains an extensive digital repository of Lincoln's correspondence as well as a large collection of Lincoln and Civil War photographs, a few of which are reproduced in this book. I also want to thank the Abraham Lincoln Presidential Library and Museum in Springfield, Illinois. The historians and curatorial staff there have been very helpful, not only during a visit in the early stages of my research, but also in responding to subsequent inquiries. The experts in the Old State Capitol, the Lincoln-Herndon Law Offices

State Historic Site, and the Lincoln Home National Historic Site, all in Springfield, offered their knowledge in full measure. So, too, did the men and women at Lincoln's New Salem State Historic Site and the park historians and rangers at Gettysburg National Military Park in Gettysburg, Pennsylvania. Many years ago, I discovered the Abraham Lincoln Association, and since that time, its members and their publications on Lincoln have moved my research forward. I'm grateful to all these people.

Many fine biographers and scholars have written books about Lincoln, and I've benefited greatly from their efforts. I'm particularly indebted to the work of William Herndon and Jesse Weik, John Nicolay and John Hay, Carl Sandburg, Emanuel Hertz, Benjamin Thomas, Richard Hofstadter, Allen Guelzo, Stephen Oates, Douglas Wilson, Rodney Davis, Michael Burlingame, David Donald, Eric Foner, William Gienapp, Harold Holzer, James McPherson, Ronald White, Doris Kearns Goodwin, Don and Virginia Fehrenbacher, Richard Carwardine, Garry Wills, Joshua Wolf Shenk, and William Lee Miller.

Until recently, there has been much less scholarly interest in Frederick Douglass. But the historians and biographers who've studied the nineteenth-century abolitionist have made a tremendous difference to my work. I want to thank Philip Foner, whose five-volume edition of Douglass's writings is a critical resource; John Blassingame, whose more recent edition of Douglass's papers has become indispensable; David Blight, whose work on American slavery, the Civil War, and Douglass himself has inspired and enriched my own; Henry Louis Gates, Jr., for his essential Library of America edition of Douglass's three autobiographies; William McFeely and John Stauffer, for their biographical studies of the antislavery activist; Manisha Sinha, whose ambitious study of the history of abolition has broadened my understanding of this vital movement; and Nathan Huggins, who long before I became a professional historian imbued me with a sense of the richness of our past, and of the African-American experience in particular. I'm also grateful to the National Portrait Gallery of the Smithsonian Institution, the Old Courthouse Museum in Vicksburg, Mississippi, the Library Company of Philadelphia, and the Virginia

Historical Society for permission to reproduce specific photographs from Douglass's life and the history of slavery.

Among readers in the United States, Dietrich Bonhoeffer is the least well known of the five leaders here. And I might never have made his acquaintance, but for Eberhard Bethge's magisterial biography of the German pastor, which I stumbled on in 2005. Bethge's other work on Bonhoeffer, including his edition of the clergyman's letters and papers from prison, was equally compelling. And before long, I was hooked on this honorable and thoughtful clergyman. I discovered the multivolume edition of Bonhoeffer's writings, published by Fortress Press, and this became my research lifeline. I owe a huge debt of gratitude to the many scholars, translators, and other experts who've worked together with Fortress to skillfully bring Bonhoeffer's letters, papers, sermons, and other work into the world. I also want to thank Fritz Stern and Elizabeth Sifton, whose poignant book about the relationship between Hans von Dohnanyi and Dietrich Bonhoeffer continues to inspire my work on leadership as well as my understanding of these two courageous men. Victoria Barnett's careful research on the history of German churches under the Third Reich is required reading for anyone trying to make sense of the stage on which Bonhoeffer worked. I've also benefited from Charles Marsh's biography of the Nazi resister. I'm grateful to the United States Holocaust Memorial Museum for its research on the Third Reich's onslaught against the Jews and other people deemed enemies of the state. I'd also like to thank Maria von Wedemeyer and her sister Ruth-Alice von Bismarck for bringing the correspondence between Bonhoeffer and his fiancée into publication. I'm indebted as well to the Bonhoeffer House, Memorial, and Place of Encounter in Berlin for permission to reproduce one of the photographs here.

There are surprisingly few studies of Rachel Carson's life. But anyone undertaking research on this leader, myself included, is deeply indebted to Linda Lear, whose 1997 biography is the seminal book on the biologist and author. I'm also grateful to Ms. Lear for her other work on Carson. I've learned a great deal from Paul Brooks's elegant account of the scientist at work, from Martha Freeman's edition of Carson's correspondence with her close friend Dorothy Freeman, and from William Souder's biography. The work of former vice president Al Gore, biologist E. O. Wilson, and other environmentalists and scientists, who've brought Carson's contributions into our time, helped me understand her lasting impact. I'm also grateful to Susan Cain for her insights about the power of introverts. I want to thank the United States Fish and Wildlife Service, the Rachel Carson Council, and the Crossett Library at Bennington College in Bennington, Vermont, for permission to reproduce photographs from Carson's life.

Other people and institutions moved my work along. I'm indebted to Phyllis Korkki, formerly of the *New York Times*, who helped me clarify my thoughts about the modern relevance of Shackleton, Lincoln, and Carson's leadership in three articles I wrote for the *Times* between 2011 and 2013. I'm grateful to that organization for permission to use some of this material in my book.

In writing a popular history book that offers real-life lessons for today, I've benefited greatly from being a faculty member at the Harvard Business School, an institution with a rich history of learning from the past to inform the present. I thank the School's Division of Research for providing financial support for this project. This support began with the HBS case I wrote on Shackleton, continued with a second case I wrote in 2005 on Abraham Lincoln, and included all the intervening stages of this work. I'm also thankful to Harvard Business School Press for permission to use some of the material from those cases in this book.

In 2008, I worked with the school's Media Services group to make a short film about the leadership lessons of Abraham Lincoln's life, and this project helped crystallize several ideas in this book. I want to thank David Habeeb and Ivan Audouin for their expertise, creativity, and good company in this enterprise. I'm very grateful to Ann Moore, A. G. Lafley, Arkadi Kuhlmann, and Jeanette Wagner, all of whom agreed to be interviewed for the film and provided powerful insights about what Lincoln offers leaders sitting in the corner office. Thank you, Jeanette, as well, for your unflagging support and friendship these many years.

I want to express my gratitude to hundreds of MBA and Harvard Kennedy School students who read and discussed early drafts of my work on all of these leaders as part of their course work with me. Their observations, questions, and engagement with these stories were very important in helping me test my ideas.

I could never have written a book covering so much historical ground without the extraordinary staff and collections of the Harvard University library system. For more than three decades, my development as a professional historian has been greatly influenced by the vast resources of the university's libraries—resources that not only enable but also encourage the curious student of the past to ask broad questions and then to try to answer them with depth, rigor, and accessibility. I owe a particular debt to the women and men of the Widener and Baker Libraries: these people helped me locate books, diaries, letters, newspapers, magazines, photographs, government documents, and more than a few nineteenth-century statistics.

I want to thank Erica Helms, Katy Miller, and Phillip Mead for their research assistance on the Shackleton and Lincoln cases. They helped me track down information from books, diaries, and other sources, offering up smart ideas and valuable research in the process.

Many colleagues and friends helped this book become a reality. For more than twenty years, Tom Watson, Janet Riccio, Brian Emsell, Dan O'Brien, Dan Maher, and Sharon Gordon have created and managed a world-class program to help busy, curious executives in the advertising business become stronger and better. Not long after I began teaching in this program, these colleagues suggested I bring my work on Shackleton—and then Lincoln and later Howard Schultz of Starbucks—into the curriculum, thus enabling scores of (unforgettable) case-method conversations about what these three individuals, two from the past and one from the present, have to teach leaders and managers today. The depth, humanity, and jaw-dropping insights that emerged during our work together have had a profound impact on this book. I'm no less grateful for the support, friendship, and humor that Tom, Janet, Brian, Dan, Dan, and Sharon have so consistently offered.

As the book slowly began to take shape, I shared my thoughts with good friends and fellow teachers. These people gave generously of their time and expertise. At Harvard Business School, Len Schlesinger,

Jim Heskett, Frances Frei, Tom Delong, and Youngme Moon provided encouragement and inspiration. Tess O'Toole of the Harvard Institute for Learning in Retirement urged me to create a history of leadership course as a living laboratory to test my emerging ideas about the book. At the Kennedy School, Graham Allison welcomed me to the Applied History Working Group, where I've benefited from the perspectives of policymakers and other scholars interested in using the past as a lens into the present. For six years, David Gergen has offered his deep knowledge of history and how it matters to the art and craft of present-day leadership. I'm very grateful as well for his generosity of spirit, wisdom, and abiding friendship.

The team at Boston Public Radio, particularly Jim Braude, Margery Eagan, and Chelsea Merz, gave me plenty of opportunities to explore my thoughts about these five leaders. On and off the air, their questions, comments, and smart speculations helped me hone the lessons of these stories and make them more accessible. I thank them as well for the pleasure of their company in almost four years of working together.

A project that takes more than ten years to come into the world requires stamina and faith—in greater reserves than I could have summoned on my own. I'm thankful to a number of people who helped me keep going when my confidence flagged or when I found myself wandering around in the wilderness. Mollie McDonald blew wind behind my wings when I doubted that I could complete a book this ambitious. Michael Kaplan kept reminding me that stories of courageous leadership are becoming more important as the world grows increasingly turbulent. Several years ago, Leonard Miller offered me his energetic friendship in full measure; I'm grateful for this and the ongoing encouragement that came with it. At various moments when I needed practical help and emotional reinforcement, Philip McLaughlin answered the call, insisting that I would write an interesting book and serving up large helpings of Irish wit in the process. For more than seven years, Steve Cunningham has supported my book and me, never letting me forget that goodness often moves in mysterious ways. I owe additional debts to the people and animals of Arrowhead Farms, all of whom helped me understand—again and again—that writing a worthy book, like riding and jumping horses, requires perseverance, forgiveness, and plenty of laughter.

From the first time she encountered the stories here, Kelly McNamara believed in the power of what Shackleton, Lincoln, Douglass, Bonhoeffer, and Carson could offer to all kinds of people today. She had no less conviction about my ability to bring this book across the finish line in a manner that matched the integrity of its subjects. Time and time again, she offered inspiration and assurance that the book deserved everything I could give it and that everything I had was enough for the job at hand. Equally important were Kelly's research, editorial, and organizational contributions. She helped me understand and then reconstruct the life of Frederick Douglass. She read scores of chapter drafts, editing at least fifteen of these and making all manner of suggestions, large and small, that improved the final work. At several points, when I found myself at an impasse in trying to tell these stories, Kelly's knowledge of and deep affinity for the five people here helped me navigate around the impasse and get back onto open ground. I'm thankful as well for her invaluable assistance editing and proofing the notes, preparing the manuscript to go to publishers, and helping keep track of hundreds of sources. Her friendship and humor were invaluable gifts. Bless you, Kelly.

A small team of talented, dedicated women and men helped produce this book. At Harvard, Alexandra Kesick applied her prodigious intellect, organization, and creativity to seeing the final manuscript through to completion. She helped format the pages, secure permissions to publish the photographs, think through cover possibilities, and strategize about my role in publicizing the book.

In late 2015, the heavens smiled down on me, sending me to William Morris Endeavor and the indomitable Tina Bennett. As my literary agent, Tina has offered her keen intelligence, careful eye, and great deftness to virtually all aspects of bringing this book into the world. Add in her thoughtfulness and unmistakable decency, and well, I've been richly blessed to work with her and her amazing colleague Svetlana Katz.

Goodness usually begets goodness, and so it has been with this book. Tina brought my literary child and me to Scribner, where I've been privileged to work with an extremely talented group of men and women. From the first time he read the manuscript, executive editor Rick Horgan understood the book and what it might be. He has brought this understanding as well as his exceptional gifts to all aspects of editing and producing the book—from the content of the introduction to the chapter layout to the publicity strategy. I'm also very grateful to Nan Graham, whose commitment to publishing books that elevate the public conversation as well as our collective sense of civility has helped make this book a reality. Roz Lippel, Colin Harrison, and Brian Belfiglio have added their expertise and experience to a range of issues, and I thank them. I'm also indebted to Lauren Lavelle, for her skill and care in publicizing the book. Finally, I'm grateful to Jaya Micelli for her elegant cover design and to Emily Greenwald for all manner of logistical and administrative support.

My biggest debts in completing this book are to a few close friends and colleagues who've both inspired and supported me for many years. Jane Lynch helped me clarify all kinds of thoughts about what this book might be and what I might become—as a historian and human traveler—in the writing of it. I owe her more than I have space here to say. Since I wrote my first Harvard Business School case on Starbucks more than twenty years ago, the company's evolution and its most important leader, Howard Schultz, have fascinated me. I've had the privilege of observing Howard's impact and humanity in a wide range of contexts, and both have taught me a great deal about the possibilities of courageous leadership in a volatile, uncertain world. I want to thank Howard, in particular, for his deep interest in history and the lessons it teaches. On more than one occasion, Howard invited me to present my work on the leaders in this book to Starbucks partners and other stakeholders, and I learned a great deal from these experiences. Howard's advice on framing this book as one about the character and integrity of leadership has been invaluable, as has his advice on a range of other issues. Thank you, Howard.

When I came near to giving up on the enterprise of this book, as I did at several moments, Shannon Alexander was there to catch me, dust me off, and send me back to work. She has always known what the larger purpose of the work is and she made certain I didn't lose sight of it. Moreover, her support and savvy counsel have enriched my life and work in countless ways.

This book was written in my study in Concord, Massachusetts, and I was fortunate to have two Welsh springer spaniels to keep me company through early mornings and late nights. Their companionship, loyalty, and sheer joy in being fortified me, time and time again. I'm blessed to have both Bono and Gavin in my life.

This book is dedicated to my dear friend Kelly Close, whose extraordinary faith in my book and me has made all the difference. For more than twenty years, Kelly has motivated me, cajoled me, and, at times, literally pushed me to be better than I imagined I could be. She has done this partly by example, creating and leading a company and a foundation dedicated to stopping the diabetes and obesity epidemics. Her energy, intelligence, and commitment to a worthy mission have been ongoing sources of inspiration. Equally important has been her never-ending willingness to read my work, articulate its relevance to our world today, and then not let up until she knew I was making the book better. Her abundant gifts to me also include well-timed flower deliveries and targeted fashion advice. At various moments in the last decade, I've stopped to ask myself what I did to deserve such a friend and colleague. I remain stymied for an answer. But since the start she has been there for this book and me—with passion, intelligence, will, and goodness. And I'm deeply grateful.

Notes

Introduction: The Call of History

7 "opposite of boring": David Foster Wallace, "Up, Simba," in *Consider the Lobster and Other Essays* (Boston: Little, Brown, 2006), 224.

7 "on our own": Ibid., 225.

8 "wanted to please": Ibid.

9 "in the game": A. G. Lafley, interviewed on camera for video *Lincoln's Journey: Lessons for Leadership* (President and Fellows of Harvard College, 2011), 3:30–4:30.

Part One: Bring the Team Home Alive—Ernest Shackleton's Challenge

13 north and west: Caroline Alexander, *The Endurance: Shackleton's Legendary Antarctic Expedition* (New York: Knopf, 1999), 71.

14 "for the ship": F. A. Worsley, 26 October 1915, in Roland Huntford, *Shackleton* (New York: Carroll & Graf, 1998), 446.

14 "witness her torture": A. H. Macklin, 28 October 1915, ibid., 447.

14 the dying ship: "After long months of ceaseless anxiety and strain," Shackleton wrote in his diary that evening, "after times when hope beat high and times when the outlook was black indeed, the end of the *Endurance* has come. But though we have been compelled to abandon ship, which is crushed beyond all hope of ever being righted, we are alive and well, and we have stores and equipment for the task that lies before us. It is hard to write what I feel. To a sailor his ship is more than a floating home, and in the *Endurance* I had centred [sic] ambitions, hopes, and desires. Now, straining and groaning, her timbers cracking and her wounds gaping, she is slowly giving up her sentient life at the very outset of her career." Ernest Shackleton, *South: A Memoir of the Endurance Voyage* (New York: Carroll & Graf, 1998), 75.

14 "loss of life": Ibid., 77.

14 "to the future": A. H. Macklin, "Shackleton as I Knew Him," unpublished manuscript, in Huntford, *Shackleton*, 455.

15 "party to civilization": E. H. Shackleton, 29 October 1915, ibid., 456.

16 "waste of ice": Shackleton, *South*, 82.

16 "her forever:" Ibid., 99.

17 "desolation more complete": Ibid.

17 "write about it": E. H. Shackleton, 21 November 1915, in Huntford, *Shackleton*, 464.

19 man mastering nature: Ibid., 10.

19 "with his books": O. T. Burne to H. R. Mill, 10 May 1922, ibid., 16.

19 "ever come across": H. R. Mill, *The Life of Sir Ernest Shackleton* (Boston: Little, Brown, 1923), 33.

19 the merchant marine: Ibid., 31. The term *merchant marine* refers to a nation's ships and crew used for commercial, rather than military, purposes.

19 "very good fellow": A. B. Armitage, memorandum for H. R. Mill, in Huntford, *Shackleton*, 29.

20 "as sailors do": J. A. Hussey to H. R. Mill, 19 June 1922, ibid., 21–22.

20 "increase of vitality": Ibid., 22.

20 "human, very sensitive": Ibid.

20 "strangle his individuality": J. A. Hussey to Hugh Robert Mill, 27 July 1922, ibid., 25.

21 vitamin C deficiency: *Encyclopaedia Britannica Online*, s.v. "Scurvy," https://www.britannica.com/science/scurvy.

21 belongs to Antarctica: Cool Antarctica, http://www.coolantarctica.com/Antarctica%20fact%20file/antarctica%20fact%20file%20index.htm.

22 pushed him on: Huntford, *Shackleton*, 109.

23 "a dead lion": Margot Morrell and Stephanie Capparell, *Shackleton's Way: Leadership Lessons from the Great Antarctic Explorer* (New York: Viking, 2001), 6.

23 "in 1906]. Amen": E. H. Shackleton, 9 January 1909, in Huntford, *Shackleton*, 273.

23 "that one biscuit": F. R. Wild, 31 January 1909, ibid., 280.

24 "energy can accomplish": Roald Amundsen, "The South Pole: An Account of the Norwegian Antarctica Expedition in the Fram," 1910–12, in Huntford, *Shackleton*, 350.

25 fifteen years combined: Ibid., 353.

25 a national hero: Ibid.

25 "sea to sea": Ibid., 350.

26 "the frozen waste": Margery Fisher and James Fisher, *Shackleton* (London: Barrie, 1957), 302.

26 "me young again": E. H. Shackleton to Elspeth Beardmore, 13 January 1914, in Huntford, *Shackleton*, 363.

27 of the time: Ibid., 367.

28 much as £80,000 ($10.6 million): Fisher and Fisher, *Shackleton*, 306.

28 London-based *Daily Chronicle*: Alexander, *Endurance*, 10.

28 a lifelong friend: Huntford, *Shackleton*, 375.

30 the "composition cake": Fisher and Fisher, *Shackleton*, 319.

30 need per day: Ibid.

30 "case of success": Huntford, *Shackleton*, 365.

30 money on advertising: Ibid.

30 at five thousand: Fisher and Fisher, *Shackleton*, 308.

31 "chaps they were": Bridges Adams to James Fisher, 31 July 1955, in Huntford, *Shackleton*, 386.

31 "Mad," "Hopeless," and Possible": Mill, *Life of Sir Ernest Shackleton*, 195.

31 "I'll take you": R. W. James to M. F. Fisher, October 1955, in Fisher and Fisher, *Shackleton*, 312.

32 want to interfere: Mill, *Life of Sir Ernest Shackleton*, 202; Fisher and Fisher, *Shackleton*, 324.

33 "and deceptively friendly": Huntford, *Shackleton*, 403.

33 "than Shackleton ashore": R. W. James to H. R. Mill, 12 May 1922, ibid., 386.

34 "rightness with him": A. H. Macklin, recorded conversation with James Fisher, 12–13 March 1956, in Fisher and Fisher, *Shackleton*, 336.

34 "ever read Browning": Ibid., 336–37.

34 "went to Wild": A. H. Macklin, interview with James Fisher, in Huntford, *Shackleton*, 422.

34 tensions had arisen: Alexander, *Endurance*, 57

35 herring and rabbit: Alfred Lansing, *Endurance: Shackleton's Incredible Voyage* (London: Weidenfeld & Nicolson, 1999), 27.

35 a clear run: Huntford, *Shackleton*, 409.

35 *Endurance* was trapped: Ibid., 410.

37 "a perfect juggler": Alexander, *Endurance*, 64.

37 the overland party: Ibid., 64–65.

37 "running the expedition": Huntford, *Shackleton*, 417.

38 "of false pride": T. H. Orde-Lees, 16 December 1914, ibid., 425.

38 and moral collapse: Ibid., 422–23.

38 make meteorological observations: Fisher and Fisher, *Shackleton*, 339.

39 was still ahead: Huntford, *Shackleton*, 428.

39 "greatest optimists living": Alexander, *Endurance*, 68.

40 meat and blubber: Lansing, *Endurance*, 37.

40 from the ceiling: Ibid., 43.

41 "our personal appearance": Frank Worsley, "Diary of *Endurance* Expedition," unpublished manuscript, in Fisher and Fisher, *Shackleton*, 343–44.

41 "the ice keeps": F. A. Worsley, *Endurance: An Epic of Polar Adventure* (New York: W. W. Norton, 1931), 4.

41 "was an agony": A. H. Macklin, 28 October 1915, in Huntford, *Shackleton*, 446.

41 "of the sea": Alexander, *Endurance*, 89.

42 "annihilating the ship": Shackleton, *South*, 76.

42 "vital mental medicine": L. D. A. Hurley, *South with Shackleton*, (London: Sampson Low, 1949), 65.

42 "end of everything": Lionel Greenstreet, recorded conversation with James Fisher, 11 October 1955, in Fisher and Fisher, *Shackleton*, 350.

42 "penalty of leadership": Frank Hurley, "Shackleton's Argonauts," in Charles F. Laseron and Frank Hurley, *Antarctic Eyewitness* (Sydney: Angus & Robertson, 1999), 231.

42 "than anything else": L. Greenstreet, interview with James Fisher, in Huntford, *Shackleton*, 456.

45 slide into arrogance: Ibid., 436–37. Greenstreet described Shackleton's tent assignments: "He collected with him the ones he thought wouldn't mix with the others . . . they were not so easy to get on with, the ones he had in his tent with him—they were quite a mixed bag." Alexander, *Endurance*, 103. See also Lansing, *Endurance*, 73–74.

45 had rigged up: Lansing, *Endurance*, 80–82.

46 watery hot cocoa: Ibid., 81.

46 bags before dark: Ibid., 82.

46 made his rounds: Ibid.

46 vegetables, and jam: Ibid., 71.

46 "onto the ice": Hurley, "Shackleton's Argonauts," in Laseron and Hurley, *Antarctic Eyewitness*, 235–36.

46 changing his mind: Ibid., 236.

47 "his last shot": Alexander, *Endurance*, 44.

47 "Patience Patience Patience": Fisher and Fisher, *Shackleton*, 357.

47 "it at once": Alexander, *Endurance*, 110.

48 *away* from land: Ibid., 110.

48 to the west: Lansing, *Endurance*, 90.

48 "as a tick": Ibid., 91.

48 the *Endurance* sank: Alexander, *Endurance*, 112.

49 they reached port: Ibid., 112–113.

49 "cause of discontent": Huntford, *Shackleton*, 476.

49 "attempt to escape": Shackleton, *South*, 107.

49 "fearless, faithful & diligent": Alexander, *Endurance*, 115.

50 "I ever had": R. W. James, 2 February 1916, in Huntford, *Shackleton*, 491.

50 "how it goes": F. A. Worsley, 2 March 1916, in ibid., 492.

50 "fed & happy tonight": Alexander, *Endurance*, 117.

53 "emotion and judgment": Huntford, *Shackleton*, 497.

54 "neighbour, Elephant Island": Shackleton, *South*, 119.

54 the *Stancomb Wills*: Huntford, *Shackleton*, 506.

54 "would come together": Alexander, *Endurance*, 119.

54 "a tremendous force": Shackleton, *South*, 126.

54 in the ice: Ibid.

54 to -7° Fahrenheit: Alexander, *Endurance*, 124.

55 "a terrible disappointment": Ibid., 123.

55 "hopes and thoughts": Shackleton, *South*, 135.

55 "their salt-encrusted faces": Ibid.

56 "rather severely frostbitten": T. H. Orde-Lees, 14 April 1916, in Huntford, *Shackleton*, 511.

56 "land since December 5, 1914": Fisher and Fisher, *Shackleton*, 370.

56 "reached the land": Lansing, *Endurance*, 179.

57 "and tattered tents": Shackleton, *South*, 156.

57 "be our objective": Ibid., 158–59.

57 from glacial ice: Ibid., 164–65.

58 "of the blizzard": Frank Hurley, 8 May 1916, in Huntford, *Shackleton*, 532.

58 "tried my best": Ernest Shackleton to Frank Wild, 23 April 1916, in Lansing, *Endurance*, 191.

58 traveled forty-five miles: Alexander, *Endurance*, 144.

59 "surged around us": Shackleton, *South*, 168.

59 "or handling sails": Alexander, *Endurance*, 144.

59 change places frequently: Lansing, *Endurance*, 223.

59 "was buried alive": Worsley, *Endurance*, 108.

60 of open sea: Ibid., 126.

60 from the masthead: Ibid., 110.

60 bailed the vessel: Ibid., 113.

60 "the greatest advantage": Ibid., 106.

61 "was going overboard": Ibid., 119.

61 "life beneath us": Shackleton, *South*, 176–77.

62 "a splendid moment": Ibid., 183.

63 "journeys ever accomplished": Alexander, *Endurance*, 153.

64 from boat screws: Worsley, *Endurance*, 143.

64 together with rope: Alexander, *Endurance*, 159.

64 "it. We'll slide": Worsley, *Endurance*, 155.

64 solemnly shook hands: Ibid., 156.

64 "merges into death": Shackleton, *South*, 203.

65 arrived at civilization: Worsley, *Endurance*, 162.

65 "that hot bath": Ibid., 163.

65 "world is mad": Shackleton, *South*, 208.

66 "the waiting men": Worsley, *Endurance*, 169.

66 named the *Emma*: Huntford, *Shackleton*, 612.

67 "he was grey-headed": Worsley, *Endurance*, 172–73.

67 called the *Yelcho*: Lansing, *Endurance*, 277.

67 the Antarctic Peninsula: Alexander, *Endurance*, 182.

68   "semi hysterical . . . inmates": Frank Hurley, 30 August 1916, in Huntford, *Shackleton*, 620.

68   "stood before us": Worsley, *Endurance*, 179.

68   "and talk[ed] of": Shackleton, *South*, 221.

68   "been through Hell": E. H. Shackleton to Emily Shackleton, 3 September 1916, in Huntford, *Shackleton*, 625.

70   "do our bit": T. H. Orde-Lees, 30 August 1916, ibid., 623–24.

70   officer Alfred Cheetham: Alexander, *Endurance*, 195.

70   in the war: Ibid., 190.

70   off Shackleton's creditors: Ibid., 190–91.

71   with their leader: Ibid., 191–92.

72   "on his order": Worsley, *Endurance*, 295–98. Since the late 1990s, the tremendous resurgence of interest in Ernest Shackleton and the *Endurance* story has resulted in a host of books and films, the formation of Shackleton societies in numerous countries, and even the establishment of an American charter school dedicated to the ideals of the Antarctic explorer. Recent media productions include an A&E movie, a PBS/NOVA movie, a giant-screen film, and an exhibit at the American Museum of Natural History. Other publications include two business volumes focused on the explorer's leadership strategies, at least fifteen children's titles, and dozens of historical books about the expedition.

Part Two: Save and Transform the Nation—Abraham Lincoln's Challenge

79   wounded, or captured: James M. McPherson, *Tried by War: Abraham Lincoln as Commander in Chief* (New York: Penguin, 2008), 98.

80   "and of money": Adam Gurowski, September 1862, *Diary from March 4, 1861 to November 12, 1862* (Boston: Lee & Shepard, 1862), 235.

80   "must die sometime": Orville Hickman Browning, *The Diary of Orville Hickman Browning*, ed. Theodore Calvin Pease and James G. Randall, 2 vols. (Springfield: Illinois State Historical Society, 1925), 1:559–60.

81   "not surprise me": Carl Sandburg, *Abraham Lincoln: The Prairie and the War Years*, 3 vols. (New York: Dell Publishing, 1954), 2:217.

82   could have imagined: Public Broadcasting System, "Timeline: Significant Civil War Battles," http://www.pbs.org/wgbh/americanexperience/features/timeline/death/.

82   "touching the ground": Geoffrey C. Ward with Ric Burns and Ken Burns, *The Civil War: An Illustrated History* (New York: Alfred A. Knopf, 1991), 121.

83   "be and live": Henry C. Deming, *Eulogy of Abraham Lincoln* (Hartford, CT: A. N. Clark, 1865), 40.

84   "defeat is inevitable": Michael Burlingame, *Abraham Lincoln: A Life*, 2 vols. (Baltimore: Johns Hopkins University Press, 2008), 2:324.

84   "lose the game!": Francis Carpenter, *Six Months at the White House: The*

Story of a Picture (New York: Hurd & Houghton, 1866; repr., 1999), 20–21.

84 "proclamation before them": Ibid., 21.

84 "make no difference": Eric Foner, *The Fiery Trial: Abraham Lincoln and American Slavery* (New York: W. W. Norton, 2010), 218.

85 "cry for help": Carpenter, *Six Months*, 21–22.

85 "had entirely overlooked": Ibid.

88 "any larger game": Abraham Lincoln, "Autobiography Written for John L. Scripps," in *The Collected Works of Abraham Lincoln*, ed. Roy Basler, Marion Dolores Pratt, and Lloyd A. Dunlap, 9 vols. (New Brunswick, NJ: Rutgers University Press, 1953), 4:62.

88 "to the world": Dennis Hanks to William H. Herndon, 13 June 1865, in *Herndon's Informants: Letters, Interviews, and Statements about Abraham Lincoln*, ed. Douglas L. Wilson and Rodney O. Davis (Urbana: University of Illinois Press, 1998), 40.

88 about his mother: For one of Lincoln's infrequent references to his mother, see Henry B. Rankin, *Personal Recollections of Abraham Lincoln* (New York: G. Putnam's Sons, 1916), 320.

88 "what I say": Abraham Lincoln to Fanny McCullough, 23 December 1862, in *Collected Works of Abraham Lincoln*, 6:16–17.

89 into dispirited gloom: Michael Burlingame, *The Inner World of Abraham Lincoln* (Urbana: University of Illinois Press, 1994), 93.

89 "as he walked": William H. Herndon, "Analysis of the Character of Abraham Lincoln," *Abraham Lincoln Quarterly* 1 (September 1941): 359.

89 "and without jealousy": David Herbert Donald, *Lincoln* (New York: Simon & Schuster, 1995), 28.

89 "I requested him": Sarah Bush Lincoln to William H. Herndon, 8 September 1865, in *Herndon's Informants*, 107.

90 "go on again": Ibid.

90 than a year: Lincoln, "Autobiography Written for John L. Scripps," 4:62.

91 "and the like": Elizabeth Crawford, "Public statement at Lincoln City, Indiana," 4 July 1865, in Francis Marion Van Natter, *Lincoln's Boyhood: A Chronicle of His Indiana Years* (Washington, DC: Public Affairs Press, 1963), 36.

91 to his peers: See, for example, Elizabeth Crawford to William H. Herndon, 16 September 1865, in *Herndon's Informants*, 126–27.

91 "in the world": Burlingame, *Inner World of Abraham Lincoln*, 95.

91 "painful than pleasant": Abraham Lincoln to John D. Johnston, 12 January 1851, in *Collected Works of Abraham Lincoln*, 2:97.

94 nickname Honest Abe: Burlingame, *Abraham Lincoln*, 1:60.

94 "to take part": Robert L. Wilson to William H. Herndon, 10 February 1866, in *Herndon's Informants*, 202.

94 "not forget again": Thomas Reep, *Lincoln at New Salem* (Petersburg, IL: Old Salem Lincoln League, 1927), 55.

94 of manual labor: Herndon, "Analysis of the Character of Abraham Lincoln," 356.

94 four hundred pounds: Ibid., 357.

94 over his head: Kenneth J. Winkle, *The Young Eagle: The Rise of Abraham Lincoln* (Dallas: Taylor Trade, 2001), 64.

96 "all were amazed": Robert B. Rutledge to William H. Herndon, 1 November 1866, in *Herndon's Informants*, 384.

97 "labors to compensate": Abraham Lincoln, "Communication to the People of Sangamo[n] County," 9 March 1832, in *Collected Works of Abraham Lincoln*, 1:8–9.

97 "he ever met": Donald, *Lincoln*, 42.

98 the "national debt": Ibid., 54.

98 the job himself: Robert B. Rutledge to William H. Herndon, 1 November 1866, in *Herndon's Informants*, 385.

98 "Lincoln man then": Burlingame, *Abraham Lincoln*, 1:80.

99 "of your votes": J. Rowan Herndon to William H. Herndon, 28 May 1865, in *Herndon's Informants*, 8.

99 "as a brother": Charles Maltby, *The Life and Public Services of Abraham Lincoln* (Stockton, CA: Daily Independent Steam Power Print, 1884), 44.

99 "of them nonetheless": Burlingame, *Abraham Lincoln*, 1:82–83.

99 "of floating driftwood": William H. Herndon and Jesse William Weik, *Herndon's Lincoln: The True Story of a Great Life*, 3 vols. (Chicago: Belford, Clarke, 1889), 1:79.

100 "devoured [the *Commentaries*]": Alban Jasper Conant, *My Acquaintance with Abraham Lincoln* (New York: De Vinne Press, 1893), 172.

100 "he met them": Burlingame, *Abraham Lincoln*, 1:91.

100 "other one thing": Abraham Lincoln to Isham Reavis, 5 November 1855, in *Collected Works of Abraham Lincoln*, 2:327.

101 "scourging [the opposition]": Burlingame, *Abraham Lincoln*, 1:122.

101 "wear this one?": Harold Holzer, "If I Had Another Face, Do You Think I'd Wear This One?," *American Heritage* 34, no. 2 (February–March 1983): 56.

102 known to exist: Donald, *Lincoln*, 57.

102 after his death: For a summary of the larger scholarly debate about Lincoln's relationship with Ann Rutledge, see David Herbert Donald, *We Are Lincoln Men: Abraham Lincoln and His Friends* (New York: Simon & Schuster, 2003), 20–24.

102 both were crying: Burlingame, *Abraham Lincoln*, 1:100.

102 a deep depression: For an incisive analysis of Lincoln's depression after Ann Rutledge's death, see Douglas L. Wilson, *Honor's Voice: The Transformation of Abraham Lincoln* (New York: Alfred A. Knopf, 1998), 119–25.

102 "somewhat temporarily deranged": William G. Greene to William H. Herndon, 30 May 1865, in *Herndon's Informants*, 21.

102 have considered suicide: Burlingame, *Abraham Lincoln*, 1:100.

102 labeled "the hypo": James M. McPherson, *Abraham Lincoln* (New York: Oxford University Press, 2009), 6.

103 during his presidency: See, for example, Joshua Wolf Shenk, *Lincoln's Melancholy: How Depression Challenged a President and Fueled His Greatness* (New York: Houghton Mifflin, 2005), 191–210.

103 "in his pocket": Robert L. Wilson to William H. Herndon, 10 February 1866, in *Herndon's Informants*, 205.

103 of his generation: Joshua Wolf Shenk, "Lincoln's Great Depression," *Atlantic* 296, no. 3 (October 2005): 54.

105 "Speed, I'm moved": Joshua F. Speed, statement for William H. Herndon, c. 1882, in *Herndon's Informants*, 590.

106 "talking, to himself": Burlingame, *Abraham Lincoln*, 1:91.

107 "of the mind": Herndon, "Analysis of the Character of Abraham Lincoln," 431.

107 "look in this": Herndon and Weik, *Herndon's Lincoln*, 2:315.

107 $5,000 a year: Burlingame, *Abraham Lincoln*, 1:333.

107 the 1860 census: Ibid.

107 charging him $2: Ibid.

108 his good character: Ibid.

108 "of a horse": Ibid., 326.

109 "evoke order from": Henry C. Whitney, *Life on the Circuit with Lincoln: With Sketches of Grant, Sherman and McClellan, Judge Davis, Leonard Swett, and Other Contemporaries* (Union, NJ: Lawbook Exchange, 2001), 42.

110 "in a ditch": Herndon and Weik, *Herndon's Lincoln*, 2:334.

110 and carefully written pleadings: Brian Dirck, "Abraham Lincoln: American Lawyer-President," *Social Education* 73, no. 1 (January/February 2009): 24.

111 made as president: Brian Dirck, *Lincoln the Lawyer* (Urbana: University of Illinois Press, 2007), 165–72.

111 opinion could change: Geoffrey C. Ward, "Before He Became a Saint," *New York Times*, October 22, 1995, http://www.nytimes.com/1995/10/22/books/before-he-became-a-saint.html?pagewanted=1.

111 "be business enough": Abraham Lincoln, "Notes for a Law Lecture," c. July 1850, in *Collected Works of Abraham Lincoln*, 2:81.

112 "a merry dance": Herndon and Weik, *Herndon's Lincoln*, 2:208.

112 "creature of excitement": Ronald C. White, *A. Lincoln: A Biography* (New York: Random House, 2010), 108.

112 "forget his prayers": Katherine Helm, *The True Story of Mary, Wife of Lincoln: Containing the Recollections of Mary Lincoln's Sister Emilie (Mrs. Ben Hardin Helm), Extracts from the War-Time Diaries, Numerous Letters and Other Documents now First Published* (New York: Harper and Brothers, 1928), 81.

112 "nature—and culture": Donald, *Lincoln*, 85.

113 "her social set": Helm, *True Story of Mary*, 84.

114 the engagement ended: On the scholarly controversy about the breakup, see Douglas L. Wilson, "Abraham Lincoln and 'That Fatal First of January,'" *Civil War History* 38, no. 2 (June 1992): 101–30.

114 got cold feet: Donald, *Lincoln*, 86.

114 would hurt himself: Not all of Lincoln's friends at the time were as worried as Speed about Lincoln's emotional health. "He was very sad and melancholy," a fellow legislator recalled, "but being subject to these spells, nothing serious was apprehended." Ibid., 87.

114 "appears to me": Abraham Lincoln to John T. Stuart, 23 January 1841, in *Collected Works of Abraham Lincoln*, 1:229.

115 "of Jany, '41": Abraham Lincoln to Joshua F. Speed, 27 March 1842, ibid., 1:282.

115 "as you are?": Abraham Lincoln to Joshua F. Speed, 5 October 1842, ibid., 1:303.

115 with Mary Todd: Burlingame, *Abraham Lincoln*, 1:195.

115 "Eyes & Ears": Elizabeth Todd Edwards, interview with William H. Herndon, c. 1865–66, in *Herndon's Informants*, 444.

115 "of profound wonder": Abraham Lincoln to Samuel D. Marshall, 11 November 1842, in *Collected Works of Abraham Lincoln*, 1:305.

116 "trotting harness on": Herndon and Weik, *Herndon's Lincoln*, 3:477.

116 to each other: Donald, *Lincoln*, 107–9; Jean Harvey Baker, *Mary Todd Lincoln: A Biography* (New York: W. W. Norton, 2008), 99–129.

117 children as "brats": Helm, *True Story of Mary*, 102.

118 "to its parents": Donald, *Lincoln*, 109.

119 "knew no rest": Herndon and Weik, *Herndon's Lincoln*, 2:375.

119 "law office entirely": Ibid., 2:272.

121 "mass of names": Abraham Lincoln to C. U. Schlater, 5 January 1849, in *Collected Works of Abraham Lincoln*, 2:19.

122 "own [burning] effigies": Stephen Douglas, "Speech of Senator Douglas: Delivered July 17, 1858, at Springfield, Illinois," in Abraham Lincoln and Stephen A. Douglas, *Political Speeches and Debates, 1854–1861* (Chicago: Scott, Foresman, 1896), 124.

123 "never been before": Lincoln, "Autobiography Written for John L. Scripps," 4:67.

123 speech on slavery: On October 4, 1854, Lincoln delivered a speech at Springfield that contained the major arguments he made in the Peoria speech twelve days later. But only press reports of his earlier speech have come down to us. The Peoria speech, which Lincoln prepared for publication after he delivered it, survives in its entirety. So it is usually cited as his first major address on slavery.

124 "ONLY BY NECESSITY": Abraham Lincoln, "Speech at Peoria, Illinois," in *Collected Works of Abraham Lincoln*, 2:275.

124 "action but *self-interest*": Ibid., 2:255.

124 pursuit of happiness: Ibid., 2:265–66.

125 to be upheld: Foner, *Fiery Trial*, 68.

125 "disregard the constitution": Lincoln, "Speech at Peoria, Illinois," 2:269.

125 "of the saving": Ibid., 2:276.

125 "expansion of slavery": Foner, *Fiery Trial*, 69.

127 "for office again": Donald, *Lincoln*, 184.

128 "alloy of hypocracy [*sic*]": Abraham Lincoln to Joshua Speed, 24 August 1855, in *Collected Works of Abraham Lincoln*, 2:323.

128 "reckon it's him": Whitney, *Life on the Circuit*, 80.

129 or false modesty: Donald, *Lincoln*, 193.

129 "bound to respect": *Scott v. Sanford*, 6 March 1857, 60 US 393, Taney, C.J., Opinion of the Court, 407.

129 "wicked" and "abominable": Don E. Fehrenbacher, *The Dred Scott Case: Its Significance in American Law and Politics* (Oxford: Oxford University Press, 1978), 417.

129 open-air slave markets: Donald, *Lincoln*, 200.

129 "infamous and tyrannical": "The Decision of the Supreme Court," *Liberator* 11 (March 13, 1857): 42.

130 even more oppressed: Donald, *Lincoln*, 201.

130 "than it is": Abraham Lincoln, "Speech at Springfield, Illinois," 26 June 1857, in *Collected Works of Abraham Lincoln*, 2:404.

130 "not be notified": Abraham Lincoln to B. Clarke Lundy, 5 August 1857, ibid., 2:413.

131 "the latter condition": Abraham Lincoln, "'A House Divided': Speech at Springfield, Illinois," 16 June 1858, ibid., 2:461–62.

133 "a different image": Donald, *Lincoln*, 213.

134 "grotesque, as Lincoln's": Carl Schurz, "The Lincoln-Douglas Debate at Quincy, Illinois," *McClure's Magazine* 28 (January 1907): 253.

134 "in the world": Fergus M. Bordewich, "How Lincoln Bested Douglas in Their Famous Debates," *Smithsonian* 39, no. 6 (September 2008).

135 "invent the others": Stephen Douglas, "Second Debate with Stephen A. Douglas at Freeport, Illinois," 27 August 1858, in *Collected Works of Abraham Lincoln*, 3:55.

135 "starved to death": Abraham Lincoln, "Sixth Debate with Stephen A. Douglas at Quincy, Illinois," 13 October 1858, ibid., 3:279.

136 "the white race": Abraham Lincoln, "Fourth Debate with Stephen A. Douglas at Charleston, Illinois," 18 September 1858, ibid., 3:145–46.

136 "let her alone": Ibid., 3:146.

136 "gone through college": White, *A. Lincoln*, 280.

136 "to an end": Abraham Lincoln, "Fifth Debate with Stephen A. Douglas at Galesburg, Illinois," 7 October 1858, in *Collected Works of Abraham Lincoln*, 3:225–26.

137 "same tyrannical principle": Abraham Lincoln, "Seventh and Last Debate with Stephen A. Douglas at Alton, Illinois," 15 October 1858, ibid., 3:315.

137 their collective will: Michael Sandel, "Political Liberalism," in *Justice: A Reader*, ed. Michael Sandel (New York: Oxford University Press, 2007), 368–69. See also Allen C. Guelzo, *Lincoln and Douglas: The Debates That Defined America* (New York: Simon & Schuster, 2008), xix–xxi.

137 of the seats: Historical sources differ on the final voting percentages for the general assembly. David Donald puts the Democratic seats at 53 percent: Donald, *Lincoln*, 227–28; Michael Burlingame puts the final percentage at 54 percent: Burlingame, *Abraham Lincoln*, 1:547.

138 "of hopeless despair": Whitney, *Life on the Circuit*, 27.

138 "except Billy [Herndon]": Henry C. Whitney to William H. Herndon, 18 July 1887, in *Herndon's Informants*, 622.

138 "I am gone": Abraham Lincoln to Anson G. Henry, 19 November 1858, in *Collected Works of Abraham Lincoln*, 3:339.

139 "for the Presidency": Abraham Lincoln to Samuel Galloway, 28 July 1859, ibid., 3:395.

139 "very great many": Abraham Lincoln to Samuel Galloway, 24 March 1860, ibid., 4:34.

140 "their first love": Ibid.

140 "much of me": Abraham Lincoln to Jesse W. Fell, "Enclosing Autobiography," 20 December 1859, in *Collected Works of Abraham Lincoln*, 3:511.

140 "a finished statesman": Rufus Rockwell Wilson, *Intimate Memories of Lincoln* (Elmira, NY: Primavera Press, 1945), 258.

141 "to his arguments": Henry Villard, *Memoirs of Henry Villard: Journalist and Financier, 1835–1900*, 2 vols. (Boston: Houghton Mifflin, 1904), 1:93.

141 "of human slavery": Harold Holzer, *Lincoln at Cooper Union: The Speech That Made Abraham Lincoln President* (New York: Simon & Schuster, 2004), 115.

141 "WE UNDERSTAND IT": Abraham Lincoln, "Address at Cooper Institute, New York City," 27 February 1860, in *Collected Works of Abraham Lincoln*, 3:550.

142 "electrify as well": Theodore Stanton, "Abraham Lincoln," *Westminster Review* 135 (January–June 1891): 640.

142 "worthy of it": James A. Briggs to Abraham Lincoln, 29 February 1860, in *The Lincoln Papers*, ed. David C. Mearns, 2 vols. (Garden City, NY: Doubleday, 1948), 1:231.

142 "no trouble whatever": Abraham Lincoln to Mary Todd Lincoln, 4 March 1860, in *The Collected Works of Abraham Lincoln: Supplement, 1832–1865*, ed. Roy Basler (Westport, CT: Greenwood Press, 1974), 49.

142 "mouth a little": Abraham Lincoln to Lyman Trumbull, 29 April 1860, in *Collected Works of Abraham Lincoln*, 4:45.

143 "it to her": Charles Zane, "Lincoln as I Knew Him," *Illinois State Historical Journal* 14, no. 1–2 (April–June 1921): 83.

143 "was upon me": Gideon Welles, *Diary of Gideon Welles: Secretary of the Navy under Lincoln and Johnson*, 2 vols. (Boston: Houghton Mifflin, 1911), 1:82.

145 Lincoln now held: Doris Kearns Goodwin, *Team of Rivals: The Political Genius of Abraham Lincoln* (New York: Simon & Schuster, 2005), xvi.

145 during his presidency: Ibid., xvi–xvii.

146 was never kept: Harold Holzer, *Lincoln President-Elect: Abraham Lincoln and the Great Secession Crisis, Winter 1860–1861* (New York: Simon & Schuster, 2008), 249.

146 "each other—again": Augustus H. Chapman to William H. Herndon, 8 October 1865, in *Herndon's Informants*, 137.

146 "had ever happened": Herndon and Weik, *Herndon's Lincoln*, 3:483–84.

147 "an affectionate farewell": Abraham Lincoln, "Farewell Address at Springfield, Illinois," 11 February 1861, in *Collected Works of Abraham Lincoln*, 4:190.

147 "a free people": Abraham Lincoln, "First Inaugural Address—Final Text," 4 March 1861, ibid., 4:268.

147 "to be extended": Ibid., 4:266–69.

148 "of our nature": Ibid., 4:271.

151 "its own existence": Abraham Lincoln, "Message to Congress in Special Session," 4 July 1861, ibid., 4:426.

151 mules and horses: James M. McPherson, *Battle Cry of Freedom: The Civil War Era* (New York: Ballantine Books, 1988), 284.

152 "must have Kentucky": William E. Gienapp, "Abraham Lincoln and the Border States," *Journal of the Abraham Lincoln Association* 13, no. 1 (1992): 13.

153 "engaged in it": McPherson, *Battle Cry of Freedom*, 354.

153 known as "colonization": Eric Foner, "The Emancipation of Abe Lincoln," *New York Times* (January 1, 2013), A19.

153 "for the new": Abraham Lincoln to Nathaniel Banks, 5 August 1863, in *Collected Works of Abraham Lincoln*, 6:365.

154 "etiquette & personal dignity": John Hay, 13 November 1861, in John Hay, *Inside Lincoln's White House: The Complete Civil War Diary of John Hay*, ed. Michael Burlingame and John R. Turner Ettlinger (Carbondale: Southern Illinois University Press, 1997), 32.

155 "their neighbor's hurt": John Hay, "Life in the White House in Mr. Lincoln's Time," in Wilson, *Intimate Memories of Lincoln*, 398.

155 "wasted nervous force": Ibid., 397.

156 "plain prairie language": Alan Nevins, *The War for the Union, Volume II: War Becomes Revolution* (New York: Charles Scribner's Sons, 1960), 193.

156 "of the day": Mary Lincoln to Mercy Levering Conkling, 19 November 1864, in *Mary Todd Lincoln: Her Life and Letters*, ed. Justin G. Turner and Linda Levitt Turner (New York: Alfred A. Knopf, 1972), 187.

156 "on his stomach": Ruth Painter Randall, *Lincoln's Sons* (Boston: Little, Brown, 1955), 107.

157 "*power to command*": Edward Bates, 31 December 1861, in Edward Bates, *The Diary of Edward Bates*, ed. Howard K. Beale (Washington, DC: US Government Printing Office, 1933), 220.

157 "long-armed ape": William H. Herndon to Jesse W. Weik, 6 January 1887, in *The Hidden Lincoln: From the Letters and Papers of William H. Herndon*, ed. Emanuel Hertz (New York: Viking Press, 1938), 153.

157 "a while first": Benjamin Thomas and Harold H. Hyman, *Stanton: The Life and Times of Lincoln's Secretary of War* (New York: Alfred A. Knopf, 1962), 151.

158 "have him die!": Elizabeth Keckley, *Behind the Scenes, or Thirty Years a Slave, and Four Years in the White House* (New York: G. W. Carleton, 1868), 103.

158 to his departed son: Burlingame, *Abraham Lincoln*, 2:300.

158 "send you there": Ibid., 300.

161 "Slave holders rebellion": Joseph Medill to Abraham Lincoln, 9 February 1862, Abraham Lincoln Papers at the Library of Congress, http://memory .loc.gov/cgi-bin/ampage?collId=mal&fileName=mal1/144/1445100 /malpage.db&recNum=2&tempFile=./temp/~ammem_ANZS&filecode =mal&next_filecode=mal&prev_filecode=mal&itemnum=10&ndocs=24.

162 "some troublesome creditor": Frederick Douglass, "The President and His Speeches," *Douglass' Monthly*, September 1862, in *The Life and Writings of Frederick Douglass*, ed. Philip S. Foner, 5 vols. (New York: International Publishers, 1952), 3:270.

163 "to hang himself": Edward Bates, "Remonstrance and Notes on Cabinet Meeting," in *The Civil War: The Second Year Told by Those Who Lived It*, ed. Stephen W. Sears (New York: Library of America, 2012), 429.

163 "the contest proceeds": Abraham Lincoln, "Meditation on the Divine Will," 2 September 1862, in *Collected Works of Abraham Lincoln*, 5:403–4.

164 "over to judgment": "War Meeting in Boston," *New York Times*, October 7, 1862, http://www.nytimes.com/1862/10/07/news/war-meeting-boston-speech-hon-charles-summer-faneuil-hall-his-views-emancipation.html.

164 "of rebel power": Frederick Douglass, "Emancipation Proclaimed," *Douglass' Monthly*, October 1862, in *Life and Writings of Frederick Douglass*, 3:273–75.

165 "hope of earth": Abraham Lincoln, "Annual Message to Congress," 1 December 1862, in *Collected Works of Abraham Lincoln*, 5:537.

165 "battles and delays": Zachariah Chandler to Letitia Grace Douglass Chandler, 18 December 1862, in Ward with Burns and Burns, *Civil War*, 174–75.

165 "am in it": Burlingame, *Inner World of Abraham Lincoln*, 105.

165 "this place for?": J. E. Gallaher, *Best Lincoln Stories, Tersely Told* (Chicago: M. A. Donohue, 1898), 84.

166 "of harassing care": Noah Brooks, "How the President Looks," 4 December 1862, in *Lincoln Observed: Civil War Dispatches of Noah Brooks*, ed. Michael Burlingame (Baltimore: John Hopkins University Press, 1998), 13.

166 "signing this paper": Don E. Fehrenbacher and Virginia Fehrenbacher, *Recollected Words of Abraham Lincoln* (Stanford, CA: Stanford University Press, 1996), 397.

166 "bill of lading": Richard Hofstadter, "Abraham Lincoln and the Self-Made Myth," in Richard Hofstadter, *The American Political Tradition* (New York: Vintage, 1989), 169.

167 of freed blacks: Foner, *Fiery Trial*, 245.

168 "of African descent": 37th Cong., 2nd Sess. ch. 201, *US Statutes at Large* 12 (1862): 599.

169 "hold in earnest?": Abraham Lincoln to Andrew Johnson, 26 March 1863, in *Collected Works of Abraham Lincoln*, 6:149–50.

169 "given the Confederacy": Ulysses S. Grant to Abraham Lincoln, 23 August 1863, Abraham Lincoln Papers at the Library of Congress, https://memory .loc.gov/cgi-bin/ampage?collId=mal&fileName=mal1/257/2579900 /malpage.db&recNum=0&tempFile=./temp/~ammem_l5Ba&filecode =mal&next_filecode=mal&prev_filecode=mal&itemnum=9&ndocs=21.

169 "any other race": Edwin M. Stanton to Abraham Lincoln, 8 February 1864, ibid., http://memory.loc.gov/cgi-bin/ampage?collId=mal &fileName=mal1/1031/1031700/malpage.db&recNum=4&tempFile= ./temp/~ammem 04M8&filecode=mal&next_filecode=mal&prev _filecode=mal&itemnum=15&ndocs=26.

169 the White House: Foner, *Fiery Trial*, 257–58.

170 "men in America": John Eaton, *Grant, Lincoln, and the Freedmen: Reminiscences of the Civil War: With Special Reference to the Work for the Contrabands and Freedmen of the Mississippi Valley* (London: Longmans, Green, 1907), 176.

171 "in the rear": Charles Sumner to Francis Lieber, 17 January 1863, in Edward L. Pierce, *Memoir and Letters of Charles Sumner*, 4 vols. (Boston: Roberts Brothers, 1893), 4:114.

171 join the Confederacy: John A. McClernand to Abraham Lincoln, 14 February 1863, Abraham Lincoln Papers at the Library of Congress, https://memory .loc.gov/cgi-bin/ampage?collId=mal&fileName=mal1/217/2172700 /malpage.db&recNum=4&tempFile=./temp/~ammem_pGgP&filecode =mal&next_filecode=mal&prev_filecode=mal&itemnum=9&ndocs=27.

171 "active, *with impunity*": Frank van der Linden, *The Dark Intrigue: The True Story of a Civil War Conspiracy* (Golden, CO: Fulcrum, 2007), 57.

172 "the country say!": Noah Brooks, *Washington in Lincoln's Time* (New York: Century, 1896), 57–58.

172 "moment at least": George Templeton Strong, 6 July 1863, in George

Templeton Strong, *Diary of the Civil War: 1860–1865*, ed. Allan Nevins (New York: Macmillan, 1962), 330.

171 "and lick him": Henry Adams to Charles Francis Adams Jr., 23 July 1863, in *Henry Adams, Selected Letters*, ed. Ernest Samuels (Cambridge, MA: Harvard University Press, 1992), 59.

173 "stand firm now": John Hay, 9 August 1863, in Hay, *Inside Lincoln's White House*, 70.

173 exchange of prisoners: Donald, *Lincoln*, 456.

173 at fifty thousand: James C. Conkling to Abraham Lincoln, 4 September 1863, Abraham Lincoln Papers at the Library of Congress, https://memory .loc.gov/cgi-bin/ampage?collId=mal&fileName=mal1/260/2604000 /malpage.db&recNum=2&tempFile=./temp/~ammem_y6iy&filecode =mal&next_filecode=mal&prev_filecode=mal&itemnum=16&ndocs=29.

174 "of black soldiers": Abraham Lincoln to James C. Conkling, 26 August 1863, in *Collected Works of Abraham Lincoln*, 6:407–9.

174 "pay the cost": Ibid., 6:409–10.

175 "tranquility and Union": Abraham Lincoln, "Proclamation of Thanksgiving," 3 October 1863, ibid., 6:497.

176 "few appropriate remarks": David Willis to Abraham Lincoln, 2 November 1863, John G. Nicolay, "Lincoln's Gettysburg Address," *Monthly Magazine* 47 (February 1894): 596.

176 with the ending: Donald, *Lincoln*, 461.

177 "from the earth": Abraham Lincoln, "Address Delivered at the Dedication of the Cemetery at Gettysburg," Final Text, 19 November 1863, in *Collected Works of Abraham Lincoln*, 7:23.

177 "annals of man": William E. Barton, *Lincoln at Gettysburg: What He Intended to Say; What He Said; What He Was Reported to Have Said; What He Wished He Had Said* (New York: Peter Smith, 1950), 116.

177 "word and comma": Ibid., 117.

177 "in two minutes": Edward Everett to Abraham Lincoln, 20 November 1863, Abraham Lincoln Papers at the Library of Congress, http://memory.loc .gov/cgi-bin/ampage?collId=mal&fileName=mal1/281/2813300/malpage .db&recNum=2&tempFile=./temp/~ammem_Dtq3&filecode=mal&next _filecode=mal&prev_filecode=mal&itemnum=9&ndocs=22.

177 nothing about equality: Donald, *Lincoln*, 465.

177 "founded the government?": "The President at Gettysburg," *Chicago Times*, November 23, 1863, http://teachingamericanhistory.org/library/document /the-president-at-gettysburg.

178 Declaration of Independence: Garry Wills, *Lincoln at Gettysburg: The Speech That Remade America* (New York: Simon & Schuster, 1992), 100–103.

178 "from the earth": Lincoln, "Address Delivered at the Dedication," 7:23.

181 "give to everybody": Milton H. Shutes, *Lincoln and the Doctors: A Med-*

ical Narrative of the Life of Abraham Lincoln (New York: Pioneer Press, 1933), 86.

182 "of the melee": Gordon C. Rhea, *The Battles for Spotsylvania Court House and the Road to Yellow Tavern, May 7–12, 1864* (Baton Rouge: Louisiana State University Press, 1997), 293.

182 "hate and murder": Ibid.

182 "ever to end": "Schuyler Colfax," *Reminiscences of Abraham Lincoln: By Distinguished Men of His Time*, ed. Allen Thorndike Rice (New York: North American, 1886), 337.

183 "takes all summer" : Ulysses S. Grant to Edwin M. Stanton, 11 May 1864, in *The Papers of Ulysses S. Grant*, ed. John Simon, 31 vols. (Carbondale: Southern Illinois University Press, 1982), 10:422.

183 "relentless, ceaseless warfare": McPherson, *Battle Cry of Freedom*, 733.

184 "cessation of hostilities": "Democratic National Convention," in Edward McPherson, *The Political History of the United States of America during the Great Rebellion* (Washington, DC: Philp & Solomons, 1865), 419.

184 "*by our foes*": Larry F. Nelson, *Bullets, Ballots, and Rhetoric: Confederate Policy for the United States Presidential Contest of 1864* (Tuscaloosa: University of Alabama Press, 1980), 113.

184 "life is dreadful": Isaac N. Arnold, *The Life of Abraham Lincoln* (Chicago: A. C. McClurg, 1909), 375.

184 "of their senses": Walt Whitman to Louisa Van Velsor Whitman, 7 June 1864, in Walt Whitman, *The Wound Dresser: A Series of Letters Written from the Hospitals in Washington During the War of the Rebellion*, ed. Richard Maurice Bucke (Boston: Small, Maynard, 1898), 194.

185 "slavery be abandoned": Thurlow Weed to William H. Seward, 22 August 1864, Abraham Lincoln Papers at the Library of Congress, https://memory.loc.gov/cgi-bin/ampage?collId=mal&fileName=mal1/354/3549000/malpage.db&recNum=2&tempFile=./temp/~ammem_vOTM&filecode=mal&next_filecode=mal&prev_filecode=mal&itemnum=21&ndocs=26.

185 "all the States": Henry J. Raymond to Abraham Lincoln, 22 August 1864, Ibid., https://memory.loc.gov/cgi-bin/ampage?collId=mal&fileName=mal1/354/3547800/malpage.db&recNum=2&tempFile=./temp/~ammem_dnRg&filecode=mal&next_filecode=mal&prev_filecode=mal&itemnum=15&ndocs=26.

185 "place, *badly beaten*": J. K. Herbert to General Benjamin F. Butler, 11 August 1864, in Fehrenbacher and Fehrenbacher, *Recollected Words of Abraham Lincoln*, 196.

185 "come what will": Diary of Joseph T. Millis, 19 August 1864, in *Collected Works of Abraham Lincoln*, 7:507.

185 became "almost irresistible": McPherson, *Battle Cry of Freedom*, 770.

186 "him try me": Abraham Lincoln to Charles D. Robinson, 17 August 1864, in *Collected Works of Abraham Lincoln*, 7:501.

186 "you serious damage": Frederick Douglass to Theodore Tilton, 15 October 1864, in *Life and Writings of Frederick Douglass*, 3:423.

187 "and fairly won": W. T. Sherman to Major General Dix, 4 September 1864, reprinted in "The Fall of Atlanta: The Official Report of Maj. Gen. Sherman," *New York Times*, September 5, 1864.

187 urban professional men: Donald, *Lincoln*, 544.

187 "bales of cotton": Major General William Tecumseh Sherman to President Abraham Lincoln, 22 December 1864, National Archives Catalog, https://catalog.archives.gov/id/301637.

187 and the president: Foner, *Fiery Trial*, 328.

188 "and felt him": Thomas Morris Chester, *Black Civil War Correspondent: His Dispatches from the Virginia Front*, ed., with a biographical essay and notes, R. J. M. Blackett (Baton Rouge: Louisiana State University Press, 1989), 297.

188 "to the laws": *Conversations with Lincoln*, compiled, edited, and annotated by Charles M. Segal (New York: G. Putnam's Sons, 1961), 382.

190 "man in America": James M. Scovel, "Thaddeus Stevens," *Lippincott's Monthly Magazine: A Popular Journal of General Literature, Science and Politics* 61 (January–June 1898): 550.

190 "for several minutes": *Congressional Globe*, 38th Cong., 2nd Sess., January 31, 1865, 531.

190 "cause as soldiers": Abraham Lincoln, "Last Public Address," 11 April 1865, in *Collected Works of Abraham Lincoln*, 8:403.

191 supported black suffrage: Foner, *Fiery Trial*, 331.

191 scene with light: Donald, *Lincoln*, 566.

191 "of prosperous peace": Salmon Chase to Mary Todd Lincoln, 4 March 1865, Abraham Lincoln Papers at the Library of Congress, http://memory.loc.gov/cgi-bin/query/P?mal:1:./temp/~ammem_t3dq.

191 "the war came": Abraham Lincoln, "Second Inaugural Address," 4 March 1865, in *Collected Works of Abraham Lincoln*, 8:332.

192 "with the lash": Ibid., 8:333.

193 "with all nations": Ibid.

193 "to tell it": Abraham Lincoln to Thurlow Weed, 15 March 1865, ibid., 8:356.

193 "you liked it": Frederick Douglass, *The Life and Times of Frederick Douglass*, ed. Henry Louis Gates Jr. (New York: Library of America, 1994), 804.

194 "honor from him": "President Lincoln Visits City Point and Petersburg, March 24–April 8, 1865," National Park Service, http://www.nps.gov/pete/learn/news/upload/Lincoln-at-Pete-and-CPrev2.pdf.

195 "been very miserable": Mary Todd Lincoln to Francis Bicknell Carpenter, 15 November 1865, in *Mary Todd Lincoln*, 284–85.

197 "would have done": Michael Beschloss, "When T.R. Saw Lincoln," *New York Times*, May 21, 2014, https://www.google.com/search?q=When+T.R.+

Saw+Lincoln+NYT&oq=When+T.R.+Saw+Lincoln+NYT&aqs
=chrome..69i57.829 5j0j7&sourceid=chrome&ie=UTF-8.

198 a bloody war: Don E. Fehrenbacher, "The Anti-Lincoln Tradition," *Journal of the Abraham Lincoln Association* 4, no. 1 (1982): 6–28.

199 "father's child has": Abraham Lincoln, "Speech to One Hundred Sixty-Sixth Ohio Regiment," 22 August 1864, in *Collected Works of Abraham Lincoln*, 7:512.

200 "be reckoned with": Fehrenbacher, "The Anti-Lincoln Tradition," 25.

Part Three: End Slavery Forever—Frederick Douglass's Challenge

203 "to regain possession": John Stauffer, *Giants: The Parallel Lives of Frederick Douglass and Abraham Lincoln* (New York: Twelve, 2008), 91.

204 "of the slaveholder": Frederick Douglass to William Lloyd Garrison, 1 January 1846, in *The Life and Writings of Frederick Douglass*, ed. Philip S. Foner, 5 vols. (New York: International Publishers, 1950), 1:127.

205 "me an insult": Ibid.

205 "Hold of me": Frederick Douglass, "Letter to William A. White," 30 July 1846, ibid., 1:183.

206 "that oppressed people": Frederick Douglass, "Farewell Speech to the British People," March 1847, ibid., 1:231–32.

209 the Chesapeake Bay: Like most slaves, Frederick Douglass never knew his exact birth date. Slave owners sometimes recorded the dates of the births and deaths of their human property, but civil law did not recognize these events as having any status, and thus there was often no legal record. In his first autobiography, Douglass wrote that he believed he had been born in early 1818. Some of his biographers and editors have dated this event a year later. Research by writer Dickson Preston has offered strong evidence that Douglass was born in 1818. Dickson J. Preston, *Young Frederick Douglass: The Maryland Years* (Baltimore: Johns Hopkins University Press, 1980), 8–9.

210 "to disturb me": Frederick Douglass, *My Bondage and My Freedom*, ed. Henry Louis Gates Jr. (New York: Library of America, 1994), 142–43.

211 the kitchen table: Ibid., 168.

211 "in the gashes": Frederick Douglass, *The Life and Times of Frederick Douglass*, ed. Henry Louis Gates Jr. (New York: Library of America, 1994), 520.

211 "disobey my orders": Frederick Douglass, *Narrative of the Life of Frederick Douglass: An American Slave*, ed. Henry Louis Gates Jr. (New York: Library of America, 1994), 19.

212 "be mine next": Douglass, *My Bondage*, 176–77.

213 "magnificence and satiety": Douglass, *Life and Times*, 506–507.

213 "wonder and admiration": Ibid., 522.

214 "will toward you": Douglass, *My Bondage*, 215.

214 "same narrow examination": Douglass, *Narrative of the Life*, 46.

214 "*mystery* of reading": Douglass, *My Bondage*, 216.

214 "her own child": Ibid., 217.

215 "away with himself": Ibid.

215 "slavery to freedom": Ibid., 218.

215 "revealed her apprehension": Douglass, *Narrative of the Life*, 40.

215 "its early happiness": Douglass, *My Bondage*, 222.

216 "me a lesson": Ibid., 224.

216 "lump of chalk": Douglass, *Narrative of the Life*, 44.

216 "the oldest son": Douglass, *My Bondage*, 235.

217 "his officers farewell": William S. McFeely, *Frederick Douglass* (New York: W. W. Norton, 1991), 34–35.

217 "the horrible pit": Douglass, *Narrative of the Life*, 42.

217 "ability to describe": Douglass, *Life and Times*, 534.

218 the city's population: Christopher Phillips, *Freedom's Port: The African American Community of Baltimore, 1790–1860* (Chicago: University of Illinois Press, 1997), 15.

218 operated in Baltimore: Michael Tadman, *Speculators and Slaves: Masters, Traders, and Slaves in the Old South* (Madison: University of Wisconsin Press, 1989), 5–7, 11–46.

218 "the chained gangs": Frederick Douglass, "The Meaning of July Fourth for the Negro," 5 July 1852, in *Life and Writings of Frederick Douglass*, 2:194.

219 "sons thus treated": William J. Anderson, "Life and Narrative of William J. Anderson: Twenty-four Years a Slave; Sold Eight Times! In Jail Sixty Times!! Whipped Three Hundred Times!!! or The Dark Deeds of American Slavery Revealed, 1857," in *The Making of African American Identity, Vol. I, 1500–1865* (Durham, NC: National Humanities Center, 2007), 5.

219 "weeping mother now": Josiah Henson, *Truth Stranger than Fiction: Father Henson's Story of His Own Life*, (Boston: John P. Jewett and Company, 1858), 12–13

220 "my heart panted": Douglass, *My Bondage*, 234.

221 "we did both": Ibid., 246.

222 "best to him": Ibid., 264–65.

222 "into a brute": Douglass, *Narrative of the Life*, 58.

223 "so, I rose": Ibid., 64.

224 "had from him": Ibid., 65.

224 "made a man": Ibid., 60.

225 "his *own* master": Douglass, *My Bondage*, 297.

226 "home of man": Ibid., 310.

226 "of horrid shapes": Ibid., 311.

226 "be my doom": Ibid., 324.

230 "your running away": Ibid., 344.

230 fund his journey: McFeely, *Frederick Douglass*, 70.

231 "I reached Philadelphia": Frederick Douglass, "My Escape from Slavery," *Century Illustrated Magazine* 23 (November 1881): 127.

231 "of this conductor": Douglass, *Life and Times*, 644.

232 "my slave life": Douglass, "My Escape from Slavery," 127–28.

232 "me unspeakable joy": Ibid., 128.

233 "the free States": Douglass, *Life and Times*, 652.

234 "time and strength": Douglass, *My Bondage*, 356.

234 "a southern port": Ibid.

235 "of my race": Ibid., 362.

237 "of interrupting him": Philip S. Foner, "Frederick Douglass: From Slavery to Freedom," in *Life and Writings of Frederick Douglass*, 1:27.

238 the assembly yelled: McFeely, *Frederick Douglass*, 88–89.

239 "or two longer": Philip S. Foner, "Anti-Slavery Agent," in *Life and Writings of Frederick Douglass*, 1:48.

239 "after Frederick Douglass": Elizabeth Cady Stanton, 21 February 1895, in *Elizabeth Cady Stanton, as Revealed in Her Letters, Diary and Reminiscences*, ed. Theodore Stanton and Harriot Stanton Blatch, 2 vols. (New York: Harper & Brothers, 1922), 2:311–12.

241 "don't know more": Frederick Douglass, "The Church and Prejudice," 3 December 1841, in *Life and Writings of Frederick Douglass*, 1:104.

241 "of the philosophy": Douglass, *Life and Times*, 662.

241 "on this way": Ibid., 663.

241 "speech than not": Ibid,

241 "and needed room": Ibid., 662–63.

242 "dispel all doubt": Ibid., 663.

242 "inspiring and terrible": David W. Blight, "Introduction: A Psalm of Freedom," in Frederick Douglass, *Narrative of the Life of Frederick Douglass, an American Slave, Written by Himself*, ed. David W. Blight (Boston: Bedford/St. Martin's, 2003), 3.

242 "of the South": Stauffer, *Giants*, 91.

244 "of us all": Frederick Douglass to William Lloyd Garrison, 16 September 1845, in *Life and Writings of Frederick Douglass*, 1:120.

244 "could reshape issues": Nathan Irvin Huggins, *Slave and Citizen: The Life of Frederick Douglass* (Boston: Little, Brown, 1980), 38.

245 chanting, "Douglass, Douglass": McFeely, *Frederick Douglass*, 148.

245 "and elevate mankind": Frederick Douglass, "To Our Oppressed Countrymen," *North Star*, December 3, 1847, in *Life and Writings of Frederick Douglass*, 1:283.

245 "held a chattel": *Frederick Douglass on Slavery and the Civil War: Selections from His Writings*, ed. Philip S. Foner (Mineola, NY: Dover, 2003), 11.

246 for their organization: For a discussion of Garrison and Phillips's response to Douglass's intention to start his own newspaper, see Philip S. Foner, *Frederick Douglass: A Biography* (New York: Citadel, 1964), 78.

246 "a publishing life": William Lloyd Garrison, "Letter from Mr. Douglass," *Liberator* 17, no. 30 (July 23, 1847): 2, http://fair-use.org/the-liberator /1847/07/23/the-liberator-17-30.pdf.

246 "to the heart": Foner, *Frederick Douglass*, 82.

248 "resources appeared inexhaustible": Douglass, *Life and Times*, 706.

248 "of English literature": Huggins, *Slave and Citizen*, 45.

248 "fiercely loyal cohort": David W. Blight, *Frederick Douglass' Civil War: Keeping Faith in Jubilee* (Baton Rouge: Louisiana State University Press, 1989), 20.

249 30,000 and 150,000: Eric Foner, *Gateway to Freedom: The Hidden History of the Underground Railroad* (New York: W. W. Norton, 2015), 4.

250 slaves to freedom: Benjamin Quarles, *Frederick Douglass* (Washington, DC: Associated, 1948), 119.

250 "heart unspeakable joy": Douglass, *Life and Times*, 710.

250 "of tyrannical legislation": Douglass, "Meaning of July Fourth for the Negro," 2:196.

250 "rapacity in check": Frederick Douglass, "The Fugitive Slave Law," 11 August 1852, http://rbscp.lib.rochester.edu/4385.

251 "permanent liberty document": Frederick Douglass to Gerrit Smith, 31 January 1851, in Blight, *Frederick Douglass' Civil War*, 33.

252 "this very hour": Douglass, "Meaning of July Fourth for the Negro," 2:192.

252 "all your hopes": Ibid., 2:201.

253 "proclaimed and denounced": Ibid., 2:192.

256 the Civil War: Manisha Sinha, *The Slave's Cause: A History of Abolition* (New Haven, CT: Yale University Press, 2016), 160–61.

257 "of popular sovereignty": Frederick Douglass, "The Kansas-Nebraska Bill," 30 October 1854, in *Life and Writings of Frederick Douglass*, 2:331.

258 "its quivering heart": Frederick Douglass, "Non-Extension versus Abolition of Slavery," *Douglass' Monthly* 2, no. 5 (October 1859): 151.

259 "of national affairs": Blight, *Frederick Douglass' Civil War*, 38.

259 "upon their pathway": Douglass, *My Bondage*, 398.

259 "incarnation of wolfishness": Frederick Douglass, "The Dred Scott Decision," 11 May 1857, in *Life and Writings of Frederick Douglass*, 2:411.

259 "system of slavery": Ibid., 2:412.

260 "its many waters": Frederick Douglass, "West India Emancipation," 4 August 1857, in *Life and Writings of Frederick Douglass*, 2:437.

261 "get out alive": Douglass, *Life and Times*, 759.

262 "destruction of slavery": Ibid., 764.

262 "was at hand": Frederick Douglass, "John Brown," 30 May 1881, http:// www.wvculture.org/history/jbexhibit/bbspro5-0032.html.

262 any slave revolt: Blight, *Frederick Douglass' Civil War*, 95.

265 "any anti-slavery work": Frederick Douglass, "The Late Election," *Douglass' Monthly* 3, no. 7 (December 1860): 370.

266 "this slaveholding rebellion": Frederick Douglass, "The American Apocalypse," 16 June 1861, in *The Frederick Douglass Papers Series One*, ed. John W. Blassingame, 5 vols. (New Haven, CT: Yale University Press, 1985), 3:440, 3:445.

266 "owes his election": Frederick Douglass, "The President and His Speeches," *Douglass' Monthly*, September 1862, in *Life and Writings of Frederick Douglass*, 3:268.

267 "the star-spangled banner": Frederick Douglass, "The Proclamation and a Negro Army," February 1863, ibid., 3:321–22.

268 "chained behind us": Frederick Douglass, "The Reasons for Our Troubles: Speech on the War," 14 January 1862, ibid., 3:204.

268 "rules the hour": Frederick Douglass, "Fighting Rebels with Only One Hand," *Douglass' Monthly*, September 1861, ibid., 3:152.

268 "the United States": Frederick Douglass, "Address for the Promotion of Colored Enlistments," 6 July 1863, ibid., 3:365.

269 attempted to escape: James M. McPherson, *Battle Cry of Freedom: The Civil War Era* (New York: Ballantine, 1988), 565–67.

270 "the n—r through": Frederick Douglass, "Our Work is Not Done," 3–4 December 1863, in *Life and Writings of Frederick Douglass*, 3:384.

270 "of the room": Ibid.

270 "[on] that point": Ibid., 3:385.

270 "of his character": Douglass, *Life and Times*, 786.

270 "my unpopular color": Ibid., 797.

271 "you serious damage": Frederick Douglass to Theodore Tilton, 15 October 1864, in *Life and Writings of Frederick Douglass*, 3:423.

272 "a sacred effort": Douglass, *Life and Times*, 804.

273 "of this event": McFeely, *Frederick Douglass*, 312.

Part Four: Resist Nazi Evil—Dietrich Bonhoeffer's Challenge

281 "the present circumstances": Dietrich Bonhoeffer to George Bell, 25 March 1939, in *Dietrich Bonhoeffer Works, Volume 15: Theological Education Underground, 1937–1940*, ed. Dirk Schulz (Minneapolis, MN: Fortress Press, 2012), 156.

281 "our ethical concepts?": Dietrich Bonhoeffer, "After Ten Years: A Reckoning Made at New Year, 1943," in Dietrich Bonhoeffer, *Letters and Papers from Prison*, ed. Eberhard Bethge (New York: Touchstone, 1997), 4.

282 ideology, or decisions: Eberhard Bethge, *Dietrich Bonhoeffer: A Biography* (Minneapolis, MN: Fortress Press, 2000), 371.

282 "toward the state": Dietrich Bonhoeffer to George Bell, 25 March 1939, in *Dietrich Bonhoeffer Works*, 15:156.

283 "filled with despair": Dietrich Bonhoeffer, "American Diary," 15 June 1939, ibid., 15:222.

283 "hardly be endured": Bonhoeffer, "American Diary," 16 June 1939, ibid., 15:223.

283 "clear to me": Ibid.

283 "brothers in struggle": See, for example, Dietrich Bonhoeffer to Paul Lehmann, 30 June 1939, ibid., 15:209.

284 "is it both": Bonhoeffer, "American Diary," 20 June 1939, ibid., 15:227.

284 "is certainly crushing": Bonhoeffer, "American Diary," 22 June 1939, ibid., 15:229.

284 "choice in security": Dietrich Bonhoeffer to Reinhold Niebuhr, late June 1939, ibid., 15:210. The original letter that Bonhoeffer wrote to Niebuhr was lost. In Elisabeth Sifton and Fritz Stern, *No Ordinary Men: Dietrich Bonhoeffer and Hans von Dohnanyi, Resisters Against Hitler in Church and State* (New York: New York Review Books, 2013), Elisabeth Sifton, who is Niebuhr's daughter, and Fritz Stern point out that these words are Niebuhr's recollections and were set down in 1945 (69).

284 "it may appear": Bonhoeffer, "American Diary," 20 June 1939, in *Dietrich Bonhoeffer Works*, 15:227.

285 "effect upon me": Bonhoeffer, "American Diary," 7 July 1939, ibid., 15:237.

286 "of shedding blood": Dietrich Bonhoeffer to Erwin Sutz, 28 April 1934, in *Dietrich Bonhoeffer Works, Volume 13: London, 1933–1935*, ed. Keith Clements (Minneapolis, MN: Fortress Press, 2007), 135.

286 "still quite unclear": Hellmut Traub, "Two Recollections," in *I Knew Dietrich Bonhoeffer*, ed. Wolf-Dieter Zimmermann and Ronald Gregor Smith (New York: Harper & Row, 1964), 159–60.

287 in Breslau, Germany: In the aftermath of World War II, Breslau was transferred to Poland and renamed Wroclaw. Today, it is the largest city in western Poland.

287 "a happy time": *Dietrich Bonhoeffer: A Life in Pictures*, ed. Eberhard Bethge, Renate Bethge, and Christian Gremmels (London: SCM Press, 1986), 29.

288 "their military service": Bethge, *Dietrich Bonhoeffer*, 17.

288 "We loved this": Sabine Leibholz, "Childhood and Home," in *I Knew Dietrich Bonhoeffer*, 20.

288 about eternal life: Ibid., 23–24.

288 "he was happy": Ibid., 22.

289 a huge impact: According to biographer Eberhard Bethge, Karl and Paula Bonhoeffer had a "happy relationship in which each partner adroitly supplemented the strength of the other. At their golden wedding anniversary, it was said that they had not spent a total of one month apart during their fifty years of marriage, even counting single days." Bethge, *Dietrich Bonhoeffer*, 17.

290 "existing as church-community": Dietrich Bonhoeffer, *Sanctorum Communio: A Theological Study of the Sociology of the Church* (Minneapolis, MN: Fortress Press, 1998), 211.

290 "means in sacrifice": Dietrich Bonhoeffer, "Sermon on 1 Corinthians 12:27, 26," 29 July 1928, in *Dietrich Bonhoeffer Works, Volume 10: Barcelona, Berlin, New York: 1928–1931*, ed. Clifford J. Green (Minneapolis, MN: Fortress Press, 2008), 509.

292 almost 33 percent: This statistic is for 1931; unemployment for nonfarm workers was 25 percent. US Department of the Census, *Historical Statistics of the United States: Colonial Times to 1970*, 2 vols. (Washington, DC: US Government Printing Office, 1975), 1:126.

292 "was refused service": Dietrich Bonhoeffer to his parents, 1 December 1930, in *Dietrich Bonhoeffer Works*, 10:258.

292 "and so on": Dietrich Bonhoeffer to Karl Friedrich Bonhoeffer, 2 January 1931, ibid., 10:269.

292 "are repressed here": Karl Friedrich Bonhoeffer to Dietrich Bonhoeffer, 24 January 1931, ibid., 10:276.

292 "slightest substantive foundation": Dietrich Bonhoeffer to Max Diestel, 19 December 1930, ibid., 10:265.

293 "others without reservation": Dietrich Bonhoeffer, "Sermon on I John 4:16," 9 November 1930, ibid., 10:581.

293 "passion and vividness": Dietrich Bonhoeffer, "Report on My Year of Study at Union Theological Seminary in New York, 1930/31. Presented to the Church Federation Office by Lecturer Dietrich Bonhoeffer," ibid., 10:315.

293 to solving problems: Bethge, *Dietrich Bonhoeffer*, 155.

293 to abiding friendship: Ibid., 155.

294 "be socially valued": Ibid., 160.

294 to daily existence: See, for example, Bonhoeffer's "Report on My Year of Study at Union Theological Seminary," 10:318–19.

294 "those who suffer": Bonhoeffer, "After Ten Years," 17.

298 "expect from us?": Wolf-Dieter Zimmermann, "Years in Berlin," in *I Knew Dietrich Bonhoeffer*, 60–61.

298 "were literally perspiring": Ferenc Lehel, "Seen with the Eyes of a Pupil," ibid., 68.

298 "its proper place": Zimmermann, "Years in Berlin," ibid., 61–62.

298 "omens are strange": Dietrich Bonhoeffer to Erwin Sutz, 8 October 1931, in *Dietrich Bonhoeffer Works, Volume 11: Ecumenical, Academic, and Pastoral Work: 1931–1932*, ed. Victoria J. Barnett, Mark S. Brocker, and Michael B. Lukens (Minneapolis, MN: Fortress Press, 2012), 50.

299 reached 30 percent: Victoria J. Barnett, Mark S. Brocker, and Michael B. Lukens, "Editor's Introduction to the English Edition," ibid., 2.

299 "his psychopathic symptoms": Bethge, *Dietrich Bonhoeffer*, 258.

299 "hitherto legal limits": Ibid., 263.

300 to government censorship: Dietrich Bonhoeffer to Erwin Sutz, 14 April 1933, in *Dietrich Bonhoeffer's Works, Volume 12: Berlin: 1932–1933*, ed. Larry L. Rasmussen (Minneapolis, MN: Fortress Press, 2009), 102.

300 Nuremberg Race Laws: US Holocaust Memorial Museum, "Anti-Semitic Legislation, 1933–1939," https://www.ushmm.org/wlc/en/article.php?ModuleId=10007901.

301 sources of Christianity: Sifton and Stern, *No Ordinary Men*, 38.

301 "within forty-eight hours": Peter F. Drucker, *Adventures of a Bystander* (New Brunswick, NJ: Transaction, 2007), 161–62. On the wave of faculty dismissals in 1933, see Bethge, *Dietrich Bonhoeffer*, 276.

301 "make up for": Dietrich Bonhoeffer to Gerhard and Sabine Leibholz, 23 November 1933, in *Dietrich Bonhoeffer Works*, 13:42.

302 to their congregations: In 1933, there were about 20 million Catholics in Germany and about 40 million Protestants. US Holocaust Memorial Museum, "The German Churches and the Nazi State," https://www.ushmm.org/wlc/en/article.php?ModuleId=10005206.

303 Protestants were members: Ibid.

303 "of the wilderness": Victoria Barnett, *For the Soul of the People: Protestant Protest Against Hitler* (New York: Oxford University Press, 1992), 27.

304 "the Christian community": Dietrich Bonhoeffer, "The Church and the Jewish Question," June 1933, in *Dietrich Bonhoeffer Works*, 12:365.

304 stop such abuse: Ibid.

304 "their very existence": Eberhard Bethge, "Dietrich Bonhoeffer and the Jews," in *Ethical Responsibility: Bonhoeffer's Legacy to the Churches*, ed. John D. Godsey and Geffrey B. Kelly (Lewiston, NY: Edwin Mellon Press, 1981), 63.

305 under state control: In November 1933, for example, the German Christians held a rally at the Berlin Sportpalast. Swastikas and banners celebrating the unity of Christianity and National Socialism lined the walls of the packed meeting hall, while speakers demanded implementation of the Aryan Paragraph and removal of the Old Testament from the Bible.

305 learned with Bonhoeffer: Sifton and Stern, *No Ordinary Men*, 45–47.

306 "very much closer": Bethge, *Dietrich Bonhoeffer*, 323.

306 "retreat into silence": Dietrich Bonhoeffer to Karl Barth, 24 October 1933, in *Dietrich Bonhoeffer Works*, 13:23.

306 "small, quiet congregation": Bethge, *Dietrich Bonhoeffer*, 327.

307 "difficult for me": Dietrich Bonhoeffer to Karl Friedrich Bonhoeffer, 13 January 1934, in *Dietrich Bonhoeffer Works*, 13:81.

307 church in Germany: See, for example, Dietrich Bonhoeffer to George Bell, 14 March 1934, ibid., 13:118–19.

308 "to his Master": G. K. A. Bell, "Foreword," in Dietrich Bonhoeffer, *The Cost of Discipleship* (New York: Simon & Schuster, 1995), 11.

308 of parish governance: Barnett, *For the Soul of the People*, 65.

308 called the *Kirchenkampf*: US Holocaust Memorial Museum, "The German Churches and the Nazi State," https://www.ushmm.org/wlc/en/article.php?ModuleId=10005206.

309 "times as these?": Dietrich Bonhoeffer to Erwin Sutz, 11 September 1934, in *Dietrich Bonhoeffer Works*, 13:217.

309 "through in faith": Dietrich Bonhoeffer to Erwin Sutz, 28 April 1934, ibid., 13:135.

311 socially deviant behavior: US Holocaust Memorial Museum, "Nazi Camps," https://www.ushmm.org/wlc/en/article.php?ModuleId=10005144.

312 "exceed their strengths": "In 1934, the German army," historian John Keegan has written, "was outnumbered by the Polish and Czech armies, greatly outnumbered by the French, even outnumbered by the British and completely outmatched by the Red Army. Within the next three years, however, the balance of military power in Europe would be transformed. By September 1938 the German army, which in 1933 possessed only seven infantry and three cavalry divisions, stood at a strength of forty-six infantry divisions and five panzer (tank) divisions, with a numerical strength of six hundred thousand. By comparison the British army had only six infantry divisions and one notional tank division; many of its two hundred thousand soldiers were dispersed abroad in colonial garrisons. The Luftwaffe, with three thousand combat aircraft, already outnumbered both the Royal Air Force and the Armée de l'Air. The French army, though large, was hidebound and poorly equipped." John Keegan, *Winston Churchill* (New York: Penguin, 2007), 116–17.

312 "or related blood": US Holocaust Memorial Museum, "The Nuremberg Race Laws," https://www.ushmm.org/outreach/en/article.php?ModuleId =10007695.

312 four Jewish grandparents: Ibid.

312 any real change: See, for example, Bonhoeffer's 1934 letter to a bishop active in the ecumenical movement: "It is precisely here, *in our attitude toward the state*, that we must speak out with absolute sincerity for the sake of Jesus Christ and of the ecumenical cause. It must be made quite clear — terrifying though it is—that we are immediately faced with the decision: National Socialist *or* Christian. We must advance beyond where we stood a year ago." Dietrich Bonhoeffer to Ove Valdemar Ammundsen, 8 August 1934, in *Dietrich Bonhoeffer Works*, 13: 192.

312 happening in Germany: Bethge, *Dietrich Bonhoeffer*, 409.

312 sabbatical in India: He went far enough along this potential path to procure a letter of introduction to Gandhi from his friend George Bell. Gandhi responded directly to Bonhoeffer, writing, "With reference to your desire to share my daily life, I may say that you will be staying with me if I am out of prison and settled in one place when you come. But otherwise, if I am travelling or if I am in prison, you will have to be satisfied with remaining in or near one of the institutions that are being conducted under my supervision. If you can stay in any of the institutions I have in mind and if you can live on the simple vegetarian food that these institutions

can supply you, you will have nothing to pay for your board and lodging."
Bethge, *Dietrich Bonhoeffer: Life in Pictures*, 137.

313   Nazi-controlled state church: See, for example, Dietrich Bonhoeffer, "From
the House of Brethren to Supporters of the Seminary," 22 July 1936, in
*Dietrich Bonhoeffer Works, Volume 14: Theological Education at Finken-
walde: 1935–1937*, ed. H. Gaylon Barker and Mark S. Brocker (Minneapolis,
MN: Fortress Press, 2013), 222.

313   "the outside world": Dietrich Bonhoeffer, "To the Council of the Evangelical
Church of the Old Prussian Union, Berlin-Dahlem, Regarding the Establishment of a House of Brethren in the Preachers' Seminary at Finkenwalde,"
6 September 1935, in Bethge, *Dietrich Bonhoeffer: A Life in Pictures*, 149.

313   "burnt-out shells behind": Dietrich Bonhoeffer to Karl Friedrich Bonhoeffer,
14 January 1935, in *Dietrich Bonhoeffer Works*, 13:284–85.

314   "Low, Sweet Chariot": Bethge, *Dietrich Bonhoeffer*, 427.

314   "long run monotonous": Wilhelm Rott, "Something Always Occurred to
Him," in *I Knew Dietrich Bonhoeffer*, 134.

315   "for good jokes": H. Gaylon Barker, "Editor's Introduction," in *Dietrich
Bonhoeffer Works*, 14:26–27.

315   "forget his sickness": Rott, "Something Always Occurred to Him," 134.

315   "the opera house": Ibid., 135.

315   "life in community": Dietrich Bonhoeffer, *Life Together* in *The Bonhoeffer
Reader*, ed. Clifford J. Green and Michael DeJorge (Minneapolis, MN:
Fortress Press, 2013), 560.

316   "to good works": Ibid., 561.

316   "the moral imagination": Charles Marsh, *Strange Glory: A Life of Dietrich
Bonhoeffer* (New York: Vintage, 2014), 232.

316   Confessing Church illegal: Ferdinand Schlingensiepen, *Dietrich Bonhoeffer,
1906–1945: Martyr, Thinker, Man of Resistance* (New York: T&T Clark
International, 2010), 193. On the larger context of church politics at this
time, see Bethge, *Dietrich Bonhoeffer*, 495–98.

317   "contact with them": Schlingensiepen, *Dietrich Bonhoeffer*, 196.

318   "for us all": Dietrich Bonhoeffer, "To the Finkenwalde Brothers," 20 December 1937, in *Dietrich Bonhoeffer Works*, 15:21.

318   "the anti-Christian forces": Ibid., 15:20–21.

318   "in both respects": Dietrich Bonhoeffer, "To the Brothers of the First Session," 15 November 1935, in *Dietrich Bonhoeffer Works*, 14:119.

319   "and the soldier": Bonhoeffer, *Cost of Discipleship*, 38.

319   on their own: David Foster Wallace, "Up, Simba," in *Consider the Lobster
and Other Essays* (Boston: Little, Brown, 2006), 224.

321   "summons of God": Bethge, *Dietrich Bonhoeffer*, 600.

321   allegiance to Hitler: Ibid., 601. See also Barnett, *For the Soul of the People*,
156–58.

321   the clerical directive: Bethge, *Dietrich Bonhoeffer*, 600.

322 of its leadership: See, for example, Dietrich Bonhoeffer to Karl Friedrich Bonhoeffer, 28 January 1939, in *Dietrich Bonhoeffer Works*, 15:115.

322 labeled "subversive activity": On Nazi prohibition of Bonhoeffer's public speaking, see Bethge, *Dietrich Bonhoeffer*, 698–99.

322 "interrogations, and arrests": Sifton and Stern, *No Ordinary Men*, 65.

323 "to settle down": Bethge, *Dietrich Bonhoeffer*, 594.

323 be "total annihilation": Ibid., 631.

324 "of the children": Sabine Leibholz to Dietrich Bonhoeffer, 26 August 1938, in *Dietrich Bonhoeffer Works*, 15:63.

324 "had become numbed": Barnett, *For the Soul of the People*, 139.

324 and mass extermination: US Holocaust Memorial Museum, "Kristallnacht: A Nationwide Pogrom," https://www.ushmm.org/wlc/en/article.php?ModuleId =10005201.

324 remained largely silent: See Barnett, *For the Soul of the People*, 142–44. A number of church officials, including radical members of the Confessing Church, protested the government's actions and even more worked privately to help the Jews.

324 "sing Gregorian chants": Bethge, *Dietrich Bonhoeffer*, 607.

325 "churches will burn": Mark S. Brocker, "Editor's Introduction," in *Dietrich Bonhoeffer Works, Volume 16: Conspiracy and Imprisonment: 1940–1945*, ed. Mark S. Brocker (Minneapolis, MN: Fortress Press, 2006), 5.

326 for their actions: Bethge, *Dietrich Bonhoeffer*, 625.

326 this emotional turbulence: The photographs taken of Bonhoeffer right after his return from America convey his relief, what his colleague Helmut Traub would call "realized freedom." See Bethge, *Dietrich Bonhoeffer: A Life in Pictures*, 178.

329 "and police battalions": Sifton and Stern, *No Ordinary Men*, 70.

329 or racial enemies: US Holocaust Memorial Museum, "Einsatzgruppen (Mobile Killing Units)," https://www.ushmm.org/wlc/en/article.php ?ModuleId=10005130.

329 Hitler was assassinated: Sifton and Stern, *No Ordinary Men*, 72.

330 "for that salute!": Bethge, *Dietrich Bonhoeffer*, 681.

331 "times moral repugnance": Sifton and Stern, *No Ordinary Men*, 54.

332 "simplicity and straightforwardness": Bonhoeffer, "After Ten Years," 16–17.

333 "sake Christ suffered": Ibid., 14.

333 "this disreputable task": Bethge, *Dietrich Bonhoeffer*, 628.

334 do the same: Nancy F. Koehn, "The Brain—and Soul—of Capitalism," *Harvard Business Review* (November 2013): 44.

334 The Final Solution: In January 1942, representatives of the Nazi government met in the Berlin suburb of Wannsee to coordinate the implementation of the large-scale killing of an estimated 11 million Jews in Europe. The participants in the meeting, known as the Wannsee Conference, did not approve the Final Solution; Hitler had already decided to undertake mass extermination of

European Jews. Instead, under the leadership of Reinhard Heydrich, the meeting was devoted to planning various aspects of implementing the program, including the fate of people of mixed blood, the relationship between the evacuation of Jews in different parts of Europe and military developments, and the population of European Jews by country. Holocaust Research Project, "Minutes from the Wannsee Conference," 20 January 1942, http://www .holocaustresearchproject.org/holoprelude/Wannsee/wanseeminutes.html.

335 in German-occupied Poland: The 1941 deportations were not the first attempts at systematic annihilation of the Jews and other "enemies" of the Third Reich. As early as 1938, Einsatzgruppen, or mobile killing squads, composed of Nazi SS and police personal, had been operating in German-occupied lands to murder Jews, Gypsies, Communists, and other people deemed enemies of the Third Reich. The Einsatzgruppen shot civilians, initially men, and later women and children as well—often in large numbers and at close range. After Germany invaded the Soviet Union in June 1941, the Einsatzgruppen followed the German soldiers through Eastern Europe and far into Soviet territory, killing thousands of Jews, Gypsies, and Soviet Communists. (In one famous incident in Kiev in September 1941, Einsatzgruppen detachment 4a massacred thirty-three thousand Jews in two days.) Although Nazi killing squads continued to operate in the Soviet Union until at least 1943, Himmler, Heydrich, and other Reich officials decided that shooting Jews and other victims was inefficient and psychologically difficult for the killers and the officers overseeing the murders. By 1942, Third Reich leaders had decided to use gas chambers outfitted in concentration camps as the central mechanism in the regime's program to annihilate European Jews. US Holocaust Memorial Museum, "Einsatzgruppen."

336 "already well populated": Dietrich Bonhoeffer to Eberhard Bethge, 25 June 1942, in *Dietrich Bonhoeffer Works*, 16:329–30.

336 "losses for everyone": Marsh, *Strange Glory*, 335.

337 "now say yes": Maria von Wedemeyer to Dietrich Bonhoeffer, 13 January 1943, in *Love Letters from Cell 92: The Correspondence between Dietrich Bonhoeffer and Maria von Wedemeyer, 1943–45*, ed. Ruth-Alice von Bismarck and Ulrich Kabitz (Nashville, TN: Abingdon Press, 1995), 338.

340 about the scheme: Sifton and Stern, *No Ordinary Men*, 103.

341 "staff's vile abuse": Dietrich Bonhoeffer, "Report on Prison Life after One Year in Tegel," in *Letters and Papers from Prison*, 248.

341 "the other prisoners": Ibid., 249.

342 "the plates concerned": Ibid., 250.

343 "things as tomatoes": Dietrich Bonhoeffer to Karl and Paula Bonhoeffer, 3 August 1943, ibid., 87.

343 "in July 1939": Ibid.

343 "than I am": Dietrich Bonhoeffer to Karl and Paula Bonhoeffer, 14 April 1943, ibid., 21–22.

344 "look forward to": Bethge, *Dietrich Bonhoeffer*, 831.

344 "all be over": Ibid.

345 "Overcoming in prayer": Dietrich Bonhoeffer, "Notes, I and II," in *Letters and Papers from Prison*, 33–35.

345 of Nazi interrogation: Bethge, *Dietrich Bonhoeffer*, 832.

345 "so ever since": Dietrich Bonhoeffer to Eberhard Bethge, 18 November 1943, in *Letters and Papers from Prison*, 129.

347 "metaphor for Advent": Dietrich Bonhoeffer to Maria von Wedemeyer, 21 November 1943, in *Love Letters from Cell 92*, 118.

349 "pass over them": Dietrich Bonhoeffer, "Outlines of Letters," in *Letters and Papers from Prison*, 60–61.

350 "nightmare is over!": Dietrich Bonhoeffer to Karl and Paula Bonhoeffer, 24 June 1943, ibid., 71–72.

351 "on the earth": Dietrich Bonhoeffer to Maria von Wedemeyer, 12 August 1943, ibid., 415.

351 "the locked door?": Dietrich Bonhoeffer to Maria von Wedemeyer, 27 August 1943, in *Love Letters from Cell 92*, 73 74.

352 "the up-and-down uncertainty": Sifton and Stern, *No Ordinary Men*, 115.

352 "and the Bible": Dietrich Bonhoeffer to Eberhard Bethge, 29 November 1943, in *Letters and Papers from Prison*, 149.

352 "asked you to": Dietrich Bonhoeffer to Eberhard Bethge, 18 November 1943, ibid., 130.

353 "him for it": Dietrich Bonhoeffer to Eberhard Bethge, 15 December 1943, ibid., 162.

354 "a clear conscience": Dietrich Bonhoeffer to Eberhard Bethge, 22 December 1943, ibid., 174.

354 "bear the consequences": Ibid., 173–74.

354 "piece of self-deception": Dietrich Bonhoeffer to Eberhard Bethge, 5 December 1943, ibid., 159.

354 "like gracious spirits": Dietrich Bonhoeffer to Karl and Paula Bonhoeffer, 3 July 1943, in ibid., 73.

356 "when peace comes": Dietrich Bonhoeffer to Eberhard Bethge, 11 April 1944, ibid., 272.

356 "for us today": Dietrich Bonhoeffer to Eberhard Bethge, 30 April 1944, ibid., 279.

356 "and more ground": Dietrich Bonhoeffer to Eberhard Bethge, 8 June 1944, ibid., 325–26.

356 "give an answer": Ibid., 326.

356 "needs and conflicts": Dietrich Bonhoeffer to Eberhard Bethge, 30 June 1944, ibid., 341.

356 previously insolvable problems: Dietrich Bonhoeffer to Eberhard Bethge, 30 April 1944, ibid., 281–82.

356 death and guilt: Ibid., 282.

357 "with the world": John W. de Gruchy, "Editor's Introduction," in *Dietrich Bonhoeffer Works, Volume 8: Letters and Papers from Prison*, ed. John W. de Gruchy (Minneapolis, MN: Fortress Press, 2010), 24–25.

357 "of Christian faith": Ibid., 8:25.

357 "there for others": Dietrich Bonhoeffer, "Outline for a Book," ibid., 8:501.

357 those who suffer: Bonhoeffer, "After Ten Years," 17.

357 "and a Christian": Dietrich Bonhoeffer to Eberhard Bethge, 21 July 1944, *Letters and Papers from Prison*, 370.

360 Reich since 1938: Sifton and Stern, *No Ordinary Men*, 120.

360 in the 1930s: Ibid., 122.

361 "the whole family": Dietrich Bonhoeffer to Maria von Wedemeyer, 19 December 1944, in *Love Letters from Cell 92*, 268–69.

362 "each new day": Ibid., 269–70.

362 "is living for": Sifton and Stern, *No Ordinary Men*, 132.

362 "owe the dead": Ibid.

363 "has been consistent": Karl Bonhoeffer to Professor Jossman, 8 October 1945, in *Dietrich Bonhoeffer: A Life in Pictures*, 234.

Part Five: Protect the Earth and Its Creatures—Rachel Carson's Challenge

371 tumors sufficiently "suspicious": Rachel Carson to Marjorie Spock and Mary "Polly" Richards, 12 April 1960, in Linda Lear, *Rachel Carson: Witness for Nature* (Boston: Mariner Books, 2009), 367.

371 "bordering on malignancy": Ibid.

371 "curious, hard swelling": Rachel Carson to George Crile, 7 December 1960, ibid., 378.

372 "life in hospitals": Ibid., 379.

372 her lymph nodes: Ibid.

372 "they were different": Rachel Carson to George Crile, 17 December 1960, ibid., 380.

372 "finish this book": Rachel Carson to Dorothy Freeman, 6 January 1962, in *Always, Rachel: The Letters of Rachel Carson and Dorothy Freeman, 1952–1964*, ed. Martha Freeman (Boston: Beacon Press, 1995), 391.

373 no longer walk: Rachel Carson to Marjorie Spock and Mary "Polly" Richards, 6 February 1961, in Paul Brooks, *House of Life: Rachel Carson at Work* (Boston: Houghton Mifflin, 1972), 266.

373 "easily flicker out": Rachel Carson to Dorothy Freeman, 2 February 1961, in Lear, *Rachel Carson*, 337.

373 "and devastating wreckage": Rachel Carson to Dorothy Freeman, 24–25 February 1962, in *Always, Rachel*, 352.

373 "a nice day": Rachel Carson, "Notebooks for *Silent Spring*," in Lear, *Rachel Carson*, 384.

373 "its own [energy]": Rachel Carson to Lois Crisler, 19 August 1961, ibid., 389.

374 "as it should": Rachel Carson to Dorothy Freeman, 26 September 1961, in *Always, Rachel*, 386–87.

374 "it won't go": Rachel Carson to Dorothy Freeman, 6 January 1962, ibid., 390–91.

377 or central heat: For a detailed description of Carson's childhood home, see Lear, *Rachel Carson*, 11.

378 "shared with her": Rachel Carson, "The Real World Around Us," 21 April 1954, in *The Lost Woods: The Discovered Writing of Rachel Carson*, ed. Linda Lear (Boston: Beacon Press, 1998), 148.

378 "up stories, too": Ibid.

378 with flour-and-water paste: Lear, *Rachel Carson*, 16.

378 "tired, gloriously happy!": Rachel Carson, "My Favorite Recreation," *St. Nicholas* 49 (May 1922): 999.

380 offering to share: Lear, *Rachel Carson*, 31.

383 "strange sea world": Rachel Carson, "Memo to Mrs. Eales on *Under the Sea-Wind*," circa 1942, in *Lost Woods*, 54.

385 some months later: Lear, *Rachel Carson*, 72.

385 nearly 9 percent: Bureau of Labor Statistics, Department of Commerce, "Labor Force—Estimating Methods," *Monthly Labor Review* (July 1948): 51.

385 "once doesn't work": Rachel Carson to Dorothy Thompson, 16 October 1930, in Lear, *Rachel Carson*, 70.

386 front of them: William Souder, *On a Further Shore: The Life and Legacy of Rachel Carson* (New York: Crown, 2012), 48.

387 a larger audience: Lear, *Rachel Carson*, 77.

387 "chance [on you]": Carson, "Real World Around Us," 149.

388 "of material immortality": Rachel Carson, "The World of Waters," in Lear, *Rachel Carson*, 86.

388 "to the *Atlantic*": Carson, "Real World Around Us," 150.

389 "connecting the dots": Steve Jobs, Stanford University Commencement Address, 12 June 2005, http://news.stanford.edu/news/2005/june15/jobs-061505.html.

391 "of the layman": Edward Weeks to Rachel Carson, 8 July 1937, in Lear, *Rachel Carson*, 86–87.

392 "and eternal night": Rachel Carson, "Undersea," *Atlantic Monthly* 160 (September 1937): 322–25, in *Lost Woods*, 4.

392 of manuscript pages: Lear, *Rachel Carson*, 100.

392 "the ocean shores": Ralph Thompson, "Books of the Times," *New York Times*, November 5, 1941, 27.

392 "no false sentimentality": Arlene R. Quaratiello, *Rachel Carson: A Biography* (Westport, CT: Greenwood Press, 2004), 31.

393 "a single error": William Beebe, "Of and About the Sea," *Saturday Review of Literature*, December 27, 1941, 5, 28.

393 "with superb indifference": Carson, "Real World Around Us," 150.

393 royalties totaled $689.17: Lear, *Rachel Carson*, 105.

393 with the technology: Ibid., 113–14.

394 "write natural history": Ibid., 148.

394 "to the Sea": Rachel Carson to William Beebe, 6 September 1948, in Brooks, *House of Life*, 110.

395 "with new pleasure": Jonathan Norton Leonard, "And His Wonders in the Deep," *New York Times*, July 1, 1951, 130.

395 "of a poet": Harvey Breit, "Reader's Choice," *Atlantic Monthly* 188 (August 1951): 82–83.

395 "work of art": E. H. Martin, "Brilliant Study of the Sea," *Evening Sun*, June 30, 1951, 4.

395 "facts I hadn't": Henry Bigelow to Rachel Carson, 4 May 1951, in Lear, *Rachel Carson*, 203.

395 sold 250,000 copies: Brooks, *House of Life*, 129.

395 thousand advance copies: Lear, *Rachel Carson*, 226.

395 ocean was contagious: Ibid., 203.

396 "upon with . . . eagerness": Rachel Carson, "National Book Award Acceptance Speech," 29 January 1952, ibid., 205.

397 "out the poetry": Rachel Carson, "National Book Award Acceptance Speech," 29 January 1952, ibid., http://www.nationalbook.org/nbaacceptspeech_rcarson.html#.VcXhFIuLgqQ.

397 "of the world": Brooks, *House of Life*, 132.

397 "and forbidding woman": Ibid.

397 "expertly, but sparingly": Quaratiello, *Rachel Carson*, 61.

398 "acknowledge the fact": Rachel Carson, "*New York Herald-Tribune* Book and Author Luncheon Speech," 16 October 1951, in *Lost Woods*, 77.

398 "is about that": Rachel Carson to Dorothy Freeman, 1 February 1956, in *Always, Rachel*, 148.

398 "could do it": Rachel Carson to Marie Rodell, 13 September 1950, in Lear, *Rachel Carson*, 184.

398 signs of malignancy: Lear, *Rachel Carson*, 185.

399 accomplish her purpose: I am grateful to Kelly McNamara for her insights about Carson's health.

402 "Are you excited?": Rachel Carson to Marie Rodell, 9 September 1952, in Lear, *Rachel Carson*, 235.

402 "softness of fog": Brooks, *House of Life*, 159.

402 and marine life: Lear, *Rachel Carson*, 246–47.

402 summer of 1953: Ibid., 248.

402 "and just talk!": Rachel Carson to Dorothy Freeman, 28 September 1953, in *Always, Rachel*, 6.

403 the southern states: Brooks, *House of Life*, 159.

403 "publisher's understanding indulgence": Rachel Carson to Dorothy Freeman, 6 November 1953, in *Always, Rachel*, 9.

403 *Sea Around Us*: Lear, *Rachel Carson*, 268.

403 "open their doors": Jonathan N. Leonard, "Between the Mark of High Tide and Low," *New York Times*, October 30, 1955, BR5.

403 "imparts is profound": Quaratiello, *Rachel Carson*, 74.

403 "interlocked and encrusted": Ibid.

403 its Achievement Award: Brooks, *House of Life*, 164.

404 "of our strength": Rachel Carson, "Help Your Child to Wonder," *Women's Home Companion*, July 1956, 46.

404 "by the dozen": Rachel Carson to Dorothy Freeman, 8 August 1956, in *Always, Rachel*, 186–87.

405 "as 17 crickets": Rachel Carson to Dorothy Freeman, 24 January 1957, ibid., 214.

405 "it frightens me": Rachel Carson to Dorothy Freeman, 28 March 1957, ibid., 219.

406 "exhaustion I can't": Rachel Carson to Dorothy Freeman, 11 December 1957, ibid., 238.

406 "very many months": Rachel Carson to Paul Brooks, 4 September 1957, in Lear, *Rachel Carson*, 304.

407 to 637 million: Rachel Carson, *Silent Spring* (New York: Houghton Mifflin, 2002), 17.

407 different brand names: Ibid., 7.

408 opossums, and armadillos: Ibid., 166.

408 sows' contaminated milk: Ibid., 167–68.

409 "without . . . just compensation": *Murphy v. Benson*, 151 F. Supp. 786 (EDNY, 1957).

409 "breasts in agony": Brooks, *House of Life*, 232.

409 of baby food: Details of Carson's investigations during this period from Lear, *Rachel Carson*, 315–17.

410 "appalled I became": Brooks, *House of Life*, 233.

410 "draw their food": Lear, *Rachel Carson*, 322.

411 "something so important": Rachel Carson to Dorothy Freeman, 28 June 1958, in *Always, Rachel*, 259.

411 "hand in mine": Rachel Carson to Dorothy Freeman, 4 December 1958, ibid., 273.

411 "through to completion": Rachel Carson to Marjorie Spock, 4 December 1958, in Lear, *Rachel Carson*, 338.

413 "inflicted upon us": Rachel Carson to Paul Brooks, 14 February 1959, in Brooks, *House of Life*, 244.

414 jobs and reputations: Lear, *Rachel Carson*, 334.

414 "fallen into place": Rachel Carson to Paul Brooks, 3 December 1959, ibid., 357.

414   "most serious concern": Carson, *Silent Spring*, 237.

415   "a valuable lesson": Mrs. Thomas Duff to Paul Brooks, 24 February 1969, in Brooks, *House of Life*, 259–60.

415   "to worry about": Rachel Carson to Paul Brooks, 3 December 1959, ibid., 258.

416   "the chemical companies": Rachel Carson to Marjorie Spock and Mary "Polly" Richards, 12 April 1960, in Lear, *Rachel Carson*, 367.

417   "for another day": Rachel Carson to Dorothy Freeman, 17 January 1961, in *Always, Rachel*, 332.

417   or a movie: Public Broadcasting Service, "Rachel Carson's *Silent Spring*," *American Experience* (DVD, 2007).

418   "an insect spray": Carson, *Silent Spring*, 8.

418   "of the earth": Ibid., 7–8.

418   "its violent crossfire": Ibid., 8.

419   "with the insects": Ibid., 9.

419   "are now known": Ibid., 138.

419   "against the earth": Ibid., 297.

420   "of our earth": Ibid., 277.

420   "balance of nature": See, for example, Robert White-Stevens, assistant director of the Agricultural Research Division of American Cyanamid, in Lear, *Rachel Carson*, 434. See also Thomas H. Jukes, "People and Pesticides," *American Scientist* 51, no. 3 (September 1963): 355–61.

421   "science was male": Linda Lear, "Introduction," in Carson, *Silent Spring*, xi. See also Souder, *On a Farther Shore*, 324–25.

421   "bird in flight?": Carson, *Silent Spring*, 127.

422   "right to know": Ibid., 12–13.

422   "no such problem": Ibid.

422   "sudden but horrible": Ibid., 99.

423   "a human being?": Ibid., 99–100.

423   "supports all life": Ibid., 13.

425   "were being done": Rachel Carson to Lois Crisler, 8 February 1962, in Lear, *Rachel Carson*, 397.

425   "it each day": Rachel Carson to Dorothy Freeman, 28 March 1962, in *Always, Rachel*, 399.

426   result of radiation: Public Broadcasting Service, "Rachel Carson's *Silent Spring*."

426   "their own kind?": Carson, *Silent Spring*, 8.

426   "*Uncle Tom's Cabin*": William O. Douglas, *Book-of-the-Month Club News*, September 1962, 2–4, in Lear, *Rachel Carson*, 419.

426   "our own making": Loren Eiseley, "Using a Plague to Fight a Plague," *Saturday Review*, September 29, 1962, 18, 34.

426   "of our nation": Quaratiello, *Rachel Carson*, 109.

427   "going to be": Lear, *Rachel Carson*, 412.

427   "Miss Carson's book": Brooks, *House of Life*, 305.

427 "of persistent pesticides": White House, *Use of Pesticides: A Report of the President's Science Advisory Committee* (Washington, DC: Government Printing Office, May 15, 1963), 19.

427 "toxicity of pesticides": Ibid., 22.

428 "balance of nature": John M. Lee, "'Silent Spring' Is Now Noisy Summer," *New York Times*, July 22, 1962, 97.

428 "[Iron Curtain] parity": Louis A. McLean to William E. Spaulding, 2 August 1962, in Lear, *Rachel Carson*, 417.

428 "inherit the earth": Robert White-Stevens, in Columbia Broadcasting Service, "The Silent Spring of Rachel Carson," *CBS Reports*, April 3, 1963.

428 "over the page": Quaratiello, *Rachel Carson*, 108.

428 "that she loves": "Pesticides: The Price for Progress," *Time* 80, no. 13 (September 28, 1962): 47.

428 "will be okay": H. Davidson, Letter to the Editor, 29 June 1962, in *New Yorker* 71, no. 2 (February 20 and 27, 1995): 18.

429 "in our economy": F. A. Soraci in *Conservation News* (1962), in Frank Graham Jr., *Since Silent Spring* (New York: Houghton Mifflin, 1970), 56.

429 "a mystical cult": Frank Graham Jr., "Fifty Years After *Silent Spring*, Assault on Science Continues," *Yale Environment 360*, June 21, 2012, http://e360 .yale.edu/feature/fifty_years_after_rachel_carsons_silent_spring_assacult _on_science_continues/2544/.

429 "worried about genetics?": Public Broadcasting Service, "Rachel Carson's *Silent Spring*." See also Lear, *Rachel Carson*, 429.

429 "ahead and sue": "Milton Greenstein," *New Yorker* 67, no. 26 (August 19, 1991): 79.

429 hundred thousand copies: Quaratiello, *Rachel Carson*, 106.

430 watched the program: Lear, *Rachel Carson*, 450.

430 "steadily controlling nature": Columbia Broadcasting Service, "Silent Spring of Rachel Carson."

430 "but of ourselves": Ibid.

430 "of *Silent Spring*": Lear, *Rachel Carson*, 450.

431 "problems she raised": Public Broadcasting Service, "Rachel Carson's *Silent Spring*."

431 "is indicated, too": Rachel Carson to George Crile, February 1963, in *Lost Woods*, 226.

432 "for this morning": Rachel Carson to Dorothy Freeman, 10 September 1963, in *Always, Rachel*, 467–68.

434 "of them together": Al Gore, "Introduction," in Rachel Carson, *Silent Spring* (New York: Houghton Mifflin, 1994), viii.

435 "always in deed": E. O. Wilson, "Afterword," in Carson, *Silent Spring* (2002), 361.

435 in different forms: Susan Cain, *Quiet: The Power of Introverts in a World That Can't Stop Talking* (New York: Broadway Books, 2012), 1–15.

436 govern the planet: Linda Lear, "The Pollution of Our Environment," in *Lost Woods*, 228.

436 "generations to come": Rachel Carson, speech, Kaiser Foundation Hospitals and Permanente Medical Group, San Francisco, 18 October 1963, in *Lost Woods*, 228.

Conclusion: The Power of Courageous Leadership

442 "time of trouble": Ecclesiasticus 2:2, *The Bible: Authorized King James Version with Apocrypha* (New York: Oxford University Press, 1997), 114.

443 "sent or signed": Abraham Lincoln to George G. Meade, 14 July 1863, in *The Collected Works of Abraham Lincoln*, eds. Roy Basler, Marion Dolores Pratt, and Lloyd A. Dunlap, 10 vols. (New Brunswick, NJ: Rutgers University Press, 1953), 6:328n1.

446 "afraid of again": Ken Burns, "An Interview with Ken Burns," Public Broadcasting System, January 21, 1997, http://www.pbs.org/jefferson /making/KB_01.htm.

447 "your present distress": Abraham Lincoln to Fanny McCullough, 23 December 1862, in *Collected Works of Abraham Lincoln*, 6:16–17.

447 "and his orphan": Abraham Lincoln, Second Inaugural Address, 4 March 1865, ibid., 8:333.

Index